Fourth Edition

Persuasion

Integrating Theory, Research, and Practice

Ann Bainbridge Frymier | Marjorie Keeshan Nadler

Miami University   *Miami University*

Kendall Hunt
publishing company

Book Team

Chairman and Chief Executive Officer   Mark C. Falb
President and Chief Operating Officer   Chad M. Chandlee
Vice President, Higher Education   David L. Tart
Director of Publishing Partnerships   Paul B. Carty
Senior Developmental Coordinator   Angela Willenbring
Vice President, Operations   Timothy J. Beitzel
Senior Production Editor   Sheri Hosek
Senior Permissions Editor   Caroline Kieler
Cover Designer   Jenifer Fensterman

Cover image © Shutterstock.com

Kendall Hunt
publishing company

www.kendallhunt.com
Send all inquiries to:
4050 Westmark Drive
Dubuque, IA 52004-1840
Copyright © 2017 by Kendall Hunt Publishing Company

ISBN 978-1-5249-0736-5

Printed in the United States of America

BRIEF CONTENTS

CONTENTS

SECTION ONE INTRODUCTION TO PERSUASION   1

SECTION TWO THE PERSUASION PROCESS 59

SECTION THREE   THEORIES OF PERSUASION   153

SECTION FOUR   STRATEGIES AND TACTICS   271

SECTION FIVE   ETHICS IN PERSUASION   297

PREFACE

Persuasion and social influence are topics of interest to many students and teachers. Despite this common interest, teachers and students often approach this field differently. Students often want to know the key skills needed to persuade parents, friends, supervisors, teachers, and so on. Teachers often view a skills approach as too limiting and focus on theories of persuasion. These two approaches have often been at odds, with each winning out over the other at one time or another. Here in *Persuasion: Integrating Theory, Research, and Practice,* we reject the idea that practice and theory are dichotomous. The approach adopted here is that practice and application can serve as a means to understanding theory and, conversely, that theory can serve as a means for understanding practice and application. In other words, theory and practice are two parts of the same whole. There is no point of having a theory if it cannot be applied. Similarly, the practice of persuasion is nearly impossible if one doesn't understand the persuasion process. Therefore, theory informs practice and practice informs theory. The structure and examples used in each chapter are designed to help students and teachers alike integrate theory and practice.

Research is the third important component in this text. Research is used to illustrate the components of theory as well as the application of theory. Although some texts cite numerous research conclusions, this text explains representative studies for each theory. Our goal is to show how research is conducted and how it led to the theories and applications presented throughout the text. By understanding how the research was conducted, students can gain a clearer understanding of the theories and their limits.

ORGANIZATION OF THE BOOK

The **first section** lays the foundation by defining persuasion and its components. Persuasive messages most often target attitudes, beliefs, and/or behaviors, and Chapters 2 and 3 are devoted to understanding these constructs. Understanding these constructs is crucial to understanding both the theories and the practice of successful persuasion. It was when scholars developed a solid understanding of these constructs that persuasion theory advanced significantly.

The **second section** examines each component of the persuasion process from a communication perspective. The chapters on the source, message, channel, and receiver discuss specific factors that influence persuasiveness, such as source credibility, message sidedness, and fear appeals. Examples from research and other contexts are used to illustrate how the communication components work together to create persuasive communication.

The **third section** focuses on major theories of persuasion. It begins with a brief chapter on theory, which provides a refresher for students who have already taken a course on communication theory and provides a foundation for students who have not had such a course. The components of each theory are presented followed by research and practical examples. Depending on preference, instructors can put greater emphasis on theory, greater emphasis on research, greater emphasis on the examples and practice, or give each equal emphasis. The theories are presented as they were developed so that students can understand the progression of persuasion theory. The knowledge from one theory and its gaps is used to transition from one theory to another. The earlier chapters on communication components are frequently referenced to facilitate understanding of how theory directs the use each component in creating persuasive communication.

The last two sections each consist of a standalone chapter. Chapter 12 takes a more tactical approach to influence by discussing compliance and propaganda. This chapter can be incorporated into section two on the persuasion process or even used as part of the introduction to persuasion. The final chapter focuses on ethics and is written so that it could be read at any point in the course. Instructors can choose to address ethics early in the course so that ethical issues with each theory and component can be systematically examined. Or they can address ethics at the end of the course as a capstone, focusing on the ethical implications of persuasive messages and practice.

PEDAGOGICAL FEATURES

Each chapter begins with a brief list of **learning objectives.** These are the key concepts, functions, or issues that students should understand after they have read the chapter. The purpose of learning objectives is to provide structure and direction. The instructor will likely have additional learning objectives for each unit. Clearly communicating learning objectives helps students focus on important concepts and distinguish between primary and secondary concepts.

In each chapter you will see the **web activity** icon ⊕ with instructions for a brief activity. The web activities help students and instructors find examples of persuasion concepts or to learn more about a particular topic or research study. In the electronic version of the text, the icons link readers directly to the web. The web activities can be used to facilitate online or in-class discussions or can be turned into assignments. Numerous examples of effective and ineffective persuasion can be found on online that can be used as the basis for discussions, activities, and assignments.

At the end of each chapter there is a bulleted **summary** of key information, a list of **key terms**, **review questions**, and **discussion questions**. The review questions provide students with a guide for organizing the key concepts and issues discussed in the chapter. A student who answers each review question creates an outline of the chapter. It is recommended that students answer the review questions as they read. An instructor may use the review questions as a way of assessing recall and comprehension of the material. The discussion questions give students an opportunity to apply and analyze the content in the chapter and are designed to be answered in dyads or small groups. Students who answer each discussion question engage in critical thinking about the content, extending the content beyond the confines of the textbook. Instructors may use the discussion questions to facilitate classroom discussion, in online discussions, or in assessing higher levels of learning.

In each chapter a few *research studies* are discussed in depth to illustrate the theory and its application. Additional primary research studies could be assigned to complement each chapter if the instructor would like to put greater emphasis on persuasion research. Each chapter also contains *examples* and *illustrations* of the application of the concepts employed in that chapter. As a result, theory, research, and application are integrated within each chapter. In Chapter 11 an in-depth example of integrating theory, research, and practice is provided. Dr. Melissa Bekelja Wanzer, Professor in the Department of Communication at Canisius College in Buffalo, NY who worked with a group of students to transform a class project into a campaign to increase young males' performance of testicular self-exams. This case study provides an excellent example of how to use multiple theories in the creation of persuasive messages and events and how to evaluate the campaign through research.

ACKNOWLEDGMENTS

As with any large project, numerous people play a supporting role. First, we would like to thank our husbands, Jeff and Larry, and our children, Julia, Nicholas, Jessica, Pat, Kellie, and Cara, for their patience and support as we rode the roller coaster of writing this book and each edition. A special thanks to Janet Lowitz and Nicole Dobransky for their hard work and many contributions. We would also like to thank Holly Allen for her guidance and support in the early stages of this project. We want to thank numerous students from our persuasion course for reading chapters as they were written and for giving us feedback and helping us identify examples. We want to thank the many members of Kendall Hunt who have worked with us to make this book as good as it could be, with a special thank you to Paul Carty and Angela Willenbring. We appreciate the suggestions and insight provided by reviewers Patricia Fairfield-Artman, Brant R. Burlson, Tyler R. Harrison, Susan Kline, Katherine L. Nelson, J. D. Ragsdale, Richard A. R. Watson, Stacy Wolski, Itzhak Yanovitzky, and David Zarefsky on the first edition and whose advice continues to resonate throughout the text.

ABOUT THE AUTHORS

Ann Bainbridge Frymier is a Professor of Communication and Associate Dean of the Graduate School at Miami University and received an Ed.D. in communication studies and curriculum and instruction in 1992 from West Virginia University. Dr. Frymier's primary area of research is instructional communication, focusing on effective communication in instructional environments. Her research is published in a variety of journals including *Communication Education, Communication Quarterly, Journal of Applied Communication*, and *Communication Research Reports* and has written several book chapters. Dr. Frymier frequently teaches persuasion and research methods and has taught a wide variety of other courses, including instructional communication, interpersonal communication, organizational communication, intercultural communication, and nonverbal communication.

Marjorie Keeshan Nadler is a Professor Emerita at Miami University and received a Ph.D. in communication studies from the University of Kansas in 1983. Dr. Nadler's research focused on gender communication, persuasion, public relations, and instructional communication. She coedited a book on gender communication, and her research appeared in book chapters and journals such as *Communication Studies, Journal on Excellence in College Teaching, Women's Studies in Communication, Journalism and Mass Communication Educator,* and *Journal of the Association of Communication Administrators.* Dr. Nadler primarily taught courses in persuasion, public relations, and methods of teaching communication.

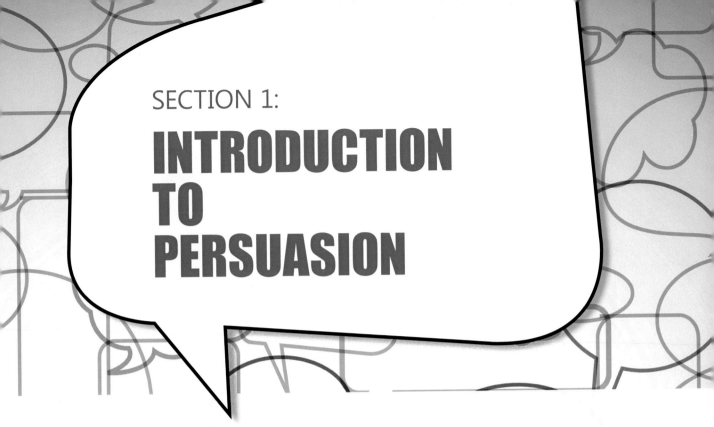

SECTION 1:
INTRODUCTION TO PERSUASION

What is persuasion all about? Answering this question is the primary purpose of this first section. The concept of persuasion is defined, the realm of social influence is explored, and the defining characteristics of persuasion are discussed in the first chapter. Additionally, Chapter 1 provides examples of different situations when persuasion is commonly used and introduces ethics in persuasion. You might want to read Chapter 13 soon after reading Chapter 1 if you'd like to consider the ethical issues more thoroughly as you progress through this text. Chapters 2 and 3 both address attitudes, beliefs, and behaviors as central concepts in the field of persuasion, and their role in the persuasion process. Chapter 2 defines attitude and differentiates it from beliefs and values. The characteristics of attitudes, as well as how attitudes are formed, are discussed. How attitudes and beliefs are measured is also addressed to help you understand the research that is discussed throughout the text and the role that attitudes play in persuasion. Chapter 3 explores the complex relationship between attitudes and behavior, and some of the situations when attitudes influence behavior. Changing attitudes, beliefs and behaviors are the focus on persuasion. Understanding these concepts is crucial to effective persuasion.

CHAPTERS

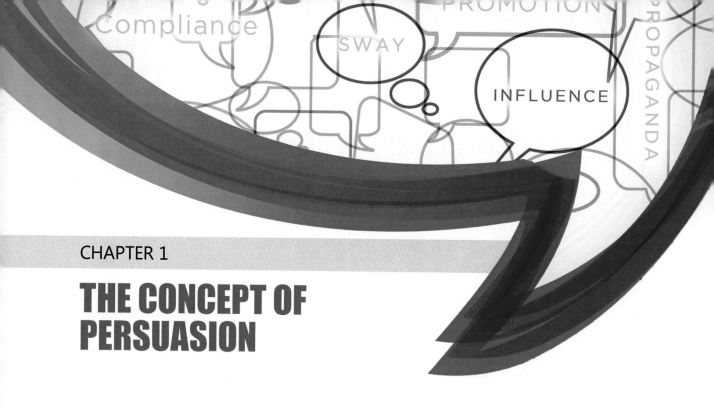

CHAPTER 1

THE CONCEPT OF PERSUASION

Shekera, a 20-year-old female and full-time student at a state university, is sitting in her nutrition class with Dr. Kalibo listening to her explain how complex carbohydrates are broken down into simple carbohydrates. Shekera loves the class and feels she has learned so much about food, diet, and health. Since the beginning of the semester, Shekera has almost quit drinking soda, has starting eating vegetables every day, and has quit adding cream to her coffee.

Jake and Melinda have been dating for 2 years and have lived together for the past 8 months. Melinda regrets moving in with Jake and has decided to move out. This evening Melinda broke the news to Jake. Jake responded with complete rage and began breaking things. Melinda yelled and pleaded with him to stop, and then Jake saw the fine porcelain Lladro figurine that her beloved grandmother had brought to her from Spain. Jake grabbed the Lladro, held it over his head and said, "Tell me you won't move out. Promise me you'll stay and I won't break it. If you leave, I break it." Melinda agreed to stay.

Nick is an 18-year-old male in his first year of college. On his way to class one day, he sees a flyer for the rowing club. It looks like fun, and Nick decides to go to the informational meeting that evening. At the meeting several members of the club spend a few minutes describing their experiences with the club, how much fun it is, and how many fun people they have met. By the end of the meeting, Nick can't wait to sign up. As he fills out the membership form, the club members congratulate him and welcome him to the rowing club.

So which of these situations involve persuasion? Is Shekera persuaded by her instructor to change her diet? Does Jake persuade Melinda to stay in the relationship? Is Nick persuaded to join the rowing club? All three of these situations involve influence, but are these examples of persuasion? One of these situations is clearly persuasion. Most scholars would agree that one situation is not persuasion, and one situation could be persuasion, but we need more information about the situation to know for sure. Let's begin discussing some of the characteristics of persuasion so that you can determine which of these situations are good examples of persuasion and which are not.

LEARNING OBJECTIVES

- DEFINE PERSUASION AND DIFFERENTIATE IT FROM OTHER FORMS OF INFLUENCE.
- DESCRIBE KEY CHARACTERISTICS OF PERSUASION.
- DESCRIBE SITUATIONS IN WHICH PERSUASION IS COMMONLY USED.
- CONSIDER THE ROLE OF ETHICS IN PERSUASION.

DEFINING CHARACTERISTICS OF PERSUASION

Persuasion has been defined in numerous ways, as is illustrated by the five definitions shown in Figure 1.1. Before we provide the definition to be used in this text, let's discuss some key characteristics that will help you understand why we define persuasion the way we do. First, **persuasion involves symbolic interaction using a shared symbol system**. Language and nonverbal behaviors are symbols, which means that communication between people involves symbolic interaction. Therefore, persuasion involves verbal and nonverbal communication. Four of the five definitions in Figure 1.1 refer to communication. The one definition that does not directly refer to communication does imply communication. Persuasive messages can be verbal and involve language (e.g., English), be nonverbal with symbols that have shared meanings (e.g., a smile, a picture of a flag), and are transmitted from a sender to a receiver. All three of the influence situations described above clearly involve communication and a shared symbol system, so all three have at least one characteristic of persuasion.

Second, **persuasion requires intent**. Without this requirement, we could argue that all communication is persuasive; however, only three of the five definitions in Figure 1.1 refer to intent in some way. When someone walks across campus and says "hello" to you, it is possible to interpret that as a persuasive intent to convince you that he or she is a friendly person and/or to convince you to respond in a friendly manner but, most often, it is nothing more than a greeting. A definition that doesn't require persuasive intent on the part of the sender doesn't help us distinguish persuasion from other related terms such as communication. The intent requirement means that persuasion focuses on messages that are intended to persuade the receiver. The second and third situations above clearly involve intent. Jake clearly intends to influence Melinda, and the rowing club clearly wants to influence Nick to join. But does Dr. Kalibo intend to influence Shekera to change her eating habits? Maybe. Assuming Shekera's teacher is like most other teachers, she wants Shekera to learn specific information about nutrition and dispel myths and misconceptions about food and diet. But that doesn't mean Dr. Kalibo intends to change Shekera's eating habits, particularly the changes that Shekera made. We would really need to ask Dr. Kalibo

BOSTROM (1983)

"Persuasion is communicative behavior that has as its purpose the changing, modification, or shaping of the responses (attitudes or behavior) of the receivers" (p. 11).

PETTY AND CACIOPPO (1981)

". . . any instance in which an active attempt is made to change a person's mind because the word is relatively neutral and because one person's propaganda may be another person's education" (p. 4).

LARSON (2013)

". . . the process of dramatic co-creation by sources and receivers of a state of identification through the use of verbal and/or visual symbols" (p. 20).

PERLOFF (2010)

". . . a symbolic process in which communicators try to convince other people to change their attitudes or behaviors regarding an issue through the transmission of a message in an atmosphere of free choice" (p. 12).

O'KEEFE (2002)

"A successful intentional effort at influencing another's mental state through communication in a circumstance in which the persuadee has some measure of freedom" (p. 5).

FIGURE 1.1 Definitions of persuasion.

if she intended to change her students' eating habits. If that indeed was her intention, then the situation would have the second characteristic of persuasion. If Dr. Kalibo simply wanted students to learn the content, and she left it up to the students to decide what to do with that information, then we would likely conclude that this really is not persuasion. Education and persuasion overlap in numerous ways, and the similarities and differences are further discussed later in this chapter.

Third, **persuasion involves two or more persons**. There has to be a sender and a receiver for persuasion to occur. Some have considered whether nonhuman animals can be involved in persuasion, whether individuals can persuade themselves through intrapersonal communication, and/or whether inanimate objects (e.g., a tree) can be persuasion agents. Although each of these arguments has supporters, the persuasion discussed in this textbook (and in most persuasion research) refers to persuasion attempts between at least two persons. All three of the influence situations involve at least two persons, so they all have this characteristic.

Finally, we need to consider the outcomes of persuasion. Miller (1980) argues that persuasion is intended to shape, reinforce, or change the responses of the receiver, and all of the definitions in Figure 1.1 refer to some type of change. We generally expect persuasive messages to involve attempts to **change** the beliefs, attitudes, and/or behavior of the receivers. For example, you have probably heard and seen numerous public service campaigns that want people to avoid texting while driving. In our situations, we can see change in behavior. Shekera changes her eating habits; Melinda stays rather than moves out; and Nick signs up for the rowing club. We also assume that Shekera's beliefs about her diet changed, which led to a change in her behavior. It's hard to say whether Melinda's beliefs about moving out changed, but her intended behavior was altered. We can also assume that Nick developed positive beliefs about the rowing club; otherwise, he wouldn't have signed up. Therefore, all three situations share this characteristic of persuasion.

Not all persuasive messages try to invoke change, however. Some attempt to **reinforce** currently held beliefs or attitudes and/or current behavioral practices. For example, Pepsi wants current Pepsi drinkers to remain loyal to the product. Political candidates speaking to members of their own party want members to remain loyal to the party and vote along party lines. Typically, speeches at the Republican and Democratic National Conventions focus on their supporters and use persuasive messages designed to reinforce current political views. Check out the 2016 convention speeches online to examine their focus. Another example is antismoking campaigns targeted at teens. Such campaigns are focused more on encouraging them *not* to start smoking than on altering current behaviors. Much of the persuasion surrounding us is attempting to reaffirm current beliefs, attitudes, and/or behaviors. The advertisement in Figure 1.2 illustrates the U.S. Potato Board's efforts to reinforce the consumption of potatoes.

Finally, some persuasion tries to shape responses. These are messages targeted toward receivers who have not developed an attitude toward an object and who often lack knowledge on the issue. For example, when a company introduces a new product, it tries to shape positive responses to that product. When Procter and Gamble introduced Febreze®, a product targeted at removing odors from fabric, the company needed to inform consumers and wanted them to think positively about such a product. Because receivers had no prior knowledge of this product, the company wasn't trying to change anything, and there was nothing there to reinforce. When AIDS was identified, the government was most concerned with shaping responses to that information. Now, the government is more concerned with reinforcing positive behaviors (e.g., safe sex) and trying to change the behaviors of those who are at risk for transmission of the disease (e.g., those who engage in sex without condoms, those who share needles). Thus, depending on the situation, the intended outcome for persuasion may be change, reinforcement, or shaping of receiver responses.

Of course, you may be wondering what is meant by "receiver responses." Depending on the situation, the desired response from the receiver may involve attitudes, beliefs, and/or behaviors. For example, at times, attitude change is desired. A political candidate may want voters to share favorable attitudes toward key campaign issues. A religious organization may want to target beliefs in receivers so that they are in alignment with the particular religion. Many times, however, behavior is the ultimate target of persuasion attempts. Advertisers ultimately want products to be purchased. Political candidates want votes and/or financial contributions. Social issue organizations often want to persuade the public about acceptable behavior (e.g., not smoking, wearing seat belts, adopting healthy exercise and eating patterns). We often expect attitudes and/or beliefs to be the basis for behavior, so targeting attitudes and beliefs may be an avenue to influence receiver behavior. As a result, when considering receiver responses, we need to consider attitudes, beliefs, and behaviors. We examine attitudes, beliefs, and behaviors in more depth in Chapters 2 and 3.

FIGURE 1.2 Potato public service announcement.

Thus, when all of these criteria are taken into account, we come to the following definition of persuasion, which draws on the multiple perspectives represented earlier: **Persuasion involves symbolic communication between two or more persons with intent to change, reinforce, or shape attitudes, beliefs, and/or behaviors of the receiver.**

At this point, we have discussed the situations presented at the beginning of this chapter in relation to the key characteristics of persuasion, but we really haven't answered the question of which of these is persuasion and which is not. We determined that

Shekera's change of eating habits might not be a result of persuasion if Dr. Kalibo did not intentionally try to influence her eating habits. However, the other two situations seemed to have all of the characteristics of persuasion. The second situation, involving Jake and Melinda, brings up another issue in distinguishing persuasion from other forms of influence—coercion. **Coercion** is social influence that involves force or threat of force. Jake uses a threat to force Melinda to stay. For this reason, this situation is a better example of coercion than it is of persuasion; however, the difference between coercion and persuasion is not always clear. Perloff's (2010) and O'Keefe's (2002) definitions of persuasion in Figure 1.1 refer to the receiver having free choice or freedom. Think of free vs. forced choice as a continuum as illustrated below.

Free choice _____ Forced choice

Having a gun pointed at your head with a demand for your laptop is clearly a forced choice. Or, in Melinda's case, the threat of a smashed treasured object is clearly force. In the third situation, Nick chose to become a member of the rowing club. No one forced or threatened Nick to sign up. Melinda's behavior was a result of force, whereas Nick's behavior was a result of choice. However, not all circumstances easily fit into one end of the continuum or the other. Consider the class you are in. The teacher controls the awarding of grades. Instructors set grading policies, work and attendance expectations, and so on. Students may choose to complete the work or not; however, there is a consequence in terms of grade received for choosing not to complete the work. Is that a free choice, or is there an element of threat in this situation? Is the public service announcement in Figure 1.3 an example of persuasion or coercion? Are you being threatened? Do you have free choice when it comes to wearing a seat belt? Situations that fall toward the forced choice end of the continuum are considered more coercion than persuasion, whereas situations that offer more free choice are considered more persuasion. However, where choice ends and force begins is not clear, making many situations ambiguous.

WHY STUDY PERSUASION?

The question of why we study persuasion is one that students may ask advisers and that researchers ask themselves. There are three major reasons people have for wanting to know more about persuasion. The most common reason students have given us for taking a class in persuasion is a very practical one. We all engage in persuasion in multiple contexts in our lives, and many want to study persuasion in order to be **more successful persuaders** themselves. That desire for mastery of the art of persuasion may be career oriented. Some career paths call for particularly strong persuasive skills, such as sales, law, marketing, public relations, and politics. In these areas, the ability to do a good job relies on strong persuasive abilities. Regardless of what career path is sought, most people want to be able to convince organizations to hire them and supervisors to promote them and award raises. People want to be able to sell their ideas to those in power and want to influence the choices made in their organizations.

In addition, we all use persuasion in our personal lives. You might try to convince your parents to send you money or to buy you a new car. You might try to persuade others to engage in social activities with you, follow you on Twitter, or to join causes you support. Perhaps you try to persuade faculty to admit you to classes or to give you a better grade. You might attempt to persuade a car salesperson to give you a better deal on your next vehicle or try to negotiate a better price for a new house. In short, because we engage in persuasion on a regular basis in multiple aspects of our lives, one good reason for studying persuasion is to be better at this process.

National Traffic highway safety.

FIGURE 1.3 Public service announcement for safety belt use.

Another common reason for studying persuasion is so that we can be better consumers of information. As we discussed previously, we are all bombarded with a broad variety of persuasive messages daily. Understanding persuasion allows us to make choices about when to be influenced and when not to be. By understanding the strategies, tactics, and methods employed by others, we can be better prepared to deal with persuasive messages targeted at us. This is particularly important in a democratic society where we trust that the typical citizen is able to process huge amounts of material and competing persuasive campaigns in order to make rational decisions about voting. Participation in a democratic society involves both the production and consumption of persuasive messages.

Finally, some people study persuasion in an attempt to better understand what they observe happening around them. When we look at behavior that doesn't fit our expectations and seems at times irrational to us, we try to understand how this can happen. Cult members engage in mass suicide in the belief that a spaceship hidden in the tail of a passing comet will take them to heaven. Seemingly useless products such as singing toy fish sell out of every store on the block. Trends in fashion come and go. Political candidates are elected to office although experts said they had no chance of being elected. A nation supports a leader conducting unspeakable atrocities, such as what happened in Germany with the Holocaust under Hitler's leadership. Studying persuasion can give us insight into these puzzling events and help to make sense of them.

The study of persuasion and the value of exploring this realm is certainly not new. Persuasion was studied and written about more than 2,500 years ago by the ancient Greeks. Arguably the most famous scholar of persuasion from that time was Aristotle. His work, Rhetoric, laid out many concepts about persuasion that are still considered valid today (Freese, 1991). Aristotle observed human interaction and persuasive attempts and taught his students how to persuade others. We discuss some of Aristotle's concepts as we explore persuasion, and much modern research draws on Aristotle's basic principles. For example, in Chapter 4, we examine source factors that influence the success and failure of persuasion and draw on Aristotle's concept of ethos, which still guides how modern researchers define source credibility. Aristotle saw persuasion as a central part of society and human interaction then, and today we still ask questions and explore persuasion as a part of interactions.

WHERE AND WHEN DO WE PERSUADE?

We suggest in this chapter that we are immersed in attempts at influence every day. The daily lives of individuals often involve persuasion in interpersonal and small-group contexts as well as in myriad forms of mass media. Students try to persuade parents to support them financially and emotionally. Roommates try to persuade each other to clean living quarters and to respect each other's privacy. Students try to convince faculty to grade them more positively. Group projects involve persuasion about meeting times, locations, and the division of labor. The multiple forms of media, such as radio, television, smartphones, newspapers, magazines, the Internet, posters, billboards, and corporate logos, surround us with messages constantly. It is hard to imagine a lack of persuasion in daily interactions for most people.

In addition, some segments of society depend on persuasion in order to achieve their goals. We have all been targeted as receivers by these segments, and some of you anticipate being senders in these contexts. We often think of advertising and marketing as bombarding us with persuasion. Certainly every form of media from television to social media to the Internet carries advertising, and it is clearly labeled as such. These advertising messages are open attempts to influence behavior, and they meet the criteria we established for persuasion. The messages are framed in words and nonverbal images that draw on culturally developed shared symbol systems. Persuasive intent is clearly involved in the purchase of advertising space, and the ads aren't always successful, but many are. The advertisements all have the purpose of changing, shaping, or reinforcing behavior toward the product or service being promoted.

Marketing encompasses advertising, but it moves beyond the purchase of advertising space in mass media outlets. Marketing can include promotional programs such as the popular, annual McDonald's Monopoly promotion. Consumers are encouraged to purchase McDonald's products in order to collect Monopoly game pieces for a chance at a variety of prizes, including a million dollars. Although the odds against winning are great, McDonald's does great business during the promotion. Marketing can also include such promotional devices as hats or T-shirts with corporate logos, special events, and more. In these cases, persuasion is operating and the receivers are generally aware that persuasion is being attempted. Marketing still involves systems of verbal and nonverbal symbols, clear persuasive intent, and attempts to influence the purchasing behaviors of receivers.

Persuasion is also used in public relations and encompasses a broad range of activities such as media relations, special events, crisis management, grassroots lobbying, and more. Here, receivers may be unaware that they are targets of persuasion. When reading a newspaper, readers often assume that more or less objective journalists write the articles. However, those articles are often influenced heavily by public relations materials that organizations have sent to the newspapers to influence content. The same is true for other forms of mass media, including news programming, talk shows, game shows, and situation comedies. These activities still meet the established criteria for persuasion. They all involve an agreed on verbal and nonverbal symbol system, intent is clearly present in the hiring of public relations professionals, and the targeted result includes changing, shaping, and reinforcing responses from the receivers.

Google CDC Health Campaigns and see the health behaviors the CDC is currently working on.

Although we often think of marketing and corporate interests as involved in persuasion, public health organizations and social issue groups also engage in persuasion. For example, the Centers for Disease Control and Prevention (CDC)_ has launched efforts to reduce smoking, encourage better eating patterns, reduce drug use, and encourage safer personal behaviors to avoid the spread of HIV. Other groups, both public and private, have launched public health campaigns around specialized issues. For example, Mothers Against Drunk Driving (MADD) has worked for years to reduce driving while under the influence of alcohol. Chances are good that one or more of these health campaigns has influenced choices you make about what to eat and how to live your life safely. Similarly, there are social issue groups that are attempting to get you to recycle more, donate to the homeless, or care about abandoned pets. These campaigns generally draw on approaches from advertising, marketing, and public relations and they all involve persuasion.

PERSUASION AS ONE OF MULTIPLE FORMS OF INFLUENCE

We have used the terms influence and persuasion, and we have used them somewhat differently. At this point we want to clarify how persuasion is different from influence as well as to clarify some related terms. **Influence** is a very general term that refers to a power that affects something. Persuasion, as we have discussed, is the use of communication to intentionally change, reinforce, or shape another's attitudes, beliefs, and/or behaviors. Clearly, persuasion is a form of influence. **Coercion** is also a form of influence that we discussed that involves force. Persuasion doesn't rely on force, although persuasion may involve pressure to change. Another term is **propaganda**. Propaganda is a term we often use to refer to persuasion attempts by those we do not agree with. When we are engaged in influence attempts, we call it persuasion. But when others are engaging in influence attempts that we disagree with, we often label that propaganda. This reflects the negative connotative meaning propaganda has for many people. In Chapter 12, we examine several propaganda tactics.. Propaganda has been defined as a type of persuasion that involves mass audiences with a purpose of achieving the goals of the persuader. It often involves emotional appeals, concealment of purpose, and a lack of sound support, which all involve ethical issues.

Education is another form of influence that can be distinguished from persuasion. Whether we consider influence to be education or persuasion is dependent on the intent of the source and the outcomes of the influence. If the source intends to change the receiver's attitudes, beliefs, or behavior (or to reinforce or shape receiver responses), it would be considered persuasion. Education does not have a persuasive intent, but instead has the intent of sharing information or knowledge. The receiver is left to decide what to do with the information. In the case of Shekera and her nutrition class, it is quite likely that sharing of information was Dr. Kalibo's primary intent. It would be rare, however, for educators not to care about how that information is used. Most educators want their students to adopt the information and use it in their lives, and that runs pretty close to shaping, reinforcing, and changing responses. Dr. Kalibo might well have been pleased by the changes in Shekera's diet. Certainly public health campaigns have the intent of doing more than sharing information. Those campaigns want to affect how receivers think about health issues, and most want specific health behaviors to be the result. Many education efforts have persuasive elements, so education and persuasion are not always easy to distinguish from one another.

We've stated several times that persuasion involves communication, but how is communication similar and different from persuasion? Communication is a broad term that encompasses a variety of messages, including those that influence people. Communication has been defined in a variety of ways; however, our preferred definition was put forth by McCroskey and Richmond (1996), who define **communication** as "the process by which one person stimulates meaning in the mind(s) of another person (or persons) through verbal and nonverbal messages" (p. 3). Our definition of persuasion refers to persuasion as a type of communication, and influence attempts involve communication. Thus, a hierarchy of terms would include communication as the umbrella term, influence next, with persuasion, coercion, and education being

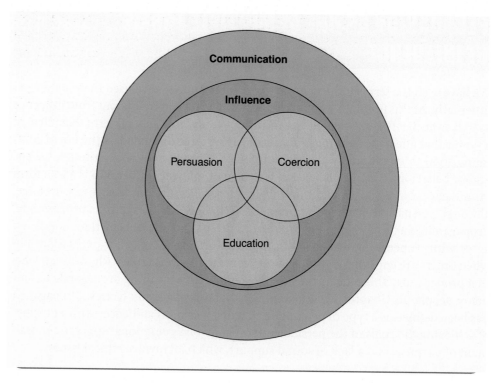

FIGURE 1.4 Venn diagram.

types of influence that overlap with one another. The Venn diagram in Figure 1.4 illustrates the relationships among communication, influence, persuasion, coercion, and education.

THE ROLE OF ETHICS IN PERSUASION

Up to this point, we have simply described types of social influence without making judgments about the appropriateness of using them. As the situation with Jake and Melinda at the beginning of the chapter illustrates, ethical implications should be considered in using and analyzing persuasion. Persuasion is a tool that can be used in an ethical or unethical manner, and it can be employed to achieve ethical or unethical ends. Although what can be done with persuasion and what has been done with persuasion are discussed throughout the book, you shouldn't lose sight of the question of what should be done with persuasion. Just because you can doesn't mean you should. Jake successfully influenced Melinda to not move out, but was that ethical?

Throughout history and across societies, ethical issues involving social influence have been raised. For example, con artists use persuasion to bilk money from vulnerable people. Hitler used persuasion to attempt world domination and to support plans to eradicate large segments of certain populations in the Holocaust. Persuasion has been employed to sell faulty products. Most people would find persuasion to be unethical in all of these cases. At the same time, persuasion has been employed to help the public stop smoking and wear seat belts. Persuasion has been used to promote the sale of useful products that benefit consumers, and persuasion is the cornerstone of our democratic system of government. Most would argue that these are important and generally ethical uses of persuasion. Persuasion is a tool, like most other tools, that can be used to benefit others or to harm them. The ethical standards of the source often determine whether persuasion is ethical or unethical.

Throughout this text, as we lay out the processes involved in persuasion and develop concepts, theories, tactics, strategies, and methods for engaging in successful persuasion, ethical implications will be considered. Questions will be raised as the book progresses, and Chapter 13 discusses ethics in more detail. We selected ethics as the topic for the last chapter, not because it is the least important, but because it is of critical importance. After you have studied all the different approaches and methods that have been and can be employed in persuasion, it is important that you consider the ethical implications of employing these approaches in multiple situations. Key perspectives on ethics are developed, and central questions are discussed. As you read the following chapters, consider whether there are or should be absolute standards in ethics. Are there guidelines (e.g., don't lie) that would be appropriate for every situation, or are ethics relative? Do the ends (e.g., a good outcome) justify any means (e.g., false evidence)? Is deceiving the receiver ever appropriate? Should the source of the message bear primary responsibility for ethics, or should the receiver share that responsibility (e.g., buyer beware)? These and other questions are discussed in Chapter 13, but you should be considering them as you read the rest of this book.

THE LAYOUT OF THE BOOK

This textbook is divided into five sections. This chapter and the next two chapters comprise the foundation of persuasion and our approach to it. Chapter 2 explores attitudes and the key concepts that underlie persuasion, and Chapter 3 explores the relationship between attitudes and behavior. With that as a foundation, the second section examines persuasion as a communication process with chapters on the source, message, receivers, and channel. The third section presents major theories of persuasion that provide guidance on how to use source, message, and channel factors. Each theory provides a different roadmap explaining how persuasion works and how to go about influencing a person. The fourth section examines interpersonal influence and propaganda. This is a tactical approach to influence. The final section examines the ethics of persuasion and presents several different perspectives.

SUMMARY

- Persuasion is a common occurrence in everyday life.
- Key concepts in the definition of persuasion include the use of symbolic interaction; intent on the part of the source of the message; two or more persons; and the intent to shape, reinforce, or change the responses of the receiver.

- Persuasion involves symbolic communication between two or more persons with intent to change, reinforce, or shape the attitudes, beliefs, and/or behaviors of the receiver.
- Persuasion is studied so that we can be more successful in persuasion attempts, be better consumers of information, and better understand what is happening around us.
- Persuasion occurs in interpersonal, small-group, and mass media settings as well as in advertising, marketing, public relations, public health issues, social issues, and other contexts of society.
- Communication is an umbrella term that includes influence. Persuasion is a type of influence along with education and coercion.
- Ethics play an important role in persuasion and should be considered throughout this book.

KEY TERMS

Coercion—social influence that involves force or threat of force.

Communication—the process by which one person stimulates meaning in the mind(s) of another person (or persons) through verbal and nonverbal messages.

Influence—general term that refers to a power that affects something.

Persuasion—symbolic communication between two or more persons with an intent to change, reinforce, or shape the attitudes, beliefs, and/or behaviors of the receiver.

Propaganda—a type of persuasion that involves mass audiences with a purpose of achieving the goals of the persuader, and it often involves emotional appeals, concealment of purpose, and a lack of sound support.

REVIEW QUESTIONS

1. How is persuasion defined?
2. What are the important characteristics of the definition of persuasion?
3. What is the difference between shaping, reinforcing, and changing responses of receivers?
4. Why is it important to study persuasion?
5. When and where does persuasion take place?
6. How do you distinguish between communication, persuasion, influence, coercion, and education?

DISCUSSION QUESTIONS

1. Compare the different definitions of persuasion. What are the strengths and weaknesses of each definition? Which do you like best? Why?

2. Brainstorm several examples of persuasion that you have encountered the past week. Use the four characteristics of persuasion to analyze your examples of persuasion. Do your examples have all four characteristics of persuasion?

3. Persuasion can be employed in many ways for many purposes. Consider the role of ethics in persuasion. What is it acceptable to do in order to persuade others? How far could you go before crossing a line into unethical behavior? What topics would influence your decision about what is ethical in persuasion? Consider ethical criteria you might develop to guide your use of persuasion.

4. Think about classes you have taken recently. To what extent was the instructor sharing information and to what extent was the instructor trying to persuade you?

5. Most people would agree that coercion in its pure form is not persuasion or, in other words, the receiver must have some degree of choice in order for the interaction to be considered persuasion. At what point does persuasion become coercion?

6. There are definitional differences between persuasion, propaganda, coercion, education, and communication. Are there also ethical differences? Do you find any of these concepts to be inherently ethical or inherently unethical? What ethical principles distinguish the five terms?

REFERENCES

Bostrom, R. N. (1983). *Persuasion.* Englewood Cliffs, NJ: Prentice-Hall.

Freese, J. H. (1991). *Aristotle: The art of rhetoric with an English translation by John Henry Freese.* Cambridge, MA: Harvard University Press.

Larson, C. U. (2013). *Persuasion: Reception and responsibility* (13th ed.). Boston, MA: Wadsworth, Cengage Learning.

McCroskey, J. C., & Richmond, V. P. (1996). *Fundamentals of human communication: An interpersonal perspective.* Prospect Heights, IL: Waveland Press.

Miller, G. R. (1980). On being persuaded: Some basic distinctions. In M. Roloff & G. Miller (Eds.), *Persuasion: New directions in theory and research* (pp. 11–28). Beverly Hills, CA: Sage.

O'Keefe, D. J. (2002). *Persuasion: Theory and research* (2nd ed.). Thousand Oaks, CA: Sage.

Perloff, R. M. (2010). *The dynamics of persuasion: Communication and attitudes in the 21st century* (4th ed.). New York, NY: Routledge.

Petty, R. E., & Cacioppo, J. T. (1981). *Attitudes and persuasion: Classic and contemporary approaches.* Dubuque, IA: Wm. C. Brown.

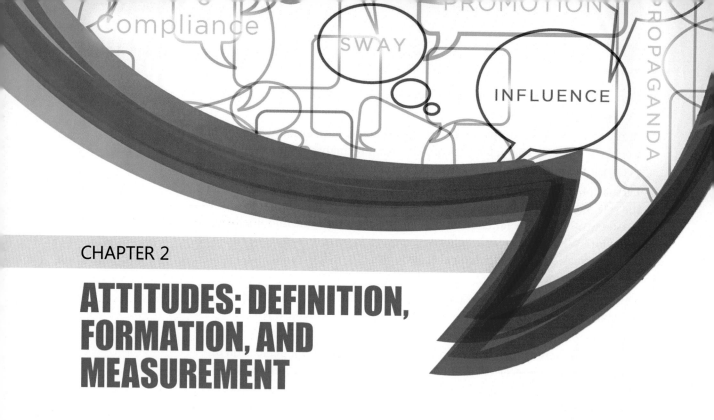

CHAPTER 2

ATTITUDES: DEFINITION, FORMATION, AND MEASUREMENT

*She has **attitude**!*

*What's your **attitude** about the war?*

*He needs an **attitude** adjustment.*

*She has a bad **attitude**.*

*Persuasion involves symbolic communication between two or more persons with intent to change, reinforce, or shape **attitudes**, beliefs, and/or behaviors of the receiver.*

Courtesy of Ann Frymier

Each of these sentences uses the term *attitude*, and the word means something a little different in each sentence. What does the term *attitude* mean to you? Is it something you can observe? We use the term *attitude* frequently in everyday life and in a variety of ways; however, the term has a specific meaning in the persuasion context. As we discussed in Chapter 1, persuasion is often about change—changing beliefs, behaviors, and attitudes. At times we also want to reinforce those things rather than change them. But before we can do either of those things, we need to understand what we are trying to influence. In this chapter we focus on those things we are most often trying to change through persuasion: **attitudes**, **beliefs**, **behaviors**, and **behavioral intentions**.

The definition of attitude is important within the study of persuasion. In just about every definition of persuasion, attitude appears as part of the desired outcome. Persuasion theories are often referred to as attitude change theories, and a great deal of research examines the relationship between attitudes

LEARNING OBJECTIVES

- DEFINE ATTITUDE AND DISTINGUISH IT FROM BELIEFS AND VALUES.
- DESCRIBE THE CHARACTERISTICS OF ATTITUDE.
- DESCRIBE AND EXPLAIN THE FUNCTIONS OF ATTITUDE.
- EXPLAIN HOW ATTITUDES AND BELIEFS CAN BE FORMED THROUGH CLASSICAL CONDITIONING, OPERANT CONDITIONING, AND MODELING.
- DESCRIBE HOW ATTITUDES ARE MEASURED.

and behavior. People often believe that our attitudes influence our behavior, so understanding attitudes can help us understand and control persuasion. Thus, it is important to have a clear understanding of the concept of "attitude" before further exploring the field of persuasion. As with the term *persuasion*, there are multiple definitions of **attitude**. Take a moment to read through the definitions of attitude presented in Figure 2.1. As you can see, all the definitions refer to the evaluation and favorableness/unfavorableness of some object. Before we fully examine the definition of attitude, let's discuss some key characteristics of attitudes so that the definition will be more meaningful for you.

CHARACTERISTICS OF ATTITUDES

These definitions lead to important characteristics of attitudes. First, attitudes involve **affect**. This means attitudes involve likes and dislikes as an affective or evaluative response as opposed to a cognitive or knowledge-based response. These evaluative responses involve feelings, likes, and dislikes and are reflected in statements that use the terms *like* or *dislike*. For example, the sentences "I like Adam Levine" and "I can't stand Adam Levine" reflect attitudes toward Adam Levine. The affective component is key in distinguishing attitudes from beliefs and is discussed later.

Second, attitudes are always **tied to an object**. Objects can refer to any item, event, person, concept, or idea. We don't hold likes or dislikes in general. Instead, we link them to objects. A person could like BMWs, dislike Star Wars, or like her relationship with her parents. Since attitudes are always linked to an object, it is important to understand the specific object in order to understand the attitude. For example, someone who dislikes Japanese food has a different attitude than someone who dislikes sushi. The more specific the object, the better we will understand the attitude.

Third, attitudes tend to be **consistent**. This does not mean they are inflexible and difficult to change, but it does mean they don't blow in the wind and move easily in either direction. Fishbein and Ajzen (1975) discuss three kinds of consistency

FISHBEIN AND AJZEN (1975)

"... learned predisposition to respond in a consistently favorable or unfavorable manner with respect to a given object" (p. 6).

EAGLY AND CHAIKEN (1993)

"... a psychological tendency that is expressed by evaluating a particular entity with some degree of favor or disfavor" (p. 1).

ALBARRACIN, ZANNA, JOHNSON, AND KUMKALE (2005)

"... attitude is reserved for evaluative tendencies, which can both be inferred from and have an influence on beliefs, affect, and overt behavior" (p. 5).

FIGURE 2.1 Definitions of attitude.

regarding attitudes. They argue that attitudes have stimulus-response, response-response, and evaluative consistency. **Stimulus-response consistency** refers to the expectation that people will have the same response to the same stimulus over time. For example, if you expressed negative attitudes about smoking in class today, we would expect you to hold negative attitudes about smoking next week in another class. Although attitudes about smoking can change over time, we don't expect them to change from one day to the next.

Response-response consistency refers to expectations that responses to stimuli will be similar over time. For example, if a friend ate plain broccoli one day (indicating a positive evaluation), then you would expect that friend to eat it in a quiche that was served the following week. Even though the broccoli was in different forms, the responses would be the same. We expect a consistency of responses from time to time.

Evaluative consistency refers to the affective tone of the attitude. For example, one can indicate a dislike for broccoli by refusing to eat it, or one can make a face when broccoli is mentioned as a central ingredient in a dish. Both represent negative responses. Although these are not the exact same responses, they are consistent in being negative responses (i.e., nonverbal, refusing to eat broccoli) to the same stimulus (broccoli). We cannot predict the exact nature of a specific response, but we can predict which part of the affective continuum (positive vs. negative) the responses will reflect. Alternatively, a person could smile when a dog walks by or could stop to pet the animal. Both represent positive responses, and both represent evaluative consistency.

A fourth characteristic is that attitudes also are **related to behavior** or, in other words, attitudes can influence behavior and behavior can influence attitudes. Early researchers believed attitudes directly caused behavior, but we know today that the relationship is not that straightforward. Also we know that behavior sometimes influences attitude formation. Several persuasion theories assume that attitudes guide behavior even though other things influence behavior too. Several things influence the way we behave, such as our genetic makeup, the situation we are in, and other people around us. However, attitude also influences behavior. For instance, if a person evaluates chocolate positively (positive attitude), he or she is likely to eat chocolate (behavior). However, your experience (behavior) with a new food (think samples in the grocery store) is often the basis of your attitude toward that food. If it tasted good, you developed a positive attitude toward it. The nature of the attitude-behavior relationship is a bit complex, so in Chapter 3 we explore this relationship in more depth.

A final characteristic is that attitudes are **learned**. Attitudes are not characteristics that people are born with. Attitudes can be learned in more than one way. Sometimes attitudes are explicitly taught by parents, teachers, peers, or significant others. If parents tell their children that dogs are nasty creatures, chances are that the children will adopt a negative attitude toward dogs. It is in this manner that many prejudices are passed on from parents to children. In addition, some attitudes can be learned from direct experience. If a person tries peas and finds them distasteful, then he or she is likely to have a negative attitude toward peas. Sometimes, attitudes are learned from observations of others. This may include the influence of mass media as well as the direct observation of those around us. If we see others eating sashimi and appearing to enjoy it, we may then hold a positive attitude toward sashimi. Similarly, many advertisements show people who purchase a particular product (e.g., toothpaste) having great experiences often involving being attractive to the opposite sex. This scenario is designed to lead viewers to hold positive attitudes about the product being featured in the advertisement.

ATTITUDE DEFINED

Another look at the definitions of attitude in Figure 2.1 should show you that these characteristics are reflected in the definitions and that there is little disagreement about what constitutes the concept of attitude (at least in the persuasion context). We have adopted Fishbein and Ajzen's (1975) very basic definition of an **attitude** as "a learned predisposition to respond in a consistently favorable or unfavorable manner with respect to a given object" (p. 6) as our preferred definition and the definition we will use in the remainder of this text.

THEORIES OF ATTITUDE AND BELIEF FORMATION

Where do attitudes come from? As discussed previously, attitudes are often learned just as we learn anything. Persuasion in general focuses on changing attitudes and related behaviors; however, there are times when we want to form attitudes rather than change existing ones. To be an effective persuader, we need to be able to influence the formation of attitudes as well as change existing attitudes. Traditional persuasion theories (such as those discussed in Chapters 8–11) focus on changing attitudes rather than on forming new ones. Learning theories are very useful to the persuader interested in attitude formation because attitudes are learned to begin with. The three learning theories discussed here were originally developed to explain how we learn behaviors, but have been expanded to explain how attitudes, beliefs, and behaviors are learned. Therefore, because these theories apply to attitudes, beliefs, and behaviors, they can help us design messages that influence attitude formation as well as change established attitudes and behavior. Although these learning theories are not a part of "traditional persuasion theories," they are very useful to persuaders. You are probably familiar with the three learning theories discussed here; however, you may never have thought of them as persuasion tools.

CLASSICAL CONDITIONING

You may be familiar with Ivan Pavlov's dogs and how he trained (conditioned) them to salivate at the sound of a bell. This theory was originally formulated to explain how people learn behavior, but it was not long before researchers realized that attitudes could be conditioned in much the same way.

Classical conditioning is based on the concept of **pairing**. Two stimuli must occur together to be paired. In Pavlov's experiments, the dogs salivated at the sight of food, which is a natural thing for dogs to do. This is not something a dog has to learn. Each time the dogs were to be fed, a bell was rung. After a few pairings of the bell and the food, the dogs would salivate at the sound of the bell alone. In this example, food is the **unconditioned stimulus** and salivating is the **unconditioned response**. These are labeled "unconditioned" because they were not learned; it is just the natural response to salivate at the sight of food. The bell is considered the **conditioned stimulus** because it was paired with the food. When the dogs salivated upon hearing the bell, the salivating was considered the **conditioned response** because the salivating was now a learned response to the sound of the bell. Therefore, the unconditioned response and the conditioned response are the same behavior (salivating), but the salivating is caused by different stimuli.

Once a behavior is conditioned, it can act like an unconditioned stimulus and be paired with yet another stimulus as is shown in Figure 2.3. This is known as **higher-order conditioning** and is how attitudes are frequently conditioned. The example in Figure 2.3 illustrates higher-order conditioning. Homemade ice cream is frequently served at church picnics and typically elicits a positive response. By serving homemade ice cream at church picnics, the unconditioned stimulus (UCS) of homemade ice cream is paired with church picnics, the conditioned stimulus (CS). After one or more pairings, church picnics elicit the same positive response as homemade ice

FIGURE 2.2

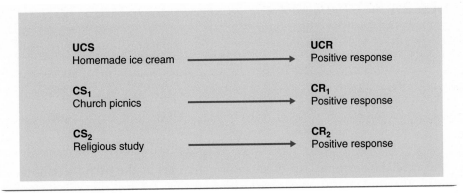

FIGURE 2.3 Higher-order classical conditioning.

cream. The positive response is considered the conditioned response (CR) because it is elicited by the church picnic rather than by the ice cream. Church picnics may then be paired with religious study. After a few pairings, religious study now elicits a positive response just as church picnics and ice cream did. There is no limit to the number of "levels" in higher-order conditioning.

Staats and Staats (1958) were some of the first to demonstrate that attitudes could be conditioned. In this study, they recruited 93 college students who were then arranged into two groups. Both groups were told that their task was to learn lists of words, with one list presented visually and the other orally. Students were told that the experiment focused on visual learning versus oral learning. The words presented visually were national names—German, Swedish, Italian, French, Dutch, and Greek—and were presented 18 times in random order. The oral words presented immediately after the words *German*, *Italian*, *French*, and *Greek* were neutral with no systematic meaning (e.g., with, chair, twelve). For one group of students, the word *Dutch* was always followed by a negative word (e.g., ugly, bitter, failure) and *Swedish* was always followed by a positive word (e.g., gift, sacred, happy). For the other group, it was just the opposite; the word *Dutch* was paired with positive words and the word *Swedish* was followed by negative words. Following the word presentations, students were asked how they *felt* about the words. Seventeen students indicated they were aware of the systematic word pairings and were excluded from the data analysis. The results are shown in Table 2.1 and indicate that Staats and Staats successfully conditioned students to have a positive attitude toward the word *Swedish* and a negative attitude toward the word *Dutch* or vice versa, depending on the group. As you can see in Table 2.1, Group 1, which heard positive words paired with the word *Swedish*, had a more positive attitude toward *Swedish* than the word *Dutch* (attitude was measured on a 7-point scale). For Group 2, the means were opposite, resulting in a more positive attitude toward the word *Dutch* than the word *Swedish*.

Classical conditioning is a rather simple way of forming a positive attitude. As a persuader, you simply pair your object of interest with something positive. You just have to make sure that the unconditioned stimulus elicits a positive response in your audience. Numerous examples of classical conditioning can be found in advertising, such as many perfume ads. These types of advertisements show a beautiful, sexy woman—something that tends to elicit a positive response from both men and

TABLE 2.1 *ATTITUDE MEANS FOR STAATS AND STAATS (1958) STUDY*

	DUTCH		SWEDISH	
	MEAN	STANDARD DEVIATION	MEAN	STANDARD DEVIATION
Group 1	2.67	0.94	3.42	1.50
Group 2	2.67	1.31	1.83	0.90

Look for advertisements for high end consumer products. What kinds of stimuli do they pair their product with?

women—and the perfume. No other information about the perfume is generally provided. The product is simply paired with an image that is likely to elicit a positive response. Advertisers hope you are exposed to the ad enough times for the conditioning to occur. Classical conditioning is often very useful, but some objects are too complicated for conditioning to work effectively. Therefore, we need additional strategies.

OPERANT CONDITIONING

The basic premise of **operant conditioning** is that learning occurs as a result of reinforcement and punishment as is comically illustrated by Dilbert in Figure 2.3. If reinforcement follows a behavior, the behavior will be learned and repeated. If punishment or no response at all (extinction) follows a behavior, the behavior will occur less frequently or disappear completely. An attitude can be formed or learned in a similar manner. For example, if a child expresses a negative view toward spiders and receives some form of verbal praise or attention for not liking spiders, the child is likely to develop a negative attitude toward spiders.

Insko (1965) demonstrated the relative ease with which attitudes can be formed using verbal reinforcement. Insko had some of his graduate students contact by phone 72 students from his Introductory Psychology course. Students were asked to strongly agree, agree, disagree, or strongly disagree with 14 statements regarding the creation of a Springtime Aloha Week at the University of Hawaii (where the experiment took place). Half of the students were verbally reinforced for indicating a positive attitude, and half were reinforced for indicating a negative attitude. The verbal reinforcement came in the form of the graduate student saying "good." Insko's graduate students were able to successfully influence students' attitude toward Aloha Week. Students receiving reinforcement for expressing a positive attitude had a significantly more positive attitude than students reinforced for expressing a negative attitude. To further test the reinforcement, a week after the phone interview, the students completed a Local Issues Questionnaire on which one item, about two-thirds through the questionnaire, asked about the Springtime Aloha Week. Once again, students who had received reinforcement for a positive attitude had a more positive attitude toward Aloha Week than did those students receiving reinforcement for expressing a negative attitude. Therefore, the reinforcement successfully formed an attitude, and the attitude continued beyond the initial experiment.

One interesting thing about the Insko (1965) study is that the reinforcement was a simple "good" coming from a complete stranger. When you receive a phone call from a telemarketer, you may notice the caller reinforcing (or at least trying to

FIGURE 2.4 Using punishment to influence behavior.

reinforce) your positive responses. Operant conditioning may be one of the strategies used to get you to say yes to their offer. For instance, the caller may initially ask you a question such as, "Do you ever read magazines?" Most people will say yes. The telemarketer follows your response with a, "Good, good. Most people do." Insko's study also demonstrates how easy it is for a researcher or polling firms to influence the audience's attitude. Such tactics may explain why different groups doing essentially the same poll can come up with such different results. This is why understanding *how* data were collected is necessary to understanding what the final results mean.

Operant conditioning is frequently used when new products are introduced. Companies often offer a variety of rewards for trying their products. Rewards may be coupons, entry into a drawing, or free samples. Reward programs are used extensively by companies such as Starbucks to keep customers coming back. Parents and teachers also frequently use operant conditioning to influence children's beliefs and behaviors. The daughters of this book's authors attended a school where all first graders receive a prize for every 25 books that they read or someone reads to them. Teachers are both reinforcing the behavior of reading as well trying to reinforce a positive attitude toward reading. Punishment can also be used to influence attitudes and behavior, although punishment is generally less effective than reward. Punishment, being negative in nature, is generally avoided by advertisers and other persuaders.

MODELING

Modeling is a learning theory that explains how we learn by observing others. If you have a younger brother or sister, there were probably times when your younger sibling mimicked everything you did, every move, every word, even your exasperated pleas to stop copying you. Your brother or sister learned to behave like you by observing you. He or she didn't learn by conditioning or by being rewarded, as discussed in operant conditioning, but rather observed a model and learned by observing. Most anyone can serve as a model. Your parents, siblings, other family members, teachers, movie stars, and other well-known people all served as models for various behaviors during your childhood. People whom we respect often serve as models. You may have been expected to serve as a model for younger siblings or cousins and were told to "set a good example." When we observe a person being rewarded for what he or she is doing, we are more likely to model his or her behavior. For example, you may observe a classmate showing interest in the professor's research and be rewarded for it by receiving more attention in class. As a result, you begin to express an interest in your professor's research in hopes of receiving the same reward. Bandura (1971) outlined four basic steps in the modeling process. The first step is **attention**. One must pay attention to a model in order to understand what the model is doing. We can't learn what we don't attend to.

The second step in the modeling process is **retention**. Once you have paid attention to what someone (a model) is doing, you have to retain that information. Think back to when you were trying to learn something such as shuffling cards. You may have asked the model to show you over and over again in an effort to attend to and retain exactly what he or she was doing.

The third step in modeling a behavior is **motor reproduction**. You must be able to reproduce the behavior. When learning to shuffle cards, you may have first learned what you needed to do but had not yet developed the motor skills to shuffle without sending the cards across the room. When learning an attitude through modeling, the motor reproduction step is not relevant because an attitude is a mental change. The last step in the modeling process is **motivation**. You have to *want* to perform the behavior. You may have watched someone smoke a cigarette numerous times and gone through the first three steps of modeling but have no desire (motivation) to smoke a cigarette; therefore, you do not take up smoking even though you have watched someone do it.

We not only learn behaviors by watching others, we also learn attitudes by observing others. As children we observe our parents' reactions and listen to their responses to a whole variety of things, events, people, and ideas. You may have learned a positive attitude toward diversity by observing your parents' positive attitudes toward diversity. A group of researchers used the principles of modeling to influence college students' attitudes toward date rape. Lanier, Elliott, Martin, and Kapadia (1998) had incoming students at a small college attend a brief play in which the actors modeled intolerance for date rape in any form. Before seeing the play, all students completed a date rape attitude survey. After completing the survey, students saw either the play on date rape or a play on multicultural issues (control group). After the play, all students completed the date rape survey a second time. Results showed that the students who had attended the date rape play viewed date rape more negatively than did students who were in the control group. Students who were initially most tolerant of date rape showed the greatest attitude change. Thus, the modeling in the play helped shape students' attitudes toward date rape.

Advertisers use modeling as well. Celebrities are often recruited to endorse a product or cause. The Dairy Association produced several advertisements over several years, such as the one in Figure 2.5, showing a variety of celebrities with a milk moustache. The association is hoping you will model the behavior of drinking milk and the apparent positive attitude toward milk being modeled in the advertisement. There is a reason advertisers use celebrities. We don't model just anyone; we tend to model those we admire and look up to. Additionally, if we observe someone being rewarded, we are more likely to model his or her behavior. If we observe someone being punished, we are less likely to model his or her behavior. Therefore, the most powerful models are those whom we admire and whom we observe being rewarded for performing the behavior or attitude of interest.

Although learning theories were not initially intended as persuasion theories, they are very useful to the persuader and their use is evident in many advertising and marketing strategies. Another approach to attitude is how people use attitudes or, in other words, how attitudes function.

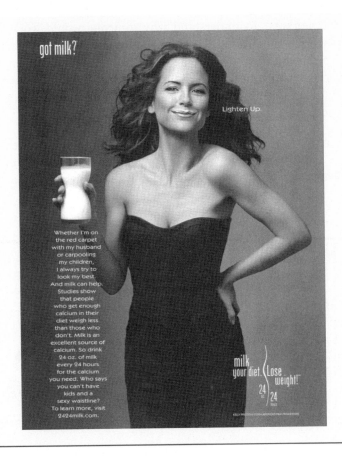

With permission of Lowe Worldwide, Inc. as agent for National Fluid Milk Processor Promotion Board.

FIGURE 2.5 How could this be viewed as modeling?

THE FUNCTIONS OF ATTITUDES

Why do people hold attitudes? It is easy to understand why researchers would be curious about this; however, those who want to be successful persuaders can be more effective if they understand the functions that attitudes serve for message recipients. If we understand why an attitude is held and how it serves the receiver, then we can better understand how to alter those attitudes and know better how to leverage those functions to achieve persuasive outcomes. As we explore each type of function, we can understand how to design persuasive appeals that would target each type.

Katz (1960) launched this line of investigation and argued that attitudes serve multiple *functions* or purposes. The first is the **ego-defensive function**. These are attitudes that are held to help people protect their sense of self and prevent the need to face unpleasant realities, as illustrated in the Dilbert cartoon in Figure 2.6. For example, Ashley might value academic achievement over sports achievement as a way to make herself feel better about her lack of athletic ability. Others might look down on a particular ethnic group or sexual orientation in order to make them feel better about their own ethnicity or sexual preference. These attitudes are tied to the individual's sense of self.

Knowledge is another function of attitudes. These are attitudes that help people understand the world around them. For example, believing that social workers are poorly paid and have bad working conditions leads to questions about why people would be social workers. To understand why someone would work for such low wages, an explanation is required. Viewing social workers as good, altruistic people helps explain social workers' willingness to work for low pay in poor working conditions. Our affective evaluations (attitudes) often help us bring understanding to the world around us, and clever persuaders offer that information in a manner designed to favor their outcomes.

A third function of attitudes is **utilitarian**. This refers to attitudes that benefit us by allowing us to avoid negative consequences and achieve positive outcomes. For example, students may like extra-credit because it benefits them personally. Faculty

FIGURE 2.6 Ego-defensiveness.

may like tenure because they see personal benefit from it. These attitudes are tied closely to the individual's sense of rewards and costs.

A fourth function of attitude is the **value-expressive function**. This function refers to attitudes that allow people to express values important to them. For example, a person who values the environment might feel positively about hybrid vehicles and solar energy. These attitudes are held as a way of expressing values.

Smith, Bruner, and White (1956) proposed an additional function of attitudes. They suggested that attitudes serve a **social-adjustive function**. These attitudes are held to help us better fit in with and relate to those around us. Many people adopt attitudes that reflect those of their peer groups to better fit in with those groups. A teenager may like rap music if most of his or her friends do and if it is a frequent topic of conversation. Similarly, a teen may dislike smoking if his or her peers view it negatively. Someone may begin viewing *The Walking Dead* as a good television show because everyone else is talking about it. Holding attitudes consistent with those of one's peers can help a person fit in socially.

Persuaders who understand how their audience uses attitudes can better understand how to persuade those individuals. The social-adjustive and value-expressive functions have received the most attention and have been the focus of a **functional matching** approach to persuasion. The idea here is that if an attitude serves a social-adjustive function for an individual, that person will be more receptive to social adjustive messages that emphasize how others view the attitude object and how holding a particular attitude helps one fit in. If an attitude serves a value-expressive function, that person will be more receptive to messages that emphasize expressing and attaining one's values. Lavine and Snyder (1996) demonstrated the effectiveness of functional matching in an experiment. They identified people whose attitude toward voting served a social-adjustive function, and they identified people whose attitude toward voting served a value-expressive function. They then created two sets of messages about voting: 1) a *value-expressive message* that argued that voting provides a way for people to express their support for values such as freedom and democracy; and 2) *a social-adjustive message* that informed participants that the majority of their peers were voting in an upcoming election and that voting enhanced a person's popularity and attractiveness. Half of each group received a social-adjustive message and half received a value-expressive message. Those who received a message that matched their attitude function perceived the message as higher quality, had a more positive attitude toward voting, and were more likely to vote than those who received a message that did *not* match how their attitude functions.

Thus, if we understand how an attitude functions for an individual or a group we can more easily create a message to influence that attitude. You may not always know how an attitude functions for a group of people. One way to deal with this is to incorporate both value-expressive and social-adjustive messages into the same message. An example of this approach is Rock the Vote campaigns. These messages appeal to the democratic values of free speech, inclusion, and participation in the democratic process. But these messages also make it cool and desirable to vote, and portray it as the "in" thing to do. Lavine and Synder (1996) tested this approach by including a *mixed message* (one that incorporates multiple attitude functions) in their experiment. They found that mixed messages were not as effective as *pure messages* (ones

Go to YouTube and search for "Rock the Vote." What attitude functions do you think they are appealing to?

that completely matched the attitude function); however, mixed messages were more effective than messages that did not match. So, matching your message to how the attitude functions for a person is most effective, but when this isn't possible, creating a mixed message is an effective alternative.

How might you go about using the functional matching approach? Imagine you are creating an advertisement for cars. What kind of information and images would you include for people whose attitude toward cars serves a value-expressive function as compared to those who held a social-adjustive attitude?

ATTITUDE AND RELATED CONCEPTS

Our discussion of persuasion has involved several concepts. Persuasion means changing or shaping attitudes, beliefs, and behaviors. Although we frequently hear the terms *attitudes, beliefs,* and *values* used together, these are three different concepts. We need to differentiate attitude from these other concepts before we continue with our discussion of attitudes and persuasion.

Behavior must be distinguished from attitude. **Behavior** refers to overt physical actions on the part of an individual. Attitudes are psychological in nature. Attitudes are held inside the mind of each individual, and we don't know what attitude a person holds until he or she engages in observable behavior. We often infer attitudes from what people say (verbal behavior), from their facial expressions (nonverbal behavior), or from actions they take (e.g., eating broccoli). We often learn about individuals' attitudes from their responses on a questionnaire. This is also a behavior because the act of responding to questions is what gave us information about the attitudes. Of course, our inferences from behavior may be inaccurate, and some people may give responses on questionnaires that don't actually reflect their attitudes. Behavior is related to attitude, but it is not the same thing as an attitude.

Related to behavior is the concept of **behavioral intention**. Fishbein and Ajzen (1975) proposed this concept as a step between the psychological construct of attitude and overt behavior. They describe behavioral intention as "a person's intention to perform various behaviors" (p. 12). In the sashimi example mentioned earlier, the individual had a positive attitude toward sashimi and intended to eat sashimi (behavioral intention) before actually eating the sashimi (behavior). Yet, those who like sashimi sometimes do not intend to eat it, and sometimes when we intend to eat sashimi, we don't. Concerns about diet or others' disapproval of sashimi may keep us from either intending to eat sashimi or not eating it when we intend to. Therefore, attitudes and behavioral intentions are not perfect predictors of behavior. We discuss the concept of behavioral intentions again in Chapter 10 in relation to the theory of reasoned action.

Another concept related to attitudes is belief. Beliefs deal with the cognitive or informational dimension, whereas attitudes deal with the affective or feeling dimension. **Beliefs** "link an object to some attribute" (Fishbein & Ajzen, 1975, p. 12). Often, what people say they know as truth actually reflects a belief. Faith in the existence (attribute) of God (object) is a belief. Fire (object) is hot (attribute) is a belief. Beliefs reflect our way of thinking about the world and are related to attitudes. "Fire is hot," reflects a belief. Not liking to be burned reflects an attitude. Avoiding fire is a resulting behavior.

Beliefs and attitudes have similar characteristics. Beliefs are also learned rather than innate, and they can be learned in many of the same ways attitudes are learned. Parents can pass along beliefs about religion or desired moral behaviors. Peers and the media can pass along beliefs, and some beliefs are formed by direct experience. Some of you learned that fire was hot by getting burned (direct experience), whereas others of you took your parents' word for it (indirect experience). Also, like attitudes, beliefs are generally consistent. They can be altered, but they don't shift back and forth easily.

Fishbein and Raven (1962) proposed two classes of beliefs: beliefs-in and beliefs-about. **Beliefs-in** refers to beliefs in the existence of a concept. It could refer to beliefs in the existence of God, global warming, or the Tooth Fairy. **Beliefs-about** refers to beliefs about characteristics of a concept. For example, believing in God is a "belief-in" type of belief, and believing that God is all-powerful is a "belief-about" type of belief. Fishbein (1967) argued that beliefs-about involve a relationship "between the object of the belief and some other object, concept, value, or goal" (p. 259).

Some beliefs about relationships may be *prescriptive*. When people say that school (object) should be required (attribute) for all children, they are expressing a prescriptive belief. Prescriptive beliefs generally indicate that something should or should not occur. Secondly, some beliefs about relationships may be *descriptive*. An example of a descriptive belief is that the sky (object) is blue (attribute). Descriptive beliefs describe characteristics of the object. Third, beliefs about relationships may be *evaluative*. Someone who says that Mary (object) is a good citizen (attribute) is expressing an evaluation based on criteria for what it takes to be a good citizen.

Beliefs can be held with varying levels of strength or importance. **Peripheral beliefs** tend to include issues that are less important to a person. For example, fashion often involves peripheral beliefs. Hairstyles and clothing choices that are believed to be fashionable one year may be totally rejected the next year. Core beliefs are the opposite of peripheral beliefs. **Core beliefs** tend to be strongly held and hard to change. They are often formed early in life and are part of an individual's sense of self. These beliefs are hard to change because of either constant reinforcement or a total lack of experience. If a child grows up in a religious family, attends services regularly, and is part of social groups in that religious organization, then those religious beliefs are being constantly reinforced. Similarly, someone who was raised to be prejudiced toward an ethnic group and has had no interactions with members of that group will have beliefs that have never been challenged by actual experience. When considering beliefs, it is important to consider how strongly they are held. Very strongly held core beliefs and values are harder to change, whereas peripheral beliefs are generally much easier to change.

Core beliefs are sometimes referred to as **values**. Rokeach (1968) defined values as "an enduring belief that a specific mode of conduct or end-state of existence is personally and socially preferable to alternative modes of conduct or end-states of existence" (p. 160). Examples of values are "people should take initiative" (mode of conduct) and

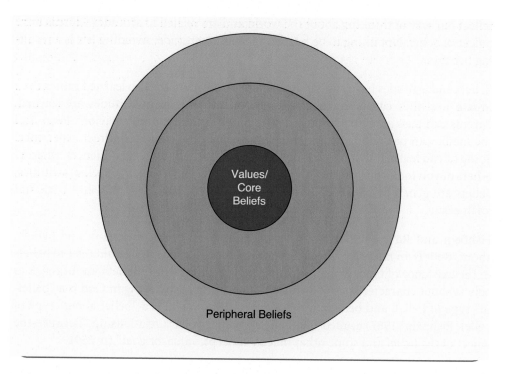

FIGURE 2.7 Core beliefs and peripheral beliefs.

"the best people are well educated" (end-state of existence). Values are types of beliefs generally closely linked to our identities and our sense of self. For example, most educators value education, as it represents core beliefs that are interwoven with their life choices. To have that value overturned would lead to serious questions about their life, so it would be difficult to persuade them to alter that value. Values tend to be broad core beliefs that offer the foundation for many other beliefs and attitudes. Figure 2.7 depicts the relationship between values, core beliefs, and peripheral beliefs. Imagine an onion with many layers. The core of the onion represents values and core beliefs. As you move to the outer rings, each layer is less central to your identity and easier to change. Peripheral beliefs are found in the outer layers of the onion.

Attitude, behavioral intention, behavior, belief, and *value* are all terms used throughout this text. An understanding of these terms is an important foundation for understanding persuasion theories and research, as well as to the practice of persuasion.

HOW DO WE MEASURE ATTITUDES?

At this point you might think you've learned all you need to know about attitudes. However, we need to discuss one more very important issue: how to measure attitudes. Why is this so important? If you can't measure attitude and changes in it, you have no way of knowing if your persuasive strategies work. This is true for the research conducted by scholars, and it is true for those practicing persuasion as a profession (e.g., sales, marketing, lawyers). Professional practitioners of persuasion are often most interested in influencing behaviors—they want you to vote, buy, donate, and so on—so why would they be interested in measuring attitudes? Attitudes are linked to behaviors and you often need to know how your audience feels (their attitude) in order to create persuasive messages that will impact behavior. Additionally, behaviors can be hard to measure. For example, imagine you work for the Democratic presidential campaign and you develop campaign messages targeted at the residents of Ohio the summer before the election. You are going to need to know before the election if your message worked. Your ultimate goal is for people to vote for your candidate, but there is no voting during the summer, and voting is a private behavior anyway. So what do you do? You poll people and measure their attitude before and after being exposed to the message. If the attitude is more positive after hearing the message, you keep your job and keep using that message. In lots of situations, behavior is either difficult or impossible to measure directly, so instead we measure attitudes, beliefs, or behavioral intentions to help us determine the effectiveness of our persuasive attempt.

We have devoted a good deal of time to defining and describing attitudes and to discussing the ways attitudes can be formed. One thing you may have noticed about attitudes is that they exist inside people and cannot be seen, heard, touched, smelled, or tasted. So, if an attitude cannot be directly observed, how can it be measured? The measurement of attitudes is challenging and has been the focus of much research. Attitudes have been measured with a variety of methods, some better than others. No measure of attitude is perfect. No current technology can measure psychological concepts with the precision and accuracy that we measure physical phenomena. However, just because a measure is not perfect does not mean it is useless. Social scientists are always looking for ways to measure attitudes more accurately and precisely; however, the current measures provide enough information to draw useful conclusions and make meaningful judgments. We outline some of the most frequently used measures of attitude in the following sections.

One last comment about attitude measures: As stated previously, attitudes cannot be "seen" or "touched"; therefore, it is important to recognize that all measures of attitude involve inferring attitude from some behavior, with some being more direct and some being more implicit. In other words, we measure something that is related to or results from the attitude. First, we describe measures that are considered "direct," and then we discuss a new generation of measures that are "implicit" measures. Direct measures are those that explicitly ask people to report how they feel about some object. These include the Thurstone, Likert, and semantic differential scales. Implicit measures are those that measure attitudes unobtrusively—people don't know their attitude toward a particular object is being measured.

THURSTONE SCALES

Let's start with one of the first methods of measuring attitudes. Louise Thurstone (1928) developed what has come to be known as the Thurstone scale to measure attitude. The **Thurstone scale** consists of several items, each representing a different level of favorableness or unfavorableness toward the attitude object. Each statement has a scale value representing the intensity of favorableness or unfavorableness. See Table 2.2 for an example of the scale drawn from Thurstone's (1929) work. To develop a Thurstone scale, you first need to write a large number of belief statements related to

TABLE 2.2 *THURSTONE SCALE*

SCALE VALUE	ITEM
1.2	I believe the church is a powerful agency for promoting both individual and social righteousness.
2.2	I like to go to church because I get something worthwhile to think about and it keeps my mind filled with right thoughts.
3.3	I enjoy my church because there is a spirit of friendliness there.
4.5	I believe in what the church teaches but with mental reservations.
6.7	I believe in sincerity and goodness without any church ceremonies.
7.5	I think too much money is being spent on the church for the benefit that is being derived.
9.2	I think the church seeks to impose a lot of worn-out dogmas and medieval superstitions.
10.4	The church represents shallowness, hypocrisy, and prejudice.
11.0	I think the church is a parasite on society.

Note: On an actual questionnaire the items would be in random order and the scale values would not be shown.

the attitude. Then you have a large number of judges (50 to 300) categorize the statements into categories ranging from *extremely favorable* to *extremely unfavorable*. Items that are consistently judged to be in the same category are kept and the others are discarded. Based on this sorting procedure, a scale value is determined for each item. Once the final set of items is selected, research participants check each statement they agree with. Research participants do not see the scale values. To obtain an attitude score, the scale values are added for each of the items checked. Theoretically, there is an equal distance between each scale item, which creates a stronger scale. A major problem with the Thurstone scale is that participants sometimes agree with statements that represent both a favorable and an unfavorable attitude. This is largely because the scale items are belief statements and two people holding the same attitude can have different beliefs. Another disadvantage of this scale is that it is very time consuming, expensive, and difficult to develop. The Thurstone scale is rarely used anymore for these reasons. Better methods for measuring attitudes have been developed and are discussed next.

LIKERT SCALES

In 1932, Rensis Likert developed a scale similar to Thurstone's scale but simpler to construct and use. A **Likert scale** consists of several statements with which participants indicate their level of agreement. Usually a five-point scale is used with strongly agree, agree, no opinion, disagree, and strongly disagree being the options, although four-point and seven-point versions are also used. See Table 2.3 for an example of a Likert scale. One difference between a Likert scale and a Thurstone scale is that, with a Thurstone scale, you want items that reflect a middle-of-the-road position as well as very favorable and very unfavorable positions. With a Likert scale, you want all your items to reflect either a very favorable or very unfavorable position—you don't want middle-of-the-road items.

TABLE 2.3 *LIKERT SCALE—BASED ON THE SHORT FORM OF THE ATTITUDES TOWARD WOMEN SCALE*

THE STATEMENTS LISTED BELOW DESCRIBE ATTITUDES TOWARD THE ROLE OF WOMEN IN SOCIETY THAT DIFFERENT PEOPLE HAVE. THERE ARE NO RIGHT OR WRONG ANSWERS, ONLY OPINIONS. YOU ARE ASKED TO EXPRESS YOUR FEELING ABOUT EACH STATEMENT BY USING THE FOLLOWING SCALE TO RESPOND TO EACH ITEM.

5 = STRONGLY AGREE   4 = AGREE   3 = NO OPINION   2 = DISAGREE   1 = STRONGLY DISAGREE

1. _____ Swearing and obscenity are more repulsive in the speech of a woman than of a man.

2. _____ Women should take increasing responsibility for leadership in solving the intellectual and social problems of the day.

3. _____ Both husband and wife should be allowed the same grounds for divorce.

4. _____ Intoxication among women is worse than intoxication among men.

5. _____ Under modern economic conditions with women being active outside the home, men should share in household tasks such as washing dishes and doing the laundry.

6. _____ There should be a strict merit system in job appointment and promotion without regard to sex.

7. _____ Women should worry less about their rights and more about becoming good wives and mothers.

8. _____ Women earning as much as their dates should bear equally the expense when they go out together.

9. _____ It is ridiculous for a woman to run a locomotive and for a man to darn socks.

10. _____ Women should be encouraged not to become sexually intimate with anyone before marriage, even their fiancés.

11. _____ The husband should not be favored by law over the wife in the disposal of family property or income.

12. _____ The modern girl is entitled to the same freedom from regulation and control that is given to the modern boy.

Note: These items were presented by Spence, Helmreich, and Stapp (1973, pp. 219–220), from *Bulletin of the Psychonomic Society.*

One advantage of a Likert scale is that participants can respond on a range of agreement-disagreement and are not forced to either agree or disagree, which may make them more comfortable. Likert scales are relatively easy to construct and use and are more reliable than Thurstone scales of a similar length. One thing to note about both Thurstone scales and Likert scales is that they rely on belief statements for scale items. To develop these scales, the researcher must understand what beliefs are consistently associated with both a negative and positive attitude toward the object in question, which is extremely difficult to do for diverse audiences. As a result, Likert and Thurstone scales are not very good measures of attitude. However, Likert scales are very useful for measuring beliefs. Likert scales have also been adapted for other uses such as measuring personality characteristics. Therefore, familiarity with Likert scales is important for understanding persuasion and communication research.

SEMANTIC DIFFERENTIAL SCALES

One of the most popular scales used to measure attitude is the **semantic differential scale**. Osgood, Suci, and Tannenbaum (1957) developed this scale. Participants are asked to evaluate the attitude object with a series of paired adjectives as shown in Table 2.4. There are typically five to seven spaces between each adjective, with each space assigned a value (as shown in Table 2.4). These ratings are then added together to create an attitude score. Almost any attitude object can be evaluated with these scales. The ease and flexibility offered by the Semantic Differential scale contribute to its popularity. The semantic differential scale is also very reliable. One strength of the semantic differential scale is that belief statements are not involved.

Another strength of the semantic differential scale is that it allows us to measure attitude intensity. Selecting a number in the middle indicates less strength than selecting a number close to an adjective. Likert scales also measure strength, but Thurstone scales do not. One commonality among these three scales is that they are all self-report; in other words, participants use the scale to describe how they feel from their point of view. An argument for the self-report method is that because attitudes cannot be seen, heard, touched, smelled, or tasted, the only person who really knows your attitudes is you. Therefore, if we want to know how you feel about something, the most direct way of finding out is to ask you. The problem with self-report scales is that you may complete the scales in the way that seems most desirable or in a way that hides your real feelings. People often want to hide attitudes that are socially unacceptable, such as racial prejudice. Because of this weakness of self-report measures, researchers have created implicit measures of attitude.

IMPLICIT MEASURES

Researchers have long tried to develop ways to measure attitudes that avoided the problems of response bias and social-desirability bias. One early attempt was to measure people's physiological response to an attitude object. Rankin and Campbell (1955) used **galvanic skin response (GSR)**, which is the change in electrical resistance of the skin and is related to the amount of sweat being produced. People sweat more when they are anxious or emotionally aroused. A major problem with GSR is that it does not differentiate between a positive response and a negative response, making it not a particularly useful measure of attitude. Another physiological response that we have little control over is pupil dilation. Hess and Polt (1960) demonstrated that pupil

TABLE 2.4 *SEMANTIC DIFFERENTIAL SCALE*

GUN CONTROL							
Good	7	6	5	4	3	2	1	Bad
Pleasant	7	6	5	4	3	2	1	Unpleasant
Strong	7	6	5	4	3	2	1	Weak
Heavy	7	6	5	4	3	2	1	Light
Fair	7	6	5	4	3	2	1	Unfair

size was related to the interest value of stimuli. Hess and Polt found that women's pupils dilated at the sight of partially nude men and that men's pupils dilated at the sight of partially nude women. Although pupil dilation is an interesting phenomenon, it is not a highly reliable measure of attitude. A person's pupils don't always constrict when viewing negative stimuli, and pupil dilation can sometimes be a response to surprise (Himmelfarb, 1993). Over the years, researchers have developed a wide variety of strategies to unobtrusively measure attitude, with most of them not being very successful, but two implicit measures of attitude have been used quite successfully.

The first is **evaluative priming** (Fazio, Jackson, Dunton, & Williams, 1995) and is based on the idea that the presentation of an attitude object automatically activates an evaluation that is held in memory. Over several trials, participants are presented with a prime (the attitude object) that is followed by negative or positive evaluative words. Participants indicate the connotation of the words as quickly as possible. If the prime (a picture of a spider) activates a negative evaluation, then participants should be able to more quickly indicate the connotation of negative words (e.g., mean, creepy, dishonest) than they could for positive words (e.g., friendly, warm, attractive). Participants typically indicate the connotation of a word by pressing a computer key marked "good" or "bad" and are given less than a second to respond, so they don't have time to contemplate the word. The amount of time it takes to respond to the evaluative words serves as the measure of attitude. Fazio et al. (1995) used evaluative priming to examine racial attitudes. Students were shown a series of color photos of black, white, and Asian students with each followed by positive or negative words. For white students, response time was faster when positive words followed pictures of white people than for black people. The opposite pattern was found for black students, and the evaluative priming task was deemed a valid measure of attitude in this study. The priming task occurs among several tasks so to reduce participants' awareness of what is being measured. For instance, in the Fazio et al. study, participants completed six tasks involving adjectives and/or photos with the priming task being the fourth task in the experiment.

A second implicit measure that is frequently used is the **implicit association test (IAT)** and, like priming, it relies on automatic associations and participants' response times (Brunel, Tietje, & Greenwald, 2004). The IAT involves identifying two opposing attitude objects such as Macs and PCs. Using a keyboard to provide their responses (which are measured in milliseconds), participants categorize words or images as being associated with each object. The left arrow key may be assigned for Mac and the right arrow key for PC. For example, participants might be given the Apple logo and categorize it as associated with Macs by pressing the left arrow key. After several trials of this task, participants are given a similar task where participants are given a series of words to classify as "pleasant" or "unpleasant," where the left key is assigned to "pleasant" and the right key to "unpleasant." Then participants are asked to combine the two tasks. Participants are given a new set of words or images to categorize, but now the left arrow key is used for both "Mac" and "pleasant" and the right arrow is used for both "PC" and "unpleasant." In a later task, the key assignments are changed so that the left arrow is for "Mac" and "unpleasant" and the right arrow is for "PC" and "pleasant." People with a positive attitude toward

Macs will be able to classify words and pictures faster when the same key is used for "Mac" and "pleasant." The difference in response time between these two tasks serves as the measure of attitude.

Evaluative priming and IAT are similar, but involve different tasks. Evaluative priming uses a single attitude object (the prime) followed by a number of tasks that involve evaluating the connotation of words. IAT uses two opposing attitude objects (Mac vs. PC; pro-life vs. pro-choice) and opposing adjectives (pleasant vs. unpleasant) and then combines the tasks. Both priming and IAT rely on the assumption that attitudes are held in memory so that evaluations that are consistent with one's attitude are made faster than evaluations that are inconsistent with one's attitude. Implicit measures are most often used when investigating attitudes where social desirability is a particular problem such as racial prejudice or sexual mores.

SUMMARY

- Persuasion involves attempts to change attitude, beliefs, behavioral intentions, or behaviors.
- Attitude is defined as a learned predisposition to respond in a consistently favorable or unfavorable manner with respect to a given object.
- The five key characteristics of attitudes are affective, tied to an object, consistent, learned, and related to behavior.
- Behavioral intention is a person's intention to perform a behavior.
- Attitudes can serve five functions: ego-defensive, value-expressive, knowledge, utilitarian, and social-adjustive.
- Functional matching is a persuasive strategy of matching the message with the attitude function.
- Behavior refers to overt physical actions by a person.
- A belief links an object to some attribute.
- Beliefs-in refers to believing in the existence of an object. Beliefs-about refers to believing that an object has some characteristic.
- Beliefs about objects can be prescriptive, descriptive, or evaluative.
- Values are core beliefs that serve as a foundation for many other beliefs and attitudes.
- Attitudes can be formed through classical conditioning in a process of pairing an unconditioned stimulus with a conditioned stimulus.
- Attitudes are frequently conditioned through a process of higher-order conditioning.
- Attitudes can be formed through operant conditioning with the use of reinforcement.
- Attitudes can be formed through modeling, which involves four steps: attention, retention, motor reproduction, and motivation.

- All measures of attitude involve inferring attitude from some behavior, with some being more direct and some being more implicit.
- Direct measures of attitude include the Thurstone scale, the Likert scale, and the semantic differential scale. The semantic differential scale is frequently used to measure attitude today.
- Implicit measures of attitudes include evaluative priming and the implicit association test.

KEY TERMS

Attitude—a learned predisposition to respond in a consistently favorable or unfavorable manner with respect to a given object.

Behavior—an individual's overt physical actions.

Behavioral intention—a psychological concept best described as an expectation or a plan. An intention is a plan for how you are going to behave.

Belief—a belief links an object to some attribute.

Beliefs-about—beliefs about characteristics of a concept.

Beliefs-in—beliefs in the existence of an object.

Conditioned response—a learned response.

Conditioned stimulus—a new stimulus that is paired with an unconditioned stimulus until it elicits the same response as the unconditioned stimulus.

Core beliefs—beliefs that are strongly held and hard to change.

Ego-defensive function—attitudes that are held to help people protect their sense of self and prevent the need to face unpleasant realities.

Evaluative consistency—consistent affective feeling toward an object.

Evaluative priming—a commonly used implicit measure of attitude.

Functional matching—when the persuasive message is matched to the function the relevant attitude serves for the audience.

Higher-order conditioning—when a conditioned stimulus acts like an unconditioned stimulus and can be paired with another stimulus.

Implicit association test (IAT)—a commonly used implicit measure of attitude.

Knowledge function—attitudes that help people understand the world around them.

Likert scale—consists of several statements with which participants indicate their level of agreement.

Peripheral beliefs—beliefs about issues that are less important to a person.

Response-response consistency—expectations that responses to stimuli will be similar over time.

Semantic differential scale—consists of a series of paired adjectives.

Social-adjustive function—attitudes that are held to help us better relate to those around us.

Stimulus-response consistency—the expectation that people will have the same response to the same stimuli over time.

Thurstone scale—consists of several items each representing a different level of favorableness or unfavorableness toward the attitude object.

Unconditioned response—an automatic or natural response (one that is not learned).

Unconditioned stimulus—a stimulus that elicits an unconditioned response.

Utilitarian function—attitudes that benefit individuals by allowing them to avoid negative consequences and achieve positive outcomes.

Value-expressive function—attitudes that allow people to express values that are important to them.

Values—enduring beliefs that specific modes of conduct or end-states of existence are personally and socially preferable to alternative modes of conduct or end-states of existence.

REVIEW QUESTIONS

1. What is an attitude and what are the five key characteristics of attitudes?
2. What is an example of the ego-defensive function of attitudes? Of the value-expressive function? Of the knowledge function? Of the utilitarian function? Of the social-adjustive function?
3. What is functional matching?
4. What are examples of prescriptive, descriptive, and evaluative beliefs?
5. What is a value, and how does it relate to beliefs and attitudes?

6. How is an attitude formed through classical conditioning?

7. How is an attitude formed through operant conditioning?

8. How is an attitude formed through modeling?

9. Is the Thurstone, Likert, or semantic differential scale most commonly used? Why is it preferred?

10. Why are implicit measures of attitude used?

DISCUSSION QUESTIONS

1. Are there ethical implications for targeting attitudes that serve different functions? Is it as acceptable to target value-expressive attitudes as it is to target social-adjustive attitudes?

2. Consider your attitude toward your college education, toward your favorite car, and toward beer. What functions do these attitudes serve for you (consider the five functions discussed in this chapter)?

3. Consider the concept of capitalism and your attitude toward it. Is your attitude positive, negative, or neutral toward capitalism? Now list the beliefs you have about capitalism. How do your beliefs about capitalism relate to your attitude toward it?

4. Is it ethical to employ classical conditioning and/or operant conditioning in persuasion? Should persuaders be more concerned with rational arguments, or is it all right to condition your target audience to respond positively to you?

5. Think about your attitude toward math. Which theory of attitude formation discussed in this chapter best explains how your attitude toward math was formed?

6. Is it ethical to intentionally try to change a person's values and core beliefs? Why?

REFERENCES

Albarracin, D., Zanna, M. P., Johnson, B. T., & Kumkale, G. T. (2005). Attitudes: Introduction and scope. In D. Albarracin, B. Johnson, & M. P. Zanna (Eds.), *The handbook of attitudes* (pp. 3–19). Mahwah, NJ: Lawrence Erlbaum.

Bandura, A. (1971). Analysis of modeling processes. In A. Bandura (Ed.), *Psychological modeling: Conflicting theories* (pp. 1–62). Chicago: Aldine-Atherton.

Brunel, Tietje, & Greenwald. (2004).

Eagly, A. H., & Chaiken, S. (1993). *The psychology of attitudes.* Fort Worth, TX: Harcourt Brace Jovanovich College Publishers.

Fazio, R. H., Jackson, J. R., Dunton, B. C., & Williams, C. J. (1995). Variability in automatic activation as an unobtrusive measure of racial attitudes: A bona fide pipeline? *Journal of Personality and Social Psychology, 69,* 1013–1027.

Fishbein, M. (1967). A consideration of beliefs, and their role in attitude measurement. In M. Fishbein (Ed.), *Readings in attitude theory and measurement* (pp. 257–266). New York: Wiley.

Fishbein, M., & Ajzen, I. (1975). *Belief, attitude, intention, and behavior: An introduction to theory and research.* Reading, MA: Addison-Wesley.

Fishbein, M., & Raven, B. H. (1962). The AB scales: An operation definition of belief and attitude. *Human Relations, 15,* 35–44.

Hess, E. H. (1965). Attitude and pupil size. *Scientific American, 212,* 46–54.

Hess, E. H., & Polt, J. M. (1960). Pupil size as related to interest value of visual stimuli. *American Association for the Advancement of Science. Science, 132,* 349–350.

Himmelfarb, S. (1993). The measurement of attitudes. In A. H. Eagly & S. Chaiken (Eds.), *The psychology of attitudes* (pp. 23–87). Fort Worth, TX: Harcourt Brace Jovanovich.

Insko, C. A. (1965). Verbal reinforcement of attitude. *Journal of Personality and Social Psychology, 2,* 621–623.

Katz, D. (1960). The functional approach to the study of attitudes. *Public Opinion Quarterly, 24,* 163–204.

Lanier, C. A., Elliott, M. N., Martin, D. W., & Kapadia, A. (1998). Evaluation of an intervention to change attitudes toward date rape. *Journal of American College Health, 46*(4), 177–180.

Lavine, H., & Snyder, M. (1996). Cognitive processing and the functional matching effect in persuasion: The mediating role of subjective perceptions of message quality. *Journal of Experimental Social Psychology, 32,* 580–604.

Likert, R. (1932). A technique for the measurement of attitudes. *Archives of Psychology, 140,* 5–53.

Milgram, S., Mann, L., & Harter, S. (1965). The lost letter technique: A tool of social research. *Public Opinion Quarterly, 29,* 437–438.

Osgood, C. E., Suci, C. J., & Tannenbaum, P. H. (1957). *The measurement of meaning.* Urbana: University of Illinois Press.

Perloff, R. M. (1993). *The dynamics of persuasion.* Hillsdale, NJ: Lawrence Erlbaum.

Rankin, R. E., & Campbell, D. T. (1955). Galvanic skin response to Negro and White experimenters. *Journal of Abnormal and Social Psychology, 51,* 30–33.

Rokeach, M. (1968). *Beliefs, attitudes, and values: A theory of organization and change.* San Francisco: Jossey-Bass.

Smith, M. B., Bruner, J. S., & White, R. W. (1956). *Opinions and personality.* New York: John Wiley.

Spence, J. T., Helmreich, R., & Stapp, J. (1973). A short version of the attitudes toward women scale (AWS). *Bulletin of the Psychonomic Society, 2,* 219–220.

Staats, A. W., & Staats, C. K. (1958). Attitudes established by classical conditioning. *Journal of Abnormal and Social Psychology, 57,* 37–40.

Thurstone, L. L. (1928). Attitudes can be measured. *American Journal of Sociology, 33,* 529–554.

Thurstone, L. L. (1929). Theory of attitude measurement. *Psychological Bulletin, 36,* 222–241.

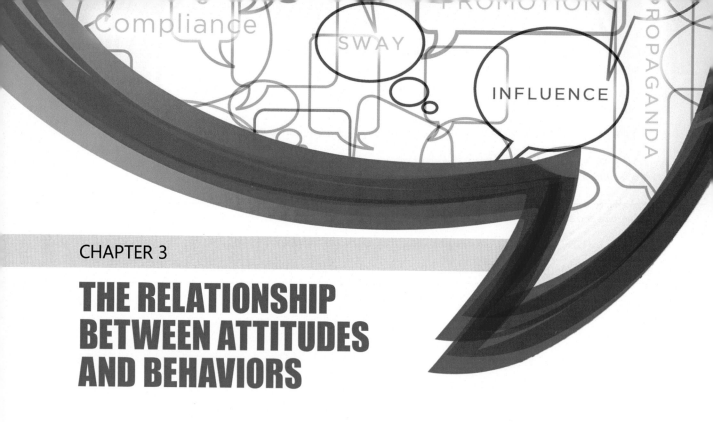

CHAPTER 3

THE RELATIONSHIP BETWEEN ATTITUDES AND BEHAVIORS

Julie: Hi, Mary. Is this your new dog? She is so cute! How old is she?

Mary: Thanks. Her name is Tillie. She's 7 weeks old. I got her yesterday from the shelter. She was abandoned. Someone just dumped her off on the side of the road.

Julie: That's terrible! People are so irresponsible with their pets. People get a puppy, don't get it neutered, and then they have puppies they don't want and can't keep. If people would just have their pets neutered, the world would be a better place!

Mary: I agree completely! Everyone except for breeders should neuter their pet. It's the only responsible thing to do.

Julie: I agree! Well, have fun with Tillie! I'll see you later.

One year later:

Mary: Hi, Julie. How are you? Would you like to get another dog?

Julie: Not really. Charlie and Lamar are all I can handle. Why?

Mary: Tillie had puppies last month, and I'm trying to find homes for them. I'm going to have to take them to the shelter if I can't find homes for them soon.

In the previous chapter, we said that attitudes are related to behaviors; however, the scenario depicted above in Julie and Mary's conversation is not all that unusual. Here, Mary expressed an attitude toward the need to neuter pets, but she did not act on that attitude. In some situations, attitudes lead to behavior; yet in other situations, people seem to act in ways that show no relationship between attitudes and behavior.

LEARNING OBJECTIVES

- EXPLAIN HOW THE MEASUREMENT OF ATTITUDES CAN INFLUENCE HOW WELL ATTITUDES PREDICT BEHAVIOR.
- DESCRIBE ATTITUDE FORMATION FACTORS THAT INFLUENCE THE ATTITUDE–BEHAVIOR RELATIONSHIP.
- EXPLAIN HOW ATTITUDE ACCESSIBILITY AND RELEVANCE AFFECT THE ATTITUDE–BEHAVIOR RELATIONSHIP.
- EXPLAIN HOW INDIVIDUAL AND SITUATIONAL FACTORS AFFECT THE ATTITUDE–BEHAVIOR RELATIONSHIP.

In this chapter, we discuss factors that determine when attitudes are good predictors of behavior, as well as additional factors that influence behavior. As persuaders we are often interested in influencing other people's behavior as well as their attitudes and beliefs. To do that successfully, we need to understand behavior and the factors that influence it.

DO ATTITUDES INFLUENCE BEHAVIOR?

It makes sense that attitudes should guide behavior. Humans are intelligent creatures, and we expect reasons to exist for our behavior. Most people assume that attitudes influence behavior. For example, if someone speaks favorably about a presidential candidate, we expect him or her to vote for that candidate. Scholars are in the business of challenging assumptions, so it wasn't long before this assumption was tested. In the early 1930s, Richard LaPiere conducted one of the more famous studies. LaPiere traveled with a Chinese couple around the United States to see whether they would be accepted as guests at hotels, restaurants, and auto-camps. (During the 1930s in the United States, there was considerable bias against people from China.) They visited 251 establishments and only once were they refused service. Six months after visiting each establishment LaPiere (1934) sent a questionnaire to the proprietor asking "Will you accept members of the Chinese race as guests in your establishment?" (p. 233). Despite having been consistently "treated with what I judged to be more than ordinary consideration" (LaPiere, 1934, p. 232), over 90 percent of respondents indicated they would not accept Chinese as guests. LaPiere concluded that attitudes did not influence behavior.

You don't need to be a genius to see some flaws in the methods LaPiere used. Consider what other explanations there might be for these findings besides attitudes not influencing behavior. Did the same person fill out the questionnaire who served

3.1 ABOUT CORRELATIONS

In this chapter we frequently refer to correlations. A correlation is a simple statistical measure of the relationship between two things. The letter "r" is shorthand for the word *correlation*, and a correlation can range from –1.0 (a perfect negative relationship) to 1.0 (a perfect positive relationship). A correlation of 0 indicates no relationship. A positive relationship means that as one thing increases or decreases, so does the other. For example, as attitude becomes more positive about recycling, recycling behavior increases. A negative relationship means that as one thing increases, something else decreases. For example, as attitude toward eating a healthy diet increases, eating of sugary and fatty foods decreases.

Correlation should not be confused with causation. Just because two things are correlated, or happen at the same time, does not mean that one causes the other. At one time, people believed that breathing swamp air *caused* malaria because being around swamps was *correlated* with contracting malaria. We now know that mosquitoes live in swamps and can carry the microscopic malarial parasite and can transmit it in their bites. Thus, there is a *correlation* between breathing swamp air and contracting malaria, but breathing swamp air is not the *cause* of the disease. Being bitten by an infected mosquito is what *causes* malaria.

FIGURE 3.1

the Chinese couple? Could the servers' attitudes about politeness, not creating a fuss, or the desire for money have been stronger than their discriminatory attitudes? Others have suggested that having a white man with the Chinese couple set up a different situation. You can probably find other problems as well. Although this was only one study, it received a lot of attention and challenged the assumption that attitudes influence behavior. Over the next few decades, research continued with mixed results. Sometimes a relationship was found between attitudes and behaviors, and sometimes it wasn't.

In a review of 42 studies, Wicker (1969) made a case for the lack of an attitude–behavior relationship. He reviewed studies examining attitudes and behaviors toward blacks and other ethnic groups, jobs, breastfeeding, and other issues. Some of these studies found attitudes to be strongly correlated to behavior (as high as $r = .60$); others found correlations close to zero. Most of the correlations were quite low, however, leading Wicker to conclude, "taken as a whole, these studies suggest that it is considerably more likely that attitudes will be unrelated or only slightly related to overt behaviors than that attitudes will be closely related to actions" (p. 65).

Wicker's (1969) article created a real fracas among scholars. Wicker drew on studies that were primarily experimental studies conducted in artificial laboratory settings. Critics noted that the laboratory settings might not reflect actual situations where attitudes and behavior would be related. Other studies that used surveys outside the traditional laboratory in "real world" settings found stronger and more consistent relationships between attitudes and behavior. For example, a study of voting behavior found that attitudes toward political candidates were closely related to voting behavior (Campbell, Converse, Miller, & Stokes, 1960). Polls are used frequently during election years, and political candidates rely heavily on them. Even though poll results are occasionally in error, there is evidence of a strong relationship between attitudes and behavior in this context. Schuman and Johnson (1976) reviewed a broader base of studies including the survey research methods described above, and they concluded that the correlation between attitude and behavior was small to moderate. Thus, at times attitudes have been linked to behavior, and at times attitudes don't appear to have much of a relationship to behavior. One key result of Wicker's (1969) and Schuman and Johnson's (1976) reviews was a renewed interest in the relationship between attitudes and behaviors. Because the reviews found that attitudes and behaviors were *sometimes* correlated, the focus of research turned from "are attitudes correlated with behavior?" to "*when* are attitudes correlated with behavior?" and "what else influences behavior?" Thus, there are times when attitudes are linked to behavior, but it is not a simple relationship. Additionally, attitudes are not the only factor that influences behavior.

INFLUENCING BEHAVIOR

Behavior is often the outcome of interest in both persuasion research and practice, and because attitudes are thought to affect behavior, attitude has been a central focus of persuasion. However, the relationship between attitudes and behaviors is complex, and multiple factors must be considered. These factors fall into five categories: measurement issues, perceptions of behavioral control, attitude formation, cognitive processing, and situational factors. Understanding these factors will allow us to better understand how to shape, reinforce, and change both attitudes and behaviors, which are central persuasion goals.

MEASUREMENT FACTORS

To determine whether attitudes predict behavior, it is important to understand *which* attitudes and *which* behavior. **Measurement factors** were a problem with much of the early attitude research. Attitude was measured in a rather general way (as it was in LaPiere's study) whereas the behavior was measured very specifically. A general attitude is predictive of a general pattern of behavior. For instance, if José expresses a positive attitude toward the environment (a general attitude), then we could expect any combination of several behaviors from José. He might recycle, drive a hybrid vehicle, install solar panels on his house, eat locally grown food, or walk to work.

However, it would be very difficult to predict which of these behaviors he would perform. This was one of the problems with early research—attitudes and behaviors were measured with different levels of specificity. When measuring attitudes and behavior, we want to measure both with the same **level of specificity**. A specific attitude predicts a specific behavior.

Ajzen and Fishbein (1977) identified four factors that should be taken into account when measuring attitudes and behaviors, and these factors help us increase the level of specificity. These four factors allow us to be very detailed about the kinds of behaviors that are expected, and thus we can examine more specific attitudes. The first factor is the **action** performed. This refers to the specific behavior, such as recycling or eating locally grown food. The second factor is the **target** of the action; or in other words, what object the behavior targets. If we focus on recycling, then what object is the action directed toward? Is it paper, glass, plastic, or used oil? Each target modifies the specific action performed. Third, the **context** of the action must be considered. Context can refer to the location of the action or the situation. For example, is the context recycling at home, at work, or on campus? The specific context helps specify attitudes that can lead to behavior. The final factor identified by Ajzen and Fishbein is **time**. When is the action to be performed? For example, is it recycling during the annual "Recycle Mania" or on a daily basis? When you vary the context, target, or time, the action varies. Therefore, to predict a specific behavior, you must have a specific attitude. You might want to think of the four factors as a series of choices you need to make to appropriately focus your measurement, as illustrated in Figure 3.2. Measuring attitude and behavior with the same level of specificity will allow you to gather data to demonstrate the effectiveness of your campaign or other persuasive messages.

When attitudes and behaviors are measured with the same level of specificity (that is, the action, target, context, and time all match), measurement specificity is greater. Greater **measurement specificity** results in a stronger attitude–behavior relationship. In other words, if you measure the attitude with the same level of detail (or specificity) as you measure the behavior, the attitude is more likely to predict (or be correlated with) the behavior. In LaPiere's (1934) study, the action was serving

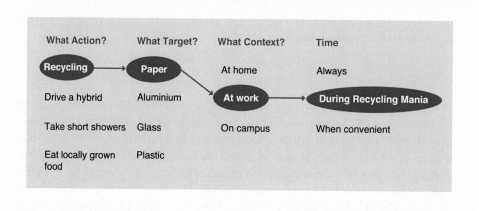

FIGURE 3.2 Example of attitude factors for predicting environmental behavior.

Chinese people. This was as far as that study went in specificity. Had LaPiere examined attitudes concerning serving (action) a Chinese couple (target) in the establishment when the couple is well dressed and in the company of a Caucasian (context) at dinnertime (time), the results may have been different. This kind of specificity can lead to stronger relationships between attitude and behavior and greater ability to predict the behaviors we attempt to influence through persuasion.

The correlation between attitude and behavior increased when researchers began measuring attitudes and behaviors with the same level of specificity. For example, Davidson and Jaccard (1979) conducted a study dealing with attitudes and behaviors regarding birth control. They measured the attitudes of 244 women toward birth control, birth control pills, using birth control pills, and using birth control pills in the next 2 years. They then followed up to see which women used birth control pills during those two years (specific behavior). Table 3.1 displays the correlations among the four attitudes with the behavior of using birth control pills during a two-year period. The first attitude in Table 3.1 is the most general; the fourth is the most specific and is measured with the same level of specificity as the behavior. Note that the more specific the attitude, the larger the correlation with the behavior. Thus, the more specific the measures were on the action, target, context, and time dimensions, the better the attitude predicted behavior. Ajzen and Fishbein's (1977) review of more than 100 studies further supported this conclusion by finding that the highest correlations between attitudes and behaviors occurred in the studies that measured behavior and attitude with the same level of specificity.

The four factors discussed above refer to using a specific attitude to predict a specific behavior. What if we measured more than one behavior? Would attitude be a better predictor of behavior if we measured multiple behaviors? In our earlier example, we noted that if José had a positive attitude toward the environment we could expect him to perform one or more of several behaviors. Ajzen and Fishbein (2005) describe the **principle of aggregation**, which states that a general attitude will predict a **behavioral domain**, but not a specific behavior. A behavioral domain is a set of related behaviors. Earlier we listed several behaviors that José may engage in because he has a positive attitude toward the environment. All of these environmental behaviors taken together are a behavioral domain. Therefore, it is important to distinguish between specific behaviors and behavioral domains. If you are

TABLE 3.1 *ATTITUDE AND BEHAVIOR SPECIFICITY*

ATTITUDE MEASURE	CORRELATION WITH BEHAVIOR (USING BIRTH CONTROL PILLS DURING A 2-YEAR PERIOD)
1. Attitude toward birth control	.083
2. Attitude toward birth control pills	.323
3. Attitude toward using birth control pills	.525
4. Attitude toward using birth control pills during the next 2 years	.572

Note: Data from Davidson and Jaccard (1979).

interested in influencing a specific behavior, then you need to work with the attitude specific to that behavior (match on action, target, context, and time) both in regard to your persuasive message and the measurement. If you are interested in influencing a behavioral domain, then a general attitude is sufficient. Again, how the attitude and behavior are measured affects our ability to predict behavior from attitudes.

BEHAVIORAL CONTROL BELIEFS

What a person believes about a behavior can also influence whether he or she will perform that behavior. Ajzen (1985) identified perceived behavioral control as a factor that influences behavior. **Perceived behavioral control** refers to an individual's perception of the level of control he or she has over a behavior. For example, a person could have a favorable attitude toward losing weight, yet not believe he or she is capable of engaging in that behavior. Wanting to lose weight but believing that it isn't possible means that attitudes in favor of weight loss would not be reflected in behavior. Although many have successfully managed to lose weight, the key issue here is whether the specific recipients of the message *believe* (or *perceive*) that this would be possible for themselves. Many people have become aware of the need for a good night's sleep, yet many fail to achieve it. This failure may be due to perceptions that because of a busy lifestyle or other factors, individuals have little personal control over getting more sleep. In this case, in addition to measuring a person's attitude toward sleeping more, you would need to measure the person's *perceived* behavioral control with regard to modifying his or her sleep patterns.

Messages can directly address the issue of perceived behavioral control. Including information about how to take control over an issue, such as how to lose weight successfully, can help increase the chances that the target of the persuasive message will perceive the ability to control that behavior. For example, an article on a popular medical information website provided advice on how to lose weight and focused on beliefs. It is targeted at helping individuals feel in control of their eating behavior, with statements such as, "Picture yourself thin," "Have realistic expectations," and "Set small goals." It is written in the form of an article, but the goal of the author is clearly to change what a person believes about weight loss and one's ability to lose weight. When the perceptions of control increase, so does the likelihood that the overall persuasive message will be more successful.

FORMATION FACTORS

The way an attitude is formed can also affect whether attitudes influence behavior. When attitudes are formed through **direct experience**, they tend to have more influence on behavior. Here's an example of an attitude being formed through direct experience: Someone has a positive attitude toward Greek olives because he or she ate them. The person has direct experience with the attitude object and believes that they have a good taste. Attitudes formed through direct experience tend to be better predictors of future behavior than attitudes formed through **indirect experience**. A person who forms an attitude through indirect experience does not directly interact with the attitude object, but learns about it secondhand through reading about it or hearing about it from others. A person who has a negative attitude toward Greek olives because his or her siblings said the olives tasted bad (but has never actually tasted a Greek olive) is an example of an attitude formed through indirect experience.

Regan and Fazio (1977) examined attitude formation in a naturalistic setting. Because of a shortage of housing at Cornell University, many freshmen were forced to spend their first few weeks of school in temporary facilities including cots in dormitory lounges. Other freshmen moved directly into permanent housing, but the issue of the housing shortage was discussed among students and in the college newspaper. The freshmen who lived in temporary facilities had **direct experience** with the issue, and they formed attitudes based on the housing situation they experienced. The freshmen who lived in permanent housing formed attitudes through **indirect experience** by reading about it and discussing it with others.

Regan and Fazio surveyed a random sample of students in temporary housing and students in permanent housing. Survey questions measured attitudes about the housing situation and offered students the opportunity to take six actions: (a) sign a petition to the administration, (b) get other students to sign the petition, (c) report interest in attending a meeting to discuss proposals to deal with the housing situation, (d) report interest in joining a committee of students to research the situation and make recommendations to the administration, (e) list recommendations or suggestions for solving the housing problems, and/or (f) write a letter expressing opinions about the housing problems to the Housing Office. (Note that behavior was measured with multiple acts.) The researchers indicated they would forward the items and information to the administration.

Both groups (those in temporary facilities and those in permanent housing) had similar attitudes about the situation. Even though the attitudes were the same, the behavioral responses were not. Regan and Fazio found that those who formed their attitudes through direct experience (those in temporary housing) were more willing to act (an attitude–behavior correlation of $r = .42$) than those who formed their attitudes through indirect experience (an attitude–behavior correlation of $r = .03$). In other words, when the attitude was formed through indirect experience, it didn't seem related to behavior, but when the attitude was formed through direct experience, it was related to behavior. Additional research conducted on this issue (Fazio & Zanna, 1978; Regan & Fazio, 1977) found similar results. Fazio and Zana (1981) concluded.

> Generally speaking, the picture that emerges is that attitudes formed through direct experience are stronger than those formed through indirect experience. There is evidence to suggest that direct experience attitudes are more clearly defined, held with greater certainty, more stable over time, and more resistant to counterinfluence. (p. 185)

This research challenges the traditional model that attitude causes behavior as is illustrated in the top panel of Figure 3.3. The research on direct experience along with contemporary views of attitude suggest that behavior can be the basis of attitude formation. Or, in other words, behavior can cause an attitude to form (Dillard, 1993). The lower panel of Figure 3.3 illustrates behavior leading to an attitude, which in turn influences future behavior. This issue has practical implications for persuaders.

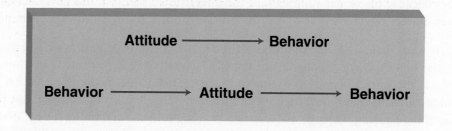

FIGURE 3.3 Two views of the attitude–behavior relationship.

If direct experience leads to attitude formation, then persuaders might plan efforts to include behavior first. This is done in grocery stores that routinely give away samples of food products. In this case, the behavior (customers eating the food) comes first, and the grocers hope positive attitudes will result that will lead to future behavior (customers purchasing the food). Stores continue this practice despite the expense because it results in greater sales of sampled items. Another example of this issue is the use of seat belts. For years the government tried to convince Americans to wear seat belts at all times when driving (change attitude to influence behavior). Focusing on attitude toward seat belts didn't result in a sufficient rate of seat belt usage, so the government changed their strategy. A law was passed making seat belt use mandatory, and resulted in people wearing seat belts, even though they didn't want to (held a negative attitude toward seat belts). For many people, they performed the behavior (wearing seat belts), which in turn positively influenced their attitude toward seat belts. Today seat belt usage is much greater than it was 30 years ago. Two theories of persuasion, cognitive dissonance theory and self-perception theory (Chapter 9), involve behavior serving as the basis for influencing attitude. In that chapter we more thoroughly discuss exactly how behavior influences attitude.

Thus, when we are trying to influence behavior, we need to consider how related attitudes were formed in addition to the level of perceived behavioral control. Additionally, how attitudes are cognitively structured influences the relationship between an attitude and a behavior.

COGNITIVE PROCESSING FACTORS

We all have attitudes on a variety of topics. Some attitudes we use regularly and are at the forefront of our thoughts. Other issues we think about infrequently and it can take time to recall our attitudes on a topic when it is raised. Think of the human mind as a kind of filing cabinet. Attitudes we use frequently are in the front of the cabinet, and this information is easy to find, it is accessible. Attitudes used infrequently are elsewhere in the cabinet, and it can take a while to locate them in the filing system. This concept is referred to as **attitude accessibility**. Only attitudes that are activated can affect behavior, and highly accessible attitudes are more easily activated. Making an attitude accessible is sometimes more important than changing an attitude.

Fazio, Chen, McDonel, and Sherman (1982) argue that attitude accessibility is related to direct experience. They suggest that direct experience makes an attitude more accessible, or more easily retrieved. These researchers measure attitude accessibility by timing how quickly subjects are able to retrieve attitudes in response to questions. Attitudes that are retrieved the fastest are the most accessible, and those attitudes are better predictors of behavior. Attitudes used most often are also easier to retrieve, or in other words, more accessible.

Attitude accessibility has been tested in research examining a presidential campaign (Fazio & Williams, 1986) and environmental attitudes (Kallgren & Wood, 1986). Results have consistently supported attitude accessibility as an important factor in the attitude–behavior relationship. It makes sense that people who talk about an issue frequently are more likely to engage in behavior consistent with their attitudes than those who rarely consider an issue, but other factors come into play here. Clearly, attitude formation based on direct experience and/or vested interest would influence attitude accessibility. Issues that individuals have had experience with and stand to gain from (as in the housing study) are retrieved more easily than issues with indirect experience or no vested interest. Attitude accessibility is a cognitive processing factor, but it is influenced by how the attitudes are formed.

Attitude accessibility is also related to the **relevance** of the attitude to the behavior for the individual. Snyder and Kendzierski (1982) propose this model: For behavior to be influenced by attitude, the attitude in question must first be accessible for a person, and second must be perceived as relevant to the behavior. This model essentially states that attitude accessibility is not enough for attitudes to influence behavior—a person also has to perceive that the attitude is relevant to the behavior. For instance, if I go out to buy a lawn mower, my attitude toward air quality and emission of pollutants would only influence my purchasing behavior if first it was accessible and second if I perceive it as relevant. If I think of my attitude toward emission standards as only relevant to cars, trucks, buses, and manufacturing plants, I probably won't even consider the emissions of the different models of lawn mowers. Snyder (1982) describes relevance as an action structure that links the attitude to the behavior. If it is pointed out to me that some models of lawn mowers produce an inordinate amount of air pollution, it serves to link my attitude toward emission standards to my lawn mower purchase and allows me to act on my attitude. An implication of Snyder and Kendzierski's (1982) model is that attitude–behavior consistency can be increased if the receiver is reminded of his or her attitude (enhance accessibility) and the relevance of the attitude to the behavior is noted. An example of this is shown in Figure 3.4. This announcement was distributed to faculty at the authors' institution. Note that in the brief message appealing to professors to announce the speaker to their classes, the source attempts to make professors' positive attitudes toward class discussion relevant to announcing the speaker to their classes.

Snyder and Kendzierski (1982) demonstrated that when receivers perceived their attitude toward affirmative action as relevant to decision-making behavior, receivers' behavior was more consistent with their attitude. Snyder and Kendzierski concluded that if a person perceives an attitude as relevant to a behavior, that attitude is automatically accessible. Therefore, as a source, you can focus your energy on enhancing the relevance of an attitude to a behavior. If you are successful in making the attitude relevant to the behavior, you will also be successful in making it accessible to the receiver.

DEAR MIAMI PROFESSOR:

Campus Activities Council Lecture Board is composed of 12 students, and we have worked very hard to bring a diverse set of speakers to Oxford's campus. We hope that as professors, you will encourage your students to expand their education outside of the classroom. By attending lectures and widening their knowledge, students will be able to contribute increasingly in class discussions. Please take the 15 seconds that is needed to announce the following lecture; our board and your classes will appreciate it. We want to work with you, and are asking you to meet us halfway.

KERSHAUN SCOTT

TO LIVE & DIE IN L.A.

Kershaun Scott—gang name Lil' Monster, an original gangster from South Central's Eight Tray Crips—has become a familiar face to Americans following the violent aftermath of the Rodney King verdict. Scott offers profound insight into the causes and reasons for gang violence. Drawing on his own personal experience, Scott articulates the attraction gang life has for the young men and women growing up in ghetto environments in Los Angeles and other American cities. Scott was instrumental in implementing the gang truce so many thought impossible.

"Bright and articulate . . . I liked him very much and was extremely impressed with a great deal of what he had to say and the passion with which he says it."

— Ted Koppel, ABC NEWS

FIGURE 3.4 The source attempts to make the professors' positive attitude toward class discussion relevant to announcing the speaker to their classes.

Similar to relevance is vested interest. If you have a **vested interest** in something, it has some impact on you and you are interested because you have something to gain or lose. Thus, attitudes formed through vested interest are better predictors of future behavior. Sivacek and Crano (1982) studied college student responses to a proposed raise in the legal drinking age (a topic with which college students were expected to have had direct experience and a vested interest) and student responses to proposed comprehensive exams as graduation requirements for themselves (vested interest) or others (non-vested interest). In both studies, the relationship between attitudes and behavior was strongest for those participants with a vested interest in the topic. Relevance and vested interest both create links between an attitude and a behavior, creating a stronger relationship between the attitude and the behavior.

Attitudes that are particularly relevant to an individual and to the behavioral choices he or she faces are those most likely to be used frequently and to be accessible. If an attitude is also formed through direct experience with an object, and the object is one in which the individual has a vested interest, the attitude-behavior relationship is further strengthened.

SITUATIONAL FACTORS

Situational factors are the final set of factors to examine in understanding when and how attitudes predict behavior. **Situational factors** are characteristics of the situation in which an individual performs the behavior in question. Abelson (1982) divided situational factors that affect the attitude–behavior relationship into three categories: **individuated situations**, **deindividuated situations**, and **scripted situations**. As the situation is altered, the expected relationship between attitudes and behavior is altered as well.

Individuated situations are situations that encourage individuals to focus on their internal states, including attitudes, beliefs, and values. Often, individuated situations cause individuals to take more responsibility for their own actions, and it is less possible for individuals to be part of an anonymous group in these kinds of situations. When individuals focus more on their own attitudes and feelings, they tend to act on those attitudes and, hence, attitude and behavior are related. In addition, when individuals feel more responsibility for their own actions as opposed to being part of a group, their attitudes are more consistent with their behavior. Research has supported this (Carver, 1975; Pryor, Gibbons, Wicklund, Fazio, & Hood, 1977). A person choosing to write a letter to the editor of the local newspaper about a political candidate is acting in an individuated situation. There is individual responsibility, and the person is more likely to think about his or her stand on the issue than a person who is part of a citizen's group that intends to endorse a political candidate.

Deindividuated situations are situations that offer an individual more anonymity and encourage less focus on internal states such as attitudes and feelings. When participating in a group, people tend to adopt the group perspective and often don't have to take as much responsibility for individual actions. As a result, there is less correspondence between attitudes and behaviors in deindividuated situations. Rioters, looters, and people who engage in nonnormative social behavior (e.g., mass suicide in religious cults) are all examples of actions in deindividuated situations (Sherman & Fazio, 1983). In these cases, people are more likely to engage in behavior that the group as a whole is engaging in without considering their own thoughts and feelings (beliefs and attitudes) about the behavior. Individuals who participate in riots and looting may be doing so simply because everyone else is doing it. However, deindividuated situations are not necessarily so extreme. Anytime we are part of a group, our behavior is apt to be more influenced by the group than by our own individual attitudes and beliefs.

The third type of situation is **scripted situations**. Do you ever respond automatically without thinking? Do you ever say "I'm fine" when someone asks how you are, even when you feel terrible? Doing so is an example of a scripted situation—in other words, a situation in which individuals know the expected behavior and therefore do not need to think in order to behave. For example, when you walk into a classroom for the first time, you don't need to think about whether you should sit at the desk in the front of the room or at a seat facing that area. You also don't need to be told to quiet down when the teacher begins speaking, and you expect the teacher to take the initiative to start the class. This is a scripted situation in which you don't need to think about your behavior, but instead you follow what is expected from you. Similarly, many of us rely on scripts when grocery shopping. We often reach for the same brand or the same size of products each time we go, so we don't need to ponder each of the 100 or more decisions we make. These scripts often serve us well, but sometimes we buy the wrong thing or pay a higher price because we rely on a script, rather than on our attitudes toward costs or nutrition. For example, if you always buy a gallon of milk because it is cheaper per ounce, and don't look at the price, you will miss out on sales where two half gallon jugs are cheaper than the gallon size. Scripted behavior is guided less by an individual's attitudes and more by social norms, habits, or previously thought out patterns. Thus, attitude–behavior correlations are much weaker in scripted situations.

As a persuader, you can use all of these situational factors to enhance your persuasive success. Persuaders may take advantage of deindividuated group events to get people to jump on the bandwagon to join their cause, buy their product, or adopt their beliefs. Some unethical persuaders will plant "converts" to speed up the deindividuating process and encourage audience members to join the cause. A persuader can create a link between some existing attitude or value, and then ask the audience to look deep into their soul, creating an individuated situation that encourages the audience to act on their attitudes, beliefs, or values. Persuaders also take advantage of the scripts we use. For example, manufacturers try to maintain product placement and brand names so that purchase habits are reinforced. They may also reduce the contents of a package yet keep the size of the box or bag the same to encourage scripted responses. If a new, smaller package was designed to reflect the reduction in contents, the consumer might think about the purchase rather than grab the product as usual.

All five factors that affect the attitude–behavior relationship are important, and all five factors have considerable support from research studies. What started out as a fairly simple proposition in Chapter 2 (attitude influences behavior) has become a bit more complicated. It takes more than simply influencing attitude in order to affect behavior. When you are designing persuasive messages, these factors should be considered. If you consider that attitudes formed through direct experience are more predictive of behavior, you might choose to give customers free samples. Alternatively, if you consider that when attitudes are accessible and relevant they have more impact on behavior, you may choose to remind people of the importance they place on the environment before asking them to sign a petition to increase taxes on gas guzzling vehicles. Understanding the relationship between attitudes and behavior may be very important, but by itself it is insufficient to be a successful persuader. In the following chapters we discuss source and message factors, which are your primary means for influencing attitudes, beliefs, and behaviors. The theory chapters that follow in section three provide explanations that help us put all the pieces together.

SUMMARY

- Early research, including the LaPiere (1934) study, suggested that attitudes did not correlate with behaviors.
- Other research, especially in naturalistic situations, found support for attitudes predicting behavior.
- Determining when and under what circumstances attitudes are related to behavior involves factors in five categories: measurement issues, perceived behavioral control, attitude formation, cognitive processing, and situational factors.
- Measurement factors include the action performed, the target, the context, time, and types of behavioral criteria.

- Specific attitudes predict specific behaviors; general attitudes predict behavioral domains.
- Perceived behavioral control influences behavior and can sometimes be addressed in a persuasive message.
- Attitudes formed through direct experience are more predictive of behavior than attitudes formed through indirect experience.
- Factors related to cognitive processing include attitude accessibility, relevance, and vested interest.
- Situational factors include individuated, deindividuated, and scripted situations.
- The attitude-behavior relationship must be considered when creating persuasive messages.

KEY TERMS

Attitude accessibility—the availability of an attitude in a person's mind.

Attitude relevance—how related or connected an attitude is to a behavior.

Behavioral domain—a set of related behaviors.

Deindividuated situations—situations that offer the individual more anonymity and that tend to encourage less focus on internal states such as attitudes and feelings.

Direct experience—when an audience forms an attitude as a result of engaging with the attitude object.

Indirect experience—when an audience forms an attitude by observing or learning about the object from a secondary source.

Individuated situations—situations that encourage individuals to focus on their internal states, including attitudes, beliefs, and values.

Level of specificity—refers to measuring both attitude and behavior with the same amount of detail.

Measurement factors—how attitudes and behaviors are measured. How they are measured can influence whether attitudes and behavior are related.

Measurement specificity—the extent to which both attitude and behavior are measured in the same way with regard to the action, target, context, and time.

Perceived behavioral control—an individual's perception of the level of control he or she has over a behavior.

Principle of aggregation—states that a general attitude will predict a behavioral domain but not a specific behavior.

Scripted situations—situations in which individuals know the expected behavior and therefore do not need to think in order to behave.

Situational factors—characteristics of the situation in which an individual performs the behavior in question.

Vested interest—having a personal stake in the outcome of a situation.

REVIEW QUESTIONS

1. What does LaPiere (1934) conclude about the relationship between attitudes and behavior? What are problems with this research?
2. How does measurement of attitude and behavior impact their relationship with one another?
3. How do action, target, context, and time improve the measurement of attitudes and behavior?
4. What is meant by perceived behavioral control? How does it affect the behavior?
5. How do direct and indirect experience affect the attitude–behavior relationship?
6. How does cognitive processing affect the attitude–behavior relationship?
7. How are attitude accessibility and relevance related? What impact do they have on the attitude–behavior relationship?
8. How are vested interest and relevance similar?
9. What is the difference between individuated, deindividuated, and scripted situations? How does each affect the attitude–behavior relationship?

DISCUSSION QUESTIONS

1. Would a research study such as LaPiere's be acceptable today? If not, how could you ethically modify this study to replicate or check on the validity of the findings today?
2. How much do you think your attitudes influence your behavior? Describe a time when your behavior influenced your attitude. When has your behavior influenced your attitude?
3. Think of a time you behaved in a way that was inconsistent with a related attitude. Use the factors that affect the attitude–behavior relationship in explaining why your behavior was inconsistent with your attitude.
4. What are some of the scripts you use frequently? When do they serve you well, and when don't they?
5. Many factors affect the attitude–behavior relationship. Do you have ethical concerns about targeting any of these aspects? For example, is it ethical to manipulate situations to create more of a deindividuated situation to enhance persuasive pressure? Can a persuader ethically create an artificial situation so that a target audience has direct experience in order to enhance persuasive success? Where would you draw the line?

REFERENCES

Abelson, R. P. (1982). Three modes of attitude-behavior consistency. In M. P. Zanna, E. T. Higins, & C. P. Herman (Eds.), *Consistency in social behavior: The Ontario Symposium* (Vol. 2, pp. 131–146). Hillsdale, NJ: Lawrence Erlbaum.

Ajzen, I. (1985). From intentions to actions: A theory of planned behavior. In J. Kuhl & J. Beckman (Eds.), *Action control: From cognition to behavior* (pp. 11–39) Heidelberg, Germany: Springer.

Ajzen, I., & Fishbein, M. (1977). Attitude-behavior relations: A theoretical analysis and review of empirical research. *Psychological Bulletin, 84,* 888–918.

Ajzen, I., & Fishbein, M. (2005). The influence of attitudes on behavior. In D. Albarracin, B. T. Johnson, & M. P. Zanna (Eds.), *The handbook of attitudes* (pp. 173–221). Mahwah, NJ: Lawrence Erlbaum.

Campbell, A., Converse, P. E., Miller, W. E., & Stokes, D. E. (1960). *The American voter.* New York: Wiley.

Carver, C. S. (1975). Physical aggression as a function of objective self-awareness and attitudes toward punishment. *Journal of Experimental Social Psychology, 11,* 510–519.

Davidson, A. R., & Jaccard, J. J. (1979). Population psychology: A new look at an old problem. *Journal of Personality and Social Psychology,* 31, 1073–1082.

Dillard, J. P. (1993). Persuasion past and present: Attitudes aren't what they used to be. *Communication Monographs, 60,* 90–97.

Fazio, R. H., Chen, J., McDonel, E. C., & Sherman, S. J. (1982). Attitude accessibility, attitude-behavior consistency, and the strength of the object-evaluation association. *Journal of Experimental Social Psychology,* 18, 339–357.

Fazio, R. H., & Williams, C. J. (1986). Attitude accessibility as a moderator of the attitude-perception and attitude-behavior relations: An investigation of the 1984 presidential election. *Journal of Personality and Social Psychology,* 51, 505–514.

Fazio, R. H., & Zanna, M. P. (1978) Attitudinal qualities relating to the strength of the attitude-behavior relationship. *Journal of Experimental Social Psychology, 14,* 398–408.

Fazio, R. H., & Zanna, M. P. (1981). Direct experience and attitude-behavior consistency. In L. Berkowitz (Ed.), *Advances in experimental social psychology* (Vol. 14, pp. 162–202). New York: Academic Press.

Kallgren, C. A., & Wood, W. (1986). Access to attitude-relevant information in memory as a determinant of attitude-behavior consistency. *Journal of Experimental Social Psychology, 22,* 328–338.

LaPiere, R. T. (1934). Attitudes vs. action. *Social Forces, 13,* 230–237.

Pryor, J. B., Gibbons, F. X., Wicklund, R. A., Fazio, R. H., & Hood, R. (1977). Self-focused attention and self-report validity. *Journal of Personality, 45,* 514–527.

Regan, D. T., & Fazio, R. H. (1977). On the consistency between attitudes and behavior: Look to the method of attitude formation. *Journal of Experimental Social Psychology,* 13, 38–45.

Schuman, H., & Johnson, M. P. (1976). Attitudes and behavior. *Annual Review of Sociology,* 2, 161–207.

Sherman, S. J., & Fazio, R. H. (1983). Parallels between attitudes and traits as predictors of behavior. *Journal of Personality, 51,* 308–345.

Sivacek, J., & Crano, W. D. (1982). Vested interest as a moderator of attitude-behavior consistency. *Journal of Personality and Social Psychology, 43,* 210–221.

Snyder, M. (1982). When believing means doing: Creating links between attitudes and behavior. In M. P. Zanna, E. T. Higgins, & C. P. Herman (Eds.), *Consistency in social behavior: The Ontario Symposium* (Vol. 2, pp. 105–130). Hillsdale, NJ: Lawrence Erlbaum.

Snyder, M., & Kendzierski, D. (1982). Acting on one's attitudes: Procedures for linking attitudes and behavior. *Journal of Experimental Social Psychology, 18,* 165–183.

Wicker, A. (1969). Attitude versus actions: The relationship of verbal and overt behavioral responses to attitude objects. *Journal of Social Issues, 25*(4), 41–78.

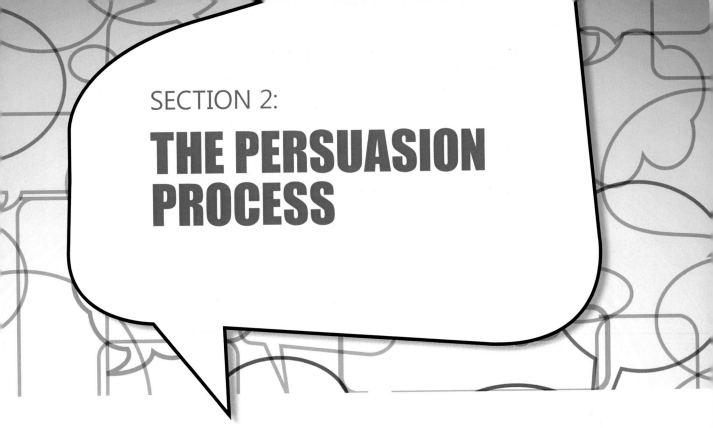

SECTION 2:
THE PERSUASION PROCESS

The focus of this section is on the components of the persuasion process. Persuasion is a communication process, and the components of the communication process serve as the framework for examining persuasion in this section. The basic components of the communication process include the source, receiver, message, and channel. Persuasion research involving each of these components is the basis for the chapters in this section. Chapter 4 focuses on characteristics of the source, primarily source credibility and related variables. Chapter 5 addresses message characteristics, including evidence and emotion. Chapter 6 addresses channel and receiver characteristics. Source, message, receiver, and channel factors serve as the building blocks of persuasion messages.

CHAPTERS

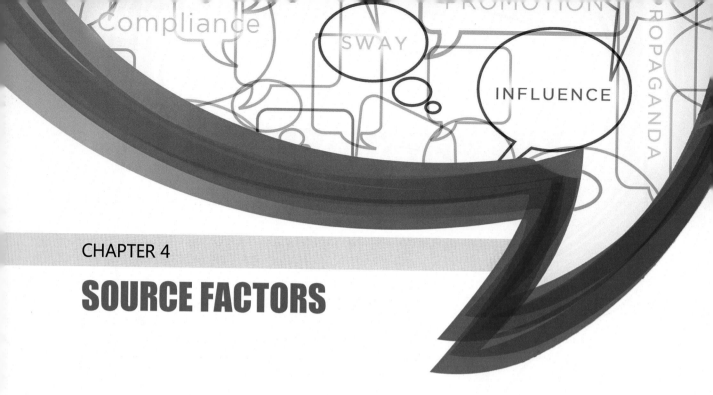

CHAPTER 4

SOURCE FACTORS

It's the first day of school. You enter class, look around to see if you know anyone in the class, and wait for the instructor. A few minutes later a young woman walks in, introduces herself as Ms. Brown, the instructor, and states that she is a graduate student and this is the first class she has ever taught. What is your response? What expectations do you have for the class? How knowledgeable do you think Ms. Brown is? Do you assume she is competent or incompetent? Now, let's rewind and do this again. A middle-aged woman walks in, introduces herself as Dr. Brown, the instructor, and states that she is a professor and this is her 15th year of teaching. What is your response? How knowledgeable and competent do you think Dr. Brown is? You may have had experiences similar to these. Do you give more attention to your instructors who are experienced professors? Are you more likely to challenge your instructors who are graduate students and assume they don't know what they're talking about?

Compare your assessment of instructor credibility with how you assess the credibility of various media such as the Internet or social media. What makes a news report, a website, a tweet, a Facebook posting, a blog, or other computer-mediated communication credible? Are you persuaded by more credible sources in these contexts? Does your decision about who is a credible source vary in these contexts, or do you rely on the same factors you used in the instructor example? Just as you may be more willing to listen to an instructor you perceive as credible, we are often more persuaded by sources we perceive as credible across contexts.

In this chapter we examine what makes a source credible and what impact that has on persuasion. Source credibility has received far more attention than any other source factor; however, there are other source factors to consider as well. This chapter is the first of four chapters that examine the parts of the persuasion process (source, message, channel, receiver). Recall from Chapter 1 that persuasion is a communication process, so we draw on the basic communication model of a source sending a message through a channel to a receiver who responds with feedback to the source.

LEARNING OBJECTIVES

- DEFINE CREDIBILITY AND DIFFERENTIATE THE MODERN DEFINITION WITH ARISTOTLE'S DEFINITION.
- DESCRIBE FACTORS THAT INFLUENCE PERCEPTIONS OF CREDIBILITY.
- EXPLAIN HOW CREDIBILITY AFFECTS PERSUASION.
- EXPLAIN THE TYPES OF POWER.
- DESCRIBE MILGRAM'S RESEARCH ON OBEDIENCE AND AUTHORITY AS A SOURCE FACTOR.
- EXPLAIN HOW SOURCE SIMILARITY, ATTRACTIVENESS AND LIKEABILITY AFFECT PERSUASION.

The **source** is the individual creating and/or delivering a message. The characteristics of a source are important to persuasion. If two different people delivered the same persuasive message, they would not necessarily be equally successful. There are a number of source characteristics that influence persuasion. Some of these source characteristics can be controlled, at least to some extent; others we have little control over. One important thing to keep in mind as you learn about source characteristics is that there are specific source qualities or behaviors, and there is how an audience *perceives* those qualities and behaviors. Just as two people delivering the same message may not be equally persuasive; two people listening to the same source will not have the same perceptions of the source.

CREDIBILITY

One of the most studied source factors is credibility. This concept will also make appearances in later chapters, specifically Chapters 9 and 11. A simple definition of **credibility** is that it is a perception of believability. If you are credible, you are believable. The concept of source credibility has been studied for thousands of years and there has been much disagreement and confusion about exactly what it means to be a credible source. To complicate matters, the concept of source credibility is not stable. Perceptions of a source's credibility can change during the course of a single message or from one message to another. For example, you may perceive your communication professor as highly credible when he or she is talking about persuasion theory. But if your professor gave you advice on what cell phone to purchase, your perception of his or her credibility may not be so high.

Let's first examine how perceptions of credibility can change over the course of a message. There are two types of source credibility: initial and derived. **Initial credibility** refers to the level of source credibility apart from any specific message—that is, the credibility of a source prior to the presentation of a persuasive message. **Derived credibility** refers to the level of source credibility during and after the presentation of a particular message. Although these two types of credibility may be the same at times, they are often different. For example, have you ever read a blog and, as a result of what you read, perceived the source as more credible than you did initially? This is an example of derived credibility increasing as a result of the message. The reverse can also be true. Have you ever perceived someone as having less credibility after your read his or her tweet or blog? Thus, when we consider source credibility, we must also consider both initial and derived forms.

ARISTOTLE'S APPROACH

A quick examination of the references in this book might lead you to guess that serious attention to the study of persuasion did not start until the mid-20th century. Nothing could be farther from the truth. Although many of the currently held theories and much of what we know from social scientific approaches to persuasion were developed in the last century, the study of persuasion itself is more than 2,500 years old. Writings by ancient Greeks serve as the foundation for much of our current understanding of persuasion. In particular, Aristotle gave us great insight into how persuasion works, and he did so from observing human behavior at that time. Much has changed over the last two millenniums, but the basics of human response to persuasive messages appear to have some enduring characteristics, and the nature of source credibility is one that has lasted.

Aristotle argued that persuasion has three important components: ethos, logos, and pathos. **Ethos** refers to the nature of credibility of the source, and some current credibility researchers use the term *ethos*. **Logos** refers to the nature of the arguments and structure of the message, and **pathos** refers to the emotional appeals of the message. We will discuss logos and pathos in Chapter 5. In this chapter, we focus on ethos.

DIMENSIONS OF CREDIBILITY

Source credibility is a multidimensional concept. Three dimensions, or parts, make up what we perceive as the credibility of the source. We must understand these dimensions in order to clearly understand the concept of credibility. The notion of source credibility having multiple dimensions is not new. Aristotle in ancient Greece argued that source credibility or ethos was composed of three dimensions: **good character, goodwill,** and **intelligence.** Good character refers to the moral nature, the honesty and goodness, of the source. **Goodwill** refers to the speaker's intent toward the audience. If the speaker has good intentions and has the receivers' best interest in mind, then the speaker has goodwill toward the audience. Intelligence refers to the knowledge base of the speaker, or, in other words, a source's expertise. To have the maximum level of credibility, a source would need to be perceived as having all three characteristics: good character, goodwill, and intelligence.

Aristotle identified these dimensions from observing human behavior and watching what it took for speakers to be perceived as credible by audiences at that time. These are also dimensions that Aristotle thought *should* be considered when evaluating speakers, and he taught those principles to his students. These three dimensions were assumed to be true for many years. Then in the 1960s, scholars began to question Aristotle's approach and used modern research and statistical methods to re-examine credibility. A statistical technique known as factor analysis was developed that was designed to identify the dimensions of a construct. Factor analysis is a statistical method that allows researchers to identify which items of a scale measure the same thing. Items that measure the same thing are called *factors* or *dimensions*. Wanting to develop a better understanding of credibility and to test Aristotle's conceptualization of credibility, researchers used factor analysis in several studies to identify the dimensions of credibility. Many items, usually in the form of semantic differential scales (see Chapter 2), were developed to measure credibility and, with the use of factor analysis, various dimensions of credibility were identified.

Unfortunately, this research that was intended to improve our understanding of credibility resulted in making things more confusing. Several other dimensions of credibility were identified such as dynamism, charisma, and safety. As a result, different scholars measured source credibility differently, making it difficult to compare results and draw conclusions. In 1981, McCroskey and Young published an article that reviewed the previous 30 years of research on source credibility and the methods used. They argued that these "new" dimensions of credibility were perceptions related to credibility, but not actual components of credibility. Additionally, they argued that Aristotle and other scholars had sufficiently conceptualized source credibility as consisting of intelligence, character, and goodwill. McCroskey and Young concluded that when measuring credibility, goodwill collapsed with character; therefore, character and intelligence were the two primary components of source credibility. But the saga continued. In 1999, McCroskey and Teven again examined the construct of source credibility, particularly the goodwill dimension. They drew on research on teacher caring and argued that the concept of goodwill was represented in the caring construct. McCroskey and Teven conducted a study with 783 participants who reported on 1 of 10 sources. Using factor analysis, they were able to successfully identify goodwill, in the form of caring, along with intelligence and character, as dimensions of credibility, confirming Aristotle's original definition of credibility from 2,500 years ago. Over the years the term "intelligence" has changed to "expertise" to better reflect the idea that it is what a source knows rather than his or her ability to know. Similarly, the term "character" has changed to "trustworthiness" to better reflect perceptions of honesty and integrity. The scale developed by McCroskey and Teven to measure expertise, trustworthiness, and caring is shown in Figure 4.1 and is the most contemporary measure of credibility.

The debate about how to define and measure source credibility may or may not have concluded. However, because of this long debate about how to measure source credibility, credibility research has used many different measures. The problem is that, because different measures were used, drawing conclusions about the role of source credibility in persuasion is a bit like trying to conclude the color of apples when yellow, red, and green varieties are included in the sample. In the following paragraphs we review research on source credibility. Keep in mind, though, that a vast majority of research on source credibility was conducted before any kind of consensus was reached on how credibility should be measured.

CREDIBILITY AND PERSUASION

So far, we have discussed how to define source credibility and its dimensions. We have not yet discussed the extent that credibility is useful when persuading someone. Your common sense probably tells you it is important. However, if you were to look at all the research conducted on credibility in persuasion, you would find that sometimes researchers concluded that credibility was very important and useful in changing receivers' attitudes. In other research, you would find that credibility seemed irrelevant to persuasive success. Finally, you would find in some research that credibility was actually a liability and inhibited persuasive success. Why the

From Communication Monographs, Vol. 66, 1999, by McCroskey and Teven.

Expertise								
Intelligent	1	2	3	4	5	6	7	Unintelligent
Untrained	1	2	3	4	5	6	7	Trained
Inexpert	1	2	3	4	5	6	7	Expert
Informed	1	2	3	4	5	6	7	Uninformed
Incompetent	1	2	3	4	5	6	7	Competent
Bright	1	2	3	4	5	6	7	Stupid
Goodwill								
Cares about me	1	2	3	4	5	6	7	Doesn't care about me
Has my interests at heart	1	2	3	4	5	6	7	Doesn't have my interests at heart
Self-centered	1	2	3	4	5	6	7	Not self-centered
Concerned with me	1	2	3	4	5	6	7	Unconcerned with me
Insensitive	1	2	3	4	5	6	7	Sensitive
Not understanding	1	2	3	4	5	6	7	Understanding
Trustworthiness								
Honest	1	2	3	4	5	6	7	Dishonest
Untrustworthy	1	2	3	4	5	6	7	Trustworthy
Honorable	1	2	3	4	5	6	7	Dishonorable
Moral	1	2	3	4	5	6	7	Immoral
Unethical	1	2	3	4	5	6	7	Ethical
Phony	1	2	3	4	5	6	7	Genuine

FIGURE 4.1 McCroskey and Teven's (1999) measure of source credibility.

variation in results? In a nutshell, credibility functions differently in different situations. Fortunately, research and theory help us explain and understand the complexities of credibility. The cognitive dissonance theory (Chapter 10) and the elaboration likelihood model (Chapter 11) will help us better understand the inconsistent research.

PERSISTENCE OF SOURCE CREDIBILITY EFFECTS OVER TIME

In early credibility research, Hovland and his colleagues (Hovland, Lumsdaine, & Sheffield, 1949) observed a strange phenomenon. They conducted experiments comparing the persuasiveness of sources with high and low credibility. Their experiment involved exposing an audience to either a high or low credibility source and measuring attitude immediately after hearing the message. They measured attitude again about a week later. Hovland and his colleagues found that the high credibility source was more persuasive initially—no surprise here. But when they measured attitude a week later, the receivers who had heard the low credibility source had a more positive attitude than the first time! They labeled this phenomenon the **sleeper effect**.

Kelman and Hovland (1953) tested the sleeper effect with a message advocating lenient treatment for juvenile delinquents. The high credibility source was a judge with experience with juvenile delinquents and who had authored several books on the topic. The low credibility source was a man off the street who appeared to be rather obnoxious and who had gotten into multiple problems as a youth. The topic was pretested with participants, and those in both the high credibility and low credibility conditions had similar views on the subject before being exposed to the message. When the participants were tested right after the message was presented, those exposed to the message from the highly credible source reported significantly more agreement with the message than did those exposed to the message from the low credibility source. However, when these same participants were asked their opinion about the topic (more lenient treatment for juvenile delinquents) three weeks later, both sets of attitudes had changed. Those who had been exposed to the message from the highly credible source reported attitudes that were less positive than right after the message. Those who had been exposed to the low credibility source reported more positive attitudes than right after hearing the message three weeks earlier. This sounds like something from a spy novel!

The sleeper effect describes the situation where receivers exposed to a low credibility source develop more positive attitudes over time, but when exposed to a high credibility source, receivers' attitudes become less positive over time. After enough time passes, the attitudes of those who heard the message from a high credibility source and those who heard the low credibility source tend to be the same. The sleeper effect is illustrated in Figure 4.2.

Why does the sleeper effect occur? The discounting model explains this phenomenon. It states that the effects of source credibility are temporary. The **discounting model** assumes that initial attitude change is a result of both source credibility and message content; however, permanent attitude change is based on message content

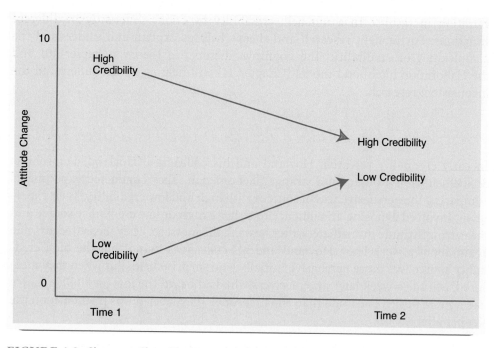

FIGURE 4.2 Sleeper effect. The impact of source credibility on attitude change wears off over time.

(Allen & Stiff, 1998). After three weeks, the receivers remembered the content of the message, but not the source of the message. In other words, the effect of source credibility wore off after three weeks, and just the effects of the message content remained. To test this hypothesis, in another study, receivers were reminded of the credibility of the message source, and the sleeper effect was offset. The high credibility source generated a greater attitude change than the low credibility source with this reminder, but the attitude still decayed somewhat over time. Many of us remember information but often fail to remember where we read it or heard it. That lack of connection between source and message means that the effects of source credibility are temporary. However, a persuader can maintain the influence of source credibility by continuing to remind the target audience of the source supporting the message.

INTRODUCTIONS AND CREDIBILITY

Perceptions of credibility judgments are affected by the information the audience has about the source, such as the source's **education** and **experience**. When the introduction of a speaker includes information about the source's education and experience, perceptions of credibility are often increased. For example, in an early study of credibility conducted during the communist scare of the 1950s, Hovland and Weiss (1951) devised a message about atomic-powered submarines. The high credibility condition attributed the message to Robert Oppenheimer, a PhD physicist who directed the Manhattan Project, which led to the creation of the United States' atomic bomb. In the low credibility condition, the message was attributed to *Pravda,* a Russian propaganda publication. As expected, Oppenheimer turned out to be a significantly more credible source, and the message attributed to him resulted in greater attitude change. Multiple studies have manipulated credibility using similar types of methods. A common manipulation is to describe one source as a university professor with years of experience in a topic area (high credibility manipulation) and describe the other source as a high school sophomore (low credibility manipulation) (Hewgill & Miller, 1965). These studies indicate that sharing relevant information about the source's credentials is a quite effective means of enhancing perceptions of credibility.

When posting information online in the form of tweets, comments on websites, and consumer reviews of products, you have the option of providing information about yourself or choosing a name that allows you to remain more anonymous. Although we know from prior research that how you introduce yourself matters, the question is what kind of credibility do we perceive for those who post with less personal information? Xie, Miao, Kuo, and Lee (2011) researched this question in the context of consumer online reviews of hotels. They found that those who included personal identifying information (their real name, where they lived, dates for the hotel stay) were rated as more credible than those who did not include this information (such as traveler@hotmail.com). In addition, the reviews with personally identifying information led to greater influence on behavioral intentions about staying at the hotel being reviewed than those who failed to include the aspects of source introductions. Thus, source introductions of any kind are important in online contexts as well.

In most contexts, providing a source's education and experience to the receiver enhances perceptions of credibility to the extent that education and experience are positive qualities. What if the source doesn't have much education and lacks experience? It would be unethical to lie or mislead the audience about the source's background. So what do you do? As it turns out, *when* you provide the audience with this information about the source determines how much impact it has. If the audience is given the source's credentials first, that information has maximum impact on source credibility. If the source's credentials are given after the message is presented, the information has minimum impact on source credibility. When the credentials are introduced at the end of the message, high and low credibility sources are about equally effective. In this situation, the persuasive success or failure of the message is a result of other factors (Husek, 1965; O'Keefe, 1987). Thus, it is best for high credibility sources to establish their credentials at the beginning of the message, or certainly no later than the middle of the message. On the other hand, sources with low credibility are better off introducing their credentials at the end of the message and relying on message factors to persuade the audience. Why do you suppose this occurs?

When credibility manipulations are introduced *after* the message has been processed, the message has already been processed and information about the source will have little impact. Regardless of what factors of the message or situation affected the processing of the message, that process has already occurred before the credibility is introduced. If the receiver is paying attention and processing the message, the receiver is focusing on the content of the message without regard to the credibility of the source. Additionally, we tend to give strangers the benefit of the doubt and assume anyone speaking on a particular topic is at least moderately credible. It is probably a cultural characteristic that we have at least some trust in strangers, so this phenomenon may not be observed in other cultures. This assumption of at least moderate credibility enhances the persuasive effectiveness of low credibility sources when that lack of credibility is not introduced until the message has already been processed.

MESSAGE VARIABLES

Message variables refer to the content and structure of a message. Perceptions of credibility are based on characteristics and behaviors of the source, but what the source says (the message) also impacts perceptions of credibility. We will discuss message variables in greater detail in Chapter 5. At this point, however, we discuss how message variables interact with source credibility. A central variable is **message discrepancy**, which will be discussed again in Chapter 8. Message discrepancy refers to the difference between the advocated message and the receiver's position on a topic. For example, a source may advocate for making all abortions illegal, and the receiver's position might be that abortion should be legal during the first trimester—there is a discrepancy between the message and the receiver's position. You might think that highly credible sources could get away with more message discrepancy and this is true at least some of the time (Sternthal, Philips, & Dholakia, 1978). However, when a message was more discrepant and counter-attitudinal for receivers (a message that went against their attitude), highly credible sources were more persuasive than less credible sources. The opposite was true for pro-attitudinal messages (messages that support the audience's attitude) that were low in discrepancy. In this case, low credibility sources were more persuasive than high credibility sources (Chabet, Filiatraut, Laroche, & Watson, 1988; Harmon & Coney, 1982).

Humor is another variable affecting evaluations of source credibility, depending on how effectively it is employed in the message. Tamborini and Zillmann (1981) evaluated instructor use of humor in the college classroom. As with other researchers (e.g., Houser, Cowan, & West, 2007), they found that limited and appropriate use of humor could enhance receiver liking and trustworthiness of a source but not the expertise dimension. However, the type of humor must also be considered. Hackman (1988) found that the use of self-disparaging and other disparaging humor reduced perceptions of credibility. Wrench, Brogan, Wrench, and McKean (2007) found that religious leaders were perceived as more credible when they were also perceived to use humor. In another study, however, Wrench, Millhouse, and Sharp (2007) found that flight attendants who used humor in their preflight safety briefing were perceived as less credible. Humor is a complex variable that can be interpreted very differently by different people. Humor can generate positive perceptions, but it can also very easily offend some members of the audience. In general, humor should be used with great caution in persuasive situations.

Not only can the content of the message affect perceptions of source credibility, but the **delivery of the message** can influence source credibility judgments as well. Speakers who are quite fluent in their speaking style are perceived as having more expertise than those who are less fluent (Burgoon, Birk, & Pfau, 1990; Engstrom, 1994). The rationale is that we assume fluency and knowledge go together.

Objectively we know this is not necessarily true, but we still perceive speakers who are fluent and polished as more credible. Speakers who pause frequently, use fillers like "uh," or have more mistakes in delivery are assumed to be less knowledgeable, and therefore as less credible. Thus, improving your speaking patterns and eliminating unnecessary movements (e.g., shifting weight; fiddling with rings, watches, keys) can enhance perceptions of your credibility.

Some scholars have examined the message with regard to the source's best interest. Some evidence suggests that **message incongruity** with the source's interest interacts with source credibility. Messages that appear to go against the source's best interests tend to enhance the source's credibility overall and tend to win greater persuasive success (Walster, Aronson, & Abrahams, 1966). If we heard the head of the National Rifle Association arguing in favor of gun control or the leader of a labor union arguing in favor of reduced labor benefits, we would tend to believe them because these ideas are not what we would expect them to say to protect their own interests. This is particularly true for low credibility sources. If you have high credibility to begin with, using message incongruity doesn't help you. You can only be so credible. We tend to be more skeptical if people advocate for themselves, but we expect it to happen that way. When sources advocate against their own interests, we tend to believe them.

CHANNEL FACTORS

Not only do the characteristics of the message impact perceptions of source credibility, but the channel used to deliver the message does as well. Chapter 6 examines channel effects in more detail; here we look at the credibility of the delivery channel. We know receivers trust some messages more than others due to the nature of the source and channel of delivery. What channels of information people trust has changed dramatically in recent years. Social media and Internet sources have surged in credibility, while traditional media have declined. However, the trust we have in a channel depends on the type of information we are seeking. As shown in Figure 4.3, when it comes to commercial brands, Americans trust Facebook as much as they do newspapers. Age also makes a difference. It comes as no surprise that younger Americans trust social media more than do older Americans. Additionally, people differ across the globe. Figure 4.4 illustrates that traditional media is trusted at differing levels around the world, and that trust changes over time. The illustration in Figure 4.4 shows how levels of trust in media have risen or decreased between 2011 and 2012 alone.

Researchers have started examining the role of credibility in social media channels. For example, interest in credibility's role for tweets has increased as the popularity of Twitter has grown. Phelps (2012) reported the results of Microsoft research into Twitter that identified factors associated with both low and high credibility tweets. High credibility was generally associated with sources that had expertise in the topic (as demonstrated on the Twitter bio), were influential (as assessed by a larger number of followers, retweets, and mentions by others), had a history on the topic (such as tweeting about the topic often, having posted material about the topic online outside of Twitter, or being in a locations relevant to the topic of the tweet), and who had a

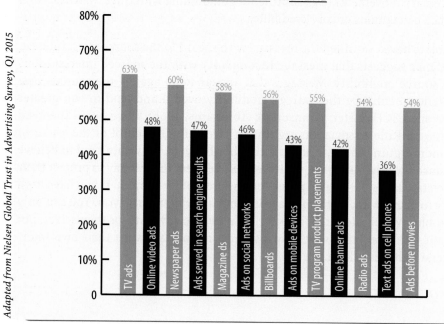

PERCENT OF GLOBAL RESPONDENTS WHO COMPLETELY OR SOMEWHAT TRUST ADVERTISING FORMAT
TRADITIONAL vs. *ONLINE*

Adapted from Nielsen Global Trust in Advertising Survey, Q1 2015

TV ads: 63%
Online video ads: 48%
Newspaper ads: 60%
Ads served in search engine results: 47%
Magazine ds: 58%
Ads on social networks: 46%
Billboards: 56%
Ads on mobile devices: 43%
TV program product placements: 55%
Online banner ads: 42%
Radio ads: 54%
Text ads on cell phones: 36%
Ads before movies: 54%

FIGURE 4.3

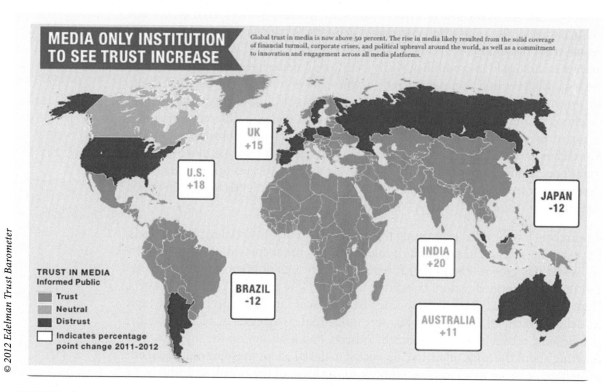

FIGURE 4.4 Global Trust in Media

reputation (being someone the receiver follows or has heard of). In addition, users who used a photo of themselves rather than a cartoon character or other avatar were considered more credible. The topic area of the tweets also made a difference. Those who posted about science were viewed as more credible than those who posted about politics or entertainment. Those whose Twitter names were more related to the topic were the most credible. For example, Phelps noted that "@AllPolitics" is more specific and thus more credible than "@Alex_Brown," which in turn is more specific and thus more credible than "@tenacious27." Johnson (2011) looked at how instructor tweets affected faculty credibility with students. Their study exposed students to social tweets, scholarly tweets, or a combination of social and scholarly tweets from a professor. Their results indicated that students who received the social tweets rated the professor higher on credibility.

Twitter is just one form of social media, and those in the influence business (e.g., public relations, advertising, strategic communication) have a great deal at stake in figuring out how credibility works in social media. A major public relations firm, Burson Marsteller, has noted that those who carry influence online carry a great deal of weight. "Representing 8% of the internet population (about 9 million users), this group influences more people on more topics than other online users. And, they are eight times more effective at communicating their views than Roper's traditional 'influentials'" (Kirwan, 2012, p. 6). It is important to consider the impact the channel has on a source's credibility and influence with the targeted receivers.

OTHER SOURCE FACTORS

Source credibility has received the bulk of research attention and is certainly an important factor in the persuasion process. But other source factors also affect the persuasion process. Persuaders such as advertisers make strategic choices about whom the source of the message should be in order to maximize the persuasive impact of their messages. These factors have received less research attention than credibility has, but they also contribute to our understanding of the persuasion process.

POWER

Power is the ability to get others to do what you want (see Figure 4.5) and is a broad-based concept that includes many ways of communicating. Sources who are perceived as powerful are influential, and receivers will often accept their messages because of the source's power. Power and credibility are sometimes linked, but not always. We may completely distrust someone in power, or perceive them as uncaring and incompetent. A commonly used description of power is the one provided by French and Raven (1959). They identified five **power bases**: reward, coercive, legitimate, referent, and expert. **Reward power** is one's ability to use rewards to influence another's behavior. If your professor offers you 10 bonus points for attending a lecture, he or she is using reward power. **Coercive power** is the ability to use punishment to influence a person's behavior. If your professor said you would lose 10 points if you did not attend the lecture, it would be an example of coercive power. **Legitimate power** is the power one has because of his or her title or position. When your mom says, "Do it because *I* said so," she is using her legitimate power as your parent. This power base exists primarily because we believe that person has a right to tell us what to do. Referent and expert power are different from the three previous power bases. **Referent power** is based in the relationship between two persons. When people have referent power, others are willing to do what is asked of them because they like and/or respect that person. When your boss asks you to do something and you do it because you respect your boss, you are primarily influenced by referent power. Referent power is more implicit than reward and coercive power. Rarely do people with referent power actually refer verbally to the relationship when making requests. The power derived from the relationship is communicated implicitly. The last power base is **expert power**, which is based on how knowledgeable a person is. When our technology guru neighbor tells us to buy a specific router to solve our wireless problem, we do exactly as told because of the expertise we perceive our neighbor as having.

As you might guess, the power bases are not equal. Having power increases your ability to influence people, particularly short-term behavior. Coercive and reward power are generally effective at getting short-term behavior change, but not so good for changing attitudes and beliefs. For example, imagine a dishwashing dispute between two roommates, Fred and Barney. Barney wants Fred to wash his dishes after he eats and not just leave them in the sink. Barney might wield power by offering to drive Fred to class (reward power), and Fred may agree. However, this is not likely to change Fred's attitude about washing dishes or his beliefs about the importance of taking care of one's dirty dishes. Coercive and reward power are quite useful in gaining compliance from receivers, which is something we will discuss more extensively in Chapter 12. Referent and expert power are a different matter. These two bases of power are developed over time as a result of how we conduct ourselves and are much more useful for influencing attitudes and beliefs. People are more apt to pay attention to sources when they are perceived as having referent or

For Better or For Worse®   **by Lynn Johnston**

FIGURE 4.5 Power can be communicated explicitly or implicitly.

expert power, and these two power bases are closely linked to credibility. Referent power is linked to perceptions of caring and trustworthiness. Expert power is clearly linked to expertise. Legitimate power is a bit different than the other bases of power. Legitimate power has to do with your position and title. When we perceive someone as having legitimate power, we believe they have the authority or right to tell us what to do. Legitimate power is the reason people often "obey" authority figures such as police officers and teachers. The reasons people obey authority figures are not well understood; however, there is a great deal of evidence that people obey authority figures quite consistently.

AUTHORITY AND OBEDIENCE

In 1963, Stanley Milgram published a study on obedience that shocked the world. You may be familiar with this study. The procedure involved recruiting research participants to take part in an experiment on the effects of punishment on learning. On entering the experimental setting, the participant was told he (all participants were male) would play the role of teacher, and a confederate was introduced as another research participant who would play the role of learner. Electrodes were attached to the arm of the confederate, and the research participant was instructed to test the confederate on recalling word pairs. For each wrong answer, the participant was to administer a shock, with the first being 15 volts. With each wrong answer, the shock was increased by 15 volts, with 450 volts being the maximum. The confederate did not actually receive any shock but gave progressively more intense responses with increased voltage, such as progressively louder grunts, followed by asking for it to stop, screaming in pain, and claiming that his heart was bad, and finally being unresponsive. A researcher dressed in a white coat (authority figure) was present, and if the research participant expressed concern or a desire to stop, would urge the participant to continue. Milgram (1963) reported that 65 percent continued administering shocks until 450 volts was reached.

Milgram's (1963, 1974) research drew a great deal of attention for two reasons. First, because most people found it very unsettling to think that such a large proportion of normal people would obey the authority figure and administer electrical shocks. We like to think that only criminals or *bad people* would do such a thing. Second, the ethics of the research procedures were seriously questioned. Milgram put research participants into a difficult and stressful situation and reported that participants showed definite signs of stress, with three participants having seizures. As a result of the ethical concerns, this line of research was not continued. However, Milgram's study was replicated by Shanab and Yahya (1977) in Jordan with children. Shanab and Yahya replicated Milgram's procedures exactly with 192 children ranging from 6 to 16 years old. Shanab and Yahya reported that 73 percent of participants delivered shock until the last step, which is similar to that reported by Milgram (1963). Shanab and Yahya also reported no sex or age differences, meaning that sex and age did not influence whether the participants obeyed or not.

You may be thinking that a lot has changed since the 1960s, and even 1977, and that people are not as obedient now as they were back then. In response to such comments, Burger (2009) partially replicated Milgram's (1963) study. Burger created an experiment exactly like Milgram's except that it ended at 150 volts when the confederate yelled to stop and that his heart was bad. After observing whether the research participant was going to continue administering shocks or not, Burger stopped the experiment. Burger conducted extensive screening to ensure that all research participants were mentally healthy and free from previous experiences that might result in negative experiences for the participants as well as provided extensive debriefing with a clinical psychologist. Burger (2009) reported that 70 percent continued after the 150-volts point, whereas Milgram reported 83 percent continued beyond this point. Although this difference looks substantial, it was not a significant difference (was probably a result of chance rather than a real difference). Burger also reported no differences in obedience between male and female participants. He concluded that people today are just as likely to obey an authority figure as they were in 1963.

Sources who have legitimate power are perceived as having authority and receivers are more likely to obey them, even when it goes against their better judgment. Sources with authority need to consider their legitimate power and understand the ethical implications of their power. In Chapter 13 we discuss the ethics of persuasion.

NORMATIVE INFLUENCE AND SIMILARITY

Are you more likely to be influenced by someone who is similar to you or different from you? Are you willing to go against the group? Do you look to those you admire for direction? We are referring to a set of related factors that include normative influence, identification, and similarity. Deutsch and Gerard (1955) introduced the **normative influence** concept when studying group influences and group dynamics theory (see Chapter 7). Deutsch and Gerard found that normative influences from group membership affected receivers' judgments, but only when the group was present and/or knew about the receivers' response. You might observe the impact of normative influence the next time you cross the street against the light. When a crowd is waiting to cross and one person starts off across the street against the light, do you and others follow? Lefkowitz, Blake, and Mouton (1955) used this situation to test normative influence. The norm is to wait until the light reads *walk* to cross the street (more so in cities than on college campuses). It is nonnormative behavior to walk against the light (not to mention dangerous). Lefkowitz et al. found that more people crossed against the light when well-dressed confederates (a confederate is someone working with the researcher) crossed than when poorly dressed confederates crossed against the light. Although not involving a traditional persuasive message, this study did illustrate the power of normative influence to direct behavior in a natural setting. Similar to normative influence, Kelman (1961) described **identification** as a form of influence. When we identify with an individual, we find that person more socially attractive and we are more willing to allow that person to influence us. We often identify with those in roles we value, such as the president of the United States, the CEO of a valued organization, or a celebrity. With normative influence and identification, we are influenced because we associate ourselves with a group or individual we value.

The perceived **similarity** of the source to the receiver is a source factor that enhances persuasion in some instances. We tend to think that we are more likely to be influenced by those similar to us, but the research on this idea is split. At times, similarity on the part of the speaker can lead to greater persuasive success (Brock, 1965), but, at other times, similarity reduces persuasive effectiveness (Infante, 1978) or seems to have no effect (Klock & Traylor, 1983). For similarity to enhance persuasion, the similarity must be relevant to the persuasive goal. For instance, Brock (1965) conducted an experiment with salespeople selling paint. Salespeople indicated they were either similar to the customer in terms of the type of painting they had done recently, or they were dissimilar in terms of the type of painting they had done recently. Brock found that similar sources were more successful at influencing the type of paint purchased by customers. If the similarity is irrelevant to the persuasive goal, such as noting a similarity in painting experience when trying to persuade someone to buy insurance, use of similarity is generally ineffective.

Similarity also appears to influence our willingness to model a source's behavior. Recall our discussion of modeling in Chapter 2 and that we model people we like and respect. Similarity also plays a role in our willingness to model someone. Anderson and McMillion (1995) illustrated this in a study of African American women's intentions to perform breast self-examination. The study used two educational videos on breast self-examination (BSE). One video was targeted at a broad audience and used a white male physician and women of various races modeling BSE. The other video was targeted at African American women and used an African American female physician and African American women modeling BSE. A third video was used with a control group. Anderson and McMillion found that the participants who viewed the similar videotape (African American physician and African American models) had greater intentions to perform BSE than those who viewed the diverse video or the control video. Participants also rated the African American female physician as more credible with regard to BSE than the white male physician. When a source is similar to the receiver in some relevant way, persuasion is often enhanced. Additionally, similar sources are often viewed as more credible. The AIDS message shown in Figure 4.6 is targeted at young African Americans and uses similarity. The creators of this message are hoping that young African Americans will model the couple in the ad and seek HIV testing. Similarity is another source factor that affects the persuasion process and is useful when you are involved in influence attempts.

PHYSICAL ATTRACTIVENESS

The **physical attractiveness** of the source is another source factor that plays a role in the persuasion process. Are physically attractive people more or less persuasive than unattractive people? If you spend a few minutes looking at the advertisements in any magazine, you'll conclude that only attractive models are used. Certainly, we prefer looking at attractive people more than unattractive people, particularly when they are strangers. But does physical attractiveness make you a more effective persuader? The answer, as with so many persuasion variables, is sometimes. Evidence suggests that physically attractive people are more effective persuaders in many situations (Chaiken, 1986). Widgery and Ruch (1981) had research participants read a persuasive message with a picture of the source attached to the message. Half of the participants read a message from an attractive source, the other half from an unattractive source. As expected, participants who read the message from the attractive source were more persuaded than those who read the same message from the unattractive source. Why would an attractive source be more effective than an unattractive source? Physical attractiveness may serve as a simple cue (Chaiken, 1986). By *cue* we mean a simple rule or shortcut for assessing a message. We tend to associate attractive things with good things. So the attractive source attached to the message served as simple reason to believe the message. Source attractiveness is not so important when receivers devote a lot of attention and effort to the message. Additionally, physically attractive people are often perceived as more credible (Widgery, 1974). Therefore, attractiveness often contributes to perceptions of credibility. By itself, physical attractiveness probably has a small impact on persuasion, but because it contributes to perceptions of credibility, it becomes more important. Sources that are not physically attractive need to be aware of this fact and emphasize other qualities such as education, experience, trustworthiness, and caring to offset any negative effects of their physical appearance.

What are additional reasons for using physically attractive sources in persuasion? In order to influence someone, you have to have their attention. Physically attractive people tend to draw attention. A physically attractive model will draw attention to an advertisement. Getting the audience's attention is often half the battle in our advertisement-saturated environment. Besides drawing attention, we generally respond positively to attractive things, be they people, animals, art, or other objects. Pretty things elicit positive feelings and affect. Recall our discussion of classical conditioning in Chapter 2. By pairing a product, organization, or idea with a physically attractive source, the advertisement may result in the receiver

City of Los Angeles, AIDS Coordinator's Office.

Ready to do **things differently?**

I have a boyfriend.

We've been going out and we really like each other.

We're using condoms to be safe.

Our friends are getting tested for HIV, and we are ready to test too.

That's right, we're ready and we're doing it together...

So we can know the results together.

After all,

it's time to do things differently.

Get Tested Together ~ Share the Results

For more information, contact:
California AIDS Hotline
1-800-367-AIDS
TDD: 1-888-225-AIDS
www.LaCityAIDS.org

Message brought to you by the City of Los Angeles - AIDS Coordinator's Office

FIGURE 4.6   Ready to do things differently?

being conditioned to have a positive response to the product, organization, or idea. Pick up a magazine of your choice and look at the models in the advertisements. How are the advertisers using attractiveness? To gain attention? As a simple cue? To enhance credibility?

LIKEABILITY

A final source factor is the **likeability** of the source. Liking of the source has been related to trustworthiness in some research studies, and it makes sense that we would trust those we like more. Generally, sources we like are more effective than those we dislike, and generally liking is related to the trustworthy dimension of credibility. However, research has indicated that when liking and credibility come into conflict (e.g., when we like a source who has low credibility), then credibility outweighs liking. Wachtler and Counselman (1981) studied the size of damage awards in a personal injury lawsuit. Sources were portrayed as warm and friendly or cold and stingy. Participants were given messages attributed to one of the two sources who advocated a large award or a small award. Results indicated that participants liked the warm and friendly source more, but the cold and stingy source was rated as more credible and resulted in higher awards when advocating a large award. Advocating against one's best interest led to greater credibility attributions, and those outweighed the dislike for the source. Thus, liking the source can be a factor; however, it is not as important as source credibility and other persuasion factors.

SUMMARY

- The two kinds of source credibility are initial credibility and derived credibility.
- Aristotle studied persuasion more than 2,500 years ago and focused on ethos, logos, and pathos. Ethos is the study of a source's credibility.
- Aristotle argued that good character, goodwill, and intelligence are the dimensions of source credibility.
- McCroskey and Teven (1999) developed a measure of credibility that included expertise, trustworthiness, and caring.
- The discounting model explains the sleeper effect phenomenon.
- The discounting model states that receivers forget the source of the message, but remember the content.
- The timing of the source introduction determines whether credibility will play a role in processing the message.
- Message variables that interact with source credibility include message discrepancy, use of humor, and delivery of the message.
- The channel of message delivery can affect source credibility and how credibility is established.

- Sources with greater levels of power are more influential. Referent and expert power are the most effective power bases.
- Milgram's (1963) study of obedience revealed the power of authority.
- Sources that are perceived as similar are sometimes more effective, particularly when the similarity is relevant to the persuasive goal.
- Attractive sources are sometimes more effective, because they may gain attention and be associated with good things through classical conditioning.
- The likeability of a source is important, with more likable sources being more generally effective than disliked sources.

KEY TERMS

Authoritarianism—a personality trait regarding to the degree to which individuals rely on authority figures and sources to guide their lives.

Credibility—a perception of believability.

Derived credibility—the nature of the credibility of a source during and after the presentation of a particular message.

Discounting model—assumes that initial attitude change is a result of both source credibility and message content; however, permanent attitude change is based on message content.

Dogmatism—a personality trait regarding how closed minded a person is.

Ethos—the nature of the source's credibility and composed of three dimensions: good character, goodwill, and intelligence.

Expertise—a primary dimension of credibility that refers to the perceived knowledge and intelligence of the source.

Identification—occurs when a target accepts influence from an agent because he or she wants to be associated with the agent.

Initial credibility—the credibility of a source prior to the presentation of a persuasive message.

Goodwill—a dimension of credibility that refers to the perceived caring on the part of the source.

Locus of control—the degree to which an individual perceives his or her life is controlled by internal factors or external factors.

Logos—the nature of the arguments and structure of the message.

Message discrepancy—the difference between the position being advocated by a message and the preferred position of the receiver.

Message incongruity—when a message goes against (is not congruent with) the source's interests or needs.

Normative influence—a factor that can influence perceptions of credibility; refers to the influence from group norms; also referred to as identification and similarity.

Pathos—the emotional appeals of the message.

Power—the ability to get others to do what you want.

Power bases—includes five types of power: reward, coercive, legitimate, referent, and expert.

Sleeper effect—suggests that high credibility sources have more persuasive impact immediately following the message than do low credibility sources but that, over time, the effects of credibility wear off.

Topic saliency—how important the topic of a persuasive message is to receivers.

Trustworthiness—a primary dimension of credibility that refers to receivers' perceptions of the source's honesty.

REVIEW QUESTIONS

1. What is the difference between initial credibility and derived credibility?
2. What are ethos, pathos, and logos? How do they relate to the definition of credibility?
3. What are the three dimensions of source credibility?
4. What is the sleeper effect?
5. What is the discounting model and how does it explain the sleeper effect?
6. How does the timing of the source introduction affect credibility's role in persuasive success?
7. How do message and channel factors affect perceptions of source credibility?
8. What are the five bases of power?
9. How did Milgram (1963) study obedience? How does obedience relate to power?
10. How do similarity, likeability, and physical attractiveness affect persuasion?

DISCUSSION QUESTIONS

1. Think of a teacher you perceive as credible, a family member you perceive as credible, and a public figure you perceive as credible. Why do you perceive each of these individuals as credible? How similar or different are your reasons for perceiving these three individuals as credible?

2. Imagine yourself giving a presentation to a group of senior managers at your place of employment. Assume you have been with the company for only 2 weeks. What could you do during your presentation to enhance your credibility?

3. The sleeper effect can be used to introduce ideas from less-than-credible sources that will gain acceptance as people forget about the source of the message. Is it ethical to introduce persuasive concepts from low credibility sources and count on time passing to remove negative impact of low credibility? Can you think of examples where this occurred? How do you rate the ethics of those situations?

4. Is it ethical for a low credibility source to purposely delay the introduction of her or his credentials in order to reduce the impact of their low credibility? When would this practice be acceptable? When would you find it unacceptable?

5. Think of a persuasive situation in which you believe it would be important for the source to be highly credible. Think of another situation in which high source credibility would not be so important. What are the differences between the two situations?

6. Does a source with authority have greater ethical responsibility for their messages?

7. What source factors do you pay the most attention to in advertisements? What about for your professors?

REFERENCES

Allen, M., & Stiff, J. B. (1998). An analysis of the sleeper effect. In M. Allen & R. W. Preiss (Eds.), *Persuasion: Advances through meta-analysis* (pp. 175–188). Cresskill, NJ: Hampton Press.

Anderson, R. B., & McMillion, P. Y. (1995). Effects of similar and diversified modeling on African American women's efficacy expectations and intentions to perform breast self-examinations. *Health Communication, 7,* 327–343.

Applebaum, R. L., & Anatol, K. W. (1972). The factor structure of source credibility as a function of the speaking situation. *Speech Monographs, 40,* 231–237.

Berlo, D. K., Lemert, J. B., & Mertz, R. J. (1969). Dimensions for evaluating the acceptability of message sources. *Public Opinion Quarterly, 33,* 563–576.

Brock, T. C. (1965). Communicator-recipient similarity and decision change. *Journal of Personality and Social Psychology, 1,* 650–654.

Burgoon, J. K., Birk, T., & Pfau, M. (1990). Nonverbal behaviors, persuasion, and credibility. *Human Communication Research, 17,* 140–169.

Chabet, J. C., Filiatraut, P., Laroche, M., & Watson, C. (1988). Compensatory effects of cognitive characteristics of the source, the message, and the receiver upon attitude change. *Journal of Psychology, 122,* 609–621.

Chaiken, S. (1986). Physical appearance and social influence. In C. P. Herman, M. P. Zanna, & E. T. Higgins (Eds.), *Physical appearance, stigma, and social behavior: The Ontario Symposium, Vol. 3* (pp. 143–177). Hilsdale, NJ: Lawrence Erlbaum.

Deutsch, M., & Gerard, H. (1955). A study of normative and informative influences upon individual judgment. *Journal of Abnormal and Social Psychology, 54,* 629–636.

Engstrom, E. (1994). Effects of nonfluencies on speaker's credibility in newscast settings. *Perceptual and Motor Skills, 78,* 739–743.

Fogg, B. J., Soohoo C., & Danielson, D. (2002). *How do people evaluate a Web site's credibility? Result from a large study.* Retrieved February 26, 2009, from http:www.consumerwebwatch.org/ dynamic/web-credibility-reports-evaluate-abstract.cfm

Hackman, M. Z. (1988). Audience reactions to the use of direct and personal disparaging humor in informative public address. *Communication Research Reports, 5,* 126–130.

Harmon, R. R., & Coney, K. A. (1982). The persuasive effects of source credibility in buy and lease situations. *Journal of Marketing Research, 19,* 255–260.

Hewgill, M. A., & Miller, G. R. (1965). Source credibility and response to fear-arousing communications. *Speech Monographs, 32,* 95–101.

Houser, M. L., Cowan, R. L. and West, D. A. (2007). Investigating a new education frontier: Instructor communication behavior in CD-ROM texts—do traditionally positive behaviors translate into this new environment? *Communication Quarterly, 55,* 19–38.

Hovland, C. I., Janis, I. L., & Kelley, H. H. (1953). *Communication and persuasion.* New Haven, CT: Yale University Press.

Hovland, C. I., Lumsdaine, A., & Sheffield, F. (1949). *Experiments in mass communication.* Princeton, NJ: Princeton University Press.

Hovland, C., & Weiss, W. (1951). The influence of source credibility on communication effectiveness. *Public Opinion Quarterly, 15,* 635–650.

Husek, T. R. (1965). Persuasive impacts of early, late, or no mention of a negative source. *Journal of Personality and Social Psychology, 24,* 125–128.

Infante, D. A. (1978). Similarity between advocate and receiver: The role of instrumentality. *Central States Speech Journal, 29,* 187–193.

Johnson, K. (2011). The effect of *Twitter* posts on students' perceptions of instructor credibility. *Learning, Media and Technology, 36*(1), 21–38.

Kelman, H. C. (1961). Processes of opinion change. *Public Opinion Quarterly, 25,* 57–78.

Kelman, H. C., & Hovland, C. I. (1953). Reinstatement of the communicator in delayed measurement of opinion change. *Journal of Conflict Resolution, 2,* 51–60.

Kirwan, P. (2012). Selected findings: How to measure your social media impact and ROI. Retrieved from http://usefulsocialmedia.com/impact/selected-findings.php.

Klock, S. J., & Traylor, M. B. (1983). Older and younger models in advertising to older consumers: An advertising effectiveness experiment. *Akron Business and Economic Review, 14,* 48–52.

Lefkowitz, M., Blake, R., & Mouton, J. (1955). Status factors in pedestrian violation of traffic signals. *Journal of Abnormal and Social Psychology, 51,* 704–706.

Marketing Charts (2012). Americans trust traditional sources of info most; wary of SocNets. Retrieved February 23, 2013, from http://www.marketingcharts.com/television/americans-trust-traditional-info-sources-most-wary-of-socnets-22387/.

McCroskey, J. C. (1966). Scales for the measurement of ethos. *Speech Monographs, 33,* 65–72.

McCroskey, J. C., & Teven, J. J. (1999). Goodwill: A reexamination of the construct and its measurement. *Communication Monographs, 66,* 90–103.

McCrosky, J. C., & Young, T. J. (1981). Ethos and credibility: The construct and its measurement after three decades. *Central States Speech Journal, 32,* 24–34.

O'Keefe, D. J. (1987). The persuasive effects of delaying identification of high- and low-credibility communicators: A meta-analytic review. *Central States Speech Journal, 38,* 63–72.

Petty, R. E., Cacioppo, J. T., & Goldman, R. (1981). Personal involvement as a determinant of argument based persuasion. *Journal of Personality and Social Psychology, 41,* 847–855.

Phelps, A. (March 16, 2012). Think fast: Is that tweet true or false? How we use credibility cues to make decisions. Nieman Journalism Lab. Retrieved February 23, 2013, from http://www.niemanlab.org/2012/03/think-fast-is-that-tweet-true-or-false-how-we-use-credibility-cues-to-make-decisions/?utm_source=feedburner&utm_medium=feed&utm_campaign=Feed%3A+NiemanJournalismLab+%28Nieman+Journalism+Lab%29.

Princeton Survey Research Associated. (2002, January). *A matter of trust: What users want from Web sites. Results of a national survey of Internet users for Consumers Web Watch.* Retrieved February 26, 2009, from http:www.consumerwebwatch.org/web-credibility-reportsa-matter-of-trust-abstract.cfm.

Schweitzer, D., & Ginsburg, G. P. (1966). Factors of communicator credibility. In C. W. Backman & P. F. Secord (Eds.), *Problems in social psychology* (pp. 94–102). New York: McGraw-Hill.

Steinfatt, T. M. (1987). Personality and communication: Classical approaches. In J. C. McCroskey & J. A. Daly (Eds.), *Personality and interpersonal communication* (pp. 42–126). Newbury Park, CA: Sage.

Sternthal, B., Philips, L. W., & Dholakia, R. (1978). The persuasive effect of source credibility: A situational analysis. *Public Opinion Quarterly, 42,* 285–314.

Tamborini, R., & Zillmann, D. (1981). College students' perceptions of lecturers using humor. *Perceptual and Motor Skills, 52,* 427–432.

Wachtler, J., & Counselman, E. (1981). When increased liking or a communicator decreases opinion change: An attribution analysis of attractiveness. *Journal of Experimental Social Psychology, 17,* 386–395.

Walster, E., Aronson, E., & Abrahams, D. (1966). On increasing the persuasiveness of a low prestige communicator. *Journal of Experimental Social Psychology, 2,* 325–342.

Warnick, B. (2004). Online ethos: Source credibility in an "authorless" environment. *American Behavioral Scientist, 48,* 256–265.

Widgery, R. N. (1974). Sex of receiver and physical attractiveness of source as determinants of initial credibility perception. *Western Speech, 38,* 13–17.

Widgery, R. N. & Ruch, R. S. (1981). Beauty and the Machiavellian. *Communication Quarterly, 29,* 297–301.

Wilson, E. J. & Sherrell, D. L. (1993). Source effects in communication and persuasion research: A meta-analysis of effect size. *Journal of the Academy of Marketing Science, 21,* 101–112.

Wrench, J., Brogan, S., Wrench, J., & McKean, J. (2007, November). *The relationship between religious followers' functional and relational goals and perceptions of religious leaders' use of instructional communication.* Paper presented at the annual National Communication Association Conference, Chicago.

Wrench, J. S., Millihouse, B., & Sharp, D. (2007). Laughing before takeoff. Humor sex and the pre-flight safety briefing. *Human Communication, 10,* 381–399.

Xie, H., Miao, L., Kuo, P., & Lee, B. (2011). Consumers' responses to ambivalent online hotel reviews: The role of perceived source credibility and pre-decisional disposition. *International Journal of Hospitality Management, 30,* 178–183.

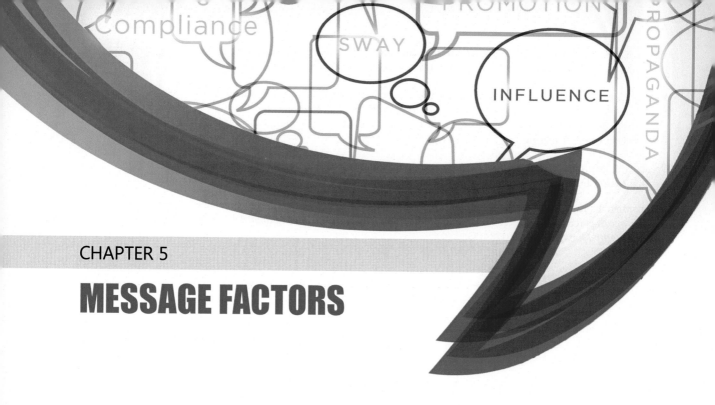

CHAPTER 5

MESSAGE FACTORS

And so, my fellow Americans, ask not what your country can do for you; ask what you can do for your country. My fellow citizens of the world, ask not what America will do for you, but what together we can do for the freedom of man.

John F. Kennedy, January 20, 1961

I have a dream that one day this nation will rise up and live out the true meaning of its creed: "We hold these truths to be self-evident; that all men are created equal."

I have a dream that one day on the red hills of Georgia the sons of former slaves and the sons of former slave owners will be able to sit down together at the table of brotherhood.

Martin Luther King, Jr., August 28, 1963

What is it about these words, these messages that influenced millions of people? These messages were delivered more than 50 years ago and both men have long passed, yet the messages are still repeated and discussed and continue to influence people. In the previous chapter, we laid out the approach to organizing persuasion research by looking at source, message, receiver, and channel factors. In this chapter, we examine the impact that message factors have on persuasive success. Message factors involve anything dealing with the content and structure of the message itself, such as the strategies or arguments being employed, the language used to frame the message, the evidence employed to support claims, and the structure of the message. Messages can be written or oral and involve both verbal and nonverbal elements. Watching a video of President Kennedy or Reverend King giving these famous speeches reveals that the nonverbal messages each used were as important as the verbal messages. In this chapter, we discuss some of the many choices one must make when constructing a persuasive message.

LEARNING OBJECTIVES

- DISTINGUISH BETWEEN LOGICAL AND EMOTIONAL APPEALS.
- DESCRIBE THE EXTENDED PARALLEL PROCESSES MODEL AND HOW IT IS USED.
- EXPLAIN HOW EVIDENCE IS USED TO PERSUADE.
- EXPLAIN HOW LANGUAGE CHOICES AFFECT PERSUASION.
- EXPLAIN HOW INOCULATION THEORY AND FOREWARNING DEVELOP RESISTANCE.

WHAT I SAY: MESSAGE CONTENT

When constructing a message, you must make many decisions. One major decision is what content to include in the message. Obviously, the content is in part dictated by the topic of your message; however, you can never include everything about a topic, so you must choose what content to include and what to exclude. Other choices you must make are whether to use emotion, such as fear, in your message, to take a logical approach, or to use both.

LOGICAL VERSUS EMOTIONAL APPEALS

Two general types of persuasive messages are based on logical appeals and emotional appeals. A **logical appeal** is a persuasive message that relies on logic and reasoning to be persuasive; an **emotional appeal** is a persuasive message that relies on emotion to be persuasive. Aristotle identified three means of persuasion—ethos (the nature of the source), pathos (the emotion of the audience), and logos (the nature of the message presented by the source) (McCroskey, 1997). We addressed ethos, or the nature of the source, in Chapter 4 when we discussed source characteristics such as credibility and attractiveness. Pathos and logos correspond with emotional appeals and logical appeals, respectively. Although these three means of persuasion are unique and distinguishable from one another, they often overlap somewhat. In other words, emotional appeals often contain logical elements, and logical appeals often contain emotion.

Both logical and emotional appeals can be effective, but the context or situation should be considered. For instance, Wilson (2003) recorded the logical and rational persuasive strategies students used while working in teams on class projects over a 3-month period. Students rated the effectiveness of these strategies using face-to-face and e-mail messages. Emotional strategies were perceived as slightly more effective than logical strategies in e-mail interactions, whereas logical strategies were perceived as more effective than emotional strategies in face-to-face interactions. Thus, the context of the interaction can play a crucial role in the effectiveness of the type of message used. Wilson did not examine what emotions were targeted in the messages the students constructed, which also needs to be considered. Similarly, advertisers make regular decisions about what images to use in messages. A study by Harris Interactive (2010) found that Americans reported that puppies tugged at their heartstrings most, with images of babies following as a close second. These results were more pronounced for women than men, and all ages seemed to respond to puppies, whereas those in the 35 to 54 age range were more affected by images of babies than other age groups. Thus, context and receiver characteristics that are discussed further in Chapter 6 must be considered to understand the impact of emotional and logical appeals.

Humans experience many emotions, and nearly all of these emotions could potentially be used in a persuasive message. An example of an emotional appeal is a story or picture of a deprived child being used to persuade an audience to give money to a charity or organization that helps children in need. Many emotions can be targeted by persuasive messages, but three have been used frequently by persuaders and explored by researchers: humor (see Figure 5.1), guilt, and fear.

HUMOR

Do you have a sense of humor? Do you like funny advertisements? Are you more likely to buy a product from or agree with someone who uses humor? Humor is used frequently in advertising (Cline & Kellaris, 1999) and in political communication such as political cartoons (see Figure 5.2), but is it effective? Humor is very effective at gaining an audience's attention (Cline & Kellaris, 1999; Weinberger & Gulas, 1992). Getting your audience's attention is an important first step in the persuasion process. With

Speed Bump used by permission of Dave Coverly and Creators Syndicate, Inc.

FIGURE 5.1 Speed Bump.

"WE NEED TO RUN BACKGROUND CHECKS TO MAKE SURE YOU'RE NOT TERRORISTS. CAN YOU TREAD WATER FOR 18 TO 24 MONTHS?"

FIGURE 5.2 Political cartoon.

the thousands of messages that bombard us every day, it is a continuing challenge for persuaders to get our attention. Humor is most effective at gaining our attention when it is relevant to the topic (e.g., product, idea) of the influence attempt. If the humor is unrelated to the persuasive topic and goal, it may take attention away from the persuasive message. Turn to Chapter 11 and review the *Check Yo Nutz* campaign that is highlighted. Dr. Wanzer and her students used humor to gain their audience's attention. The humor used in this campaign was related to the persuasive goal of increasing the number of young men who regularly performed testicular self-exams. Had they used sexual humor (which is unrelated to the persuasive goal), it would have gained attention but not for the important message accompanying the humor. Research has provided few consistent findings about humor, but the one consistent finding is that humor must be relevant to the persuasive goal to be useful.

Humor generates positive emotions and tends to reduce negative reactions to being persuaded (Slaski, Tamborini, Glazer, & Smith, 2009). In other words, people often resist attempts to change their attitudes, beliefs, and behaviors and may feel annoyed or angry at the source. The positive emotion generated by humor can counter the negative reaction to being persuaded.

The positive emotion generated by the humor can also lead to enhanced liking for the source (Weinberger & Gulas, 1992), and liked sources are perceived as more credible (Nabi, Moyer-Guse, & Byrne, 2007). But, as mentioned in Chapter 4, humor does not necessarily increase perceptions of credibility, and may even decrease them (Hackman, 1988). Being liked can help you be more persuasive, but being perceived as credible is probably more important. One problem with studying humor is its many forms—cartoons, jokes, puns, riddles, and so on—and genres—sexual, political, self-disparaging, other-disparaging, and so on. Because humor varies so greatly, it is difficult to study. As a result, research findings are often contradictory, making it difficult to make generalizations about the use of humor. Humor elicits positive feelings in receivers, which is why funny people are liked. However, humor can be very offensive too. We have all been offended by humor at one time or another. Humorous put downs targeted at people we like or at groups we associate with are usually perceived as offensive.

The research on humor can be confusing, but we have three recommendations. First, know your audience before using humor so you can avoid offending them. Don't assume that you and your audience will find humor in the same things. Second, make the use of humor relevant to your persuasive goal. The humor needs to help your audience process the message and not distract them from it. And third; humor alone is not persuasive. It must be combined with other message and source factors to create a persuasive message.

GUILT

Not only are positive emotions such as humor used to persuade, but more negative emotions such as guilt are used as well. You may be very familiar with this emotion and its use as a persuasive tool. Some people rely on this strategy extensively to accomplish their goals. In Chapter 12 we discuss compliance gaining, and in Tables 12.2 and 12.3 guilt is listed as a compliance-gaining technique. What we mean specifically by **guilt** in the persuasion context is when you believe that your behavior does not meet your own standards and so you experience feelings of guilt (O'Keefe, 2002). Like other emotions, guilt occurs on a continuum, so you may experience a little bit of guilt, a lot of guilt, and everything in between.

We often think our behavior doesn't meet standards and thus we feel guilty. Advertisers may attempt to take advantage of this guilt by offering products or services that help alleviate the guilt. A study by Huhmann and Brotherton (1997) found that over 5 percent of the ads in magazines contained guilt appeals. For instance, mothers working outside the home often feel guilty for not spending more time with their children and for not doing things "a good mother should." A cookie maker may use the guilt a mother experiences for not baking homemade cookies to sell expensive cookies that are "better than homemade." Buying these cookies may help working mothers alleviate some of the guilt they feel. As noted, guilt is not a positive emotion. It seems risky to use a negative emotion to influence people; they might get mad at the source. Coulter and Pinto (1995) conducted a study on this very issue. They examined three levels of guilt (low, moderate, and high) and measured participants' emotional responses as well as their attitudes toward the products: bread and dental floss. Coulter and Pinto found that advertisements with a high level of guilt resulted in anger and feelings of being manipulated. They concluded that moderate levels of guilt might be the most effective at both gaining the audience's attention and eliciting an acceptable level of guilt. When a guilt appeal is explicit, persuasion is usually reduced (O'Keefe, 2002). Guilt appeals that are implicit and elicit a low to moderate amount of guilt are probably the most effective.

In a similar study, Turner and Underhill (2012) tested high, moderate, and low guilt appeals in emergency preparedness messages. Turner and Underhill specifically examined whether participants felt angry with the source when exposed to a guilt appeal. Anger was the highest for the high guilt appeal. However, higher guilt was associated with perceiving emergency preparedness as important. So guilt appeals can be a double-edged sword. Receivers may be more influenced by higher levels of guilt, but they also are angrier at the source and situation.

HIGH GUILT

Have you thought about preparing for an emergency . . . but said "I'll get to that later"? You don't know when the next attack or natural disaster will happen—What if later is too late?

If you haven't prepared, YOU could be putting your loved ones in jeopardy. How will you look your family in the eyes and tell them you were too busy? Think of the weight on your conscience. It's not worth the regret. You need to have emergency supplies, including items like food, water, and a first aid kit. Develop a communication plan with your family in case of emergency. If you don't take the initiative to prepare your family, who will? Be responsible and don't let your loved ones down. Go to ready.gov and learn about how to prepare. The website provides simple, achievable steps that you can do!

Do it today, so you don't regret it tomorrow.

Take the time to get prepared—or prepare to live with the consequences.

MODERATE GUILT

Have you thought about preparing for an emergency . . . but said "I'll get to that later"? You don't know when the next attack or natural disaster will happen—What if later is too late?

If you haven't prepared then YOU might be putting your loved ones at risk. You want to look your family in the eyes and know you took care of them. Avoiding planning is just not worth the regret. You need to have emergency supplies, including items like food, water, and a first aid kit. Develop a communication plan with your family in case of emergency. If you don't take the initiative to prepare your family, who will? Go to ready.gov to learn more about how to prepare. The website provides simple, achievable steps that you can do! It's your responsibility to make sure your family is prepared for emergencies.

Do it today, and you won't regret it tomorrow.

Take the time to get prepared—or prepare to live with the costs.

LOW GUILT

Have you thought about preparing for an emergency . . . but said "I'll get to that later"? It's hard to predict when the next attack or natural disaster will happen—don't let later be too late.

If you haven't prepared for terrorism, what are you waiting for? Your loved ones depend on you. Make sure you can look your family in the eyes and tell them you are prepared. You don't want to let them down when they need you the most. You need to have emergency supplies, including items like water, food, and a first aid kit. Develop a communication plan with your family in case of emergency. If you don't take the initiative to prepare your family, who will? Go to ready.gov to learn more about how to prepare. The website provides simple, achievable steps that everyone can do!

Your loved ones need you. Make sure that your family is prepared for an emergency like a terrorist attack.

Take the time. Get prepared. No regrets.

NEUTRAL

Resolve to be ready in 2017. Prepare for emergencies before they happen. Taking simple steps can ensure the safety of you and your loved ones in the case of a disaster of any kind.

You need to have emergency supplies, including items like food, water, and a first aid kit. Take the initiative to prepare your family. All Americans should have a plan in case of a disaster. Before an emergency happens, be sure to sit down with your family and decide how you will get in contact with each other, where you will go, and what you will do in an emergency. Keep a copy of this plan in your supply kit or another safe place. Go to ready.gov and learn more about how to prepare. The website provides simple, achievable steps that you can do!

Prepare, plan, and stay informed!

FIGURE 5.3 Turner & Underhill (2012) Guilt Appeal Messages.

From Communication Quarterly, Volume 60(4), September, 2012 by Monique Mitchell Turner and Jill Cornelius Underhill. Copyright © 2012 Routledge. Reprinted by permission of Eastern Communication Association, www.ecasite.org.

Moderate levels of guilt are overall better than high levels. Turner and Underhill also suspect that personality interacts with guilt, such that different types of people react differently to guilt appeals. The specifics of such interactions have not been studied. Additionally, we should consider the ethics of using guilt appeals. Is it ethical to elicit guilt to persuade? The same question can be asked about another negative emotion that is frequently used to persuade: fear.

FEAR

One of the most widely used emotional appeals in applied settings, and certainly the most researched of all the emotional appeals, is fear appeals. A **fear appeal** is a type of emotional appeal that relies on fear to persuade the audience; however, fear appeals often have many qualities of logical appeals as well. Kim Witte (1994) provides a current and useful definition of fear appeals: "a persuasive message that attempts to arouse the emotion of fear by depicting a personally relevant and significant threat and then follows this description of the threat by outlining recommendations presented as feasible and effective in deterring the threat" (p. 114). The first portion of Witte's definition describes a fear appeal as a message that arouses the emotion of fear. This part of the definition is probably along the lines of what you were expecting. You may not have anticipated the second part of the definition that refers to an outline of recommendations that deter the threat. This second part of the definition reflects our current understanding of what an *effective* fear appeal is. There are many examples of messages that arouse fear (or at least are intended to arouse fear) but do not mention how to eliminate the threat. For example, for many years anti-drug campaigns have relied on fear to get their message across. These messages may or may not have aroused fear in you, but rarely do they provide specific recommendations on how to avoid drug use. Current research indicates that simply arousing fear in the audience is not sufficient to influence attitudes, intentions, or behaviors (Witte, 1992, 1994). Therefore, we are including recommendations that deter the threat in our discussion of fear appeals.

Web Activity: Go to YouTube and search for anti-drug commercials. How many generate fear?

Early research in fear appeals found that sometimes fear appeals worked, sometimes they didn't, and sometimes they had a boomerang effect (the audience did the opposite of what the source was advocating). In an attempt to understand why fear appeals worked sometimes and not others, Leventhal (1970) offered the **parallel response model**, which proposed that people had one of two responses when they were exposed to a fear appeal. One response was described as a **fear control response**, which is an emotional response. For example, if you are the recipient of a fear appeal that makes you feel fearful, and you respond by focusing on how to reduce the fear, you are having a fear control response. Your focus is on the emotion you are experiencing and how to eliminate this unpleasant emotion (fear) so that you can feel better. The most common ways people reduce fear is to deny that they are really in danger and to downplay the threat. These strategies are quite successful at eliminating the fear, but these strategies don't eliminate the threat or the cause of the fear. For example, suppose you are a smoker. You hear a fear appeal targeted at getting you to quit smoking, and you have a fear control response. You downplay the threat of smoking and the likelihood that you'll be negatively affected by smoking. You are unlikely to take steps to stop smoking. A fear control response rarely, if ever, results in receivers changing their attitudes or behavior.

If after receiving the fear appeal you focus on eliminating the threat from your life, you are having a **danger control response**. A danger control response is considered a cognitive response (the fear control response was an emotional response), because you focus on assessing the threat and how to eliminate it. So, if you take a danger control response to a fear appeal on smoking, you focus on ways to quit smoking so that you can eliminate the threat to your health.

Leventhal's parallel response model provided a new level of understanding of fear appeals and provided an explanation for why fear appeals sometimes worked and sometimes did not. When the audience has a fear control response, they probably will not adopt the source's recommendations (e.g., quit smoking, wear their seat belts). When the audience has a danger control response, however, the fear appeal is more likely to be successful because the audience is more likely to adopt the source's recommendations as a means of eliminating the threat. Although Leventhal's parallel response model was very useful in explaining *why* and *how* fear appeals worked, it did not provide sufficient detail to predict *when* receivers would take a danger control response rather than a fear control response and hence limited the ability to elicit a danger control response from the audience.

EXTENDED PARALLEL PROCESS MODEL

Building on Leventhal's parallel response model and the protection motivation theory developed by Rogers (1975, 1983), Witte (1992) developed the **extended parallel process model (EPPM)**. The EPPM builds on the concept that people have either a danger control response or a fear control response when exposed to a fear appeal. Additionally, Witte (1992, 1994) specifically outlines the message components that are necessary for an *effective* fear appeal and explains how the audience's perceptions of the message differ with a danger control response and a fear control response. The greater explanation of the EPPM has led to a greater ability to predict when receivers will have a danger or fear control response and provides guidance on how to construct a message that elicits the danger control response.

The EPPM is illustrated in Figure 5.4. An effective fear appeal must have these four components: severity, susceptibility, response efficacy, and self-efficacy. **Severity** refers to the grimness of the threat presented in the message. Imagine a message that shows the consequences of not wearing a seat belt. The message depicts a driver going through the windshield and being killed. This is pretty grim, pretty severe. An effective fear appeal must depict a threat the audience perceives as severe. Related to this is the second component, susceptibility. **Susceptibility** refers to how probable it is that the threat will affect the audience. In our seat belt fear appeal example, if you perceive that you are at risk for going through the windshield, you will feel susceptible to the threat. If you perceive the threat as unrealistic or not applicable to you, you will not feel susceptible to the threat. For fear to be elicited, you must perceive the threat depicted in the message as severe and you must perceive yourself as susceptible to the threat. If after appraising the message you believe that the threat is not severe *or* that you are not susceptible, then no fear is elicited and you are not likely to be motivated to process the message further or to take any action. In Chapter 4 we discussed source credibility. A threat is more effective if it is delivered by a highly credible source, in part, because high credibility sources make the threat appear

Web Activity: Google distracted driving. Do current messages that discourage distracted driving successfully convey severity and susceptibility to create perceived threat?

Threat + Severity = Perceived Threat

Response Efficacy + Self-Efficacy = Perceived Efficacy

If Perceived Threat > Perceived Efficacy = Defensive Motivation = Fear Control Response

If Perceive Efficacy > Perceived Threat = Protection Motivation = Danger Control Response

Excerpt from "Putting the Fear Back Into Fear Appeals" by K. Witte, *Communication Monographs*, Vol. 59, 1992.

FIGURE 5.4 Witte's 1992 extended parallel processing model.

more credible itself. Hearing a homeless person wander the streets and threaten that a terrorist attack is imminent has little credibility. However, having the secretary of state or the president of the United States hold a press conference and say that a terrorist attack is imminent will have much more impact and believability. Thus, a highly credible source can enhance the effectiveness of a threat.

For a fear appeal to be effective there must be more than just a threat. The third component of the EPPM is response efficacy. **Response efficacy** refers to how effective the recommended response is in eliminating the threat. The recommended response is what you want your audience to do, such as wearing a seat belt or refraining from using drugs. The audience also has to be convinced that the recommended response will be effective at eliminating the threat. Examine the message in Figure 5.5. The source provides five things parents can do to reduce the likelihood of their teen abusing prescription drugs. This is a good example of response efficacy. Going back to our earlier example, wearing a seat belt almost completely eliminates the threat of going through the windshield in the event of an accident. You must perceive the recommended response as effective in order for the fear appeal to be effective. If you perceive the recommended response as ineffective in eliminating the threat, you are unlikely to adopt the recommended response.

The fourth component of the EPPM is self-efficacy. **Self-efficacy** refers to the extent the audience believes they are capable of performing the recommended response. If your response to the seat belt fear appeal was "I could never stand to wear a seat belt all the time," your self-efficacy regarding the recommended response would be quite low. It is unlikely that you would begin wearing a seat belt (the recommended response). On the other hand, if your response was along the lines "It takes two seconds to wear a seat belt. What's the big deal? I can wear a seat belt," then you would have high self-efficacy and be very likely to begin wearing your seat belt. So when a person is exposed to a fear appeal containing these four components, the person first appraises the threat to determine the severity of the threat and his or her susceptibility. If the threat is perceived as moderate or severe, the person is motivated to assess the efficacy of the recommended response and his or her self-efficacy, or ability to perform the recommended response. The greater the perceived threat, the more motivated the person is to assess the efficacy of the recommended response. If the threat is perceived as trivial or irrelevant, the person will give little attention to the recommended response.

When teens want to get high
YOUR PRESCRIPTION IS AVAILABLE FOR PICK UP.

TEENS ARE ABUSING PRESCRIPTION DRUGS THEY FIND AT HOME.
HERE'S WHAT THEY ARE DOING—AND HOW PARENTS CAN STOP IT.

It can be medication left over from your last surgery. Maybe they're the pills you keep on the dresser or tucked inside your purse. Teens are finding prescription drugs wherever people they know keep them—and abusing them to get high. In fact, 70 percent of persons age 12 and older who abuse prescription painkillers say they get them from a relative or friend[1]—leading to several troubling trends:

- **Every day, 2500 kids age 12 to 17 try a painkiller for the first time.**[2]
- **Prescription drugs are the drugs of choice for 12 and 13 year olds.**[3]
- **Teens abuse prescription drugs more than any illicit street drug except marijuana.**[4]

What's also disturbing is they don't realize these drugs can be as dangerous as street drugs. So kids who would never try street drugs might feel safe abusing prescription drugs. Misperceptions about prescription drug abuse have serious consequences. In fact, drug treatment admissions for prescription painkillers increased more than 300 percent from 1995 to 2005.[5] Now that you know prescription drug abuse is a problem, here are ways parents can keep it from affecting their kids' lives:

- **Safeguard** all drugs at home. Monitor quantities and control access.
- **Set clear rules** for teens about all drug use, including not sharing medicine and always following the medical provider's advice and dosages.
- **Be a good role model** by following the same rules with your own medicines.
- **Properly conceal and dispose** of old or unused medicines in the trash.
- **Ask friends and family** to safeguard their prescription drugs as well.

Following these steps is a start. Let your teen know where you stand.
When you talk about drugs and alcohol, include prescription drugs in the conversation.
To learn more, visit **THEANTIDRUG.COM** or call 1-800-788-2800.

1. 2006 National Survey on Drug Use and Health, SAMHSA, September 2007.
2. Ibid. 3. Ibid. 4. Ibid. 5. 2005 Treatment Episode Data Set, SAMHSA, 2007.

Office of National Drug Control Policy.

FIGURE 5.5 Response efficacy example.

So when does a person have a danger control response and when does he or she have a fear control response? As long as the perception of efficacy (efficacy of recommended response and self-efficacy) is greater than the perception of threat, the danger control process will dominate and the person will focus on how to eliminate the threat (accept the recommended response). If the perception of the threat is greater than the perception of efficacy, the fear control processes will dominate and the person will focus on eliminating the fear (become defensive and deny he or she is at risk). The perception of the threat determines the intensity of the reaction to the fear appeal; the perception of efficacy determines whether fear control or danger control processes will be initiated (Witte, 1992). Therefore, for a fear appeal to be effective, the message must portray the threat as sufficiently severe and likely to occur so that the audience perceives the threat as substantial. The message must also convince the audience that the recommended response will effectively eliminate (or reduce) the threat and that the audience is capable of performing the recommended response. Examine the advertisement in Figure 5.6. Is this an effective fear appeal? The advertisement appeared in a women's magazine. Do you think women seeing the ad would perceive threat? Would they perceive efficacy?

USING THE EXTENDED PARALLEL PROCESS MODEL

The EPPM not only explains when and why an audience will have a danger control response versus a fear control response but also gives us specific guidance on how to create an effective fear appeal. Mark Morman (2000) applied the EPPM in developing messages to convince young men to perform testicular self-exams in order to increase early detection and decrease deaths due to testicular cancer. Testicular cancer is the most common malignancy among American white males between the ages of 24 and 34 and the second most common in other age groups of white males (Morman, 2000). (Rates of testicular cancer are much lower for African American, Hispanic, and Asian American males.) Additionally, testicular cancer is on the rise, up 51 percent from 1973 to 1995 (Morman, 2000). Morman's goal was to motivate young men to perform the testicular self-exam (TSE) regularly. Additionally, Morman wanted to test the EPPM and to examine whether a fact-based or narrative-based message would be most effective.

First, Morman developed four versions of a fear appeal advocating the regular performance of TSE. The four messages are displayed in Figure 5.7. One message used a fact-based approach and used high efficacy. The second message also used a fact-based approach but used low efficacy. As you can see, the high-efficacy message explicitly states that performing a TSE reduces the threat of testicular cancer and gives specific information on how to perform the TSE. The low-efficacy message is much more vague and general in presenting the TSE as a means of reducing the threat of testicular cancer. The third message was a narrative-based approach that used high efficacy. The narrative approach was written as a personal story. The fourth message also used a narrative-based approach but had low efficacy.

Morman (2000) recruited 80 male students at a Midwestern university and a Midwestern community college. All participants were between the ages of 18 and 32 (men ages 15 to 35 are most at risk for testicular cancer). The men were told that the purpose of the study was to evaluate testicular cancer and TSE awareness materials

Expose the Truth

In the U.S. a woman will die from breast cancer, on average, every 13 minutes.
We must stop this, here and around the world. Research today saves lives tomorrow.

The
Breast
Cancer
Research
Foundation.

Funding the fight to prevent and cure breast cancer in our lifetime.
The Breast Cancer Research Foundation
Founded in 1993 by Evelyn H. Lauder
www.bcrfcure.org, 1.866.FIND.A.CURE

FIGURE 5.6 Is this an effective fear appeal? How would the components of the EPPM be applied here?

in the early stages of development. The participants were then randomly assigned to read one of the four messages. After reading the message, the men were asked to respond to a variety of questions that assessed fear arousal, susceptibility, severity, response efficacy, and self-efficacy, along with other questions.

Some guys are so macho they'd never stoop to having their testicles checked.

They'd die first.

Testicular cancer is the most common cancer among men ages 20–34. With a 96 percent malignancy rate, it is also the most fatal cancer for men in this same age group.

- Testicular cancer will develop in about 6,000 men this year.
- The rate of testicular cancer has doubled in the last two decades.
- It can develop without any warning signs.
- If not detected, it can kill you.
- If detected early, it can be cured.

If you are age 18 or older, protect yourself from the threat of testicular cancer by learning how to perform the Testicular Self-Exam, or TSE. Ninety-six percent of all testicular tumors are discovered by men performing the routine self-exam. Here's how to do it:

- Once a month, after a warm shower, gently roll each testicle between the thumb and fingers.
- Feel for hard lumps or bumps.
- If you notice a change in your testicles, have pain, or find a lump, see your doctor immediately.

If detected early, testicular cancer patients show a 94 percent survival rate. For free information to learn more about testicular cancer and the TSE, just call The Men's Clinic at:

816-***-MEN 1

Appointments for free professional testicular examinations are also available on the first three Fridays of each month.

Learn the TSE and perform it once a month.

It will save your life.

Some guys are so macho they'd never stoop to having their testicles checked.

They'd die first.

Testicular cancer is the most common cancer among men ages 20–34. With a 96 percent malignancy rate, it is also the most fatal cancer for men in this same age group.

- Testicular cancer will develop in about 6,000 men this year.
- The rate of testicular cancer has doubled in the last two decades.
- It can develop without any warning signs.
- If not detected, it can kill you.
- If detected early, it can be cured.

If you are age 18 or older, and especially if you are a white male, you face an increased risk of developing testicular cancer. For a majority of men, the cancer in your testicles will spread to other areas of your body and show up in places like your liver, kidneys, or lymph nodes. Once the cancer has spread, the chances of survival significantly decrease.

Testicular cancer can affect your ability to have sex, maintain an erection, or even maintain a romantic relationship. It also might affect your ability to urinate properly or keep control of your bladder. Usually, the diseased testicle is surgically removed, and the follow-up chemotherapy normally causes significant hair loss, decreased energy levels, and a loss of appetite.

You can protect yourself from the threat of testicular cancer by learning how to perform the Testicular Self-Exam, or TSE. Ninety-six percent of all testicular tumors are discovered by men performing the routine self-exam.

Just because men don't talk about things like this, doesn't mean testicular cancer can't kill you.

NARRATIVE-BASED HIGH EFFICACY MESSAGE
Macho Pride and Getting Cancer

My name is Kyle. I'm 21 years old and a senior business major at the University of Kansas. At this point in my life, I thought I had everything under control—I had a great girlfriend, solid job prospects, a nice apartment, lots of money, and loyal friends. What I didn't have under control was developing cancer. But not just any cancer, testicular cancer, which I had no clue was the most common form of cancer in guys ages 20–34. It's also the most fatal form of cancer for men in this age group.

What is really ironic is that last year, a doctor from the Men's Clinic came to a fraternity meeting and told us all about testicular cancer and this procedure called the testicular self-exam or TSE. He said we should do it to check for tumors in our testicles. But I thought, "no way," "how embarrassing," and "how disgusting to feel around on yourself like that." None of my buddies ever talked about it, and I guess none of them did the exam either. You know, guys just don't talk about things like that.

Anyway, I started to have some pain in my left testicle. After about a month, I finally went to the doctor because my girlfriend made me go. And he found cancer. With a 96 percent malignancy rate and a 19 percent death rate for guys like me, I knew I was in big-time trouble.

I lost my testicle. I couldn't have sex with my girlfriend anymore because I had trouble getting and keeping an erection. Plus, with only one testicle, I just felt so humiliated and embarrassed. We broke up last week. I dropped out of my frat, and I stopped playing on the intramural basketball team, mainly because I don't have any energy anymore and because my so-called friends treat me different now. The chemotherapy made me lose my hair, my grades have crashed, and I feel sick all the time. The really bad news is that the cancer has spread to my liver, and the doctor gives me only a 20 percent chance of beating it. I keep thinking, I'm only 21 years old, this isn't supposed to be happening!

My doctor said if I had caught the tumor earlier, I might have really improved my chances of beating it. But I was so macho, so stupid, really, that I didn't listen and I let my male ego guide my actions. Now, what do I have to show for such a childish attitude? No girlfriend, no sex, no friends, no energy, no hair, only one testicle, and slim chance of living. This male ego thing isn't all it's cracked up to be.

Listen, dude, don't make my mistake. Don't let your pride and ego keep you from doing the self-exam. It's really simple: once a month, after a warm shower, roll each testicle gently between your thumb and fingers. Feel for any hard lumps. If you have pain in your testicles, or if you find a lump, go see your doctor immediately, He tells me there is a 94 percent chance of survival if it's caught early.

Look, just because guys don't talk about things like this doesn't mean testicular cancer can't kill you. Learn the TSE and do it once a month. It will save your life.

The Men's Clinic Kansas City, MO 64111

816-*-MEN 1**

From Journal of Applied Communication Research, 28, 91–116. Reprinted by Permission of Taylor & Francis Ltd. http://www.tandf.co.uk/Journals

NARRATIVE-BASED LOW EFFICACY MESSAGE

Macho Pride and Getting Cancer

My name is Kyle. I'm 21 years old and a senior business major at the University of Kansas. At this point in my life, I thought I had everything under control—I had a great girlfriend, solid job prospects, a nice apartment, lots of money, and loyal friends. What I didn't have under control was developing cancer. But not just any cancer, testicular cancer, which I had no clue was the most common form of cancer in guys ages 20–34. It's also the most fatal form of cancer for men in this age group.

What is really ironic is that last year, a doctor from the Men's Clinic came to a fraternity meeting and told us all about testicular cancer and this procedure called the testicular self-exam or TSE. He said we should do it to check for tumors in our testicles. But I thought, "no way," "how embarrassing," and "how disgusting to feel around on yourself like that." None of my buddies ever talked about it, and I guess none of them did the exam either. You know, guys just don't talk about things like that.

Anyway, I started to have some pain in my left testicle. After about a month, I finally went to the doctor because my girlfriend made me go. And he found cancer. With a 96 percent malignancy rate and a 19 percent death rate for guys like me, I knew I was in big-time trouble.

I lost my testicle. I couldn't have sex with my girlfriend anymore because I had trouble getting and keeping an erection. Plus, with only one testicle, I just felt so humiliated and embarrassed. We broke up last week. I dropped out of my frat, and I stopped playing on the intramural basketball team, mainly because I don't have any energy anymore and because my so-called friends treat me different now. The chemotherapy made me lose my hair, my grades have crashed, and I feel sick all the time. The really bad news is that the cancer has spread to my liver, and the doctor gives me only a 20 percent chance of beating it. I keep thinking, I'm only 21 years old, this isn't supposed to be happening!

My doctor said if I had caught the tumor earlier, I might have really improved my chances of beating it. But I was so macho, so stupid, really, that I didn't listen and I let my male ego guide my actions. Now, what do I have to show for such a childish attitude? No girlfriend, no sex, no friends, no energy, no hair, only one testicle, and slim chance of living. This male ego thing isn't all it's cracked up to be.

Look, just because guys don't talk about things like this doesn't mean testicular cancer can't kill you.

The Men's Clinic
Kansas City, MO 64111
816-***-MEN1

FIGURE 5.7 Morman (2000) fear appeal messages.

Morman (2000) found that the men who read the high-efficacy messages had greater intentions to perform the TSE than those men who read the low-efficacy messages. Men in the two groups reported an equal amount of fear in response to the severity of the message. The difference was in the response efficacy and self-efficacy communicated in the messages. The men who read the high-efficacy messages had a danger control response and therefore intended to perform the TSE. These men perceived their efficacy as greater than the severity of the threat, resulting in the danger control response. The men reading the low-efficacy messages had a fear control response and focused their energy on reducing the fear rather than developing intentions to perform the TSE. These men perceived the threat as greater than their efficacy in dealing with the threat, resulting in the fear control response. Morman was also interested in whether a fact-based or narrative-based message would be more effective. Morman found that both message types were equally effective.

The EPPM has been employed in many contexts, and it has been integrated with specific individual factors that can affect the success or failure of persuasive messages based on the topic. For example, Wong and Cappella (2009) used Witte's EPPM in a study of antismoking messages in conjunction with smokers' readiness to quit. For smokers with a low readiness to quit smoking, threat and efficacy were critically important for influencing receivers' intention to quit smoking. However, for smokers with a high level of readiness to quit, efficacy was the most important factor. Those ready to quit did not require a high threat message because they had been convinced of the threat by prior messages. For them, messages directed at convincing recipients about their own ability to quit were most important.

Fear appeals are a useful means of persuasion and have been used a great deal with health topics. As we have discussed, fear alone is insufficient for an effective message. The fear-inducing components of the message (severity and susceptibility of threat) must be accompanied by response efficacy and self-efficacy information. The efficacy component of the message is necessary for the audience to be motivated to adopt the recommended response. If the efficacy component is missing, the audience will most likely focus on eliminating the fear (an emotional process) rather than on eliminating the danger (a cognitive process). Witte's extended parallel process model not only does a good job of explaining why fear appeals work but also provides specific guidelines for how to develop an effective fear appeal. Recent research has found that the EPPM also works when the fear appeal threat is directed toward others. Roberto and Goodall (2009) used the EPPM model to test doctors' intentions and behavior toward testing patients for proper levels of kidney functioning in response to threats to patient health from kidney disease in combination with efficacy messages about the role of early detection. Their research found that Witte's model works even when the receiver isn't the direct target of the threat. Emotion is an important element when deciding what content to include in a message. Pathos is not the only content issue that must be considered; as Aristotle noted, logos, or the nature of the message, must also be considered.

USE OF EVIDENCE

A logos-based choice regarding the content of the message is whether or not to use evidence. You may be most familiar with the use of evidence in court cases. We frequently hear about DNA evidence either being the basis for convicting someone of a crime or setting someone free who was wrongly convicted. DNA evidence is one form of physical evidence, but there are other forms of evidence as well. Evidence is an important element in logical appeals. McCroskey (1969) defined **evidence** as "factual statements originating from a source other than the speaker, objects not created by the speaker, and opinions of persons other than the speaker that are offered in support of the speaker's claims" (p. 170). DNA evidence would be considered an object not created by the speaker. Essentially, evidence is something created by someone else, and that *something* could be an opinion, a factual statement, or some type of object. Just because something is a piece of evidence does not mean it is necessarily "good evidence." Whether or not a piece of evidence is considered good or strong is largely a matter of opinion. At a minimum, however, the evidence must be *relevant* to the topic in order to be considered good evidence. If the evidence is irrelevant to the topic, it is clearly poor evidence.

Should you use evidence when creating your persuasive message? That depends. It depends largely on the source and nature of the evidence. McCroskey conducted a series of experiments on the impact of evidence on attitude change and on audience perceptions of source credibility. In summarizing more than 20 studies on evidence, McCroskey (1969) drew five conclusions about the use of evidence in persuasive messages.

The first conclusion was that the use of good evidence has little if any impact on attitude change or source credibility if the source has initial high credibility. In other words, if your audience perceives you as highly credible from the beginning, using evidence in your persuasive message isn't more effective than using your own opinions. If you are highly credible, including evidence will not enhance your persuasiveness with an audience. However, evidence may enhance your persuasiveness if your audience is really focused on your message rather than on you. If you have low to moderate initial credibility, using evidence helps increase your credibility, and thus helps you be more persuasive.

A second conclusion from McCroskey's research is that evidence has little impact on attitude change if the evidence is delivered poorly. If you stumble, lose your place, fidget, mumble, or perform other distracting behaviors, the audience is likely to disregard the good evidence you used in your message. Similarly, in a written message, if it has grammatical errors, misspelled words, or is poorly organized, the audience will likely dismiss your message. So, for evidence to be effective in changing an audience's attitude, the evidence must be well delivered.

A third conclusion is that evidence has little impact on attitude change or source credibility if the audience is familiar with the evidence. In other words, the audience must be unfamiliar with the evidence in order for it to affect attitude change and source credibility. Why? The audience processed the evidence the first time they were exposed to it. At that point, either the audience was influenced by the evidence or they discarded it. In a sense, the influence of that evidence gets used up on the first exposure. In the second exposure, the evidence no longer has any influence left.

To summarize these three conclusions, using good evidence in a persuasive message can enhance attitude change and increase source credibility when the source has moderate-to-low initial credibility, the evidence is delivered well, and the audience is unfamiliar with the evidence.

McCroskey (1969) also concluded that the use of good evidence might increase sustained audience attitude change regardless of the source's credibility. This means that if you deliver a persuasive message containing evidence to an audience and influence their attitude, the audience's attitude change will more likely last than if you did not use evidence. This is consistent with the discounting model discussed in Chapter 4. Recall that the discounting model assumes that initial attitude change is a result of both source credibility and message content; however, permanent attitude change is based on message content (Allen & Stiff, 1998). Therefore, if you are interested in obtaining long-term attitude change in your audience, including evidence in your message is a good idea, even if you are a highly credible source.

The last conclusion drawn from McCroskey's program of research is that the mode of transmission—audiotape, videotape, or live—has no impact on the effectiveness of evidence. Evidence is equally effective regardless of which of these three channels of communication the source uses. However, McCroskey did not test the effectiveness of evidence in print as compared to audio, video, and live modes of transmission, nor did he test computer-mediated communication. Based on decades of research, Reynolds and Reynolds (2002) concluded overall that persuaders who cite evidence are more effective than those who don't.

When constructing a persuasive message, the content you choose is obviously very important. It is generally a good strategy to provide evidence for the claim you are making. Certainly many persuasive messages don't use evidence, and many of them are effective; however, using evidence may help change your audience's beliefs as well as their attitude, making the attitude change more enduring.

NARRATIVE VERSUS STATISTICAL EVIDENCE

We just concluded that using evidence is generally a good strategy when constructing a persuasive message, but what type of evidence should you use? Evidence can take several forms. As the definition describes, evidence can be in the form of factual statements, opinions, or physical objects. Two specific types of evidence are statistical evidence and narrative evidence. **Statistical evidence** refers to a summary of many cases that is expressed in numbers and is used to support a claim. An example of statistical evidence is telling an audience that 73 percent of people wearing a seat belt survived an accident compared to 44 percent of people who were not wearing a seat belt in the year 2000 (car-accidents.com). This information is based on many cases (all reported accidents within the United States) and is presented as a summary in the form of percentages.

Narrative evidence refers to case stories or examples used to support a claim. An example of using narrative evidence is providing a story of an individual who was wearing his or her seat belt and survived a terrible auto accident. Previously, we discussed Morman's (2000) study of fear appeals and his comparison of fact-based and narrative-based messages. The fact-based messages shown in Figure 5.7 use statistical evidence (e.g., "96 percent of all testicular tumors are discovered by men performing the routine self-exam"). The narrative-based messages tell a story about a young man named Kyle who was diagnosed with testicular cancer and are examples of narrative evidence.

Narrative evidence is more vivid and personal than statistical evidence. However, narrative evidence is usually an example of one. In other words, it describes one incident that may or may not be representative of other cases. Statistical evidence is based on many cases and is relatively uninfluenced by exceptional cases. You may conclude from this discussion that statistical evidence is better than narrative evidence. Statistical evidence does provide more information about the issue than narrative evidence, but that does not necessarily mean it is more persuasive.

One strength of narrative evidence is that it tends to be more vivid than statistical evidence and may generate a more concrete image in the minds of the audience. Kazoleas (1993) found that participants exposed to a message containing narrative evidence retained greater attitude change 2 weeks later than did participants exposed to a message containing statistical evidence. Additionally, some audience members may not fully understand the meaning and implications of statistics, but do understand the meaning and implications of the narrative. Both narrative and statistical evidence have their strengths, so is one more persuasive? This question has frequently been asked and addressed by researchers; however, a clear answer has not really evolved. Allen and Preiss (1997) identified 16 studies that specifically compared statistical and narrative evidence. Of those, 10 studies found statistical evidence to be more effective, 4 studies found narrative evidence to be more effective, and 2 studies found no difference. Using a procedure call meta-analysis that summarizes the effects of several studies, Allen and Preiss concluded that statistical evidence was slightly more effective in terms of persuasion than narrative evidence.

Keep two things in mind about the Allen and Preiss findings. First, the studies they examined and summarized all took place in the United States and used college students or other fairly well educated people as participants. In other words, there was a great deal of cultural similarity among the participants used in the 16 studies examined by Allen and Preiss. As Allen and Preiss point out, people belonging to cultures with different expectations for what constitutes proof may very well respond differently to narrative and statistical evidence than the people represented in the research studies. Hornikx and de Best (2011) pursued this question with regard to students from two universities in India, and they found remarkably similar responses to evidence between these participants and the results from Western research. Of course, this is one study in one culture, and we need to be aware that there may be wider cultural differences with other populations.

The second thing to keep in mind is that there is no need to have to choose between narrative and statistical evidence. In most cases, the two forms of evidence can be combined in a single message. Combination may very well be the most effective approach; however, researchers have not addressed this point directly. Combining the two forms of evidence may allow the persuader to create a message that is vivid, memorable, and more persuasive than using either type of evidence alone.

ONE-SIDED VERSUS TWO-SIDED MESSAGES

Regardless of the topic of persuasion, there is almost always an opposing side. If you work for a political candidate, he or she will have an opponent; if you work in advertising, your product will have a competitor; if you work for a nonprofit organization, other nonprofit organizations will be competing for the same dollars you are. Your audience may or may not know a lot about your competitor. When you are constructing a persuasive message, one issue that arises is whether to address your competitor. For example, imagine you work for a political candidate who is running for the U.S. Senate and wants to abolish the death penalty. When constructing a persuasive message for the campaign, do you only provide reasons why the death penalty should be abolished, or do you also acknowledge or address the reasons why the death penalty should exist? If you choose to address only the reasons for abolishing the death penalty, you are constructing a one-sided message. A **one-sided message** only presents arguments in favor of a particular issue. A **two-sided message** presents arguments in favor of an issue but also considers opposing arguments. This should not be confused with a balanced presentation of the issues in a controversy. A two-sided message in this context still clearly advocates for one side of the issue, but it acknowledges counter arguments and sometimes refutes them. If you choose to use a two-sided message, one issue that arises is how you should address the opposing arguments in your two-sided message. Do you just mention them and let the audience do with them as they wish? Or should you refute them? A two-sided message that presents opposing arguments and then refutes them is a **refutational two-sided message**. A message that simply mentions the opposing arguments but does not refute them is a **non-refutational two-sided message**.

So which type of message should you use? After reviewing and analyzing (using meta-analysis) 70 studies, Allen (1998) concluded that a refutational two-sided message was overall more effective than either a one-sided message or a non-refutational two-sided message. Allen et al. (1990) found further evidence of the superiority of the refutational two-sided message in an extensive study. Why is a refutational two-sided message more effective than the other message types? The theory that best explains this is the inoculation theory, which is discussed later in this chapter. In addition to being more persuasive, sources of refutational two-sided messages are perceived as more credible than sources of one-sided and non-refutational two-sided messages (Allen et al., 1990). When a source provides reasons for his or her position and also discusses and refutes the opposition's arguments, he or she is displaying knowledge of the topic, which increases perceptions of expertise. As we discussed in Chapter 4, expertise is a key component of source credibility.

HOW I SAY IT: LANGUAGE STYLE

In the preceding sections, we discussed the issue of what type of content to include in a persuasive message. Should we use evidence, should it be in the form of statistical or narrative evidence, and should we use fear-inducing content? These important issues dramatically affect the effectiveness of your persuasive message. However, in addition to the content you include in your message, the *style* of how you say it also affects the persuasiveness of your message. By **language style** we mean the types of words you choose to present your message. For example, let's take the statement "The university has an innovative diversity plan that will enhance the quality of education for students." If we change it to "The university has an ingenious diversity plan that will create an innovative and distinctive educational experience for students," we have not changed the logical meaning of the statement. We have changed the style of the message, however, and an audience would most likely interpret the two statements differently. There are two issues in language style we will discuss. One involves choosing words that communicate power rather than powerlessness. The second issue is language intensity.

POWERFUL VERSUS POWERLESS SPEECH

We discussed types of power in Chapter 4 and defined power as the ability to get others to do what you want. When a person has power, he or she is perceived as having status and is likely to also be perceived as credible. Among other factors, the words you choose contribute to whether you are perceived as powerful or not.

Several language features contribute to **powerless speech**. Four such features that have been studied include *hedges* or *qualifiers* ("sort of," "kinda," "I guess"), *hesitation forms* ("uh," "well, you know"), *tag questions* (". . . , don't you think?"), and *disclaimers* ("This may sound odd, but"). The absence of these features has been defined as **powerful speech**. When a person's speech contains these features, he or she will likely be perceived as less credible and be less persuasive than if those features are not present (Burrell & Koper, 1998).

Johnson and Vinson (1990) wondered how a person would be perceived if he or she began with powerless speech but then switched to powerful speech. Would the switch to powerful speech overcome the negative effects of the powerless speech? Similarly, they also wondered about the consequences of starting off with powerful speech but then switching to powerless speech. Johnson and Vinson designed an experiment that manipulated the number of hedges and hesitations in a transcribed testimony. They also manipulated whether the hedges and hesitations occurred at the beginning of the testimony, at the end, or throughout. In all, they had four conditions: powerful (no hedges or hesitations), powerless (hedges and hesitations throughout), powerful beginning (hedges and hesitations in the last third of the testimony), and powerful ending (hedges and hesitations in the first third of the testimony). They found that it did not matter where the powerless language was placed. All three groups of testimony that contained powerless language were less persuasive and were perceived as less credible than the powerful testimony.

In a second study, Johnson and Vinson (1990) wondered if a small number of powerless features would have a negative impact or if a person could get away with a few powerless features in her or his speech. Again, Johnson and Vinson created four conditions: a powerful condition (no hedges or hesitations), moderate power (10 powerless features), low power (19 powerless features), and powerless (39 powerless features). Their results indicated that even the small number of powerless features contained in the moderate power condition resulted in reduced persuasiveness.

These two studies are consistent with other research on powerless speech, and we should conclude that using powerless speech in the form of hedges, hesitations, disclaimers, and tag questions reduces persuasiveness and should be avoided. Powerless speech is usually only a concern in oral messages, such as when you are giving a persuasive speech or when you are in a one-on-one or small-group situation. It would be truly rare to find powerless speech in formal written persuasive messages. For some people the use of powerless speech has become a habit.

Women have historically been afforded less power in American society. In 1975, Lakoff argued that women used language differently than men and were discriminated against because of this difference in language use. Lakoff described women as using a different vocabulary (e.g., women have a larger repertoire of colors); as using empty adjectives (e.g., "cute," "sweet," "divine"); as using more tag questions, more polite forms of speech, more hedges, more intensives (e.g., "so," "very," "really"); and using hypercorrect grammar. It has often been assumed that women use more powerless language; however, in a more recent study when Grob, Meyers, and Schuh (1997) examined the use of powerless language among males and females in group interactions, there were few differences between men and women, and, when differences did exist, men were found to use more powerless language. In another study, Bradac and Mulac (1984) examined how people perceived males and females who were interviewing for a job and used various forms of powerless language. Bradac and Mulac found no differences in how men and women were perceived when using powerless language. If women use powerless language, they can expect to be perceived as less credible and less persuasive, but the same holds true for men. Being aware of the words you choose when speaking is an important part of being an effective persuader. In addition to considering the power your message is communicating, be aware of the intensity of the language you use when constructing a message.

INTENSE LANGUAGE

Language intensity refers to language characteristics that indicate the extent the source deviates from neutrality. Two language features determine whether language is intense or not. The first is **emotional intensity**, which is the amount of affect expressed in the language choices of the source. The word *incredible* is more emotionally intense than the word *good*; *catastrophic* is more emotionally intense than *terrible*, which in turn is more emotionally intense than *bad*. The second feature is **linguistic specificity**. Linguistic specificity is "the degree to which a source makes precise reference to attitude objects in a message" (Hamilton & Stewart, 1993). Words that are specific have more narrow meaning and are more precise. Words that are less specific are more vague, have broader meaning, and provide less precise information. Specific language is more likely to bring a vivid picture to mind. For example, describing an object as "6 feet wide and 8 feet tall" is more specific and vivid than describing an object as "quite large"; however, both descriptions are accurate. Combining specific language with emotional language creates intense language.

A study by Buller et al. (2000) tested different messages (high intensity vs. low intensity and deductive vs. inductive organization) and their effectiveness in influencing parents to protect their children and themselves from the harmful effects of sun exposure. Buller and his colleagues found that parents were most influenced by the deductive message that used intense language. They concluded that the intense message was more effective because it was more memorable. Intense language is more vivid because it is more likely to bring a specific picture to mind. It is easier to remember a message that we have associated a picture with in our mind.

Research has suggested that high credibility sources can successfully employ more intense language, but that low credibility sources are less effective when they use intense language (Bradac, Bowers, & Courtright, 1979). This doesn't necessarily hold true for obscenity, which is a form of intense language; some evidence suggests that sex plays a role in this interaction. In general, males can successfully use more intense language than females, so care should be exercised in applying this principle too literally. Still, language choice is a message variable that interacts with source credibility in determining persuasive success.

Language intensity has also been explored in computer-mediated contexts. Andersen and Blackburn (2004) found that more intense language in an e-mail request to complete a survey resulted in a higher compliance rate. Andersen and Blackburn created two different e-mail requests—one with high intensity language and one with low intensity language (see Figure 5.8). The response rate was 35 percent for the low intensity message and 47.6 percent for the high intensity message. This is an important finding because as persuaders we often need information from our target audience (audience analysis) and we often obtain that information by conducting surveys. Getting people to complete surveys is an ongoing battle for researchers of all stripes. Using more intense language appears to be more effective in getting people to complete those surveys.

THE HIGH INTENSITY MESSAGE

Note: Italicized portions differed between low and high intensity versions

Subject Line Said: *Important: SDSU Mascot*

Dear <<First_Name>>,

We are sure you have heard that on September 27, the Associated Students Council voted to retire the 'Aztecs' name, logo and the mascot, 'Monty' Montezuma. The decision is not final and will ultimately be decided by President Stephen L. Weber. Our office *has been swamped* with calls about this resolution; however, we are still looking for additional input from alumni.

The president has assured me that he will take into account input from many constituents including: alumni, students, faculty, and staff. In order to better represent the opinions of our alumni regarding this resolution, I ask that you give me *some vital input* relating to three specific areas: the name 'Aztecs,' the logo, and the human mascot 'Monty' Montezuma.

If you care at all about this issue, pro or con, please answer the three questions to help us understand the collective sentiment of 179,000 alumni. *Please submit your crucial* answers to me by simply using the "Reply" function of your email program and identifying which answer you choose. *These essential* questions are divided in three segments:

Aztec Name:

1. I am in favor of retaining the name 'Aztecs'

   I am opposed to retaining the name 'Aztecs'

   I have no opinion

Aztec Logo:

2. I am in favor of retaining the 'Aztec' logo

   I am opposed to retaining the 'Aztec' logo

   I am in favor of modifying the 'Aztec' logo

   I have no opinion

Mascot:

3. I am in favor of retaining the human mascot, 'Monty' Montezuma

   I am opposed to retaining the human mascot, 'Monty' Montezuma

   I am in favor of modifying the human mascot, 'Monty' Montezuma

   I have no opinion

Sample images of the Aztec logo and mascot can be viewed on the SDSU website, www.sdsu.edu. I would like to commend and thank you for expressing your interest on the Associated Students resolution. As the alumni director, I assure you your voice will be heard.

Sincerely,

Jim Herrick

THE LOW INTENSITY MESSAGE

Subject Line Said: *SDSU Mascot1*

Dear <<First Name>>

As you may be aware, on September 27, the Associated Students Council voted to retire the 'Aztecs' name, logo and the mascot, 'Monty' Montezuma by the end of the current academic year. The decision is not final and will ultimately be decided by SDSU President Stephen L. Weber. Our office has *received a high volume* of calls about this resolution: however, we are still looking for additional input from alumni.

The president has assured me that he will take into account input from many constituents including: alumni, students, faculty, and staff. In order to better represent the opinions of our alumni regarding this resolution, I ask that you give me *some input* relating to three specific areas: the name 'Aztecs,' the logo, and the human mascot 'Monty' Montezuma.

Below are three questions that will help us understand the collective sentiment of our 179,000 alumni. *You can submit* your answers to me by simply using the "Reply" function of your email program and identifying which answer you choose. *Questions are* divided in three segments:

Aztec Name:

1. I am in favor of retaining the name 'Aztecs'

    I am opposed to retaining the name 'Aztecs'

    I have no opinion

Aztec Logo:

2. I am in favor of retaining the 'Aztec' logo

    I am opposed to retaining the 'Aztec' logo

    I am in favor of modifying the 'Aztec' logo

    I have no opinion

Mascot:

3. I am in favor of retaining the human mascot, 'Monty' Montezuma

    I am opposed to retaining the human mascot, 'Monty' Montezuma

    I am in favor of modifying the human mascot, 'Monty' Montezuma

    I have no opinion

Sample images of the Aztec logo and mascot can be viewed on the SDSU website, www.sdsu.edu. I would like to commend and thank you for expressing your interest on the Associated Students resolution. As the alumni director, I assure you your voice will be heard.

Sincerely,

Jim Herrick

From Communication Reports, Vol. 17, No. 2, Summer 2004 by Peter A. Anderson and Tammy R. Blackburn. Used by permission of the publisher.

FIGURE 5.8 A high language intensity message used by Andersen and Blackburn.

Intense language is not always appropriate. Whether to use intense language and how intense to be are decisions you must make with the topic and the context of the message in mind. Some issues are so inherently emotional that using intense language with them could potentially be explosive. In other cases, using intense language may be perceived as being in poor taste or as manipulative. To be an effective persuader, you must constantly be considering the characteristics of your audience and the persuasive context as you decide how to construct your message.

RESISTANCE TO PERSUASION

How a message is constructed is an important element in persuasion. It is also an important element in how resistant your audience is to persuasion. Why in the world would we want to make our audience resistant to persuasion? Well, we don't want our audience to be resistant to *our* persuasion—it's our opponent we want our audience to be resistant to. Imagine you work in sales and have successfully influenced a group of customers to believe that your product is superior to your competitor's product. On your departure, your customers become the recipients of your opponent's persuasive message. All your hard work may go down the drain if your opponent successfully influences your customers. Practitioners of persuasion are interested not only in successfully influencing their audience, but also in how to make their audience resistant to counter-persuasion (influence from the opponent). How you construct your message can influence your audience's resistance to your opponent. Two areas of research have addressed the issue of resistance: inoculation theory and forewarning.

INOCULATION THEORY

In all likelihood, you have been inoculated or immunized against several diseases and are familiar with the general theory behind immunizations. In the early 1960s, William McGuire suggested that the general theory of immunizing against disease (e.g., polio, smallpox) could also be applied to persuasion and termed this **inoculation theory**. To make an audience resistant to counter-persuasion, they could be given a small, weakened dose of arguments supporting the opposition. This is analogous to injecting a small, weakened dose of the smallpox virus into a person. When injected with the smallpox virus, the human body reacts by producing antibodies that will attack and kill the virus, making the person much more resistant to the smallpox virus if ever exposed to it. Giving an audience a few weak opposing arguments would give the audience the opportunity to develop counterarguments (similar to antibodies), making them resistant to the opposition's persuasive messages. More specifically, McGuire (1961, 1962) proposed that exposing a receiver to opposing arguments would threaten his or her existing beliefs and motivate the person to generate counterarguments. Just exposing a receiver to opposing arguments is not quite enough to create resistance to counter-persuasion. The source must also refute the opposing arguments. This threat combined with the refutation of the counterarguments is fundamental to inoculation theory (Pfau, 1992). The threat motivates individuals to bolster their existing attitude, and the refutational component helps them develop the counterarguments they need to shoot down the opposition.

Initially, McGuire (1961) tested four message types: supportive-only, refutational-only, supportive-refutational, and refutational-supportive. A **supportive message** is a one-sided message that only presents arguments in favor of one side of a particular issue. A **refutational message** is a message that argues against or proves false the opposing arguments and refutes them. This should not be confused with a balanced presentation of the issues in a controversy. The opposing views are presented and refuted. McGuire found that a supportive-plus-refutational message (it didn't matter if the supportive part of the message came first or second) was the most effective in creating resistance. The refutational portion of the message served to weaken the believability of the counterarguments, or, in other words, the audience was less likely to believe the opposing viewpoints. The supportive portion of the message served to bolster audience beliefs favoring the issue. This supportive-plus-refutational message tested by McGuire is essentially the same thing as a refutational two-sided message. However, one important difference between a two-sided message and inoculation is that inoculation warns the audience of an impending attack. A refutational two-sided message does not necessarily warn the audience of an impending attack. When it does, it would be considered inoculation (Pfau, 1992).

In a second study, McGuire (1962) wondered whether the amount of time between the refutational message and an attack message (a message attacking the beliefs of the audience) would be important. McGuire also wanted to compare refutational-same and refutational-different messages. A **refutational-same message** refutes the arguments contained in the opponent's attack message from the opposition. A **refutational-different message** refutes opposing arguments on an issue but not the ones contained in the attack message. In this study, participants heard either a refutational-same or refutational-different message and then heard an attack message immediately, 2 days later, or 1 week later. McGuire found that both refutational-same and refutational-different messages increased audience resistance to the attack messages, particularly when the attack occurred 2 days or 1 week after receiving the refutational message. The really interesting finding in this study was that the refutational-different message was so effective at developing resistance in the audience. This means the audience heard a message that was supportive of their existing beliefs, contained some counterarguments, and then refuted them. However, when their beliefs were attacked, the arguments used in the attack were *different* from the counterarguments given in the refutational message. The receivers were resistant to the attack even though the arguments in the attack were different. The refutational message seemed to stimulate the audience to think about their beliefs and to generate reasons why they believed as they did. So, when faced with a persuasive attack on their beliefs, they were prepared to resist, even if the arguments presented by the opposition were new. This is good news for persuaders in applied settings because it means they don't actually have to guess what arguments will be employed by competitors. In fact, they can simply choose the arguments that are weakest and thus the ones they most prefer to refute.

In a more recent study, Pfau et al. (2001) examined inoculation messages that were either cognitive or affective. By cognitive, we mean the message emphasized verifiable evidence such as statistics and research findings. Cognitive messages require analytical thinking and processing of the message. An affective message is intended to stimulate emotions. Additionally, Pfau et al. created refutational-same inoculation messages and refutational-different messages. Some of the messages used by Pfau et al. are shown in Figures 5.9 and 5.10. In this study, research participants first completed a questionnaire that measured their attitudes toward legalization of marijuana and banning handguns. Three weeks later, the participants were randomly assigned to receive a cognitive inoculation message, receive an affective inoculation message, or be placed into the control group that didn't receive any inoculation message. Participants received an inoculation message that supported their existing attitude toward either banning handguns or legalizing marijuana. Half of participants received an inoculation message that contained the same arguments (refutational-same) that they would be exposed to in the attack message. The other half of participants received an inoculation message with different arguments (refutational-different) than they would be exposed to in the attack message. Two weeks after receiving the inoculation message, some research participants received a message supportive to their existing attitude toward the topic. Four of these inoculation messages are displayed in Figure 5.9. Two weeks later, participants received an attack message—a message that attacked their existing attitudes and beliefs about either banning handguns or legalizing marijuana. Examples of the attack messages used by Pfau et al. are shown in Figure 5.10. Compare the refutational-same inoculation messages in Figure 5.9 to the attack messages in Figure 5.10. You can see that the messages use the same arguments. The inoculation-different messages use arguments different from those used in the attack messages.

REFUTATIONAL-SAME AFFECTIVE INOCULATION MESSAGE
A Handgun Ban Will Save American Lives

Handguns kill thousands of Americans each year, and as a result, many Americans support a ban on the manufacture, sale and possession of handguns. In response, gun proponents have launched an intense campaign to thwart a ban. Some of their arguments are persuasive, and may cause you to doubt the wisdom of your position.

Those who oppose a handgun ban argue that people must be able to arm themselves for protection against criminals. Yet, there are numerous examples that illustrate that handguns don't protect people from criminals, and in fact, may endanger them more. Take the case of John Reynolds. John kept a gun in his bedroom closet for protection. The only problem was that the man who came to rob John's house found the gun before John woke up. Ultimately, John was killed with his own gun. If John had not owned a gun, he may only have lost his wallet; instead, he lost his life. People like John are dead because irrational people equate owning a gun with security. These same people keep guns on the street and continue to endanger the lives of your loved ones.

Those who oppose a handgun ban also argue that any restriction of gun ownership infringes on the right to bear arms provided in the Second Amendment to the Constitution. This interpretation of the Constitution is wrong. Lawrence Ashford, an attorney for the Justice Department and a specialist on the Constitution, argues that, "The Second Amendment was designed to give states the right to form militias. It was not meant to apply to the individual citizen."

Anti-gun control supporters talk about bearing arms to feel safe, and yet their so-called cause is exactly why many Americans live in fear. The time has come for your right to feel safe from taking a back seat to their right to own a gun.

REFUTATIONAL-DIFFERENT COGNITIVE INOCULATION MESSAGE

A Handgun Ban Will Save American Lives

Handguns kill thousands of Americans each year, and as a result, many Americans support a ban on the manufacture, sale and possession of handguns. In response, gun proponents have launched an intense campaign to thwart a ban. Some of their arguments are persuasive, and may cause you to doubt the wisdom of your position.

Those who oppose a handgun ban argue that manufacture and sale of handguns are responsible for the incomes of many citizens, and that a ban would impose an economic hardship. However, the hardship to our nation can be counted in terms of an even more valuable resource—human lives. Handgun crimes and resulting deaths and injuries have increased at an alarming rate in the last few years. The Justice Department reports that violent crimes involving handguns increased more than 21 percent from 1991 to 1992. Every year more than 35,000 Americans lose their lives due to handgun homicide, accident or suicide. A ban on handguns would end this madness. A ban on handguns would reduce the total number of guns, and therefore cut the number of violent crimes involving guns. Studies indicate that those states with stricter handgun laws experience much less homicide and suicide due to firearms. Those people intent on killing others or themselves may well turn to other means if handguns are unavailable, but studies show that these alternatives are less lethal.

In addition to the loss of lives, handguns are responsible for almost 250,000 other injuries each year. This results in costly medical bills often passed on to the taxpayer. In fact, in 1992, tax dollars paid for 80 percent of the $14 billion in medical bills for gunshot injuries. American citizens are being forced to foot the bill for handgun violence. This is too high a price to pay.

Support a ban on handguns in the U.S.!

REFUTATIONAL-SAME COGNITIVE INOCULATION MESSAGE

A Handgun Ban Won't Stop Violent Crimes

Handguns are citizens' only protection against violent crime. Despite this fact, gun opponents have stepped up their campaign to ban the manufacture, sale, and possession of handguns throughout the U.S. Unfortunately, their campaign is gaining ground, and some of their arguments may cause you to doubt the wisdom of your position.

Advocates of a ban on handguns claim that it would save lives. This *assumes* a ban could reduce the total number of handguns in circulation, especially among criminals. But this assumption is oversimplified. FBI statistics reveal that there are currently 211 million firearms circulating in the United States, more than one gun for every adult. There is simply no way to remove those guns from circulation. Various local attempts to buy back handguns have been tried and failed. They succeed in getting obsolete or broken guns turned in for sure, but failed to reduce the number of functioning handguns. Moreover, if a national handgun ban is enforced, criminals will turn to an underground black market to obtain illegal firearms.

Also, restrictions on handguns would strip decent citizens of their ability to defend their homes, their families and their lives. A recent study indicates that firearms are used 2.5 million times each year to protect lives and property. Another recent survey reports that 8 million gun owners report they have used a gun to defend themselves or their family. If the ownership of guns is banned, it will send a clear message to criminals that people are defenseless against them.

In addition to taking away an individual's ability to protect their life and property, a ban on handguns would also restrict rights of American citizens granted under the Constitution. The Second Amendment to the Constitution grants all American citizens the right to keep and bear arms.

Oppose efforts to ban handguns in the U.S.!

REFUTATIONAL-DIFFERENT AFFECTIVE INOCULATION MESSAGE

A Handgun Ban Won't Stop Violent Crimes

Handguns are citizens' only protection against violent crime. Despite this, gun opponents have stepped up their campaign to ban the manufacture, sale, and possession of handguns. Unfortunately, their campaign is gaining ground, and some of their arguments may cause you to doubt your position.

Gun opponents claim a ban on handguns will reduce violent crimes. However, the fact is that a handgun ban would not cure the underlying causes of crime, and is thus doomed to fail. During the past 30 years, America has experienced alarming increases in family breakdowns, structural unemployment, drug trafficking, and especially violence on television. Brandon Cantrill, a highly-regarded expert on television violence, indicates that U.S. homicide rates rose sharply after the introduction of television, and have paralleled the steady increase in the depiction of graphic violence in television programs. Many experts say television violence glorifies violence, contributing to crime. One way to reduce violent crime is to address these causes. Handguns are just a scapegoat.

Another way to reduce violent crime is get tough with criminals, using longer prison sentences to keep offenders behind bars. Take the case of Joe Lopez. Lopez had been in and out of prison nearly a dozen times for rape and other offenses. But thanks to a tough "three strikes and you're out" sentencing law, Lopez will no longer be freed to prey upon society.

Instead of looking for a convenient scapegoat, support attempts to address the real causes of violent crime. If banning handguns won't reduce crime, then all it will accomplish is disarming good citizens who only want to feel safe in their homes. Don't let the misinformed take away your right to feel safe. Oppose the campaign to ban the manufacture, sale, and possession of handguns in the U.S.!

FIGURE 5.9 Inoculation messages.

PROTECT CITIZENS' RIGHT TO OWN HANDGUNS

A new attack is being waged against law-abiding citizens of the United States by those who support a total ban on the manufacture, sale and ownership of handguns. Although these people manipulate statistics to prove their point, the truth is that all Americans have a right to own a handgun for protection. Further, this right is guaranteed to all of us in the Second Amendment to the Constitution of the United States.

Restrictions on handguns would strip decent citizens of their ability to defend their homes, their families, and their lives. Many citizens in this country own guns in order to protect themselves and their families from unlawful intruders. A study by a prominent criminology professor at Stanford University reports that firearms are used approximately 2.5 million times per year for protection. Take the case of Thomas Nesbitt. Last March two criminals entered the Nesbitt home in the middle of the night. By threatening the intruders with his gun, Nesbitt was able to frighten them away, thus avoiding harm to his family and property. If the ownership of handguns is restricted, it would be impossible for Americans to protect themselves and their loved ones. The message this would send to criminal elements is that we as potential victims of crime are completely vulnerable. James Fendry, an official of the National Rifle Association, articulates this point: "With the crime rate soaring, we don't want to send a message to criminals that people might not have a handgun in their home, and if they do, they're violating the law and will be hesitant to use it in a crisis."

In addition to taking away an individual's ability to protect their life and property, a ban on handguns would also restrict rights of American citizens granted under the Constitution. The Second Amendment to the Constitution grants all American citizens the right to keep and bear arms. Legislation banning handguns is in direct violation of the Bill of Rights as written by our founding fathers. Wesley Horton, a constitutional law expert, explains that this debate is about preserving, what is at this time, an unpopular right. But the jurist adds: "You can't distinguish between good and bad rights. All rights under the Constitution are good." The point is clear. The right to bear arms was won for us by people willing to shed their blood and give their lives for their country.

Oppose efforts to restrict gun ownership.

A HANDGUN BAN WILL SAVE AMERICAN LIVES

Handgun crimes and resulting deaths and injuries have increased at an alarming rate in the last few years. The Justice Department reports that violent crimes involving handguns increased more than 21 percent from 1991 to 1992. Last year, more than 35,000 Americans lost their lives in gun-related felonies. As a result, more and more people believe that it is now time to ban the manufacture, sale, and possession of handguns in the U.S.

A handgun ban will reduce this carnage. A ban will reduce the total number of guns, and therefore cut the number of violent crimes involving guns. Most Americans are law abiding and would surrender their handguns as part of a buy-back policy that would be implemented in conjunction with a ban. Programs that employ a ban coupled with a buy-back policy, patterned after the Baltimore model, have enjoyed excellent success. They demonstrate that a buy-back approach will eventually reduce the overall stock and circulation of guns.

Remember that most murders are committed by people previously acquainted with their victims, and not by strangers. Take the case of one Kentucky family. Last May, 17-year-old Clay Shrout used his father's handgun to murder every single member of his family. Shrout got up early, retrieved a .380 caliber semi-automatic handgun from his father's Jeep, and returned to the house to systematically shoot his parents and 12- and 14-year-old sisters to death in their bedrooms. If no handgun was available, this situation might have proven less tragic. People who are intent on killing may well turn to other means if handguns are unavailable, but the weight of scientific research clearly indicates that other weapons are much less lethal than handguns.

As for those murders committed by total strangers, a ban would reduce them also. Granted that criminals will still possess guns, but at least they will not be able to purchase or steal them from law-abiding citizens. Each year more than one million dollars in guns are stolen from private homes and then used to commit additional crimes. In buying handguns for protection, well-intentioned people are actually providing the firepower for increased crime. Besides, the available evidence indicates that guns simply don't protect people. One study found that in the event of a break-in, a handgun in the home is more than twice as likely to result in the death or injury of the occupant than to be used successfully by the occupant to repel an intruder. Take the case of John Reynolds. John owned a gun to protect against intruders. Unfortunately, the intruder came across the gun before John woke up, and when John attempted to disarm the intruder, he ended up being killed with his own gun. If he had not owned a gun, he might only have lost his wallet; instead, he lost his life. This situation is the rule, and not the exception.

An effective handgun ban would reduce the quantity of guns in circulation and thus save thousands of lives. Let's stop the carnage! It's time to ban handguns.

Reprinted by permission of Michael Pfau.

FIGURE 5.10 Attack messages.

Pfau and his colleagues found that both refutational-same and refutational-different inoculation messages were effective at creating resistance in the audience. This finding was supportive of previous research. When exposed to a refutational message, the audience feels threatened and becomes motivated to develop counterarguments to defend their position against any arguments (whether new or old) opposing their position. Pfau and his colleagues had expected cognitive refutational messages to be more effective in conferring resistance than affective refutational messages. The study results did not support this hypothesis. Both cognitive and affective inoculation messages were effective in this case. In follow-up research, Ivanov, Pfau, and Parker (2009) also examined whether inoculation remained effective in the face of multiple counterattacks on the initial message. They found that, although the effectiveness of the inoculation effect was reduced somewhat, the refutational messages still were more effective than any other version of the message. Earlier in this chapter we discussed logical and emotional appeals. Pfau et al.'s cognitive inoculation messages in Figure 5.10 are examples of a logical appeal. The affective inoculation messages are examples of emotional appeals.

Warning your audience of an impending attack on their attitude and beliefs followed by refuting some of the opposing arguments is an effective way of making your audience resistant to your opponent. Note in the inoculation messages in Figure 5.10 that the audience is explicitly warned of the impending attack on their position. Substantial research over the past 40 years has supported inoculation theory as a means for conferring resistance in an audience. However, refutational messages are not the only means of conferring resistance in an audience. Simply forewarning your audience of impending persuasion also results in resistance.

FOREWARNING

How a persuasive message is introduced can reduce its effectiveness in changing audience attitudes. **Forewarning** an audience—or, in other words, telling the audience they are about to be persuaded—can make an audience resistant to the persuasive message. Several research studies have examined the effects of forewarning. Two meta-analyses (Benoit, 1998; Wood & Quinn, 2003) reviewed several studies on forewarning, and both concluded that forewarning audience members increased their resistance to an impending persuasive message. There are two types of forewarning messages. The first is **topic and position forewarning**. This type of message forewarns the audience of the topic of persuasion and the position (for or against) of the impending persuasive message. The second type of forewarning is **persuasive intent forewarning**. This type of message forewarns the audience that they will be receiving a message that probably will attack their attitudes and beliefs; however, the topic and position of the message is not given. A study by Jacks and Devine (2000) examined the impact of forewarning an audience. In the first stage of this study, the researchers pretested participants' attitudes toward allowing gays in the military. Those who held favorable attitudes were selected for the study. After hearing a brief introduction to the study, half of participants were forewarned by being told:

> ... that their session had been assigned to hear a speech on the side of not lifting the ban on gays in the military. So the speaker will be arguing against allowing gays to serve openly in the military.

Half of participants in this study were not warned of the impending persuasion. Those participants who were warned were more resistant and experienced less attitude change after hearing a persuasive speech advocating that gays not be allowed in the military. Consistent with previous research, Jacks and Devine found forewarning to be an effective means of creating resistance in an audience.

Jacks and Devine (2000) also examined the amount of time between the forewarning and the persuasive message. Half of research participants who were forewarned heard the persuasive message immediately following the forewarning (no delay condition). For the other half of research participants, there was a 2-minute delay between the forewarning and the persuasive message (time-delay condition). Jacks and Devine found that participants who found the topic of gays in the military to be of high importance and who experienced the 2-minute delay were *not* more resistant to the persuasive message than those who had no delay before hearing the persuasive message. However, for participants who did not find gays in the military to be an important topic, experiencing a 2-minute delay *increased* their resistance when compared to those not receiving a delay. The conclusion to be drawn from Jacks and Devine's study is that a delay between the forewarning and the persuasive message increases resistance for those who have low involvement in the issue. We know that when receivers perceive a topic as relevant or personally involving, they are more motivated to cognitively process the message. We can apply this to forewarning. If an audience is highly involved in a topic, they will be motivated to think of arguments to defend their existing attitude and beliefs if forewarned of impending persuasion. Giving them extra time probably doesn't make much difference, because one can think of only so many arguments, and one can only become so resistant. However, for those who have low involvement, forewarning them may motivate them to think about the topic. Providing these folks with a little extra time gives them an opportunity to think of reasons/arguments for why they believe as they do. Therefore, if the audience has low involvement in the issue, a time delay will probably increase resistance over no time delay.

In those instances when you want your audience members to be resistant to your opponent, forewarning them of the impending persuasion is one means of increasing resistance to your opponent's message. You also want to keep in mind the effects of forewarning when you are either introducing yourself and your topic or are being introduced. When giving speeches as well as other forms of communication, we often begin our presentation with an introduction. Although it would be unethical to lie about our intent, we should avoid explicitly stating our goal of changing our audience's attitudes and/or beliefs. Such an introduction would forewarn our audience and would most likely increase their resistance to our message.

Both the content and style of a persuasive message are important considerations when persuading an audience. In this chapter, we addressed several message factors that can be manipulated to enhance persuasion. At this point we want to again remind you of source factors. We have purposively separated source factors from our discussion of message factors to help you understand these concepts. It's too complex to try to talk about them all together. However, in real persuasion, the source and the message are closely linked and the two interact. When constructing a persuasive message, the effective persuader considers both the message and who is delivering it.

- Logical appeals rely on logic and reasoning to be persuasive.
- Emotional appeals rely on one or more emotions to be persuasive.
- Humor, guilt, and fear are emotions commonly used to persuade.
- Leventhal's parallel response model explains two responses to fear appeals: a fear control response and a danger control response.
- Witte's extended parallel process model explains how an audience processes a fear appeal and identifies four components of an effective fear appeal.
- Evidence can enhance attitude change and source credibility when the source has low to moderate initial credibility, the evidence is delivered well, and the evidence is new and unfamiliar to the audience.
- Both narrative and statistical evidence are useful, but statistical evidence is slightly more effective than narrative evidence.
- Two-sided refutational messages are more effective than one-sided messages and non-refutational two-sided messages.
- Use of powerless speech in even small amounts reduces the persuasiveness of a speaker.
- Intense language is specific and emotionally intense. Messages that use intense language are more memorable than messages that use less intense language.
- Inoculation theory proposes that an audience can be inoculated against the opposition by giving them small doses of the opposing arguments and refuting them.
- Both refutational-same and refutational-different inoculation messages are effective at creating resistance in an audience.
- Forewarning an audience of impending persuasion results in the audience being resistant to the persuasive message.
- Both types of forewarning—topic and position forewarning and persuasive intent forewarning—are effective at conferring resistance.

KEY TERMS

Danger control response—a cognitive response to a fear appeal that focuses on how to eliminate the danger or threat that is causing the fear.

Door-in-the-face (DITF)—initially making a very large unreasonable request that the target is likely to turn down, then making the critical request.

Emotional appeal—a persuasive message that relies on emotion to be persuasive.

Emotional intensity—the amount of affect expressed in the language choices of the source.

Evidence—factual statements originating from a source other than the speaker, objects not created by the speaker, and opinions of persons other than the speaker that are offered in support of the speaker's claims.

Extended parallel process model (EPPM)—developed by Witte and describes the two ways receivers process fear appeals and how different responses result from different ways of processing.

Fear appeal—a persuasive message that attempts to arouse the emotion of fear by depicting a personally relevant and significant threat and then follows this description of the threat by outlining recommendations presented as feasible and effective in deterring the threat.

Fear control response—an emotional response to a fear appeal that focuses on how to eliminate the fear.

Forewarning—when a receiver is told that he or she is about to be exposed to a persuasive message that challenges his or her beliefs.

Guilt appeal—a persuasive message intended to stimulate the emotion of guilt, which is often experienced when a person thinks his or her behavior does not meet his or her own standards.

Inoculation theory—McGuire's theory on resistance to persuasive messages.

Language intensity—language characteristics that indicate the extent the source deviates from neutrality.

Language style—the types of words a person chooses to present a message.

Linguistic specificity—the degree to which a source makes precise reference to attitude objects in a message.

Logical appeal—a persuasive message that relies on logic and reasoning to be persuasive.

Narrative evidence—case stories or examples that are used to support a claim.

Non-refutational two-sided message—a message that mentions the opposing arguments but does not refute them.

One-sided message—a message that only presents arguments in favor of a particular issue.

Parallel response model—developed by Leventhal and proposes that people have one of two responses when exposed to a fear appeal.

Persuasive intent forewarning—a message that forewarns the audience that they will be receiving a message that will probably attack their attitudes and beliefs; however, the topic and position of the message are not given.

Powerful speech—the absence of powerless language features.

Powerless speech—the use of language features such as hedges or qualifiers, hesitations, tag questions, and disclaimers that create perceptions of little power.

Refutational message—a message in which opposing views are presented and refuted in inoculation theory.

Refutational two-sided message—a two-sided message that presents opposing arguments and then refutes them.

Refutational-different message—a message that refutes opposing arguments on an issue but not the ones contained in the preceding attack message.

Refutational-same message—a message that refutes the arguments contained in the attack message from the opposition.

Response efficacy—how effective the recommended response is in eliminating a particular threat.

Self-efficacy—the extent the audience believes they are capable of performing the response recommended in a message.

Severity—the grimness of the threat presented in a message.

Statistical evidence—an informational summary of many cases that is expressed in numbers and used to support a claim.

Supportive message—a one-sided message in inoculation theory.

Susceptibility—how probable it is that a particular threat will affect the audience.

Topic and position forewarning—a message that forewarns the audience of the topic of persuasion and the position (for or against) of the impending persuasive message.

Two-sided message—a message that presents arguments in favor of an issue but also considers opposing arguments.

REVIEW QUESTIONS

1. How do emotional appeals and logical appeals differ?
2. How are humor and guilt used in emotional appeals?
3. What are the four components that a fear appeal must have to be effective?
4. Why does a person have a fear control response? Why does a person have a danger control response to a fear appeal?
5. What are the four conclusions drawn by McCroskey about the use of evidence?
6. What are the two types of two-sided messages? Which is more effective?
7. What are the strengths and weaknesses of statistical evidence and narrative evidence?
8. What are the four language features of powerless language?
9. What are the two characteristics of intense language?
10. How effective is a refutational-same inoculation message compared to a refutational-different inoculation message?
11. What are two types of forewarning?

DISCUSSION QUESTIONS

1. Look over the advertisements you see online. How many of the advertisements rely on emotion? What emotions do they try to stimulate? How effective is the message at influencing you? Do you think it would be more effective or less effective for someone else? Why?
2. Some theorists argue that emotional appeals are unethical because they subvert the priority of rational thought. What do you think? Are emotional appeals always ethical? If not always ethical, under what circumstances would you find emotional appeals to be unethical?
3. What kinds of topics do you think fear appeals work best with? Why?
4. Go to the website of a nonprofit organization that supports a cause, such as PETA or Planned Parenthood. What kind of evidence do they use to support their claims? What type of information is used as evidence? What types of evidence do you find most persuasive?
5. Quality of evidence is not included in the criteria for effective use of evidence. If your audience cannot distinguish between high and low quality evidence (as some research suggests), is it ethical to use low quality evidence in order to gain persuasive success? What role should evidence quality play in making ethical judgments about message content?
6. Think about the last time you made a request or gave your opinion. How powerful or powerless was your speech? Would you benefit from using more powerful speech when communicating with others?

7. Would manipulating language intensity in order to be more persuasive be ethical? What criteria would you suggest to help make these evaluations?
8. Find a fear appeal advertisement and analyze it according to the extended parallel processing model. Do you think the target audience would perceive threat? Would they perceive response efficacy? Would they perceive self-efficacy?

REFERENCES

Allen, M. (1998). Comparing the persuasive effectiveness of one- and two-sided messages. In M. Allen & R. W. Preiss (Eds.), *Persuasion: Advances through meta-analysis* (pp. 87–98). Cresskill, NJ: Hampton Press.

Allen, M., Hale, J., Mongeau, P., Berkowitz–Stafford, S., Stafford, S., Shanahan, W., et al. (1990). Testing a model of message sidedness: Three replications. *Communication Monographs, 57,* 275–291.

Allen, M., & Preiss, R. W. (1997). Comparing the persuasiveness of narrative and statistical evidence using meta-analysis. *Communication Research Reports, 14,* 125–131.

Allen, M., & Stiff, J. B. (1998). An analysis of the sleeper effect. In M. Allen & R. W. Priess (Eds.), *Persuasion: Advances through meta-analysis* (pp. 175–188). Cresskill, NJ: Hampton Press.

Andersen, P. A., & Blackburn, T. R. (2004). An experimental study of language intensity and response rate in e-mail surveys. *Communication Reports, 17,* 73–84.

Benoit, W. L. (1998). Forewarning and persuasion. In M. Allen & R. W. Preiss (Eds.), *Persuasion: Advances through meta-analysis* (pp. 139–154). Cresskill, NJ: Hampton Press.

Bradac, J. J., Bowers, J. W., & Courtright, J. A. (1979). Three language variables in communication research: Intensity, immediacy, and diversity. *Human Communication Research, 5,* 257–269.

Bradac, J. J., & Mulac, A. (1984). A molecular view of powerful and powerless speech styles: Attributional consequences of specific language features and communicator intentions. *Communication Monographs, 51,* 307–319.

Buller, D. B., Burgoon, M., Hall, J. R., Levine, N., Taylor, A. M., Beach, B., et al. (2000). Long-term effects of language intensity in preventive messages on planned family solar protection. *Health Communication, 12,* 261–275.

Burrell, N. A., & Koper, R. J. (1998). The efficacy of powerful/powerless language on attitudes and source credibility. In M. Allen & R. W. Preiss (Eds.), *Persuasion: Advances through meta-analysis* (pp. 203–216). Cresskill, NJ: Hampton Press.

Car-Accidents.com Get the Facts: Statistics. (n.d.). Retrieved February 12, 2003, from www.car-accidents.com/pages/stats/2000_seatbelts.html.

Cialdini, R. B., Vincent, J. E., Lewis, S. K., Catalan, J., Wheeler, D., & Darby, B. L. (1975). Reciprocal concessions procedures for inducing compliance: The door-in-the-face technique. *Journal of Personality and -Social Psychology, 31,* 206–215.

Cline, T. W., & Kellaris, J. J. (1999). The joint impact of humor and argument strength in a print advertising context: A case for weaker arguments. *Psychology and Marketing, 16,* 69–86.

Coulter, R. H., & Pinto, M. B. (1995). Guilt appeals in advertising: What are their effects? *Journal of Applied Psychology, 80,* 697–705.

Grob, L. M., Meyers, R. A., & Schuh, R. (1997). Powerful/powerless language used in group interactions: Sex differences or similarities? *Communication Quarterly, 45,* 282–303.

Hackman, M. Z. (1988). Audience reactions to the use of direct and personal disparaging humor in informative public address. *Communication Research Reports, 5,* 126–130.

Hamilton, M. A., & Hunter, J. E. (1998). The effect of language intensity on receiver evaluations of message, source, and topic. In M. Allen & R. W. Preiss (Eds.), *Persuasion: Advances through meta-analysis* (pp. 99–138). Cresskill, NJ: Hampton Press.

Hamilton, M. A., & Stewart, B. L. (1993). Extending an information processing model of language intensity effects. *Communication Quarterly, 41,* 231–246.

Harris Interactive. (November 12, 2010). Do emotional images in advertising pull at heart strings? Harris Polls, retrieved from http://www.harrisinteractive.com/NewsRoom/HarrisPolls/tabid/447/mid/1508/articleId/627/ctl/ReadCustom percent20Default/Default.aspx.

Hornikx, J., & de Best, J. (2011). Persuasive evidence in India: An investigation of the impact of evidence types and evidence quality. *Argumentation and Advocacy, 47,* 246–257.

Huhmann, B. A., & Brotherton, T. P. (1997). A content analysis of guilt appeals in popular magazine advertisements. *Journal of Advertising, 26*(2), 35–46.

Ivanov, B., Pfau, M., & Parker, K. A. (2009). Can inoculation withstand multiple attacks? An examination of the effectiveness of the inoculation strategy compared to the supportive and restoration strategies. *Communication Research, 36*(5), 655–676.

Jacks, J. Z., & Devine, P. G. (2000). Attitude importance, forewarning of message content, and resistance to persuasion. *Basic and Applied Social Psychology, 22,* 19–29.

Johnson, C., & Vinson, L. (1990). Placement and frequency of powerless talk and impression formation. *Communication Quarterly, 38,* 325–333.

Kazoleas, D. (1993). The impact of argumentativeness on resistance to persuasion. *Human Communication Research, 20,* 118.

Lakeoff, R. (1975). Language and woman's place. *Language and Society, 2,* 45–80.

Leventhal, H. (1970). Findings and theory in the study of fear communications. In L. Berkowitz (Ed.), *Advances in experimental social psychology* (Vol. 5, pp. 120–186). New York: Academic Press.

McCroskey, J. C. (1969). A summary of experimental research on the effects of evidence in persuasive communication. *Quarterly Journal of Speech, 55,* 169–176.

McCroskey, J. C. (1997). *An introduction to rhetorical communication* (7th ed.). Needham Heights, MA: Allyn & Bacon.

McGuire, W. J. (1961). The effectiveness of supportive and refutational defenses in immunizing and restoring beliefs against persuasion. *Sociometry, 24,* 184–197.

McGuire, W. J. (1962). Persistence of the resistance to persuasion induced by various types of prior belief defenses. *Journal of Abnormal and Social Psychology, 64,* 241–248.

Morman, M. T. (2000). The influence of fear appeals, message design, and masculinity on men's motivation to perform the testicular self-exam. *Journal of Applied Communication Research, 28,* 91–116.

Nabi, R. L., Moyer-Guse, E., & Byrne, S. (2007). All joking aside: A serious investigation into the persuasive effect of funny social issue messages. *Communication Monographs, 74,* 29–54.

O'Keefe, D. J. (2002). Guilt as a mechanism of persuasion. In J. P. Dillard & M. Pfau (Eds.), *The persuasion handbook: Developments in theory and practice* (pp. 329–344). Thousand Oaks, CA: Sage.

O'Keefe, D. J., & Figgé, M. (1997). A guilt-based explanation of the door-in-the-face influence strategy. *Human Communication Research, 24,* 64–81.

Pfau, M. (1992). The potential of inoculation in promoting resistance to the effectiveness of comparative advertising messages. *Communication Quarterly, 40,* 26–44.

Pfau, M., Wan, H. H., Szabo, E. A., Anderson, J., Morrill, J., & Zubric, J. (2001). The role and impact of affect in the process of resistance to persuasion. *Human Communication Research, 27,* 216–252.

Reynolds, R., & Reynolds, J. (2002). Evidence. In J. P. Dillard & M. Pfau (Eds.), *The persuasion handbook: Developments in theory and practice* (pp. 428–445). Thousand Oaks, CA: Sage.

Roberto, A. J., & Goodall, C. E. (2009). Using the extended parallel process model to explain physicians' decisions to test their patients for kidney disease. *Journal of Health Communication, 14,* 400–412.

Rogers, R. W. (1975). A protection motivation theory of fear appeals and attitude change. *Journal of Psychology, 91,* 93–114.

Rogers, R. W. (1983). Cognitive and physiological processes in fear appeals and attitude change: A revised theory of protection motivation. In J. T. Cacioppo & R. E. Petty (Eds.), *Social psychophysiology: A sourcebook* (pp. 153–176). New York: Guilford Press.

Skalski, P., Tamborini, R., Glazer, E., & Smith, S. (2009). Effects of humor on presence and recall of persuasive messages. *Communication Quarterly, 57,* 136-153.

Turner, M. M., Tamborini, R., Limon, M. S., & Zuckerman-Hyman, C. (2007). The moderators and mediators of door-in-the-face requests: Is it a negotiation or a helping experience? *Communication Monographs, 74,* 333–356.

Turner, M. M. & Underhill, J. C. (2012). Motivating emergency preparedness behaviors: The differential effects of guilt appeals and actually anticipating guilty feelings. *Communication Quarterly, 60,* 545-559.

Weinberger, M. G., & Gulas, C. S. (1992). The impact of humor in advertising: A review. *Journal of Advertising, 21,* 35–59.

Wilson, V. E. (2003). Perceived effectiveness of interpersonal persuasion strategies in computer-mediated communication. *Computers in Human Behavior, 19,* 537–552.

Witte, K. (1992). Putting the fear back into fear appeals: The extended parallel process model. *Communication Monographs, 59,* 329–349.

Witte, K. (1994). Fear control and danger control: A test of the extended parallel process model (EPPM). *Communication Monographs, 61,* 113–134.

Wong, C. H., & Cappella, J. N. (2009). Antismoking threat and efficacy appeals: Effects on smoking cessation intentions for smokers with low and high readiness to quit. *Journal of Applied Communication Research, 37*(1), 1–20.

Wood, W., & Quinn, J. M. (2003). Forewarned and forearmed? Two meta-analytic syntheses of forewarnings of influence appeals. *Psychological Bulletin, 129,* 119–138.

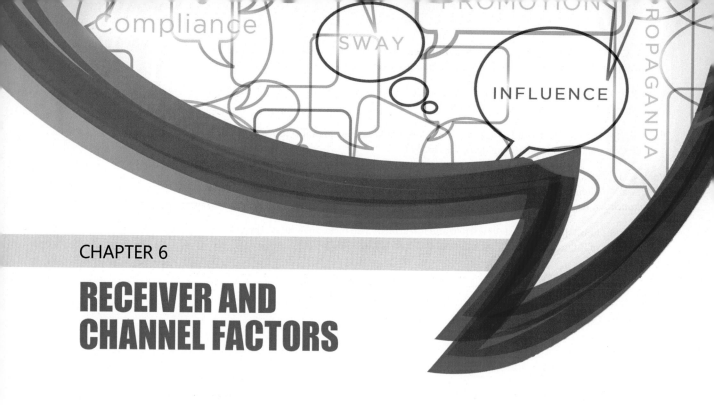

CHAPTER 6

RECEIVER AND CHANNEL FACTORS

Mila and Clive are in the audience at a political rally for the Democratic candidate for president of the United States. Both attentively listen to the 35-minute speech on foreign policy. As Mila and Clive leave the rally, they have the following conversation:

Mila: He is so right about the need for establishing closer relations with Iran!

Clive: No way! I think he is so wrong. He makes no sense at all!

Mila: He makes perfect sense. Before the rally, I would have said no way to establishing closer ties to Iran, but now I'm convinced.

Clive: I'm just the opposite. Before the rally, I had a pretty positive view of our Mideast relations, but after that speech, no way!

How is it that two people who heard the same message, at the same time, in the same situation, were influenced in different ways? How is it that a nation that heard the same political campaign messages in the 2016 presidential elections was so sharply divided into red and blue states? The message and the source were the same. What differed were the receivers. The previous two chapters focused on source and message factors that affect the persuasion process, but these factors do not explain why different receivers have different responses to the same message. Source and message characteristics have received the most research attention in part because the persuader can control the source and message factors. However, two other parts of the communication model affect the outcome of persuasive messages: receiver characteristics and message channel. Every practical guide for those engaging in persuasion suggests that audience analysis is a central factor in selecting the message source and designing the message content. This chapter explores the basis for those recommendations as it examines the role of receiver characteristics and channel factors, beginning with receiver characteristics that affect how and when individuals are influenced by persuasive messages.

LEARNING OBJECTIVES

- DESCRIBE AND EXPLAIN HOW RECEIVER CHARACTERISTICS INFLUENCE THE PERSUASION PROCESS.
- DESCRIBE AND DIFFERENTIATE PSYCHOLOGICAL, DEMOGRAPHIC, AND PHYSIOLOGICAL RECEIVER CHARACTERISTICS.
- USE PERSUASION THEORIES TO EXPLAIN WHY RECEIVERS RESPOND DIFFERENTLY TO PERSUASIVE MESSAGES.
- DESCRIBE CHANNEL FACTORS AND EXPLAIN HOW THEY INFLUENCE THE PERSUASION PROCESS.

Receiver characteristics are aspects of the target audience that influence how persuasive messages are processed and ultimately whether those messages succeed or fail. Receiver characteristics help us understand *how* to influence receivers and how different aspects of receiver experience affect responses to persuasive messages. In later chapters we will discuss the major persuasion theories, which emphasize the importance of understanding one's audience. This chapter will help you understand what aspects of your audience you need to understand. This understanding will be further expanded as you work through the theories presented in Chapters 7 through 11. Receiver characteristics include a variety of factors. We have organized them into two categories in this chapter: psychological characteristics and demographic characteristics. We discuss the impact of these receiver characteristics on persuasion and then address the role of channel factors in the persuasion process.

PSYCHOLOGICAL CHARACTERISTICS

Psychological characteristics of the receiver have received the most interest from persuasion researchers. Psychological characteristics are aspects of the receiver that vary according to some element of the audience's personality or other psychological state. Psychological characteristics influence how messages are perceived and processed. The psychological characteristics we discuss in this chapter are self-esteem, self-monitoring, and involvement but this does not exhaust the possible list.

SELF-ESTEEM AND SELF-EFFICACY

Two psychological characteristics that have been studied extensively are **self-esteem** and **self-efficacy**. Self-esteem refers to people's positive or negative attitude toward themselves (Rosenberg, 1965). People with high levels of self-esteem like and respect themselves (Crandall, 1973). They tend to be confident, optimistic, capable, and think positively about themselves. People who have low levels of self-esteem tend to feel inadequate, pessimistic, and anxious, and think negatively about themselves. Self-esteem is generally measured with a paper-and-pencil test that asks respondents to self-report their level of self-esteem. Self-esteem is similar to self-efficacy, which was discussed in Chapter 5 as a key dimension of the extended parallel process model. Where self-esteem refers to how a person feels about his or her value, self-efficacy refers to how able a person feels to perform some behavior. Self-esteem and self-efficacy are related to one another but describe different aspects of an audience. Self-efficacy is specific to a particular behavior, whereas self-esteem is more global. Self-efficacy has emerged as an important concept in persuasion, but there are also several interesting conclusions from research on the effects of self-esteem on persuasion.

Who would you expect to be easier to persuade: people with low, moderate, or high self-esteem? Many would expect people with low self-esteem to be easiest to persuade, because low self-esteem individuals would lack faith in their own judgments. You might expect persuasion to become more difficult as self-esteem increased. If this were the case, we would describe self-esteem and attitude change as having a linear relationship, as illustrated in Panel A of Figure 6.1. You might be surprised to learn that people with moderate self-esteem are the easiest to persuade and that those with either low or high self-esteem are harder to persuade. Rhodes and Wood (1992) used a technique called meta-analysis to examine several studies that explored the role of self-esteem in persuasion. This method combines data from many studies to determine the overall effect of self-esteem on attitude change. Results indicated a curvilinear relationship in the shape of an inverted U between self-esteem and attitude change rather than a linear relationship. This curvilinear relationship between self-esteem and attitude change is illustrated in Panel B of Figure 6.1. Thus, those highest and lowest in self-esteem are less likely to respond to influence attempts than those with moderate self-esteem.

The obvious next question to ask is why this pattern exists. Recall from earlier discussion that getting your audience's attention is an important first step to successful persuasion. An audience has to attend to a message before they can comprehend it. McGuire (1968) argues that people with low self-esteem are less likely to pay attention to the message and understand the content, so they are less persuaded. On the other hand, people with high self-esteem are more likely to understand the message content, but they have more faith in their own judgments and are less open to influence attempts. Thus, moderate self-esteem individuals are most open to being influenced through persuasive messages.

Meta-analysis may have found an overall curvilinear relationship between self-esteem and attitude change, but other factors are also involved. One such factor is the quality of the message. Skolnick and Heslin (1971) state that people with high self-esteem are more persuaded by high-quality arguments than low-quality arguments, whereas those with low self-esteem do not distinguish between high-and low-quality arguments. In a survey of prior studies, they found support for this claim. This finding is also consistent with McGuire's (1968) explanation that low self-esteem individuals pay less attention to the content of the message.

Johnston (1994) argues that the type of appeal used also influences how individuals with low and high self-esteem respond to a message. She suggests that those low in self-esteem are more influenced by messages based on appeals of acceptance and social belonging. Low self-esteem individuals typically have stronger needs for belonging than do high self-esteem individuals. The strong need for belonging makes low self-esteem individuals more vulnerable to appeals that suggest that complying with the persuasive message will result in being more loved, being more respected, belonging to the group, or overall societal acceptance. Johnston suggests that this is the reason people with low self-esteem are more susceptible to cult appeals that represent love and belonging for going along with cult principles.

Self-esteem also influences how individuals respond to fear appeals, which were discussed in Chapter 5. Leventhal (1970) found that high-fear appeals could be successfully used with individuals high in self-esteem, but that high-fear appeals failed with receivers with low self-esteem. Kim Witte's EPPM model discussed in Chapter 5 offers a good explanation for this phenomenon. High self-esteem receivers are confident enough to move into a danger control response mode, face the danger, and deal with it. Low self-esteem receivers tend to adopt a fear control response, because they lack the self-efficacy to deal with the threat. One's level of self-esteem can affect a person's level of self-efficacy for the behavior in question. Song, Peng, and Lee (2011) found that participants who were dissatisfied with their body image (low self-esteem with regard to body image) had lower exercise self-efficacy when they saw an image of themselves exercising. For participants who were more satisfied with their body, their exercise self-efficacy was unaffected by seeing themselves exercise. It makes sense that self-esteem would be related to self-efficacy. The more positively you feel about yourself, the more confident and capable you are likely to feel about performing a specific behavior.

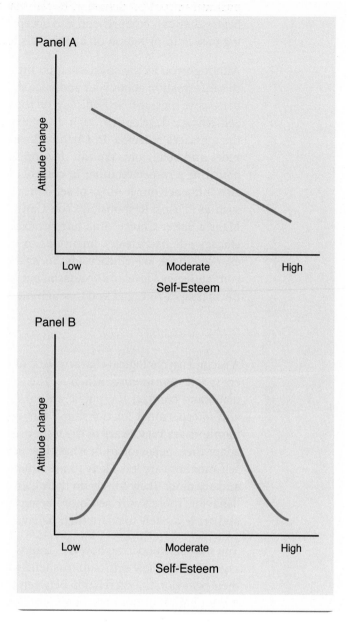

FIGURE 6.1 Self-esteem and attitude change.

High self-efficacy is also related to information seeking behavior (Thompson, Bevan, & Sparks, 2012). People with higher self-efficacy for a given behavior are more likely to seek information related to behavior. In health contexts, seeking information is often an important behavior. Recall that the audience must attend to the message before they can comprehend and accept the message. If your audience is more willing to seek information on a topic, it is likely easier to get their attention.

Although you as the source can do little to change a person's self-esteem, knowing this information about your audience should be considered when you are designing a persuasive message. Self-efficacy, on the other hand, can be influenced by the source. Self-efficacy develops through direct experience, vicarious experience, and through the messages received. In Chapter 2 we discussed modeling as a way we learn attitudes and behaviors. We can develop self-efficacy for a behavior by observing and modeling a respected other in control of the behavior. The messages we receive can also influence our feelings of self-efficacy. Lee (2010) inserted self-efficacy messages such as "Drink Responsibly, You Can Change," "You're in Charge," and "You Can Make a Better Choice" into humorous alcohol ads. Participants exposed to the high efficacy ads had greater intentions to change their drinking behaviors than those exposed to the low efficacy ads. So, as the source, there is little you can do to change your audience's level of *self-esteem*, but you can influence feelings of *self-efficacy* with the messages you send and through modeling.

SELF-MONITORING

A second psychological characteristic of receivers that has been explored by researchers is **self-monitoring**, which is "the extent to which people monitor (observe, regulate, and control) the public appearances of self they display in social situations and interpersonal relationships" (Snyder, 1987, pp. 4–5). Those who are high self-monitors are very aware of the response of others to their behavior, and they tend to adapt their behavior to fit what they perceive to be the needs of the situation. Low self-monitors are less likely to use situational and social cues to guide their behavior and are more likely to rely on their own attitudes, beliefs, and feelings to guide their behavior. Those low in self-monitoring tend to pay less attention to what others think and are less likely to adapt their behavior to the environment.

You may be wondering how this trait would affect one's response to persuasive messages. Because low self-monitors tend to rely on their attitudes and beliefs to guide their behavior, the correlation between their attitudes and behaviors is stronger than it is for high self-monitors. High self-monitors are very aware of social responses and vary their behavior to fit situations, so their behavior is less likely to be consistent with their attitudes. Thus, high self-monitors tend to have a lower correlation between attitudes and behavior (Snyder, 1982; Snyder & Swann, 1976; Snyder & Tanke, 1976).

The implications of self-monitoring go beyond attitude-behavior consistency. High and low self-monitors also respond differently to message appeals. In Chapter 2, we discussed the different functions that attitudes hold for receivers (ego-defensive, knowledge, utilitarian, social-adjustive, and value-expressive). DeBono (1987) found that high self-monitors' attitudes serve a different function than do low self-monitors' attitudes. High self-monitors' attitudes often serve a **social-adjustive** function. Recall that attitudes serving the social-adjustive function help us relate to those around us. High self-monitors use attitudes that help them respond to situations in ways that fit the expectations of those around them. These attitudes help high self-monitors fit in with others. On the other hand, attitudes held by low self-monitors often serve a **value-expressive** function. These attitudes help low self-monitors express their own values rather than altering them to fit each situation. Therefore high and low self-monitors respond differently to persuasive messages.

DeBono (1987) conducted a study that attempted to persuade receivers that people with mental illness should be treated in hospitals and institutions. A pretest found that most students were opposed to this position and preferred treatment without institutionalization. DeBono had research participants fill out questionnaires to determine their level of self-monitoring. Both high and low self-monitors were then exposed to one of two messages attributed to the same source: a professor from the University of Nebraska. One of the messages used a social-adjustive appeal by telling receivers that about 70 percent of students polled supported treating people with mental illness in hospitals and institutions. The other message used a value-expressive appeal, indicating that the values of responsibility and love toward the patients supported the need to treat those with mental illness in hospitals and institutions. After hearing the message, the participants filled out questionnaires where they reported their attitudes about treatment of people with mental illness. As DeBono predicted, the high self-monitors changed their attitude toward treatment of mental illness when they received the social-adjustive message, whereas the low self-monitors changed their attitude more when exposed to the value-expressive message. High self-monitors were more influenced by knowing what others thought than by the values expressed in the message and chose to alter their attitudes toward the position of the perceived majority. Low self-monitors were less influenced by what others thought and more influenced by a value-laden message. Thus, knowing whether receivers are high or low self-monitors can help a persuader adapt the message to fit the needs of the receivers.

This difference in approach between receivers high and low in self-monitoring has practical implications for those engaged in persuasion. Advertisers, politicians, and social interest groups can vary messages according to the characteristics of their audiences. Snyder and DeBono (1985) found that the social-adjustive function that is important to high self-monitors translates into an appreciation of image appeals in advertising, whereas the value-expressive attitude function for low self-monitors resulted in greater response to messages about product quality in advertisements. In research examining ads for whiskey, cigarettes, and coffee, high self-monitors had more positive attitudes and were more likely to purchase the products when exposed to a message using image appeal. This tactic was less effective for low self-monitors. Low self-monitors reported more favorable attitudes toward the products and stronger behavioral intentions to purchase the product after being exposed to messages about the quality of the product. Similarly, high self-monitors were willing to pay more for products sold with an image-based advertisement, whereas low self-monitors were willing to pay more for products represented as high quality in advertisements. Of course, gathering information about the self-monitoring of receivers is easy in a laboratory situation when participants fill out questionnaires for the researchers. It is much harder to gather data about the level of self-monitoring for general audiences who do not fill out questionnaires before persuasive messages are presented to them. Advertisers either have to generalize their audience characteristics from research on a sample, or cover all the options by developing both image-based and quality-based advertisements for products, candidates, and issues.

INVOLVEMENT

A third receiver characteristic in the psychological category that has received considerable research attention is **involvement**. Involvement is sometimes referred to as ego-involvement, as you will see in Chapter 8 when we discuss social judgment theory. Involvement will again be discussed in Chapter 11 on the elaboration likelihood model. The concept of involvement has been manipulated in research by stressing the importance of the task to the individual, by letting the individual know that he or she has a personal stake or something to gain or lose with the issue, or by using self-report measures of commitment to the topic. Receivers who have higher levels of involvement perceive the task as being more important, recognize a personal stake in the issue, and/or report themselves as being very concerned about the issue. Low-involvement receivers fail to find the task or issue significant, fail to see any personal stake in the issue, and/or report themselves as being unconcerned about the topic.

These different approaches to involvement have resulted in different predictions and results. Social judgment theory predicts that increased receiver ego-involvement reduces persuasion. Elaboration likelihood model predicts that increased personal involvement will increase persuasion if the audience is exposed to high quality, informative messages. These two theories make opposite predictions, but before you get frustrated, let's take a closer look at these two approaches.

Involvement has been defined differently within different theories. Social judgment theory defines *ego-involvement* as "a person's commitment to an issue and is related to a person's self-concept and self-esteem." Alternatively, elaboration likelihood model defines *personal involvement* as "the extent a topic is important or of value to a receiver." So, just what is it that we mean by *involvement*? Johnson and Eagly (1989) conducted a meta-analysis of the research on involvement and examined the different ways involvement was defined. They identified three ways that involvement has been defined: **value-relevant**, **outcome-relevant**, and **impression-relevant** involvement. Involvement works differently in the persuasion process depending on how it is defined and measured, as explained in Table 6.1.

Value-relevant involvement is equivalent to ego-involvement, which refers to a person's level of personal commitment to a topic. When value-relevant involvement is high, a person's self-concept is engaged with the topic. For example, when a person who has high value-relevant involvement in the anti-abortion topic defines themselves as a "pro-lifer," their views toward abortion are a part of their identity.

Outcome-relevant involvement is the most common way of defining involvement and probably the easiest for persuaders to measure and influence. The audience level of outcome-relevant involvement clearly impacts how receivers respond to a message. For example, receivers who have high outcome-relevant involvement in a topic tend to be more open to inoculation (see Chapter 5) against counter-persuasion,

TABLE 6.1 *TYPES OF INVOLVEMENT*

LABEL	DEFINITION	THEORY DRAWN FROM	FINDINGS
Value-Relevant Involvement	Ego-involvement; deals with central or core values of the individual; religious or controversial social issues such as abortion that are grounded in core values are topics that would use value-relevant involvement.	Social judgment theory	When value-relevant involvement (or ego-involvement) is high, persuasion is difficult regardless of message quality.
Outcome-Relevant Involvement	Personal involvement; based on how relevant the outcomes of the message are to the receiver; ELM research on comprehensive exams for college students involved outcome-relevant involvement.	Elaboration likelihood model (ELM)	When outcome-relevant involvement is high, persuasion is enhanced when strong arguments are used but reduced with weak arguments.
Impression-Relevant Involvement	Receivers' desire to express attitudes that are socially desirable; researchers convince subjects that attitudes and/or behaviors will be made public; asking students to publicly report racial attitudes results in impression-relevant involvement.	Impression management theory	When impression-relevant involvement is high, slightly harder to persuade than low levels of involvement.

thus making the effects of the persuasive message more enduring (Pfau et al., 1996). Outcome-relevant involvement influences what a person pays attention to and how much effort they are willing to put into understanding the message. When involvement is high, people are more interested in the topic, pay more attention, and think about the message more. If involvement is low, the opposite occurs. Think about the topics that are most important to you. If something related to these topics pops up on Twitter, Facebook, or any other media, your attention is piqued and you are more apt to take time to read the message.

Sawyer (1988) argued that outcome-relevant involvement affects whether advertisers should include explicit conclusions in persuasive messages or allow receivers to draw their own conclusions (implicit conclusion). For more highly involved receivers, using an implicit conclusion where receivers can draw the conclusion themselves is more effective than drawing the conclusion explicitly. For low-involvement receivers, the explicit conclusions are more effective than implicit conclusions. Thus, persuaders need to consider the level of receiver involvement in their topic or object before deciding how to structure the message conclusion.

Thus, receiver involvement in a topic or outcome is a characteristic that can significantly influence how messages are processed. Persuaders would be wise to take the level of receiver involvement into account in designing messages. Social judgment theory and the elaboration likelihood model offer guidance about how to adapt to receiver involvement levels, and successful persuaders will draw on these theoretical approaches to enhance their chances of success. Also, the way a message is structured and the arguments used can enhance the outcome relevant involvement of an audience.

Self-esteem, self-monitoring, and involvement are not an exhaustive list of psychological characteristics that can influence persuasion; however, these variables have received the most research attention. As mentioned previously, obtaining this information about an audience is often difficult. However, the source who knows his or her audience best is usually the most successful. Fortunately, not all receiver variables are as difficult to identify as the psychological characteristics.

DEMOGRAPHIC CHARACTERISTICS

Some receiver characteristics are quite visible and have been observed by census takers and others interested in society. Such characteristics are often referred to as **demographic characteristics**. Demographic characteristics are factors such as the sex, age, education, income, marital status, and cultural aspects of the targeted receivers. Unlike the psychological characteristics, demographic aspects of the audience are often obvious and can be obtained by conducting limited research on the chosen population. Marketers often collect a great deal of demographic information about their customers. A primary purpose of "reward programs" is the collection of demographic characteristics and buying behavior. With the development of powerful database software, marketers are able to track customer buying patterns and link those patterns to demographic characteristics. Three demographic characteristics that have received attention by persuaders are sex, age, and culture and are discussed in this chapter.

BIOLOGICAL SEX

The demographic characteristic that has received the most attention is receiver **sex**. There have been long-standing debates about whether males or females are easier to persuade. Historically, researchers concluded that women were easier to persuade than men (Cronkhite, 1969; Scheidel, 1963). Indeed, early researchers seemed generally to draw that conclusion. Most studies conducted before 1970 found women easier to persuade. Later research was far less likely to find this pattern (Eagly, 1978). This pattern led some scholars to suggest that the ability to influence was tied to cultural expectations and that as women's role in society changed, so did their response to persuasive messages.

This explanation was not satisfactory to everyone; therefore, further research was conducted. Eagly and Carli (1981) conducted a meta-analysis of studies that investigated sex differences in persuadability and conformity to group pressure. Eagly and Carli found a very small effect for women being more open to influence than men, but it was so small that it did not carry much weight. They found that effect accounted for less than 1 percent of the variance, which means it is a factor that has little meaning in social influence settings. A slightly more pronounced effect, however, was found for conformity in the presence of group pressure, which could be the result of women valuing relational harmony more and/or avoiding conflict more. This meant that women were more likely to comply with group pressure than men, but this effect was also very small.

The influence of receiver sex has received renewed attention as computer-mediated communication and its effect on persuasion have been investigated. Guadagno and Cialdini (2002) conducted two studies looking at the persuasive effects of e-mail versus face-to-face communication. They found in both studies that females changed their minds less often with the e-mail messages than in face-to-face situations, but that male changes in position did not differ according to the method of communication. These researchers argued that this difference was a result of women's social focus in their communication patterns, and that social cues and the values of relational harmony accounted for the differences. These differences were small, however, and the quality of the message still accounted for most of the persuasive impact for both males and females.

There is little evidence that there are general persuasion differences between men and women or, in other words, differences that hold up across persuasion topics and situations. Differences between men and women are likely much more topic or context specific. For instance, in a study of online shopping, Naseri (2011) found that overall men were more likely to make online purchases, but that it differed by product. Women were more likely to buy food, clothing, shoes, and entertainment services, whereas men were more likely to buy DVDs, financial services, computer hardware and software, and sporting equipment. Thus, sex is a factor in receiver response to messages; however, those differences are often better explained by social roles and what is personally relevant to men and women.

Although male and female receivers do not differ much in how they respond to messages in general, receivers do respond differently to male and female sources. Ward, Seccombe, Bendel, and Carter (1985) note that most sources in early research were men. These researchers suggest a cross-sex effect, where women are more persuaded by male sources than by female sources. This finding has been replicated more recently in studies examining the use of avatars and virtual sources in computer-mediated communication. Zanbaka, Goolkasian, and Hodges (2006) found that virtual characters with male or female human voices were as persuasive as real characters and that male receivers were more influenced by female sources, whereas female receivers were more persuaded by male speakers. Thus, the sex of the message source can influence the message recipient on the basis of an interaction of the two.

AGE

The **age** of the receiver is a second demographic characteristic that plays a role in how receivers respond to persuasive messages. We have all heard stereotypes and adages that imply differences in the ease of persuading based on age. "You can't teach an old dog new tricks" suggests that older people are resistant to new information, whereas "as easy as taking candy from a baby" implies that young children are easy to persuade. There is some truth behind these sayings.

Research shows that children between ages 3 and 7 are very open to persuasion in advertising settings—particularly if it involves a popular celebrity endorsing a product (Meringoff & Lesser, 1980). Children are not as able as adults to critically listen and process messages. They also have less experience to draw on in interpreting and evaluating a message. As a result, children look for simple ways to determine if they should believe a message. If the source is attractive, respected, admired, or an authority figure, children are more apt to believe the message. Advertisers certainly believe that children can be persuaded; they spend literally billions of dollars to reach this group.

At the other end of the age spectrum, scholars have argued that older people are difficult to persuade. Krosnick and Alwin (1989) suggest that older people have already processed much information and formed attitudes and beliefs so they have a more stable frame of reference. This stability makes them less open to new ideas. This argument certainly makes sense, and it does explain some limitations in persuading older individuals. However, the elderly are consistently victimized by scams and deceptive advertising. Older individuals as a group are vulnerable to scams designed to bilk them out of their money. Additionally, a huge amount of advertising is targeted at older Americans. Thus, we need to look at *what* influences this age group rather than *if* they are capable of being influenced.

Greco (1988) surveyed advertisers about their experiences with targeting older consumers. He reported that a majority of advertising practitioners found elderly spokespeople to be particularly effective in targeting elderly audiences for some products such as health issues, medicines, travel services, insurance, and financial services. In addition, these advertisers reported the use of elderly spokespeople added credibility for older consumers and helped draw attention to the products being advertised. This is evident in many drug advertisements. Drug advertising often targets older people and employs older models, as well as uses music and themes that are relevant to an older audience. Similar to sex, we can't make sweeping generalizations about how older people are different from younger people. Rather, there are likely to be differences based in experience, expectations, and interests.

People of different ages are also motivated by different things. A study by Omoto, Snyder, and Martino (2000) examined two types of messages attempting to persuade people to volunteer their time. One message attempted to motivate receivers by emphasizing the potential for developing interpersonal relationships through the volunteer experience. The second message attempted to motivate receivers by emphasizing community obligations. Omoto and his colleagues found that younger adults were more likely to volunteer when exposed to the interpersonal relationships message, whereas older adults were more motivated to volunteer when exposed to the obligations message. Thus, age plays a role in how receivers respond to messages. Once again, understanding one's audience and tailoring the message to the characteristics of the audience is important for success.

CULTURE

The vast majority of research discussed up to this point has focused on Western culture, following a predominantly Eurocentric model. Certainly some aspects of persuasion cross cultures, but, even within the United States, different subcultures respond differently to persuasive messages. **Culture** has been defined in numerous ways; however, we use Marsella's (1994) definition to frame our discussion.

Culture is shared learned behavior which is transmitted from one generation to another for purposes of promoting individual and social survival, adaptation, and growth and development. Culture has both external (e.g., artifacts, roles, institutions) and internal representations (e.g., values, attitudes, beliefs, cognitive/affective/sensory styles, consciousness patterns, and epistemologies).

Note in the definition that attitudes, beliefs, and behaviors are a part of culture and part of what distinguishes one culture from another. Therefore, different cultures will approach a message with different attitudes, beliefs, and experiences, resulting in cultures responding to the message differently. Thus, culture is a demographic receiver variable that wise persuaders will take into account when constructing persuasive messages.

As indicated in Marsella's definition, cultural factors are broad and varied and include religion, ethnic origin, geography, and economic class, among others. Even groups that share a religious orientation such as Christianity may not interpret a message in the same way because of other cultural differences. For example, many people still wrestle with the issue of same-sex marriage. Within the United States, Christian religious principles are often employed to support a ban on such marriages; however, other cultures that are also predominantly Christian, such as Canada and The Netherlands, interpret the issue of same-sex marriage quite differently.

Understanding the values of the culture or subculture to be targeted can help persuaders better adapt their messages and be more successful. For example, Han and Shavitt (1994) compared American and Korean responses to advertising slogans. The American culture values individualism, whereas the Korean culture values collectivism. Individualistic cultures emphasize the individual and independence, whereas collectivist cultures emphasize the group and supporting one's in-group. Han and Shavitt compared responses to two types of slogans. The first cluster contained slogans like, "the art of being unique" and "a leader among leaders." The second cluster had slogans like "we have a way of bringing people closer together" and "sharing is beautiful." The slogans that emphasized individualism were more effective in persuading Americans than Koreans, whereas the slogans that emphasized the group were more effective for persuading Koreans than Americans.

In a similar study, but focusing on the workplace rather than advertising, Fu and Yukl (2000) compared managers in China and the United States. Fu and Yukl were interested in what kinds of persuasive strategies were preferred by Chinese managers in comparison to American managers. Chinese managers emphasized groups and giving gifts, which is consistent with the collectivist and particularist nature of the Chinese culture. Alternatively, American managers preferred rational persuasion, which is consistent with the individualistic and universalistic nature of the U.S. culture. The strategies used by Chinese and American managers represent two very different approaches to persuasion. These differences have also been observed in interpersonal persuasion. In attempting to persuade a roommate to be quieter (Wiseman et al., 1995), Americans chose direct strategies such as, "You are making too much noise. Please be quiet." Chinese, however, chose less direct strategies and offered hints such as remarks about the enjoyment of quiet times or more group-valued approaches such as "Your noisiness shows a lack of consideration for others" (Wiseman et al., 1995). Thus, successful persuaders must understand the value system of the culture or subculture they are targeting for their persuasive messages to be effective. Culture has a tremendous impact on how we interpret messages. Persuaders who fail to appreciate the role of culture are likely to fail at persuasion when interacting with people who are culturally different from themselves. With the global nature of the business world and the increasing diversity within our society, persuaders of all types need to understand the cultural dimensions and characteristics of their audiences.

A common theme running through our discussion of receiver characteristics is that people with different characteristics have different needs, perspectives, experiences, and/or roles. In the following chapters on persuasion theory we will discuss how people process persuasive messages. How we process a message is influenced by what kinds of things we find relevant or involving, or that we feel personally responsible for, and these vary depending on who we are (male or female), our education, our culture, our age, and whether we are married and have children, etc. So, our personality and demographic characteristics often make a difference, because they influence what we view as relevant, important, involving, as well as what experiences and knowledge we have. The real value of understanding your audience is that it increases your ability to create a message that is relevant, involving, or addresses an information need of your audience. We often want to target large groups of people when we create persuasive messages, but we need to realize that the more diverse our audience, the more difficult it is to find a single message that is meaningful to everyone. Marketing, public relations, and public health professionals recognize this and often seek to segment their audience into smaller groups that have more in common and then target messages to those segments.

AUDIENCE SEGMENTATION AND TARGETED MESSAGES

At this point we have discussed several receiver characteristics and repeatedly recommended that sources consider these characteristics when developing messages. Different people respond to different messages—Figure 6.2 is a humorous illustration of this point. You need to understand your audience to develop messages that they will respond to. Because one message won't work for everyone, audiences are often segmented into smaller groups. An **audience segment** is a subgroup of the audience that has similar needs, wants, or characteristics that distinguish it from other segments. Segmentation first involves determining what variables to use to create the segments. Segmentation may be based on psychological characteristics like those discussed earlier, on demographics, or on a theoretical basis such as the theory of reasoned action (see Chapter 10). As we will discuss in Chapter 10, the theory of reasoned action directs us to understand an audiences' beliefs about a specific behavior and the social pressures the audience is experiencing to either perform or not perform the behavior. So, this theory directs us to segment our audience based on similar behavior beliefs and social pressures. The goal is to use variables that identify an audience segment that makes sense and is useful in achieving your persuasive goals. You can throw any number of variables into the pot and come out with a segment. But, unless that segment is a subgroup of your audience that makes sense

Baby Blues Partnership, King Features Syndicate.

FIGURE 6.2 Baby Blues.

for you to target and you are able to target successfully, the segmentation process is a waste of time. Segmentation is really a rather complex process and is a major topic in marketing and strategic communication. Professional persuaders often collaborate with these researchers to leverage their expertise with segmentation.

Once you have determined what variables to use in segmenting your audience, you must determine how to gather that information, or, in other words, how to analyze your audience. Sometimes audience analysis involves conducting original research in which you survey or interview a sample of the population you are interested in. If you have taken a research methods course, you are familiar with what is involved. Audience analysis may also involve using the research that others have conducted. Numerous research and marketing firms specialize in gathering information on audience characteristics (e.g., demographics, attitudes, beliefs, behaviors). The purpose of the audience analysis is learning the specific characteristics that make the target audience unique from other targets and then using that information in the development and delivery of your messages.

Audience analysis can be done in a variety of ways. Cameron et al. (2009) used focus groups to develop an in-depth understanding of beliefs about getting a flu shot among urban African American senior citizens. Influenza is a serious illness, particularly for the elderly and those with other health issues. Every year, the Centers for Disease Control and Prevention (CDC) releases information about the upcoming flu season and recommends that certain groups obtain a flu shot. African American seniors (65 and older) are less likely to receive a flu shot than white seniors. Cameron and colleagues identified a target audience of Midwestern, urban, African American seniors and conducted a series of focus groups as their method for understanding this segment. Cameron et al. relied on the extended parallel process model (EPPM) for the basis of the questions they used to facilitate discussion in the focus groups. Recall that EPPM indicates that effective messages stimulate a danger control response and include both threat and efficacy (see Chapter 5). The focus group protocol was designed to elicit information about knowledge and attitudes about influenza, past experiences with the flu shot, and reasons for choosing to either receive or forego being vaccinated, with the overall goal of understanding the audiences' perceptions of severity, susceptibility, response efficacy, and self-efficacy regarding the flu shot. Cameron and her colleagues analyzed the responses, identified knowledge and belief themes, and then developed messages to address each theme. Table 6.2 provides some examples of these messages and illustrates how data from an audience analysis is used to create messages.

Once the audience analysis is complete, persuaders may create completely different messages and campaigns for different segments. Alternatively, they may make more subtle changes to make their message more appealing to each segment. If you pick up magazines that are targeted at different audience segments, you may find different versions of the same message that are tailored to each magazine's audience. For example, Autism Speaks created a series of ads to increase the awareness of the frequency of autism. A typical ad featured a child engaged in an activity and the message presented the odds of becoming a professional or Olympic athlete and the odds of a child being diagnosed with autism. The ad that appeared in *Business Week*, a business news magazine targeted at a diverse, but primarily white, group of business owners, used an ad of a little girl in a ballerina pose in silhouette so that no racial features were distinguishable. The ad that appeared in *Black Enterprise*, a magazine targeted at African American families, professionals, and aspiring professionals, featured an African American boy swinging a baseball bat. Similarly, automakers have designed ads for the same car, but used different colors, settings, actors, and emphasized different qualities of the car to appeal to different audiences. It is not always clear what audience characteristics advertisers are targeting or using to create their

TABLE 6.2 *SUSCEPTIBILITY AND SELF-EFFICACY THEMES AND CORRESPONDING MESSAGES*

EPPM CONSTRUCT	THEME	MESSAGE
Perceived Susceptibility	Relevance of individual health status	Even healthy persons who are 65 and older are at risk for catching the flu.
	Age-related risks	As you get older, it gets harder for your body to fight the flu. Almost all of the people who die from the flu are 65 and older—just like you.
Perceived Severity	Influenza is an inconvenience, but not serious	Influenza is a serious lung infection that attacks millions of people every winter. Influenza, also called the flu, can kill you.
	Influenza can be incapacitating	Most people who get the flu feel horrible. The flu usually comes on suddenly and people have high fevers, severe headaches, extreme tiredness, a dry cough, and bad muscle aches. Often, people can't even get out of bed.
Perceived Self-Efficacy	Affordability of vaccine	Medicare covers the costs of annual influenza vaccination for all Medicare beneficiaries.
Perceived Response Efficacy	Vaccine prevents influenza or reduces severity and duration of symptoms	Getting your flu shot every year gives you the best possible protection against the flu. People who get the flu shot are much less likely to get the flu.
	Negative consequences of the vaccine	The flu shot cannot give you the flu, but some people may get a slight fever and feel a bit achy for a day or two after getting the shot. This happens because your body is working hard creating those antibodies to make you ready to fight off the flu.

Cameron et al. (2009)

messages, but it is clear that they are trying to adapt to their audience and appeal to specific characteristics. If you read magazines, look for one that is clearly targeted at a demographic group different than your own. Compare the ads with those in the magazines you typically read. You will likely find different ads for the same product. Both are examples of advertisers knowing their audience and creating messages to appeal to that audience.

Constructing messages designed to appeal to specific receiver groups is important, but the persuader also must decide how to deliver that message. The next section explores the impact that different channels of communication have on enhancing or inhibiting persuasive success.

CHANNEL FACTORS

You have analyzed your audience, perhaps identified a segment of your audience, drawn on theories and strategies of persuasion, and developed a message that appeals to your audience. Your next decision is the **channel**: how to send the message. The channel you choose for transmitting your message to your audience can also have an impact on the effectiveness of your message. The channel to be used is often a part of the audience analysis, because people often prefer one channel over another or find some channels more credible than others. Message delivery choices involve deciding whether your message should be written or oral, or face-to-face or mediated, and more often than not, several channels are used. The ways in which a message can be mediated have exploded in recent years. In the not too distant past, television, radio, and newspapers were the primary forms of media. With the development of the Internet and related technologies, the options for message dissemination have increased faster than our understanding of them. McLuhan (1964) argued "the medium is the message," and it is certainly part of the message with regard to persuasion. In this next section, we examine the traditional channels and new technology-based channels used to transmit messages. Additionally, we discuss a channel that has received much attention and is surrounded by misinformation and myth: subliminal messages. We separate the fact from the fiction and discuss what this phenomenon is really about.

MEDIUM

What was the most recent message you received? Most likely it was the previous sentence. How did you receive it? By reading this text of course. This text is an example of one of the oldest and most common media used to transmit messages. The term **medium** refers to the mode used to transmit the message from the source to the receiver and includes paper (newspapers, magazines, books), radio, television, e-mail, text, and Internet-based media such as Facebook and Twitter. The use of the Internet has grown dramatically over the past decade. In 2012, there were 2.27 billion Internet users across the world—more than double the number in 2007 (Pingdom, 2012). Internet-based media have created a host of new options for distribution of persuasive messages that are not filtered through established media outlets. Messages that appear in newspapers, magazines, radio, or television, must be deemed as *newsworthy*, or, alternatively, you must purchase advertising space to send a message clearly labeled as persuasion. The Internet offers persuaders access to mass communication, with few or no gatekeepers screening that information. The development of social media has created an entire new way of sharing information and reaching audience members that is far more interpersonal-like than traditional media. Another technological development, TiVo and DVR, that allows individuals to record television programming and skip over commercials, has changed television advertising and forced advertisers to develop news ways to get their ads in front of consumers.

You can probably list several media through which you've received messages today (e.g., Snapchat, face-to-face, Twitter, television, e-mail, texts). Which of these is the best? It is difficult to study differences in mediums because of the complexity of the differences between forms of communication. For example, if we were to compare a written format to a video and we kept the text of the message exactly the same, there are other differences beyond just the channel. The video format is visual. The nonverbal behaviors and physical appearance of the speaker are present in the video version but not in the written version of the message. Additionally, the receiver can control how quickly to receive the written message and can easily reread it. So, if we found differences in how persuaded an audience was between the two formats, we could not know for sure what was causing the difference. Was it the appearance or nonverbal behaviors of the speaker? Was it because the audience reread parts of the message? Internet-based channels introduce an additional set of differences between mediums. Messages can be placed on social media and websites in minutes or even seconds and can incorporate text and visuals in unique ways. But does this make them *more* effective than traditional mediums? Internet-based media have been compared to face-to-face communication. There are some conflicting results. Some studies find messages are equally persuasive in computer-mediated and face-to-face channels (Citera,1998; Hill & Monk, 2000). Other research, however, found that one-on-one persuasion is more effective when done face-to-face than when done through an Internet-based medium such as e-mail (Guadagno & Cialdini, 2002; Wilson, 2003). Comparing mediums is a little like comparing apples and oranges. They differ in several ways, which makes it impossible to know for sure why people react differently to them.

In reality, we rarely use the exact same language for a newspaper, a website, and television message. We automatically use more formal language in writing and tend to use more precise terms, whereas in oral messages we use less formal language, rounding of numbers, and shorter messages overall. Video messages include images—some moving and some still—but the visual component is combined with the verbal component to create the overall impact.

Despite this difficulty in comparing mediums, researchers have attempted to compare the persuasive impact of different forms of message delivery. Early research focused on the same message being presented in a written, audio-only, and video-taped format (Frandsen, 1963; Taylor & Thompson, 1982; Wilson, 1974). This research generated little support for one medium being more effective than another in overall persuasive impact. Of course, the message didn't change, and each format did not take full advantage of the potential offered by that medium. For example, the audio version included no sound effects and was just the audio portion of a person reading the message. The video format was the same person reading the message, but no additional visuals or visual effects were employed. Despite the lack of effects found in this early research, scholars were convinced of differences in persuasive outcomes among these mediums. More recent research suggests that including visual aids in presentations can enhance the persuasiveness of the message by up to 43 percent (Lynch & Golen, 2002). Do you think your response to the 2015–2016 bombings in Paris and Brussels would have been the same if you had only read about them in the newspaper and not seen the images on television and the Internet? What about the Arab Spring uprisings? Would your beliefs and interest in the events be different if you read about them only and never saw any of the corresponding video?

Chaiken and Eagly (1976) examined the interaction of message difficulty with channel on persuasion. They found that more difficult messages were most successful in changing attitudes when they were presented in a written format rather than an audio-only or video medium. The reverse was true for easy-to-understand messages. Easy messages were most effective when in a video format, followed by an audio format, and, the least effective channel, the written format. Why is this? To process a difficult message, the receiver needs the ability to think about the message in order to absorb it and to elaborate on it. The written format makes that more possible, because receivers can read it at their own pace, reread difficult sections, and pause when they need to think about an aspect of the message. The audio and video formats don't offer these options. The message is delivered once at the speaker's pace, and there is less (or no) opportunity to review difficult sections. The easy-to-understand message, however, doesn't need to be reviewed to be understood. It can be understood in the audio and video formats, and those media require less effort than the written format. For easy messages, Chaiken and Eagly (1976) found the videotaped version to be the easiest to follow, requiring the least amount of effort, making it easy for recipients to process the message. More recent research comparing testimonials and informational health messages, however, found that testimonials were more effective in an audio rather than a written format (Braverman, 2008). Low-involvement receivers who were more likely to minimally process messages attended to the vocal cues in the audio testimonials, making this format more effective.

When designing a persuasive message, you must consider the complexity of your message in relation to the medium you plan to use. There are times when you must use a certain medium to reach your audience. If you must use television, you must make your message simple and easy to process. If your message is complex, you need to communicate your message in writing. Campaigns frequently employ multiple media to reach the greatest number of people. As the source, you must be sure you adapt your message to the medium so that you take full advantage of what each medium has to offer.

In Chapter 4, we focused on source credibility, or, in other words, the believability of the source. The three major mediums also influence perceptions of credibility. Source credibility tends to be more persuasive in video rather than written messages. O'Keefe (2002) suggested that this may be caused in part by the additional information receivers have about the speaker in a video format where they can see the speaker, evaluate the voice and physical appearance, and draw on more nonverbal cues in assessing credibility than they can in a written format. Consistent with this, Chaiken and Eagly (1983) found that receivers' attitudes were not affected by the likeability of the source in written messages. In video and audio messages, however, likeability of the source had a significant impact on attitude change. The channel affects what information is available for the receiver to process and evaluate, and likely influences how motivated receivers process messages. Other research (Wanta & Hu, 1994; West, 1994) found that television overall is considered more credible than newspapers. However, the credibility of any particular medium varies for different audiences and also changes as technology changes and as technologies evolve from "new" to "mainstream." When the Internet was new, people did not generally trust information found online. Fogg, Lee, and Marshall (2002) examined how people evaluated websites for credibility. They found that the most significant factor, accounting for about 46 percent of the credibility judgment, was the design and visual appeal of the overall site. Interestingly, in all of the studies, factors such as customer service, clarity of information, and reliability weighed less than trust/credibility as a purchasing decision factor.

The topic of your message is another issue to consider when choosing a channel for communicating with your audience. For different topics, people are likely to rely more or less on different mediums of message delivery. A critical part of audience analysis involves finding out what channels are most credible for any particular group. For example, older Americans are more likely to read newspapers and rely on them for information than on television advertisements, whereas young children are more likely to be influenced by television (Bettinghaus & Cody, 1994). Some groups of people may rely on friends and family for information and not trust other channels. For example, DePietro and Clark (1984) found that teenagers relied more on peers and media for health information. Similarly, Freimuth and Marron (1978) found that elders rely more on face-to-face communication with their doctors, whereas poorer people are more likely to get their health information from television. An ongoing goal for those in public health is to persuade individuals to take better care of their health and to request certain kinds of treatments or drugs. The effectiveness of these efforts depends in part on selecting the most credible channels for delivery of the persuasive messages. Campaigns that have used multiple channels to reinforce messages, such as public service announcements being reinforced in face-to-face interactions with healthcare providers, have been the most successful. Thus, the topic of your persuasive message, along with the complexity of your message and the credibility of the channel, must be considered when choosing a channel to communicate with your audience.

The medium options have changed dramatically over the past 20 years. Each medium offers certain advantages and disadvantages. Additionally, different segments of the population prefer certain media and trust some media over others. The challenge for the persuader is to figure out what medium will best communicate the message. Some mediums work well for long complex messages; others work best for simple messages. It is important to keep in mind that, regardless of the medium used, the audience must pay attention and comprehend the message. The source and message factors discussed in Chapters 4 and 5 are central to persuasion and must be adapted to the chosen medium. The upcoming chapters on persuasion theory explain how people process messages and provide strategies for creating messages and influencing the audience. These all can be adapted to various media.

There is one more channel that we want to discuss. You have probably heard of this channel, but odds are that you don't understand it as well as you think you do. The subliminal channel is grossly misunderstood and is surrounded by much myth. Additionally, the word *subliminal* is often misused. In this next section we explore this misunderstood channel.

THE SUBLIMINAL CHANNEL

What does the word *subliminal* mean to you? Many people associate this word with sex, unethical advertising, mind control, or other such tactics. **Subliminal** simply means below consciousness. In other words, if something is subliminal, you are not conscious of it. In some ways this isn't a channel at all, because both visual and auditory stimuli can be below consciousness. Rather, the area of subliminal influence describes a type of message, a channel, and phenomenon all its own. A subliminal message is a message that is present but not within your conscious awareness. Compare this to a **supraliminal** message, which is a message within your conscious awareness. The words on this page are a supraliminal message; you are conscious of seeing them. Subliminal messages and advertising first came into the public eye in the 1950s when James Vicary claimed to have flashed the words "EAT POPCORN" and "DRINK COKE" throughout the movie *Picnic* at a drive-in theater (McConnell, Cutler, & McNeil, 1958). Vicary claimed that the theater experienced higher than usual popcorn and Coke sales and that the increase was a result of the subliminal messages. There are three things to note about Vicary's experiment. He did not have a control group (a group that was not exposed to the subliminal message for comparison purposes), he did not indicate popcorn and Coke sales for other showings of the same movie, and the findings have never been replicated (research findings are generally not accepted until they have been repeated by different researchers). Also, consider the movie in which these messages were inserted. The movie *Picnic* showed people eating and going on a picnic. You don't suppose watching people eat could have influenced popcorn and Coke sales do you?

Despite the numerous problems with Vicary's experiment, people quickly began believing that advertisers frequently used subliminal messages in advertisements. This belief was further encouraged by a book written by Wilson Bryan Key (1972) that identified numerous advertisements that supposedly had subliminal messages embedded in them. Since then, a great deal of research has been conducted on subliminal messages and subliminal influence.

Two conclusions can be drawn from the research. First, subliminal messages influence attitudes under *very specific laboratory conditions*. Second, subliminal messages *do not influence attitudes under normal conditions*. Let's begin the discussion with when subliminal messages do work. Krosnick, Betz, Jussim, and Lynn's (1992) research is a good example. In this study, 34 students from Ohio State University were recruited and came to a laboratory. They were seated in front of a screen and asked to "keep your eyes on the center of the screen" (Krosnick et al., 1992, p. 155). Students were shown a series of nine photographs of a woman doing a variety of normal activities (e.g., getting into a car, grocery shopping, studying, sitting in a restaurant). Each slide was shown for 2 seconds. Immediately preceding each slide, half of participants were shown a positive-affect-arousing photo (e.g., a bridal couple, a young ring bearer, a group of people playing cards, a group of smiling friends), whereas the other half of participants were shown a negative-affect-arousing photo (e.g., a skull, a werewolf, a face on fire, a dead body). These positive- and negative-affect-arousing photos were shown for 13 milliseconds. After viewing the slides, participants were asked to rate the woman in the slides. Krosnick et al. report that not a single participant was aware of the affect-arousing photos and that, when told of the true nature of the study, all participants expressed surprise or disbelief. Krosnick and his colleagues' findings were surprising. Participants who had been exposed to the negative-affect-arousing subliminal photos rated the woman much more negatively than the participants who had been exposed to the positive-affect-arousing subliminal photos. Images the participants were not even aware of influenced their attitude toward the woman in the pictures. Krosnick et al. conducted a second study with a shorter exposure time to the subliminal message (9 milliseconds) and with stricter controls and found the same results. This and other studies have demonstrated that subliminal messages really can influence how we evaluate something.

The laboratory conditions present in Krosnick et al.'s study are common to most studies of subliminal perception that have been successful. One procedure that was important for the subliminal message to have an effect was that there be a minimum amount of supraliminal stimuli. One characteristic of the Krosnick et al. study was that the only supraliminal stimuli were slides. No video, no sound, just still pictures. A second important characteristic of the study was that the receivers were asked to devote a great deal of attention to the message. Recall that the participants were instructed to *keep their eyes on the center of the screen*. This focus was necessary so that the receivers didn't miss the subliminal message (remember, the subliminal message lasted for less than a quarter second—you blink and you miss it). The subliminal effect has only been found in controlled settings where other stimuli are minimized and receiver attention can be focused on the stimuli. Now, let's consider applying these results to the real world. In real-world settings, such as when you're watching television at home or reading online, are these two characteristics present when you see advertisements? If you're like most people, the answer is no. More often than not, we are doing two or more things at once, and there are multiple distractions—people are talking, dogs are barking, and so on. There is a great deal of supraliminal stimuli. We don't focus our attention closely on the advertisements. Our real life is not at all similar to the laboratory conditions necessary for the subliminal influence to occur. But, of course, researchers weren't satisfied. They wanted to see if subliminal messages can work in the "real world." One such real-world situation is self-help audio programs that use subliminal messages. See Figure 6.3 for a humorous example.

Google "Subliminal Self Help" to see the latest marketing efforts to take advantage people's misunderstanding of subliminal messages.

Subliminal audio programs that promise to help you lose weight, improve your memory, improve your self-esteem, stop smoking, and other things have become popular self-help methods. Do these programs really work? Pratkanis, Eskenazi, and Greenwald (1994) conducted a study to determine the effectiveness of two subliminal programs—one to improve memory and one to improve self-esteem. To test the effectiveness of the programs, Pratkanis et al. recruited 78 students and community members who were interested in improving their memory or self-esteem. Participants were pretested and then given a set of subliminal audiotapes, either self-esteem

FIGURE 6.3 Zits.

or memory programs. Half of the tapes were mislabeled so that half of the participants who thought they were receiving the self-esteem program were actually receiving the memory program and half of the participants who thought they were receiving the memory program were actually receiving the self-esteem program. Participants were asked to listen to the programs at least once per day and were also asked to keep a listening log.

As part of the pretest, participants were asked about their beliefs regarding subliminal self-help programs, and 77 of the 78 participants expressed a strong belief in the effectiveness of subliminal programs. After listening to the subliminal programs every day for a month, participants completed a self-esteem and memory posttest. Results indicated that participants' self-esteem and memory improved regardless of which program they listened to. In other words, participants' memories and self-esteem improved because they wanted it to, not because of the subliminal messages embedded in the programs. There was no relationship between increases in self-esteem or memory and what program had been listened to. Pratkanis and his colleagues concluded that self-esteem and memory were unaffected by either of the subliminal programs.

Although the idea of subliminal messages being hidden in advertisements and music to control people's thoughts is very enticing and makes for good science fiction, there is little credible evidence to indicate that subliminal messages are at all useful in influencing people in normal circumstances. Hal Shoup, executive vice president of the American Association of Advertising Agencies, said about subliminal messages, "Those of us who practice this business find it an enduring challenge to affect the conscious, much less try to worry [about] the subconscious" (Galvin, 1996). We want you to take two basic conclusions from this section. First,

First, subliminal messages can influence attitudes in very specific laboratory controlled circumstances.

Second, subliminal messages are useless in real-world persuasion situations like advertising, public relations, and public health campaigns.

FIGURE 6.4 Subliminal Influence Conclusions

subliminal messages can influence attitudes in *very* specific laboratory controlled circumstances. Second, subliminal messages are useless in real-world persuasion situations like advertising, public relations, and public health campaigns. If advertisers or other sources do use subliminal messages, you have little to fear, they'll have no impact on you.

SUMMARY

- Receiver characteristics and channel effects are two parts of the communication model that affect persuasion.
- Receiver characteristics that influence persuasive outcomes include psychological and demographic.
- Receiver psychological characteristics include self-esteem, self-monitoring, and involvement.
- Receiver demographic characteristics include sex, age, and culture.
- It is important to analyze your audience as completely as you can in order to design the most effective persuasive message.
- Channel factors interact with the topic, the level of message difficulty, and the credibility of the medium.
- Each medium has advantages and disadvantages that persuaders need to consider when creating persuasive messages.
- Subliminal stimuli are stimuli below a person's consciousness. Supraliminal stimuli are stimuli above a person's consciousness.
- For subliminal messages to be effective, supraliminal stimuli must be kept at a minimum, and the receiver's attention must be focused on the message.
- Subliminal messages have not been successful when used in actual persuasion situations.

KEY TERMS

Age—number of years old receivers are.

Audience segment—a subgroup of the audience that has similar needs, wants, or characteristics that distinguish it from other segments.

Channel—choice of delivery system for messages.

Culture—demographic receiver variable that includes things such as differences in religion, ethnic origin, economic class, and societal values of the group membership.

Demographic characteristics—factors such as sex, age, intelligence, and cultural aspects of receivers.

Impression-relevant involvement—involvement tied to the impression that the receiver's attitudes make on a public audience.

Involvement—occurs when receivers have a personal stake in the issue, something to gain or lose, the task is important, and/or the individual has a personal commitment to the issue.

Medium—the mode used to transmit the message from the source to the receiver.

Outcome-relevant involvement—involvement levels based on how relevant the outcomes are to the receivers.

aspects of the receiver that vary according to some element of the receiver's personality or psychological state.

Receiver—the recipient of a message.

Receiver characteristics—aspects of target audiences that influence how persuasive messages are processed and, ultimately, the success or failure of those messages.

Self-esteem—how confident, optimistic, and capable individuals perceive themselves to be.

Self-monitoring—how much an individual watches (or monitors) her or his own behavior and the response of others to it.

Sex—whether a receiver is a biological male or female.

Social-adjustive—attitudes held that help individuals fit the expectations of those around them.

Subliminal—awareness that is below consciousness.

Supraliminal—conscious awareness.

Value-expressive—attitudes held that help people express their own values.

Value-relevant involvement—deals with central or core values for individuals.

REVIEW QUESTIONS

1. What are psychological and demographic receiver characteristics? How does each affect persuasion?
2. What are the types of involvement? How do the different types affect persuasive outcomes?
3. Why should a persuader analyze the audience? How should it be done?
4. What is an audience segment?
5. What are channel factors?

6. What are advantages and disadvantages of print, audio, video, and Internet-based media?

7. What is a subliminal message and how does it differ from a supraliminal message?

8. What two conditions must be met for an attitude to be influenced by a subliminal message?

DISCUSSION QUESTIONS

1. Why do you think subliminal messages have received so much attention from society?

2. Would it be ethical to employ subliminal messages if research suggested it worked? What about more subtle touches in advertising such as air brushing and computer manipulation to create images beyond the reach of the target audience? At what point does persuasion have to be openly identified for it to be acceptable?

3. Think of some examples of fear appeals you are familiar with from advertising. What level of fear is being employed? For which level of self-esteem would this be appropriate?

4. Of what practical value is knowing that personality characteristics affect persuasive success and failure? Imagine you are working on a presidential political campaign. How could you find out the personality characteristics of your target audience?

5. What are the social norms for how women should persuade? How do they differ from social norms for men?

6. Find examples of advertising targeted toward senior citizens and children. Compare the ways the persuader adapted to the age of the recipient.

7. Gather advertisements targeted at different subcultures in the United States (e.g., different religious groups, economic classes, and/or ethnic origins). Compare the values reflected in the ads as well as differences in strategies.

8. How ethical is it to seek out receiver characteristic information, such as psychological characteristics, and then employ that knowledge to enhance persuasive success? Does that constitute an invasion of personal privacy? Does that turn persuasion into manipulation? What guidelines would you suggest for ethical use of audience analysis?

9. Pick a current persuasive context. It could be a current political campaign or social issue under debate. Identify who the primary target audience would be for that issue and conduct an audience analysis using as many of the receiver characteristic factors as you can. Then consider how you would tailor a persuasive message to be most effective for the characteristics you identified.

10. What kinds of channels most influence you? Does the answer vary according to the topic? If so, how?

11. Have you studied how to evaluate the credibility of Web pages? How often do you apply these lessons to your own Web surfing? How important in terms of potential consequences is the information you work with on the Internet?

REFERENCES

Bettinghaus, E. P., & Cody, M. J. (1994). *Persuasive communication* (5th ed.). Ft. Worth, TX: Harcourt Brace College Publishers.

Bostrom, R., & White, N. (1979). Does drinking weaken resistance? *Journal of Communication, 29,* 73–80.

Braverman, J. (2008). Testimonials versus informational persuasive messages: The moderating effect of delivery mode and personal involvement. *Communication Research, 35*(5), 666–694.

Cameron, K. A., Rintamaki, L. S., Kamanda-Kosseh, M., Noskin, G. A., Baker, D. W., & Makoul, G. (2009). Using theoretical constructs to identify key issues for targeted message design: African American seniors' perceptions about influenza and influenza vaccination. *Health Communication, 24,* 316–326.

Chaiken, S., & Eagly, A. H. (1976). Communication modality as a determinant of message persuasiveness and message comprehensibility. *Journal of Personality and Social Psychology, 34,* 605–614.

Chaiken, S., & Eagly, A. H. (1983). Communication modality as a determinant of persuasion: The role of communicator salience. *Journal of Personality and Social Psychology, 45,* 241–256.

Citera, M. (1998). Distributed teamwork—the impact of communication media on influence and decision quality. *Journal of American Society of Information Science, 49*(9), 792–800.

Cooper, J., Zanna, M., & Taves, P. (1978). Arousal as a necessary condition for attitude following induced compliance. *Journal of Personality and Social Psychology, 36,* 1101–1106.

Crandall, R. (1973). The measurement of self-esteem and related constructs. In J. P. Robinson & P. R. Shaver (Eds.), *Measures of social psychological attitudes* (pp. 45–167). Ann Arbor, MI: Institute for Social Research.

Cronkhite, G. (1969). *Persuasion: Speech and behavioral change.* Indianapolis: Bobbs-Merrill.

DeBono, K. G. (1987). Investigating the social-adjustive and value-expressive functions of attitudes: Implications for persuasion process. *Journal of Personality and Social Psychology, 52,* 279–287.

DePietro, R., & Clark, N. M. (1984). A sense-making approach to understanding adolescents' selection of health information sources. *Health Education Quarterly, 11,* 419–430.

Doney, P. M., & Cannon, J. P. (1997). An examination of the nature of trust in buyer-seller relationships. *Journal of Marketing, 61,* 35–51.

Eagly, A. H. (1978). Sex differences in influenceability. *Psychological Bulletin, 85,* 86–116.

Eagly, A. H. & Carli, L. L. (1981). Sex of researchers and sex-typed communications as determinants of sex differences in influenceability: A meta-analysis of social influence studies. *Psychological Bulletin, 90,* 1–20.

Eagly, A. H., & Warren, R. (1976). Intelligence, comprehension, and opinion change. *Journal of Personality, 44,* 226–242.

Fogg, B. J., Lee, E., & Marshall, J. (2002). Interactive technology and persuasion. In J. P. Dillard & M. Pfau (Eds.), *The persuasion handbook: Developments in theory and practice* (pp. 765–788). Thousand Oaks, CA: Sage.

Frandsen, K. D. (1963). Effects of threat appeals and media of transmission. *Speech Monographs, 30,* 101–104.

Freimuth, V. S., & Marron, T. (1978). The public's use of health information. *Health Education, 9,* 18–20.

Fu, P., & Yukl, G. (2000). Perceived effectiveness of influence tactics in the United States and China. *Leadership Quarterly, 11*(2), 251–266.

Galvin, K. (1996, September 20). Put subconscious out of your mind. *The Cincinnati Enquirer.*

Greco, A. J. (1988). The elderly as communicators: Perceptions of advertising practitioners. *Journal of Advertising Research, 28,* 39–46.

Guadagno, R. E., & Cialdini, R. B. (2002). Online persuasion: An examination of gender differences in computer-mediated interpersonal influence. *Group Dynamics: Theory, Research, and Practice, 6*(1), 38–51.

Han, S., & Shavitt, S. (1994). Persuasion and culture: Advertising appeals in individualistic and collectivistic societies. *Journal of Experimental Social Psychology, 30,* 326–350.

Hill, K., & Monk, A. F. (2000). Electronic mail versus printed text—the effects on recipients. *Interacting with Computers, 13,* 253–263.

Hu, Y., Lodish, L. M., & Krieger, A. M. (2007). An analysis of real world TV advertising tests: A 15-year update. *Journal of Advertising Research, 47*(3), 341–353.

Janis, I., Kaye, D., & Kirschner, P. (1965). Facilitating effects of "eating while reading" on responsiveness to persuasive communication. *Journal of Personality and Social Psychology, 1,* 181–186.

Johnson, B. T., & Eagly, A. H. (1989). Effects of involvement on persuasion: A meta-analysis. *Psychological Bulletin, 106,* 290–314.

Johnston, D. D. (1994). *The art and science of persuasion.* Boston: McGraw-Hill.

Key, W. B. (1972). *Subliminal seduction.* New York: Signet.

Krosnick, J. A., & Alwin, D. F. (1989). Aging and susceptibility to attitude change. *Journal of Personality and Social Psychology, 57,* 416–425.

Krosnick, J. A., Betz, A. I., Jussim, L. J., & Lynn, A. R. (1992). Subliminal conditioning of attitudes. *Personality and Social Psychology Bulletin, 2,* 152–162.

Lee, M. J. (2010). The effects of self-efficacy statements in humorous anti-alcohol abuse messages targeting college students: Who is in charge? *Health Communication, 25,* 638–646.

Leventhal, H. (1970). Findings and theory in the study of fear communication. In L. Berkowitz (Ed.), *Advances in experimental social psychology* (Vol. 5). New York: Academic Press.

Lynch, D., & Golen, S. (2002). Got the picture? *Journal of Accountancy, 193*(5), 83–87.

Marsella, A. J. (1994). The measurement of emotional reactions to work: Methodological and research issues. *Work and Stress, 8,* 166–167.

Martin, P. Y., Laing, J., Martin, R., & Mitchell, M. (2005). Caffeine, cognition, and persuasion: Evidence for caffeine increasing the systematic processing of persuasive messages. *Journal of Applied Social Psychology, 35*(1), 160–182

Martin, P. Y., Hamilton, V. E., McKimmie, B. M., Terry, D. J., & Martin, R. (2006). Effects of caffeine on persuasion and attitude change: The role of secondary tasks in manipulating systematic message processing. *European Journal of Social Psychology, 37,* 320–338.

McConnell, J. V., Cutler, R. L., & McNeil, E. B. (1958). Subliminal stimulation: An overview. *American Psychologist, 13,* 229–242.

McGuire, W. J. (1968). Personality and susceptibility to social influence. In E. F. Borgotta & W. W. Lambert (Eds.), *Handbook of personality theory and research* (pp. 1130–1187). Chicago: Rand McNally.

McGuire, W. J. (1985). Attitudes and attitude change. In G. Lindzey & E. Aronson (Eds.), *Handbook of social psychology* (Vol. 2) (pp. X–X). New York: Random House.

McLuhan, M. (1964). *Understanding media: The extensions of man.* New York: Signet.

Meringoff, L. K. & Lesser, G. S. (1980). Children's ability to distinguish television commercials from program material. In R. P. Alder, G. S. Lesser, L. K. Meringoff, T. S. Roberson, J. R. Rossiter, & S. Ward (Eds.), *The effects of television advertising on children.* Lexington, MA: Lexington Books.

Miniwatts Marketing Group. (2009). *Internet world stats: Usage and population statistics.* Retrieved February 13, 2009, from: http://www .internetworldstats.com/stats.htm.

Mintz, P. M., & Mills, J. (1971). Effects of arousal and information about its source on attitude change. *Journal of Experimental and Social Psychology, 7,* 561–570.

Naseri, M. B. (2011). Role of demographics, social connectedness and prior internet experience in adoption of online shopping: Applications for direct marketing. *Journal of Targeting, Measurement and Analysis for Marketing, 19,* 69–84.

Neff, J. (2009, February 23). Guess which medium is as effective as ever: TV. *AdAge.com.* Retrieved February 23, 2009, from: http://adage.com/print?articel id=134790.

Nollis, N. (2005). Ten years of learning on how online advertising builds brands. *Journal of Advertising Research, 45*(2), 225–268.

O'Keefe, D. J. (2002). *Persuasion: Theory and research* (2nd ed.). Thousand Oaks, CA: Sage.

Omoto, A. M., Snyder, M., & Martino, S. C. (2000). Volunteerism and the life course: Investigating age-related agendas for action. *Basic and Applied Social Psychology, 23*(3),181–197.

Petty, R. E., & Cacioppo, J. T. (1984). The effects of involvement on responses to argument quantity and quality: Central and peripheral routes to persuasion. *Journal of Personality and Social Psychology, 46,* 69–81.

Pfau, M., Lee, W., Godbold, L. C., Hong, Y., Tusing, K. J., Koerner, et al. (1996). *Nuances in inoculation: The role of inoculation approach and receiver ego-involvement, message processing disposition, and gender in the process of resistance.* Paper presented at the Speech Communication Association, San Diego, CA.

Pingdom (2012). World internet population has doubled in the last five years. Accessed February 24, 2013, from http://royal.pingdom.com/2012/04/19/world-internet-population-has-doubled-in-the-last-5-years/.

Pratkanis, A. R., Eskenazi, J., & Greenwald, A. G. (1994). What you expect is what you believe (but not necessarily what you get): A test of the effectiveness of subliminal self-help audiotapes. *Basic and Applied Social Psychology, 15,* 251–276.

Quelch, J. A., & Klein, L. R. (1996). The Internet and international marketing. *Sloan Management Review, 37*(3), 60–75.

Rhodes, N., & Wood, W. (1992). Self-esteem and intelligence affect influenceability: The mediating role of message reception. *Psychological Bulletin, 111,* 156–171.

Rosenberg, M. (1965). *Society and the adolescent self-image.* Princeton, NJ: Princeton University Press.

Sawyer, A. G. (1988). Can there be effective advertising without explicit conclusions? Decide for yourself. In S. Hecker & D. W. Stewart (Eds.), *Nonverbal communication in advertising* (pp. 159–184), Lexington, MA: D. C. Heath.

Sagarin, B. J., Britt, M. A., Heider, J. D., Wood, S. E., & Lynch, J. E. (2003). Bartering our attention: The distraction and persuasion effects of on-line advertisements. *International Journal of Cognitive Technology, 8*(2), 4–17.

Schacter, S., & Singer, J. (1962). Cognitive, social, and physiological determinants of emotional state. *Psychological Review, 69,* 379–399.

Schacter, S., & Wheeler, L. (1962). Epinephrine, chlorpromazine, and amusement. *Journal of Abnormal and Social Psychology, 65,* 121–128.

Scheidel, T. M. (1963). Sex and persuadability. *Speech Monographs, 30,* 353–358.

Skolnick, P., & Heslin, R. (1971). Quality versus difficulty: Alternative interpretations of the relationship between self-esteem and persuasibility. *Journal of Personality, 39,* 242–251.

Snyder, M. (1982). When believing means doing: Creating links between attitudes and behavior. In M. P. Zanna, E. T. Higgins, & C. P. Herman (Eds.), *Consistence in social behavior: The Ontario Symposium* (Vol. 2) (pp. 105–130). Hillsdale, NJ: Lawrence Erlbaum.

Snyder, M. (1987). *Public appearances/Private realities: The psychology of self-monitoring.* New York: W. H. Freeman.

Snyder, M., & DeBono, K. G. (1985). Appeals to images and claims about quality: Understanding the psychology of advertising. *Journal of Personality and Social Psychology, 49,* 586–597.

Snyder, M., & Swann, W. B. (1976). When actions reflect attitudes: The politics of impression management. *Journal of Personality and Social Psychology, 34,* 1034–1042.

Snyder, M., & Tanke, E. D. (1976). Behavior and attitude: Some people are more consistent than others. *Journal of Personality, 44,* 510–517.

Song, H., Peng, W., & Lee, K. M. (2011). Promoting exercise self-efficacy with an exergame. *Journal of Health Communication, 16,* 148–162.

Taylor, S. E., & Thompson, S. C. (1982). Stalking the elusive "vividness" effect. *Psychological Review, 89,* 155–181.

Thompson, N., Bevan, J., & Sparks, L. (2012). Healthcare reform information-seeking: Relationships with uncertainty, uncertainty discrepancy, and health self-efficacy. *Journal of Communication In Healthcare, 5*(1), 56–66.

Wanta, W., & Hu, Y. (1994). The effects of credibility, reliance, and exposure on media agenda settings: A path analysis model. *Journalism Quarterly, 71*(1), 90–98.

Ward, D. A., Seccombe, K., Bendel, R., & Carter, L. F. (1985). Cross-sex context as a factor in persuasibility sex differences. *Social Psychology Quarterly, 48,* 269–276.

West, M. D. (1994). Validating a scale for the measurement of credibility: A covariance structure modeling approach. *Journalism Quarterly, 71*(1), 159–168.

Wilson, C. E. (1974). The effect of medium on loss of information. *Journalism Quarterly, 51,* 111–115.

Wilson, V. E. (2003). Perceived effectiveness of interpersonal persuasion strategies in computer-mediated communication. *Computers in Human Behavior, 19,* 537–552.

Wiseman, R. L., Sanders, J. A., Congalton, J. K., Gass, R. H., Sueda, K., & Ruiqing, D. (1995). A cross-cultural analysis of compliance gaining: China, Japan, and the United States. *Intercultural Communication Studies, 5*(1), 1–18.

Woodall, W. G., & Burgoon, J. K. (1983). Talking fast and changing attitudes: A critique and clarification. *Journal of Nonverbal Behavior, 8,* 126–142.

Zanbaka, C., Goolkasian, P., & Hodges, L. F. (2006). Can a virtual cat persuade you? The role of gender and realism in speaker persuasiveness. *Proceedings of the SIGCHI Conference on Human Factors in Computing Systems* (pp. 1153–1162). April 22–27, Montreal, Quebec, Canada: ACM Press.

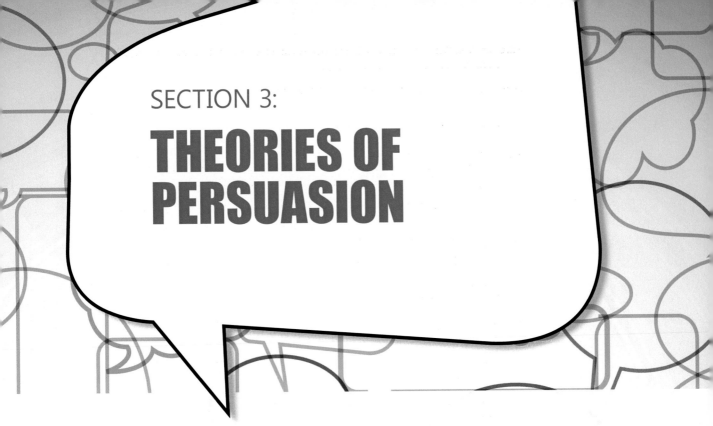

SECTION 3:
THEORIES OF PERSUASION

How, what, and when persuasion happens is the focus of this section. We begin with a general discussion of theory and a brief discussion of some classical theories of persuasion. Chapter 7 provides an overview of theory and can serve as either a refresher or a foundation, depending on your background. We then move on to in-depth discussion of the major theories of persuasion. We begin with one of the oldest theories—social judgment theory—and progress chronologically to the most contemporary theory of persuasion. In each chapter, the key components and principles of the theory are explained. The theory and its application are then illustrated with descriptions of research using that theory. The persuasion theories guide our decisions on how to use source, message, channel, and receiver characteristics to create effective persuasion messages.

CHAPTERS

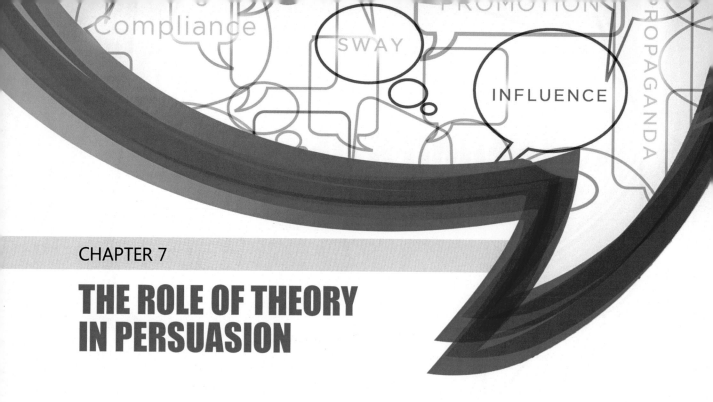

CHAPTER 7

THE ROLE OF THEORY IN PERSUASION

"Discover A Step-By-Step, Foolproof, Proven Formula To Get Anyone To Say 'Yes' To You . . . Any Time, Any Place!"

The Ultimate Persuasion Formula, 2004.

"What would YOUR life be like if you could convince people to do whatever you asked?

Anyone. Anything. Anytime.

Clients and customers at your marketing mercy.

Colleagues following your lead.

Children obeying your instructions.

Competitors on the run.

Lovers eternally loyal."

Maximum Persuasion, 2004.

Do these headlines appeal to you? Do you think these promises are legitimate? We don't recommend this source; however, it does highlight people's desire for power and control. Many of us would like the power to influence people this way, and some expect the study of persuasion to offer this power. To the casual observer, it looks like these sources are selling the power of persuasion and that the power comes from having the right skills. What they are really trying to sell is their theory of how to control the power of persuasion. They call it a "program" or "system" rather than a theory, but they are

LEARNING OBJECTIVES

- DEFINE THEORY AND EXPLAIN THE THREE CRITERIA FOR EVALUATING THEORY.
- DISTINGUISH BETWEEN SCIENTIFIC AND FOLK THEORY.
- DESCRIBE THE FIVE BASIC STEPS IN TESTING A THEORY.
- DESCRIBE THE THREE CLASSIC THEORIES OF PERSUASION.

selling their explanation for how persuasion works. The power they are pitching comes from mastery of the theory they are advancing. We are not recommending the theories these types of websites are promoting, and we seriously question the validity of their claims and their theory. Just because something is a theory doesn't mean it is useful or accurate, and in the following paragraphs we provide criteria for evaluating theory.

You may be asking how theory gives you power. Answer these questions: Would you have power if you could *explain* why things happen? Would you have power if you could *predict* when things will happen? Would you have power if you could *control* when things happen? If you answered yes to these questions, then you have agreed that theory (good, well-developed theory, that is) gives us power. Good theories give you the power to explain, predict, and control, although not perfectly as suggested in the headlines. To be an effective persuader, you must be able to explain why people are persuaded and why they are not, you must be able to predict when people will be influenced and when they won't, and you must be able control the message to persuade successfully. The extravagant promises of advertisements such as those shown previously lead people to believe that if you have the right skills or messages, you can persuade anyone at any time. Although nobody can honestly promise you that, having a repertoire of theories to choose from does give you power that most people don't have (because they haven't read this book and taken this class!).

In this chapter, we discuss the term *theory* and how theories can be useful. We also show you how theories are tested so that you can begin judging for yourself which theories are useful and which are less useful. In the last part of this chapter, we review some classic persuasion theories. These older theories serve as the foundation for the newer persuasion theories that are covered in much greater depth in Chapters 8 through 11.

It should be noted that scholars have explored persuasion in many different ways, and a wide variety of methodological approaches have been used to study persuasion. Those following in the footsteps of Aristotle and the approaches outlined in his work, *Rhetoric*, often employ methods that are considered rhetorical, qualitative, and/or humanistic. Other researchers have used more quantitative and social scientific approaches to understand how persuasion operates. These different methods draw on different paradigms and different methods of studying persuasion but often draw similar conclusions. The primary focus of this text is on research and theories using quantitative and/or social scientific approaches. A great deal of value and insight can be gained from using a variety of methods, and in some sections we draw on those principles. The chapters in this section (Chapters 7 through 11) were generated and tested primarily by quantitative and social scientific approaches to the study of social influence, and it is important to have at least a general understanding of this perspective.

WHAT IS A THEORY?

Theory is an abstract concept that means different things to different people. Many people view theory as being idealistic and unrelated to the "real world." Some people disregard the term *theory* in favor of *practice or ideas proven in the real world.* If theory is so useless, why do your professors keep insisting that you learn about theories? Maybe it's because theory really isn't so useless after all. Maybe people's criticisms of theory are based in a lack of understanding and inappropriate expectations about theory. In the following pages, we discuss what a theory is, what it is not, and how theories are useful to understanding and influencing persuasion.

Although **theory** has several definitions one of the more useful states that "a theory is any systematically related set of ideas used to describe and/or explain phenomena" (Corman, 1995, p. 4). A key term in this definition is **phenomena**, which are things a person finds extraordinary and in need of explanation. You encounter phenomena every day—the phenomenon of your roommate not doing the dishes as promised, the phenomenon of being stood up by a date, the phenomenon of a professor refusing to let you take an exam early. For each of these phenomena you may have ideas that describe and/or explain why it happened. A key phrase in the definition is "**systematically related**," which simply means that the ideas that explain the phenomenon must be related to one another in an organized way. The ideas must create a pattern and can't contradict one another. To the extent that your ideas are systematically related, you are developing and using theory to understand these phenomena and to predict when they are most likely to occur. Therefore, as an example, your ideas regarding your roommate who doesn't do dishes despite promises may be that your roommate is a lazy slob and that lazy slobs generally do not clean up after themselves and do not even notice when things need to be cleaned. These related ideas are the basis of a theory—a rather primitive theory, but a theory nonetheless.

WHY DO WE NEED THEORIES?

Theories help us explain phenomena in our daily lives, both the everyday kinds of issues that are not very important and the really big issues that can influence the quality of our lives. Theory is useful because it does three things: (a) helps us *explain* human behavior, (b) helps us *predict* what is likely to happen, and (c) helps us *control* what will happen (Andersen, 1988). To the extent a theory is able to explain, predict, and control a phenomenon, the theory is considered useful and valuable. Therefore, we judge theories on how well they satisfy these three criteria.

EXPLAINING PHENOMENA

Theory helps us explain events that we encounter in our daily lives. For example, you may observe your friend Hector being persuaded to pay $75 for a shirt of inferior quality that he doesn't need. The sales pitch consisted of a popular name brand and a reduced price (20% off the regular price). Script theory would explain this phenomenon by saying that Hector was mindlessly receiving the sales pitch and simply followed a common script: name brand equals quality, sale equals a good deal (Roloff, 1980). Hector was not influenced by the characteristics of the item or the superior arguments given by a salesperson; Hector relied on a script that led to a particular response—buying the shirt. Script theory helps us explain why Hector bought a shirt of inferior quality when he really didn't need it. More generally, theory helps us explain various events, big and small, that we encounter in our daily lives. As alluded to in the chapter introduction, being able to explain why something happens gives us power. Additionally, being able to explain why people behave the way they do helps reduce uncertainty and stress. We like to feel in control and as if we know what to expect. This statement leads us to the second reason why theory is useful.

PREDICTING PHENOMENA

Theory is useful because it helps us predict when and how a particular phenomenon will occur. When we understand the factors that cause the phenomenon and we can identify those factors, we are able to predict when the phenomenon will probably occur. In the example of Hector purchasing an unneeded $75 shirt of inferior quality, we used script theory to explain his behavior. Script theory identified a key factor, a person's mental state: whether a person mindlessly or mindfully processed the available information. Using this theory, we can predict when Hector (or any other person) will probably make unwise purchases. When Hector is mindlessly processing the available information, he will most likely rely on a script rather than mindfully process the information and determine for himself its value. The script that Hector chooses may have served him well in other situations. Buying items on sale is generally an effective way of saving money, unless of course, the "original price" is artificially inflated. Buying name brands is another script that may have worked well in the past, unless the source (shirt maker in the example) spends heavily to promote its "name" and very little to ensure the quality of the product. Hector responds differently to information when he is mindfully rather than mindlessly processing the information. This key factor allows us not only to explain his behavior but also to make some predictions. Once we can predict behavior, we have greater control over the behavior. This statement leads us to the third reason to value theory.

CONTROLLING PHENOMENA

When we understand a phenomenon and identify key factors that influence it, we can intervene and control (to some extent) those factors. One thing we need to be

"Before you grade my test, you should know about
my Theory of Life's Imprecision."

FIGURE 7.1 Life's Imprecision cartoon.

clear about here is what we mean by control. We don't mean complete and absolute control as we have over inanimate objects such as our cars and phones. For one thing, human beings cannot be completely controlled. We're speaking in relative terms. Theory allows us to have some measure of control or influence over the persuasion process. On an ethical note, it would be highly unethical to make complete control of others our goal.

Theory allows us to identify the key factors and then modify those factors to influence the process. Going back to our friend Hector, when we observe him mindlessly taking in the sales pitch, we can poke him in the ribs and say, "Hey, think about this!" and short-circuit the process that was leading him to a poor purchase. This is an example of using theory to stop or prevent persuasion. We can also use theory to enhance persuasion. Say, for instance, that after graduation a state senator who is running for reelection employs you and that your job is to get her message out to the voters. You would only work for an upstanding, ethical politician, and the senator's message consists of substantial information and not sound bites and meaningless platitudes. Therefore, you know that your audience needs to mindfully analyze the message. Script theory tells you that if voters mindlessly respond to the message, they are likely to use a script rather than actually pay attention to the senator's arguments. This leads you to construct your message to encourage voters to mindfully process the message (we'll learn more about how to do this in later chapters). In a different situation, such as selling jewelry, encouraging your customer to use a script such as "high price equals quality" may be to your advantage. One caveat: It is often unethical to encourage someone to use a script so that they don't thoroughly analyze the message. Chapter 13 deals with ethics of persuasion more thoroughly, and you may want to refer to that chapter to help you assess the ethics of using scripts as a persuasive strategy.

SCIENTIFIC VERSUS FOLK THEORY

Earlier we defined theory as "any systematically related set of ideas used to describe and/or explain phenomena" (Corman, 1995, p. 4). We provided the example of you explaining your roommate's behavior with the "lazy slob" theory. Although all theories consist of a related set of ideas, not all theories are equal. The lazy slob theory we developed to explain your roommate's behavior is considered a **folk theory** (Corman, 1995). Folk theories are the theories we develop through our own observations and experiences and knowledge. They exist in our heads, and we may occasionally verbalize them to others. We use and modify our folk theories as necessary. When a folk theory doesn't do a good job of explaining or predicting a phenomenon, we either modify the theory or write off the particular episode as an exception to the rule. Folk theories are not written down, tested, or offered up for review by others. We may not even be able to articulate the various folk theories we use to explain and predict human behavior.

Scientific theories, on the other hand, are published, tested, and offered up for review by experts. Scientific theories are the ones that make it into your textbooks, regardless of the discipline. We have high expectations for scientific theories. They must be testable, answer questions, as well as direct us toward questions and issues that will help us further understand the phenomena of interest. A scientific theory must conform to logical standards and be stated in detail. These criteria allow not only the creator of the theory but others as well to test the theory using objective and valid testing procedures. Scientific theories must stand up to rigorous testing and examination. Theories and research that meet these high standards are published in academic journals so that the larger academic community can further scrutinize and evaluate them. Our individual folk theories do not go through such a process, and it is highly unlikely that they would survive (without major revision) the rigors of testing and validation. However, it is likely that most scientific theories started out as folk theories for their originators. Scholars used the methods discussed in the next section to develop their folk theories into scientific theories.

HOW DO WE TEST THEORY?

As we described previously, theories are useful to the extent that they help us: (a) explain, (b) predict, and (c) control phenomena. These can be viewed as criteria for evaluating theory. If a theory doesn't do these three things, it's not a very good theory. To know the extent a theory really does these three things, a theory must be tested, and this is the real difference between folk and scientific theories. As we discuss each theory of persuasion, we provide examples of research that test or illustrate the theory. Research is conducted to determine how well a theory can explain, predict, and control phenomena. Many research studies are needed to test a theory, and typically years of research are required to fully develop a theory. To help you understand the research discussed in the text, we briefly outline the research process used to test theory. Quantitative and social science research generally follows the five steps discussed here. Understanding these steps makes reading and understanding research much easier.

MAKE PREDICTIONS

The first step is to make predictions, also known as forming hypotheses. The researcher uses the theory (explanation of the phenomena) to make very specific predictions. An example from Staats and Staats' (1958) study on classical conditioning (discussed in Chapter 2) is the following hypothesis: "Attitudes already elicited by socially significant verbal stimuli can be changed through classical conditioning, using other words as unconditioned stimuli" (p. 37). Staats and Staats predicted that people's attitudes toward words could be classically conditioned even when people had preexisting attitudes toward those words.

DESIGN METHODS

Once one or more hypotheses have been derived from the theory, the second step is to design an appropriate method for testing the hypotheses. For instance, to test the above-mentioned hypothesis, Staats and Staats (1958) designed an experiment in which participants (students enrolled in a psychology class) both heard and saw words. The conditioned stimulus (CS) was the words *German, Swedish, Italian, French, Dutch,* and *Greek,* and students viewed these words on a screen. After viewing each CS word, students heard and repeated a word, which served as the unconditioned stimulus (UCS). The CS words *German, Italian, French,* and *Greek* were paired with several different words that were not evaluative (e.g., chair). The CS words *Dutch* and *Swedish* were paired with evaluative words that were either positive (e.g., gift, sacred, happy) or negative (e.g., bitter, ugly, failure). Half of the students had *Dutch* paired with negative words and *Swedish* paired with positive words. The other half had the reverse—*Dutch* paired with positive words and *Swedish* paired with negative words. After the conditioning process, students were "tested" on the words and evaluated each of the CS words on a semantic differential scale (pleasant—unpleasant) and were asked to write down their thoughts about the experiment. Staats and Staats designed their method, including what would be done and how it would be done, how variables would be measured, and what subjects would be told. The method is a very important part of the research process. A poor method design results in an invalid test of the theory. Once the method has been designed, we must consider data collection.

COLLECT DATA

The third step is to collect some type of data or information that is generated from the research method. In the above example, the data were in the form of participants' written responses. Students evaluated the CS words on a semantic differential scale. The scores on these scales served as the data. Quantitative and social scientific data could also take the form of observations of behavior (what people actually did after receiving the message), or a combination of both. Data can take a variety of forms; however, any data must be in some form that can be objectively evaluated by using some valid and acceptable tool (e.g., statistics).

ANALYZE DATA

Once data have been collected, the fourth step is to analyze the data and determine whether the hypotheses were supported or rejected. The way data are analyzed depends on the type of data gathered and the type of hypotheses or research questions posed by the researchers. A major responsibility of the researcher is to analyze the data as objectively as possible by using appropriate tools (e.g., choosing the appropriate statistics). In the Staats and Staats study, the hypothesis was supported. They successfully conditioned students to feel either positively or negatively toward the words *Dutch* and *Swedish*. Sometimes research results are very clear-cut, and sometimes they are not. Having some knowledge of research methods allows you to evaluate the methods used to test the theory. You've heard the saying, "garbage in, garbage out." So, one aspect of evaluating research is determining how well the research method tested the theory. Are the results due to the theory or to the methods used?

REVISE THE THEORY

Because a test of theory rarely comes out perfectly with every aspect of the theory being supported, the fifth and last step is to revise the theory. The researcher must determine what aspects of the theory worked well and which did not. Revisions made to a theory are then tested with further research. This process continues until the theory is determined to be as useful as possible at explaining, predicting, and controlling phenomena. If you study the research conducted on a theory over the years, you will probably see the theory change as it goes through the research process.

Above we argued that theory is useful in explaining, predicting, and controlling many phenomena we encounter daily. However, theories vary in their usefulness. Some theories help us explain, predict, and control a broad range of phenomena across many contexts; others are useful for a relatively narrow range of phenomena. Theories also vary in how thoroughly they have been researched. A theory that has been extensively researched and revised tends to be more useful in explaining, predicting, and controlling phenomena. One goal of this book is to help you think critically about the theories you are learning about, and to do this you need to examine the research that has been conducted on each theory. You should ask yourself several questions such as whether specific predictions from the theory were tested. How were they tested? Do explanations other than those derived from the theory explain the results of the research? Your answers to these questions should be based on a careful and objective evaluation of the methods used to test the theory.

In this section, we explained what a theory is and how to evaluate it. In the following chapters we refer to this information a great deal. In the remainder of this chapter we discuss some of the early theories used to explain the phenomena of persuasion.

CLASSIC THEORIES OF PERSUASION

An examination of a few early theories of persuasion allows us to apply the criteria for evaluation of theories discussed above. In addition, understanding the early theories helps us understand how our knowledge about persuasion was developed. Each of the early theories contributes to our understanding of how persuasion works, but each also had limitations. By understanding the contributions of those early theories, we can better understand how later theories were developed and evolved over time.

YALE APPROACH

Carl Hovland and his colleagues at Yale University (Hovland, Janis, & Kelley, 1953) developed one of the early approaches to understanding persuasion. In attempting to explain the persuasion process and to predict what variables affected persuasive outcomes, this group of researchers conducted a series of studies examining a wide variety of factors. In what has been called the **Yale approach** (Zimbardo, Ebbesen, & Maslach, 1977), they theorized that persuasion has four components: attention, comprehension, acceptance, and retention.

Attention refers to getting the audience to focus on the message. We are all bombarded with hundreds of messages daily, and we can't possibly pay full attention to all of them. On any given day in a college classroom, you are surrounded by messages competing for your attention. There are probably T-shirts and/or hats with messages on them, flyers on bulletin boards, information from the professor and discussion in class, conversations going on in the hallway, and advertisements on web pages. Once you leave class to cross campus, there are probably more messages on shirts, more flyers and banners, more conversations surrounding you, and traffic with bumper stickers or signs on trucks. You have phone messages, e-mail messages, tweets, Facebook, and television bombarding you with many messages. Instead of trying to pay attention to all these messages, we engage in **selective attention and perception**. This refers to humans choosing, out of self-defense, to pay attention only to some of the messages bombarding them. We pay attention to messages that are particularly relevant to us in some way or that attract our attention because of their use of humor, oddity, or other similar devices.

Persuasion is no different. To be influenced by a persuasive message, you must first pay attention to it. Persuasive messages can be constructed by using a variety of tools to attract attention. Think about what makes you pay attention to a commercial on television. Is it a change in the volume, sex appeal, a clever joke, an odd picture, or is the ad about a product you are thinking about buying? For persuasive messages to be successful, the receiver has to let the message get through his or her perceptual filters to be among the messages that are cognitively processed.

Once the message has the receiver's attention, it also has to be understood. Thus, **comprehension** is the second component. To enhance comprehension, the source needs to provide clear explanations and simple messages. But, comprehension also depends on how much attention the receiver gives to the message. Sometimes, persuaders use a device for attracting attention to their message that has nothing to do with the content of the message. For example, a student in a public speaking class once said the word *sex* loudly to get the class' attention. After capturing attention, the speaker then gave a speech on the economic system in Europe. Getting attention through use of sex and then sending a message unrelated to sex does not facilitate comprehension. Attention-getting devices that are related to the message facilitate comprehension.

Several years ago, Burger King created a marketing campaign using a character named Herb. This campaign is a good example of how a lack of comprehension can affect the outcome of a persuasive message ("Big Flop," 1995). Burger King launched an advertising and public relations campaign focused on Herb, a nerd who had never tried a Burger King whopper. Lots of ads were shown nationally, Herb appeared on talk shows across the country, and the company sponsored a contest in which the first customer to spot Herb in their local Burger King won a cash prize. A great deal of coverage was given to Herb and this campaign. During the campaign, however, sales at Burger King actually decreased. Follow-up research showed that customers did not fully understand the message. They heard "Herb," "nerd," and "Burger King." Instead of associating nerds with those *not* eating at Burger King, many associated Burger King with nerds. This was a simple message, but the target audience didn't pay enough attention to clearly understand the message. Thus, the persuasive intent of the message failed.

Acceptance of the message is the third component in the persuasive process. Acceptance is used to define the success of a persuasive message. In Chapters 1 and 2 we discussed things we try to change through persuasion: attitudes, beliefs, behavioral intentions, and behaviors. Acceptance refers to the persuasive message achieving its goals, whether that's changing attitude, belief, behavioral intention, or behavior. For example, a telemarketer selling magazines would only consider purchase of one or more magazines as a successful outcome. In other cases, change in attitudes or beliefs would be considered success. A religious missionary would consider belief in the offered religion as evidence of success. Other times, behavioral intentions would be considered success. A voter who promises to vote for a certain candidate or a teen who pledges not to use drugs would be considered successful outcomes for some messages.

The acceptance step has received the most research attention. After all, the primary evaluation of persuasive messages is whether the receivers accept the message. Hovland and his colleagues (1953) researched numerous variables that influenced persuasive acceptance of messages, including source credibility and message content factors. For example, they found that high credibility sources were more effective than low credibility sources in generating attitude change and that repeating a message made the persuasive effects last longer. Indeed, this catalogue of factors laid the groundwork for later research. The Yale approach hypothesizes that attention and comprehension are necessary precursors to message acceptance.

The final component is **retention**. For many persuasive messages, being persuaded at the point of the message is not enough. The message must be retained long enough for the desired action to occur. For example, if you see an advertisement promoting toothpaste, accepting the message at the time of the ad isn't enough. You must remember that you wanted to try this product when you are in the store shopping for toothpaste. A political candidate who has successfully convinced constituents that she is the right one for office needs voters to remember this when they go into the voting booth. Mothers Against Drunk Driving want drivers to continue to remember not to drive while under the influence of alcohol rather than just right after exposure to a message. Although some persuasive messages are targeted at one-time behaviors, many require long-term retention of the persuasive message in order to be deemed successful.

The Yale approach met some of the criteria of a good theory. It *explains* why some persuasive messages are successful while others fail, and it does *predict* failure for messages that do not adequately attract receivers' attention or those that are not comprehended by the target audience. It does offer a set of factors that affect acceptance, but it does not consist of a set of related ideas to explain acceptance. It does not offer effective *control* over what happens in persuasive messages. The Yale approach is not specific enough to be able to control persuasive messages. The Yale approach's biggest strength is the focus on the attention and comprehension components. Attention and comprehension of the message as necessary conditions prior to acceptance of the message have remained important factors, and retention has been demonstrated to be of critical importance in many persuasive circumstances. The Yale approach's biggest limitation resulted from the lack of a systematic theoretical framework for control offered in the acceptance stage. Nonetheless, this theory offered a foundation other theories built on, and the next theoretical framework focused primarily on the acceptance stage of the process.

GROUP DYNAMICS

Another classic theory that focused primarily on the acceptance part of the persuasive process is called the **group dynamics** approach. Kurt Lewin (1947) argued that individuals function as a part of society, and thus, societal norms play a role in guiding our actions. This is most evident in group settings where individual attitudes and beliefs differ from group norms. Lewin argues that we change our positions to meet social norms and that we tend to evaluate ourselves according to societal standards. A persuader using group dynamics as a guide creates a sense of socially normative beliefs and/or behavior in order to pressure others to conform to these standards. Group dynamics highlights two types of social pressure: conformity and social comparison.

Web Activity: Go to YouTube and search for "Asch Conformity Experiment" to see how the experiment was done and learn more about the findings.

When we deviate from group or social norms, we feel pressured to **conform** to those norms. Asch (1956) demonstrated this in a classic research study. Asch set up a study to test conformity pressures in group settings. Each participant in this study thought he or she was part of a small group of participants. In reality, there was only one research participant in each session, and the other six to eight participants were confederates hired by the researcher to assist in the experiment. Asch told the participants that this was a study to examine people's visual perceptions. He showed them several sets of lines. In each set, one line was on the left and a set of three lines was on the right. He asked subjects to pick the line out of the three on the right that matched the length of the reference line on the left. He then asked the group members one by one to publicly state which line they thought matched the reference line. It was set up so that the confederates spoke first and the research participant was generally the last to express an opinion. For the first two trials, the confederates gave the correct answer to the question of which line matched. In the third trial, each confederate gave identical *incorrect* answers. This was repeated for multiple sets of lines. Asch wanted to see how long it took research participants to give in to peer pressure and start giving the wrong answer as well. Three-quarters of the research participants conformed to group pressure and gave wrong answers. About one-quarter of the participants conformed quickly to most of the incorrect answers given by the confederates. The majority of participants (about half of the subject pool) eventually gave in to conformity pressure and gave one or more incorrect answers in order to conform to the group's opinion. Only about one-quarter of the research participants gave all correct answers. Thus, Asch concluded that group conformity pressures are powerful motivators. When tested again privately, however, research participants reverted back to their own opinions. Therefore, participants conformed while in a group setting, but once participants were no longer in the group, they no longer conformed to the group opinion. Other researchers in similar contexts replicated this study. Thus, group pressures for conformity are considered powerful persuasive influences and are frequently used in advertisements. Consider all the ads for trucks that claim that their model is the best-selling truck in America or the political campaigns that cite polls showing more support for their candidate or their issue. These advertisements are attempting to create conformity pressures so that you'll go along with their messages.

Leon Festinger (1954) with his concept of **social comparison** illustrates the second way social pressure can be used to influence. He argued that we tend to evaluate how good our own accomplishments are by comparing ourselves to others. For example, how do we know a 4-minute mile is good? Because it is a standard that few can meet. We all do this kind of comparison in many ways. When exams are passed back, students often want to check with others to see their scores and ask what the pattern of results was for the class. In this case, a student who received 64 out of 100 on an exam might feel bad until it was announced that 64 was the high score for the class. We make social comparisons as a way to decide what is good, bad, important, unimportant, and so on.

We make social comparisons when faced with persuasive messages as well. An example of this is advertisements that lead you to believe that everyone "who is anyone" has a particular product. You may never have felt a need for the product until you compared yourself to the person in the advertisement. Your social comparison revealed that you had less than the people depicted in the advertisement. You now feel pressure to obtain the object so that you can compare favorably to others. Advertisements for many luxury products use social comparison to create a desire for their products. Thus, group dynamics involves social pressure resulting from conformity and social comparisons.

A classic study conducted during World War II illustrates the practical application of group dynamics (Lewin, 1943, 1947). The government was concerned about limited supplies of meat during the war. Government officials wanted to make sure that the greatest possible use of limited resources was the norm, but organ meats such as the brain, heart, and kidneys tended to be consumed less. The officials sponsored a research project using group dynamics theory to try to encourage more consumption of organ meats. There were two conditions in the study involving housewives, and before participating in the study all potential participants were asked if they served any of these meats. Very few did so prior to being in the study. In the first condition, housewives were given a lecture about the nutritional value of organ meats, told how to prepare them in ways that would please their family and overcome potential family objections to these meats, and told how inexpensive the cuts were. In the second condition, housewives were formed into groups and discussion leaders led discussions about the same content that was presented in the first condition. In these discussions, the housewives discussed the nutritional value of the organ meats, discussed obstacles they expected to face in serving them to their families, and then generated ways to overcome those obstacles. Discussion leaders made sure the same information that was in the lectures was introduced into the discussion at appropriate points. Both groups were asked if they intended to serve the organ meats and were contacted a week later and asked about whether they had served any of these three meats. As group dynamics predicted, those who were in the group discussion settings and subjected to peer pressure were significantly more likely to intend to serve organ meats and to have served them when contacted later. In fact, Lewin (1947) found, "A follow-up showed that only 3 percent of the women who heard the lectures served one of the meats never served before, whereas after group discussion 32 percent served one of them." (p. 335).

Group dynamics meets some criteria of a good theory, but not all of them. It does *explain* persuasion in group settings or public contexts. It does not, however, explain persuasion in private settings. As you recall, the Asch participants in the group conformity study using line lengths reverted to their own judgments in private settings, so the explanatory power of group dynamics is limited to group settings where social comparison and conformity pressures are present. This limitation makes group dynamics useful in a limited number of situations. As the organ meat study illustrates, group dynamics can *control* persuasive behavior in group setting but does not offer strategies for increasing social pressure—limiting both prediction and control. Thus, the main strength of group dynamics is its contribution to our understanding of conformity and social comparison pressures. Its greatest limitations involve the limited application of group dynamics and the lack of continued attitude change once the receiver is no longer in the group setting. Social pressures that compel someone to agree publicly to vote for a particular candidate are not effective once the individual is in a private voting booth.

BALANCE THEORY

Fritz Heider (1946, 1958) generated the first of the consistency theories. He referred to his theory as **balance theory**. This theory started out very simply and is sometimes referred to as the **"P-O-X" theory**. Heider's theory included three parts: a person (P), another person (O), and an object (X). These three elements formed a triangle with each element being linked to the other two components by a positive (+) or negative (−) evaluation.

Heider was very interested in interpersonal relationships, and the triangle was always visualized from the perspective of the person (P). The other person (O) could be anyone the person had positive or negative feelings toward. The object could be anything—third person, music, idea, product, and so on.

Heider theorized that people would try to make the relationship among the three elements balanced in order to be consistent. For example, consider Kyle to be the person, Terry to be the other person, and Taylor Swift to be the object. If Kyle liked Taylor Swift, that would be a positive evaluation. If Kyle liked Terry, that would be a positive evaluation. For the triangle to be in balance, Terry would need to like Taylor Swift (another positive evaluation), resulting in three pluses around the triangle.

However, if Terry did not like Taylor Swift that would be a negative evaluation, and the triangle would be unbalanced or inconsistent. Heider suggested that the person, Kyle, would feel pressured to balance the situation (make it consistent) by either changing his evaluation of Taylor Swift to a negative evaluation or keeping the evaluation of Swift positive and changing the evaluation of Terry to a negative evaluation. With either change, the triangle of relationships would be balanced again. Alternatively, Kyle could reconsider information and conclude that, in reality, Terry really does like Taylor Swift. In this case, Kyle might infer that Terry made the negative comments to impress a friend or to fit into a particular group, allowing Kyle to believe that Terry's true beliefs reflected support for Taylor Swift. In short, to be balanced, the triangle would have to include three positive evaluations (pluses) or two negative evaluations (minuses) and one positive evaluation (plus).

This theory makes intuitive sense for interpersonal relationships. Most of us experience the desire to evaluate positively those who share our beliefs and world views and react negatively to those who disagree with us, particularly when the issues involved are important to us. Heider's research offered support for this approach in interpersonal contexts, but it has also been used successfully in persuasion situations.

Balance theory has been used frequently in advertising and political campaigns. An example is a celebrity who endorses a product or candidate, with the assumption being that the target consumer (P) thinks positively of the celebrity (O). Because the celebrity evaluates the product (X) positively, for the triangle to be balanced the target consumer (P) should evaluate the product or candidate (X) positively. This model can be seen in Michael Phelps's endorsement of Speedo® swimwear. Because many aspiring athletes like Phelps, his positive evaluation of Speedo swimwear creates pressure on consumers to balance the triangle by evaluating Speedo positively. Another example is illustrated in Figure 7.2 with Paul McCartney identifying himself with People for the Ethical Treatment of Animals (PETA).

Balance theory made an important contribution to the development of our knowledge about persuasion by introducing the concept of consistency. Heider's work and the research of others that followed him produced clear support for this approach, but the theory had obvious limitations. Balance theory *explains* what happens in

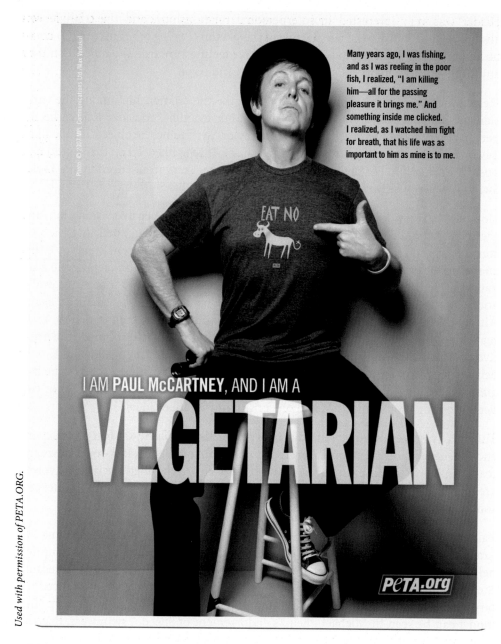

Many years ago, I was fishing, and as I was reeling in the poor fish, I realized, "I am killing him—all for the passing pleasure it brings me." And something inside me clicked. I realized, as I watched him fight for breath, that his life was as important to him as mine is to me.

EAT NO

I AM **PAUL McCARTNEY**, AND I AM A

VEGETARIAN

PeTA.org

Used with permission of PETA.ORG.

FIGURE 7.2 PETA, like other groups, seeks out celebrities to act as spokespersons for their cause.

specific situations that have sets of three involving two people and an object. Many persuasion situations involve just that, but others are more complex, so the explanatory power of the theory is limited in this sense.

Balance theory's ability to *predict* what happens even in those situations is also limited. When an imbalance exists, the theory argues that the inconsistency leads to pressure for balance or consistency, but it doesn't predict how that balance will occur. We don't know if the person will alter the evaluation toward the other person or the object. In the example of Michael Phelps and Speedo swimwear, we know that the company would like the target public to value the swimwear, but the theory also indicates that it is possible for the evaluation of Michael Phelps to change. The target public may perceive Phelps as selling out to commercial interests or supporting products that are excessively expensive. The target public may also believe that Phelps doesn't *really* like Speedo, but that the tremendous amount of money offered for endorsement is what made him do the commercials. Thus, we know that some kind of pressure for balance or consistency exists, but the inability of the theory to predict how that imbalance or inconsistency will be resolved leads to less ability to use the theory to *control* persuasion.

An additional problem is that balance theory assumes that evaluations are either positive or negative, and for an unbalanced triangle to be balanced, an evaluation must change from positive to negative or vice versa. That does happen at times, but our evaluations often do not change that dramatically. Instead, the person might feel a little less positively toward Michael Phelps and/or a little more positively about Speedo swimwear without changing the polarity of the response.

Finally, balance theory does not take into account the importance of the object or relationship involved. The theory predicts the same outcome when the object under consideration is abortion as it does for carrots. We might assume that we would feel more pressure to balance important topics, and this makes sense, but balance theory does not address the issue of topic importance.

Heider's balance theory is a bit simplistic, but it was critically important in launching research on consistency in persuasion situations. In Chapter 9 we discuss cognitive dissonance theory which was highly influenced by balance theory.

UNANSWERED QUESTIONS

These classic theories offer insight into the persuasive process. The Yale approach reminds us that the persuasion process has multiple steps. Attracting attention to a message, as well as making sure the target audience understands and retains the information, surrounds the actual acceptance of the message. Group dynamics is a stimulus-response type theory in that it involves pushing the right buttons and modifying behavior with external cues. Balance theory introduced the concept of consistency into persuasion and the pressure we feel to make our attitudes and behaviors consistent. These theories helped us understand pieces of how the persuasion process fits together, and each one works in limited situations. However, these theories don't answer broader questions about what happens internally as receivers process information in persuasive messages. What happens cognitively as we process different aspects of the message and of the source? Theories developed subsequently are called **cognitive theories**. These theories attempt to broaden our understanding of persuasion by examining the cognitive processes involved in accepting persuasive messages. These theories are discussed in more depth in the next four chapters.

SUMMARY

- Theory is very important in understanding persuasion, and good theories help us explain, predict, and control phenomena.
- We use both scientific and folk theories in explaining and predicting human behavior.
- Research helps us test theories, and research involves five basic steps: forming hypotheses, designing appropriate methods for testing the hypotheses, collecting data, analyzing the data to determine support or rejection of the hypotheses, and revising the theory.
- Classic theories of persuasion help us understand persuasion and help us understand how persuasion theories are created and evolve over time. Classic theories include the Yale approach, group dynamics, and balance theory.
- The Yale approach theorized four components to persuasion: attention, comprehension, acceptance, and retention.
- Group dynamics identified conformity and social comparison as sources of social pressure.
- Balance theory involves a person (P), another person (O), and an object (X).
- For a triangle to be balanced, it has to have three positive relationships (+) or two negative (–) and one positive (+) relationship.

KEY TERMS

Acceptance—the third step in the Yale approach which means that the persuasive message was successful in achieving its goals.

Attention—the first step in the Yale approach, referring to getting the audience to focus on the specific message.

Balance theory—the oldest of the consistency theories, sometimes referred to as the P-O-X theory.

Cognitive theories—theories of persuasion that examine the cognitive processes involved in accepting persuasive messages.

Comprehension—the second step in the Yale approach which refers to the audience needing to understand the message.

Conformity—the pressure to conform to what others in a group are doing.

Folk theory—a theory we develop through our own observations, experiences, and knowledge. It exists in our heads, and we may occasionally verbalize it to others.

Phenomena—things a person finds extraordinary and in need of explanation.

Retention—the fourth step in the Yale approach which refers to the audience remembering the message.

Scientific theory—a theory that is published, tested, and offered up for review by experts.

Selective attention and perception—our choosing, out of self-defense, to pay attention only to some of the messages bombarding us. We pay attention to messages that are particularly relevant to us in some way or those that attract our attention because of their use of humor, oddity, or other similar devices.

Social comparison—our evaluation of how good our own accomplishments are by comparing ourselves to others.

Theory—any systematically related set of ideas used to describe and/or explain phenomena.

Yale approach—theorized that persuasion has components of attention, comprehension, acceptance, and retention.

REVIEW QUESTIONS

1. What are the three criteria for evaluating theory?
2. What is the difference between a folk theory and a scientific theory?
3. What is the purpose of research in relation to theory?
4. What are the five steps in conducting research to test theory?
5. In the Yale approach, why do attention and comprehension need to occur before acceptance?
6. What are two sources of social pressure discussed in group dynamics?
7. How is balance achieved among attitudes?
8. How well do the Yale approach, group dynamics, and balance theory meet the three criteria for good theory?

DISCUSSION QUESTIONS

1. Is it ethical to try to control others? If that is one goal of theory development, is it an ethical one? What limits would you suggest to keep this within ethical boundaries?
2. What phenomenon would you like to have explained? Go to a search engine such as Google, type in the phenomenon you'd like to have explained, and see what comes up. Is there an explanation for the phenomenon?

3. What folk theory do you use to explain some aspect of communication or human behavior? How might you test this theory to see if it really explains and predicts the phenomenon?

4. One aspect of group dynamics is social comparison. Think of some examples of when social comparisons influenced your attitude toward something. In retrospect, would you have been better off if social comparison had not influenced your attitude?

5. Is it ethical to manipulate group dynamics and conformity pressures to achieve persuasive goals? Was the organ meat study approach ethical? What circumstances and/or criteria would you use to establish when it is and is not ethical to use this approach?

REFERENCES

Andersen, P. A. (1988). Philosophy of science. In P. Emmert & L. L. Barker (Eds.), *Measurement of communication behavior* (pp. 3–17). White Plains, NY: Longman.

Asch, S. E. (1956). Studies of independence and conformity: A minority of one against a unanimous majority. *Psychological Monographs: General and Applied, 70*(9), 1–70.

Big flop, (1995). *American Demographics, 17*(2), 8.

Corman, S. R. (1995). That works fine in theory, but . . . In S. R. Corman, S. P. Banks, C. R. Bantz, & M. E. Mayer (Eds.), *Foundations of organizational communication* (pp. 3–10). White Plains, NY: Longman.

Festinger, L. (1954). A theory of social comparison processes. *Human Relations, 7,* 117–140.

Heider, F. (1946). Attitudes and cognitive organization. *Journal of Psychology, 21,* 107–112.

Heider, F. (1958). *The psychology of interpersonal relations.* New York: Wiley.

Hovland, C. I., Janis, I. L., & Kelley, H. H. (1953). *Communication and persuasion: Psychological studies of opinion change.* New Haven, CT: Yale University Press.

Lewin, K. (1943). Forces behind food habits and methods of change. *Bulletin of the National Research Council, 108,* 35–65.

Lewin, K. (1947). Group decision and social change. In T. Newcomb & E. Hartley (Eds.), *Readings in social psychology.* New York: Holt.

Maximum persuasion (n.d.). Retrieved November 30, 2004 from https://secure.maxpersuasion.com/display_p.php?session=&pid=1

Roloff, M. E. (1980). Self-awareness and the persuasion process: Do we really know what we're doing? In M. E. Roloff & G. R. Miller (Eds.), *Persuasion: New directions in theory and research* (pp. 29–66). Beverly Hills, CA: Sage.

Staats, A. W., & Staats, C. K. (1958). Attitudes established by classical conditioning. *Journal of Abnormal and Social Psychology, 57,* 37–40.

The ultimate persuasion formula (n.d.). Retrieved October 8, 2004 from http://www.theultimatepersuasionformula.com/

Zimbardo, P. G., Ebbesen, E. B., & Maslach, C. (1977). *Influencing attitudes and changing behavior.* Reading, MA: Addison-Wesley.

CHAPTER 8

SOCIAL JUDGMENT THEORY

It's All Relative

Have you ever noticed that if you take a sip of coffee that is at room temperature it tastes *cold*, yet if you take a sip of a soft drink that is at room temperature it tastes *warm*. Why is this? The two beverages are the same temperature. How we perceive something depends in part on what we are comparing it to. Therefore, whether we perceive something as warm or cold depends on to what it is being compared. The "something" that we compare an experience to is referred to as an *anchor*. If our anchor is 190° F, as it probably is for hot coffee, then tasting something that is 75° F seems pretty cold. If our anchor is 40° F, as it likely is for soft drinks, then 75° F seems pretty warm. Although it is possible to perceive something without comparing it to something else, human beings almost always immediately compare what they perceive to what they already know to help them make sense of the stimuli.

FIGURE 8.1 Baby Blues.

LEARNING OBJECTIVES

- EXPLAIN THE CONCEPTS OF LATITUDE OF ACCEPTANCE, REJECTION, AND NONCOMMITMENT.
- EXPLAIN HOW ASSIMILATION AND CONTRASTING OCCUR.
- EXPLAIN HOW EGO-INVOLVEMENT AFFECTS THE JUDGMENT OF MESSAGES.
- DESCRIBE THE ATTITUDE CHANGE PROCESS FROM THE SOCIAL JUDGMENT PERSPECTIVE.

We make comparisons when understanding physical phenomena such as temperature, weight, brightness, loudness, and so on, but we also make comparisons when interpreting social phenomena. In the *Baby Blues* comic strip shown in Figure 8.1, the father was evaluating what constituted hard work by comparing between what he did at his job and the demands on him at home. Similarly, whether we perceive the media as being "liberal" or "conservative" depends greatly on what has been referred to as our **attitudinal anchors**. An attitudinal anchor is the position on a particular issue that a person finds most acceptable (Sherif, Sherif, & Nebergall, 1965). Thus, someone whose preferred political stance is at the liberal end of the continuum would have been more likely to favor Hillary Clinton for president and probably would have viewed Fox News as being too conservative. Conversely, an individual with a more conservative attitudinal anchor who supported Donald Trump would more likely have rated Fox News as being fair and well balanced but see CNN as being too liberal. Muzafer Sherif and Carl Hovland (1961) applied these principles of psychophysical judgment to the domain of attitudes in persuasion and developed **social judgment theory.** This is the first cognitive theory of persuasion that we discuss. By cognitive theory, we mean a theory that examines how persuasive messages are processed.

LATITUDES OF ACCEPTANCE AND REJECTION

A basic premise of social judgment theory is that an attitude toward an issue or object can be thought of as a range of attitudes rather than as a single point along a continuum. With this theory, a person's stance on abortion would not simply be either pro-choice or pro-life, but it would encompass a range of positions that would be acceptable and/or unacceptable. For example, at one end of the continuum of possible attitudes toward abortion is the pro-life view, with the most extreme position being that abortion should not be legal under any circumstances. At the other end of the continuum is the pro-choice view with the most extreme position being that abortion should be available upon demand at any point during a pregnancy. Between these two extreme positions are more moderate positions, some of which are more pro-life and some of which are more pro-choice. Figure 8.2 illustrates an example of a continuum of possible positions on abortion, with the midpoint of the continuum representing a neutral attitude toward the issue. This continuum has nine positions, but there is no set number of positions. Imagine that your attitudinal anchor coincides with Position 2 in Figure 8.2, which indicates that abortion should be acceptable in most cases short of gender selection of babies. This is the position you agree with most strongly and support most fully. Although Position 2 is your most preferred position, you probably find other positions acceptable as well. Let's say that you also find Positions 1 and 3 acceptable even if they don't represent your most preferred position. This range of positions is referred to as your **latitude of acceptance (LOA)**, which is simply the range of positions a person finds acceptable.

If we continue to use abortion as an example, you probably also find one position the most unacceptable. Let's say that Position 9 in Figure 8.2, where abortion is unacceptable under any circumstances, represents your most unacceptable position. You probably find some other positions unacceptable as well. For example, these may be Positions 6, 7, and 8. These positions represent your **latitude of rejection (LOR)**, which is simply the range of positions you find unacceptable. To continue our example, let's say that Positions 4 and 5 represent positions you have no real opinion on or feel neutral toward. This range of positions is the **latitude of noncommitment (LNC)**.

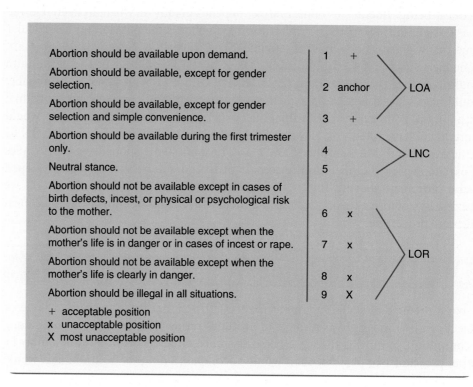

FIGURE 8.2 Latitudes of acceptance and rejection.

Social judgment theory proposes that each issue or attitude object has a range of positions that can be divided into the LOA (which contains the attitudinal anchor), LOR, and often (but not always) an LNC as well. The width, or number of positions included in any given latitude, can vary. Depending on the topic, a person's latitude may be so narrow that it includes only one position. A latitude could also be split. For example the LOR might include the extreme ends of the continuum, while the LOA includes moderate positions. The latitudes of acceptance, rejection, and non-commitment are important components of social judgment theory and are discussed further as we explore other aspects of the theory.

JUDGMENTS AND ATTITUDE CHANGE

A core assumption of social judgment theory is that your attitudinal anchor influences how you evaluate a persuasive message. This is illustrated in Figure 8.3. Let's say you are on the receiving end of a message based in Position 4 of Figure 8.3. You're likely to perceive this message as near your attitudinal anchor (Position 2). Because you perceive the message as similar to your views, you are assimilating the message. **Assimilation** means a person perceives a message as being similar to his or her attitudinal anchor and possibly closer than it really is from an objective point of view. When people assimilate a message, they are accepting the message. When people assimilate a message, they may distort it, perceiving it as being in agreement with their views when the message really may be quite discrepant. On the other hand, receivers may alter their anchor, essentially moving the anchor in the direction of the message. When assimilation occurs, receivers may perceive the message as closer to their anchor than it really is (a distortion of the message), move their anchor in the direction of the message, or some combination of the two. Therefore, a premise of social judgment theory is that assimilation facilitates persuasion.

Look once again at the continuum in Figure 8.3. If you perceived the message (based on Position 4) as being quite different from your attitudinal anchor, you would be contrasting the message. **Contrasting** occurs when a person perceives the message as being in opposition to his or her views. Like assimilation, contrasting often involves distortion, and where assimilation facilitates persuasion, contrasting inhibits persuasion. With contrasting, receivers perceive the message as being more different from their views than it really is. An objective bystander may judge the message as representing Position 3, but the receiver may distort the message and perceive it as representing Position 7 (falling in the LOR).

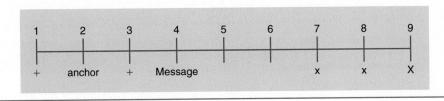

FIGURE 8.3 Assimilation and contrast effects.

A third possible way of responding to a message is the process called the **boomerang effect**. Rather than assimilating or contrasting the message, receivers may actually move their anchor away from the intended direction of the message. We often think that the worst thing that can happen if we pitch a persuasive message is that the listeners will simply fail to accept the message. The boomerang effect suggests that the message could actually be counterproductive; we could end up with receivers more opposed to our position than they were in the first place. In this case, the anchor is actually moved in the opposite direction of what we wanted.

An example of the boomerang effect can be found in politics. Rush Limbaugh, a popular conservative talk show host, was opposed to a congressional proposal to require all health insurance coverage to include contraceptives. Although much of the prior debate centered on whether there should be exemptions for religious organizations, Limbaugh's most publicized criticism focused on the defense of the proposal by a law student named Sandra Fluke. His on air comments included labeling her as a slut and a prostitute along with indicating that if public taxpayers were going to pay for her to have sex, he wanted her to post a video of it online so everyone could watch. Public outcry resulted from what was perceived to be a personal attack on a young woman, and public opinion became more favorable about insurance coverage of contraceptives. In this case, Limbaugh's message was not only rejected, but individuals' attitudinal anchors appeared to move in the opposite direction and away from the position advocated by his message. Thus, if a message is perceived as falling within the LOR, it will be rejected and the anchor may even move in the opposite of the intended direction.

Assimilation and contrasting are perceptual effects. Our preexisting attitudes and beliefs influence the way we perceive and interpret information. We selectively attend to and organize information on the basis of our attitudes and beliefs (as well as other factors). A liberal Democrat watching the nightly news is more likely to attend to comments and stories that support his or her view that the media is an extension of big business and capitalism, whereas the conservative Republican is more likely to attend to comments and stories that support his or her view that journalists are a bunch of bleeding heart liberals.

If the message is perceived as falling in the LNC, social judgment theory does not predict exactly how the message will be processed. Either assimilation or contrasting could occur. A few studies more recently have reported greater message acceptance when the message fell into the LNC; however, limited research supports this finding. Recall that prediction is a criterion of a good theory. Although social judgment theory helps us explain how people evaluate messages, it is limited in its ability to predict outcomes when messages fall into the LNC.

EGO-INVOLVEMENT

We have discussed the idea of anchors, making comparisons, and how our existing attitudes and beliefs influence our comparisons. Sherif and his colleagues identified another factor that influences how a person evaluates a message: ego-involvement. A person's ego-involvement in the issue influences how a message is evaluated and thus whether the message is assimilated or contrasted. **Ego-involvement** is a person's commitment to an issue and is related to a person's self-concept and self-esteem (Sherif et al., 1965). Recall our discussion of involvement from Chapter 6, where we identified different types of involvement. Ego-involvement is also called value-relevant involvement and is different from outcome-relevant involvement, which is discussed in Chapter 11. A person is ego-involved when his or her attitude toward an issue is closely linked to his or her identity and self-concept. For example, students might have ego-involving attitudes toward grades. It is difficult to be objective in evaluating our own work if our grade and our sense of self-value are tied up in achieving a positive outcome. Although people likely have attitudes toward thousands of different objects/issues/people, only a few of those attitudes will be ego-involving.

Social judgment theory predicts that ego-involvement will affect the persuasion process in two ways. The first prediction is that ego-involvement affects the size of the LOR and LNC. Social judgment theory predicts that as ego-involvement increases, the width of the LOR increases (includes more positions) and the LNC decreases (includes fewer positions) or disappears. Therefore, let's say that Rose defines herself as pro-life and she is highly ego-involved in the abortion issue. Rose believes that abortion should be illegal but should be available to women who are victims of violent rape and young girls who are victims of incest and that abortion should only occur during the first 6 weeks of pregnancy. Rose has thought through the issue, and she believes she is right. As a result of this involvement with the issue, there are very few, if any, positions for which she is noncommittal, making her LNC very narrow (or even nonexistent). Another result of this involvement is that her LOR expands to include all the positions she may have previously been noncommittal on as well as any position that does not fall in her LOA. Originally Sherif and Hovland (1961) hypothesized that the LOA would also be affected by ego-involvement and would become much narrower. Research indicated, however, that the LOR and LNC were affected by ego-involvement but that the LOA was not (Eagly & Chaiken, 1993).

The second prediction is that ego-involvement is thought to increase contrasting and assimilation effects. An ego-involved person is more likely to either assimilate or contrast a message; in other words, a highly ego-involved person distorts a message more than does a person who is less ego-involved. If a person is ego-involved, he or she is committed to a position and has a personal stake in the issue. Also, the ego-involved person has probably considered various positions and concluded that his or her position is the *best* position. As a result, the person tends to dichotomize the issue into the two extremes with no (or very little) middle ground. A result of this dichotomized view is that the receiver distorts (assimilates or contrasts) the message to make it fit into his or her LOA or LOR.

In an effort to demonstrate the impact of ego-involvement on message acceptance and rejection, Hovland, Harvey, and Sherif (1957) conducted a study that has become somewhat famous over the years. It took place in Oklahoma during the 1950s and, at this time, Oklahoma was a "dry" state (the sale of alcohol was prohibited). There had recently been a referendum on the issue (prohibition won), but it was still a hot topic of discussion. By drawing on statements made by various newspapers in the state, nine positions on the prohibition issue were identified and are shown in Figure 8.4. These nine statements were the basis for a measure developed by Hovland

and his colleagues and referred to as an "ordered alternatives questionnaire." This measure consists of a set of nine positions representing the continuum of positions on an issue. This measure was used to assess the latitudes of acceptance, rejection, and noncommitment. Essentially, individuals were asked to mark on the questionnaire the statement they most agreed with (their attitudinal anchor), any other statements they agreed with, the statement they disagreed with most, and any other statements they disagreed with.

Hovland and his colleagues were particularly interested in examining the hypothesis that ego-involvement would increase assimilation and contrasting effects. To test their hypothesis, they identified people with established and publicly committed stands on the wet-dry issue. They recruited 183 members of the Women's Christian Temperance Union and the Salvation Army as having high ego-involvement in prohibition (the dry stand). Hovland et al. note that recruiting individuals with high ego-involvement in repeal (wet stand) was difficult; however, they were able to recruit 25 people personally known to the experimenters or their assistants as being committed to the repeal of prohibition. Additionally, 290 college students who represented a more moderate position on the issue were recruited.

To test their hypothesis, Hovland et al. prepared three messages based on arguments actually used by prohibition and repeal advocates during the referendum. One message represented an extreme "wet" position, one an extreme "dry" position, and one a moderate position based on Position F in Figure 8.4. The wet message was presented to the dry and moderate participants, the dry message was presented to the

From Journal of Abnormal and Social Psychology (Hovland, Harvey, & Sherif, 1957).

(A) Since alcohol is the curse of mankind, the sale and use of alcohol, including light beer, should be completely abolished.

(B) Since alcohol is the main cause of corruption in public life, lawlessness, and immoral acts, its sale and use should be prohibited.

(C) Since it is hard to stop at a reasonable moderation point in the use of alcohol, it is safer to discourage its use.

(D) Alcohol should not be sold or used except as a remedy for snake bites, cramps, colds, fainting, and other aches and pains.

(E) The arguments in favor and against the sale and use of alcohol are nearly equal.

(F) The sale of alcohol should be regulated so that it is available in limited quantities for special occasions.

(G) The sale and use of alcohol should be permitted with proper state controls so that the revenue from taxation may be used for the betterment of schools, highways, and other state institutions.

(H) Since prohibition is a major cause of corruption in public life, lawlessness, immoral acts, and juvenile delinquency, the sale and use of alcohol should be legalized.

(I) It has become evident that man cannot get along without alcohol; therefore, there should be no restriction whatsoever on its sale and use.

FIGURE 8.4 Ordered alternatives questionnaire.

wet and moderate participants, and the moderate message was presented to all three groups. Approximately 3 weeks before hearing the audio-recorded message, participants indicated their latitudes of acceptance, rejection, and noncommitment regarding the positions shown in Figure 8.4. After listening to the message, participants once again indicated their latitudes of acceptance, rejection, and noncommitment on the issue. Hovland et al. were able to support their hypothesis. Participants whose view diverged greatly from that advocated by the message perceived the message as being more different from their own view than it actually was (contrasting effect). Those participants whose view was close to the position advocated by the message tended to perceive the message as being closer or more similar to their view than it really was (assimilation affect).

Hovland et al.'s (1957) study provided the first evidence that ego-involvement influenced how a message was evaluated and specifically demonstrated the assimilation and contrast effects. However, this study has also received a good deal of criticism. A primary criticism is that the participants were *presumed* to be highly ego-involved because of their group memberships. The researchers assumed that anyone who was a member of the Women's Christian Temperance Union would be highly ego-involved in the prohibition issue and that college students in journalism, speech, education, chemistry, and other classes would be only moderately involved in the issue. Furthermore, those who were recruited as wet were chosen on the basis of personal acquaintance. It is questionable whether or not Hovland et al. really examined different levels of ego-involvement. Later research, however, examined ego-involvement using different methods and found similar results: that persuasion was reduced when highly ego-involved participants were exposed to counter-attitudinal messages (Eagly & Chaiken, 1993). Therefore, it is fairly safe to conclude that ego-involvement influences how we interpret messages; however, the process and its finer points are not well understood.

CHANGING ATTITUDES WITH SOCIAL JUDGMENT THEORY

Social judgment theory proposes that attitude change is most likely to occur when the message is perceived to fall within the LOA. When a message is perceived to fall within the LOA, the position being advocated is assimilated, its content is positively evaluated, and attitude change may occur. On the other hand, if a message is perceived as falling within the LOR, contrasting occurs, the content is negatively evaluated, and the persuasion attempt fails. You may draw the conclusion that changing attitude is easy: all you have to do is make sure your message falls within your audience's LOA. Like most things that "seem easy," however, attitude change is not quite that simple. For one thing, your message may not fall within a person's LOA. The message you want your audience to accept may be highly discrepant from their initial position on the issue. We are often faced with these kinds of challenges in applied persuasion settings. A person advocating a liberal Democratic candidate for president is not likely to find many message positions that fall within the LOA of a conservative Republican.

The level of message discrepancy is a key issue in predicting attitude change within social judgment theory. **Message discrepancy** refers to the difference between the position being advocated by a message and the preferred position of the receiver. For example, let's say your audience's preferred position (anchor) is represented by Position B in Figure 8.4 (the sale and use of alcohol should be prohibited). If you present a persuasive message based on Position I (there should be no restriction on the sale and use of alcohol), your message would be much more discrepant than if your persuasive message was based on Position G (the sale and use of alcohol should be permitted with state controls and taxation). Social judgment theory makes the prediction that as message discrepancy increases, attitude change will also increase to the point where the message is discrepant enough to fall within the LOR. At this point, continuing to increase levels of discrepancy will result in reduced attitude change. This relationship between message discrepancy and attitude change is shown in Figure 8.5. With small amounts of message discrepancy, only small amounts of attitude change are likely. As the message becomes more discrepant, greater attitude change is possible; however, the possibility of the message being contrasted and rejected also increases.

A study by Siero and Jan Doosje (1993) found that messages that fell within the LNC were most persuasive. Siero and Jan Doosje presented three messages advocating using cars less in order to save the environment (this study was conducted with members of the Royal Dutch Tourist Association, which is similar to the American Automobile Association in the United States). All three messages advocated using cars less frequently but varied in their level of extremity. When a message was judged as falling within a person's LNC, attitude was most likely to change. However, little attitude change occurred when the message was judged as falling within the LOR.

A similar study was conducted on a college campus. Many universities are concerned about alcohol abuse on campus, and have searched for the most effective way to change student behavior. Smith, Atkin, Martell, Allen, and Hembroff (2006) drew on social norms surrounding drinking, and argued that messages using social norms falling in the LNC were most likely to be accepted. They researched how believable

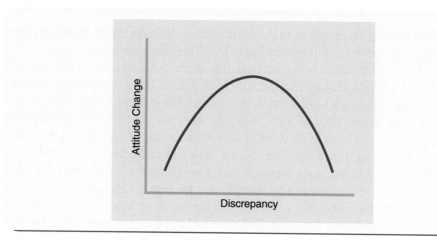

FIGURE 8.5 Discrepancy and attitude change.

students found claims about different percentages of students on campus who had five or fewer drinks when they partied. Researchers found that respondents' belief that 60 to 70 percent of campus students had five or fewer drinks when they partied represented the LNC at the upper end of the scale. They then widely disseminated ads and posters on campus that included the LNC social norm of "most (63%) drink zero to five when they party" in the message. The results showed both a shift in social norms and a reduction in the number of reported drinks that occurred during partying on that campus. This applied research did not compare the LNC-based message to ones in students' LOA or LOR, so it is difficult to claim that messages in the LNC are superior to others, but it does support the concept that, in some cases, messages falling in the LNC can result in attitude and behavior change.

Therefore, it is best to construct a persuasive message so that it falls within the receiver's LOA or LNC. If the message is judged to fall within the LOR, it will most likely be rejected. Thus, persuasion that seeks greater attitude change is not likely to occur with a single message. It would be necessary to target messages at the outer edges of the receiver's LOA or LNC in order to gradually drag the anchor toward the desired point. This process would have to be repeated over time to gradually move a receiver toward the ultimately desired goal.

Three factors can influence the relationship between discrepancy and attitude change. These are ego-involvement, source credibility, and language intensity. When ego-involvement is high, the audience will tolerate relatively little message discrepancy before attitude change decreases. People with high ego-involvement have a larger LOR, so it takes relatively little discrepancy before the message will fall into the LOR and be rejected. The second variable is source credibility. The more credible the source is perceived to be, the more accepting the audience is of message discrepancy. In other words, the audience will give more consideration to messages from highly credible sources.

Influencing attitude from the perspective of social judgment theory requires the source to structure his or her message so that it is not too discrepant from the audience's attitudinal anchor. This leads to an incremental approach to persuasion. By incremental, we mean to slowly move your audience toward your position with a series of persuasive messages. Ideally, each message is assimilated, moving the anchor in the desired direction a little each time. An example of attitudes changing incrementally is Americans' attitude toward animal rights. In the early 1970s, the idea of animals having rights was quite foreign to most Americans. Many people perceived animals existing to serve humans, and little thought was given to the ethics of using animals for testing products for human consumption. Also, wearing fur coats was popular and viewed as a status symbol. We could describe Americans' attitudinal anchor as being against animal rights (on a continuum with animals having no rights at one extreme and with animals having rights equal to humans at the other extreme). Various groups have campaigned for animal rights and presented the American people with a variety of messages about animal rights and animal testing. Over the years, Americans' attitudinal anchor has gradually shifted toward animals having rights. Today there are cosmetic lines that tout their product testing as animal-free, fur coats are not nearly as popular (however, leather coats continue to be popular), and the number of vegetarians and vegans is increasing, all indicating the change in attitude toward animals among the American public.

In Chapter 5 we discussed language intensity as a message factor. Recall that intense language is emotionally intense and specific. Language intensity also moderates the impact of message discrepancy on attitude change. Intense language enhances perceptions of message discrepancy. Messages that use intense language are interpreted as more extreme, so the distance between the receiver's position and the position being advocated by the message seems greater. Therefore, if the audience has low ego-involvement with the topic, increasing language intensity enhances attitude change, especially if the message is delivered by a credible source (Hamilton & Hunter, 1998). This is because the low involved person is less likely to reject the message, so greater discrepancy means the message has the potential to result in greater change. On the other hand, if the audience has high ego-involvement, increasing language intensity will probably reduce attitude change.

When attempting to persuade audience members, their existing beliefs and attitudes will influence how they interpret your message. If they judge your message as being "on the other side," they are likely to disregard your message and you will be unsuccessful in your influence attempt. In fact, if the boomerang effect kicks in, the persuasive attempt could be counterproductive and move the receivers in the opposite direction from what you want. On the other hand, if they perceive your message as being "on their side," they are more likely to accept your message. If they perceive your message as falling within their LNC, then they may listen to you because they haven't made up their minds yet on these positions, and you have the opportunity to influence them. People who are highly ego-involved are very difficult to influence because they have essentially "made up their minds" and are therefore generally unwilling to accept a position that varies from their LOA.

APPLYING SOCIAL JUDGMENT THEORY

Let's consider how you might apply social judgment theory in constructing a persuasive campaign. For this process, we will work through a hypothetical example involving a challenging topic: passing death with dignity legislation in the state of Ohio. The first step in the process would be to identify the range of positions on assisted-suicide for voters in Ohio similar to what Hoveland et al. (1957) did with the wet-dry issue in Oklahoma. Using a sample of Ohio voters, we would need to learn what positions were in the LOA for the majority and what attitudes were in the LOR for the majority. We would want to know not only about the majority but also about the latitudes for certain groups such as Protestants and Catholics, professional and blue collar workers, and the young and old. Some groups will be undecided. Others will hold moderate views, either in support of or in opposition to the legislation. Still other groups will feel very strongly about the topic. We would need to select representative samples of different groups and ask them to evaluate the continuum of all the possible positions.

We might expect members of the Catholic community to be strongly opposed to assisted-suicide, and the terminally ill to be in favor of such legislation. Both of these groups would likely be ego-involved in the topic. For the Catholic community, any message promoting assisted-suicide would likely be very discrepant and fall into their LOR. Finding a credible person to author a favorable message, such as a famous physician, would enhance our chances of gaining some movement with a larger message discrepancy. However, a message asking directly for support for this legislation would be expected to fail with the Catholic community because such a call would be squarely within the LOR regardless of the source of the message.

Does this mean it is hopeless? No, not as long as we take a long-term view. Proponents of civil rights faced an uphill battle initially, and gradually barriers were broken down and attitudes toward racial rights were shifted. Similarly, attitudes toward same-sex marriage have changed dramatically over the past 20 years. Radical change will not occur overnight, but can happen slowly over time. In the case of death with dignity, attitudes have changed from being "unthinkable" to being supported by many Americans. To change attitudes toward assisted-suicide, we have to consider how to tailor a message that can seek small, gradual changes toward the ultimate goal. We need to find where the edges of the LOA and/or LNC are for the groups not currently in favor of death with dignity laws and create messages targeted at those points in the attitude continuum. Given the size of the likely discrepancy between our message and the anchors of the target audience, finding highly credible sources would be important.

Google "Gay Marriage Timeline" to see a summary of how views of same sex marriage changed over the past 50 years.

We also need to keep in mind that, with this topic, the opposition is also engaged in persuasive campaigns. Just as proponents are seeking gradual progress in legalizing assisted-suicide, the opposition is also engaged in campaigns to maintain the status quo and prevent legalization of assisted-suicide. The American Medical Association

© Associated Press

FIGURE 8.6

has voiced strong opposition to right to die initiatives. However, end of life directives and do not resuscitate orders have become common and represent a moderate position. These actions represent gradual steps toward legalizing assisted-suicide. Even in the absence of opposition, movement toward social change is slow. In the presence of opposition, movement is even slower and at times is even reversed.

STRENGTHS AND LIMITATIONS

In Chapter 7, we introduced the criteria of explain, predict, and control for evaluating theory. We can use those three criteria to view the strengths and weaknesses of social judgment theory. One strength of social judgment theory is that it provides an *explanation* of how an attitudinal anchor can change over time. Slightly discrepant messages are assimilated, gradually changing the attitudinal anchor, until at some point the person holds a very different position than he or she did originally. Similarly, social judgment theory explains how and why some messages can backfire and result in a boomerang effect.

Another strength of social judgment theory is the implication it has for applied persuasion. Audience analysis is a central part of using social judgment theory effectively. The basic assumption of social judgment theory is that our existing attitudinal anchors influence persuasion. For this theory, the issue of message discrepancy and the importance of your message not being *too* discrepant from your audience's position are central concerns. The implication of these assumptions is that a source must know something about his or her audience. The source needs to know the audience's existing attitudinal anchors as well as their latitudes in order to construct a message that will not be contrasted.

An additional *explanatory* strength of social judgment theory is that it helps us understand how people process a persuasive message and why two persons holding similar initial attitudes (or attitudinal anchors) can respond to the same message in different ways. This strength of social judgment theory also leads to a limitation. We cannot predict how individuals will likely respond to a message unless we know how they evaluate the full continuum of positions. Just knowing the most preferred position or attitude toward the topic is not enough. In other words, social judgment theory is not very useful for *controlling* persuasion. Because of the enormous difficulty of applying and testing this theory, it has received relatively little research attention.

Another limitation of social judgment theory is that it does not provide a theoretical *prediction* for what happens when a message falls in the LNC. The theory predicts that a message will be assimilated if it falls into the LOA and contrasted if it falls into the LOR. Essentially, social judgment theory states that either assimilation or contrasting may occur if the message falls in the LNC, but does not specify the conditions necessary for either response, making it impossible to predict how people will respond in such a situation.

An additional limitation of social judgment theory is the ordered alternatives questionnaire. The theory is constructed with this attitude measurement device as its basis. If you examine the ordered alternatives questionnaire, it consists of a series of belief statements, similar to the Thurstone attitude scale. The problems that plagued the Thurstone scale and led many to abandon it also plague the ordered alternatives questionnaire. This approach to defining and measuring attitudes makes social judgment theory difficult to apply to real-world persuasion situations and thus represents a failure of the theory to allow us to *control* persuasion. Another major weakness of social judgment theory is that it does not address how a message should be constructed. We know where we want it to be perceived on the attitude continuum, but no guidance is offered to help us figure out how to construct a message that can be placed so precisely. This also reflects a lack of good *control* for this theory.

Like all theories, social judgment theory has both strengths and limitations. It offers good explanatory power, but its predictive power is limited and our ability to control persuasion by using this theory is also quite limited. This theory offers some guidance in the design of messages, but its power in this area is less strong than other theories. Strength in explanatory power is important enough to warrant understanding the theory and the unique contributions it has made to the study of persuasion, but the weaknesses in prediction and control make this a theory of less practical use overall.

SUMMARY

- We judge physical phenomena and communication events by comparing them to our previous experience or attitudes. These are referred to as anchors.

- The latitude of acceptance (LOA) refers to those positions on an issue that we find acceptable. The latitude of rejection (LOR) refers to those positions on an issue that we find most unacceptable. The latitude of noncommitment (LNC) refers to those positions we have little or no opinion on.

- When we are exposed to a persuasive message, we compare it to our existing attitude (or LOA). If we judge the message as being similar to our attitude (even if it's not by objective standards), we are assimilating the message. If we judge the message as being dissimilar to our attitude (even if it's not by objective standards), we are contrasting the message.

- Creating clear and explicit messages can reduce assimilation and contrasting.

- Ego-involvement is a person's commitment to an issue and is closely linked to his or her identity and self-concept. Ego-involvement increases assimilation and contrast effects, and it affects the size of the LOR and the LNC.

- Message discrepancy refers to the difference between the position being advocated and the preferred position of the receiver. As message discrepancy increases, persuasion increases to a point at which attitude change begins to decrease.

- Ego-involvement, source credibility, and language intensity are three factors thought to influence the discrepancy-persuasion relationship.

- An important strength of social judgment theory is that it places emphasis on understanding the receiver. The application of social judgment theory requires a source to understand the existing attitudes of his or her audience.

- Two primary limitations of social judgment theory are the ordered alternatives questionnaire, which was designed as the means to measure the latitudes and change them, and the difficulty of applying the theory. This reflects limited predictive and control power.

KEY TERMS

Assimilation—a person perceives a message as being similar to his or her attitudinal anchor and possibly closer than it really is from an objective point of view.

Attitudinal anchor—the position on a particular issue that a person finds most acceptable.

Boomerang effect—can happen during contrasting, when a person's anchor is moved in the opposite direction of the proposed message.

Contrasting—when a person perceives a message as being in opposition to his or her views.

Ego-involvement—a person's commitment to an issue and related to a person's self-concept and self-esteem.

Latitude of acceptance (LOA)—the range of positions along an attitude continuum a person finds acceptable.

Latitude of noncommitment (LNC)—the range of positions along an attitude continuum a person finds neither acceptable nor unacceptable.

Latitude of rejection (LOR)—the range of positions along an attitude continuum a person finds unacceptable.

Message discrepancy—the difference between the position being advocated by a message and the preferred position of the receiver.

REVIEW QUESTIONS

1. What is an attitudinal anchor?
2. What are the LOA, the LOR, and the LNC?
3. What are assimilation and contrast effects? Why are they described as perceptual effects?
4. What is ego-involvement? How does ego-involvement affect the persuasion process?
5. What does message discrepancy refer to?
6. How much discrepancy should there be between a source's persuasive message and the audience's preferred position?
7. What are the strengths and weaknesses of social judgment theory?

DISCUSSION QUESTIONS

1. Think of an issue, such as the death penalty, affirmative action, or legalization of marijuana, and write down a range of positions going from one extreme to another. Does the range of positions fit into a continuum? Are there positions that don't fit into the continuum?

2. Are assimilation and contrasting effects limited to the persuasion context, or do these phenomena occur in other situations as well? If yes, what kinds of situations? Think of examples of when assimilation and contrast have occurred.

3. Think of an issue in which you are ego-involved. How do you respond when someone tries to influence you on this issue?

4. Social judgment theory suggests that changing an audience's attitude can be incremental (a little at a time). In what kinds of issues would such an incremental approach be appropriate? In what kinds of issues would such an approach be inappropriate?

5. Consider the case of a political candidate running for the presidency of the United States. Is it ethical for that candidate to represent his or her position as less extreme than it really is in order to fall into the LOA of more people? How about casting an opponent's position as more extreme than the opponent would represent it in order to encourage it to fall into voters' LORs? Look at historical positions that candidates have taken and compare them to actual actions taken after they were elected. Did they employ social judgment theory ethically or not?

REFERENCES

Eagly, A. H., & Chaiken, S. (1993). *The psychology of attitudes.* Fort Worth, TX: Harcourt Brace Jovanovich.

Hovland, C. I., Harvey, O. J., & Sherif, M. (1957). Assimilation and contrast effects in reaction to communication and attitude change. *Journal of Abnormal and Social Psychology, 55,* 244–252.

Sherif, M., & Hovland, C. I. (1961). *Social judgment: Assimilation and contrast effects in communication and attitude change.* New Haven, CT: Yale University Press.

Sherif, C. W., Sherif, M., & Nebergall, R. E. (1965). *Attitude and attitude change: The social judgment involvement approach.* Philadelphia: W. B. Saunders.

Siero, F. W., & Jan Doosje, B. (1993). Attitude change following persuasive communication: Integrating social judgment theory and the elaboration likelihood model. *European Journal of Social Psychology, 23,* 541–554.

Smith, S. W., Atkin, C. K., Martell, D., Allen, R., & Hembroff, L. (2006). A social judgment theory approach to conducting formative research in a social norms campaign. *Communication Theory, 16,* 141–152.

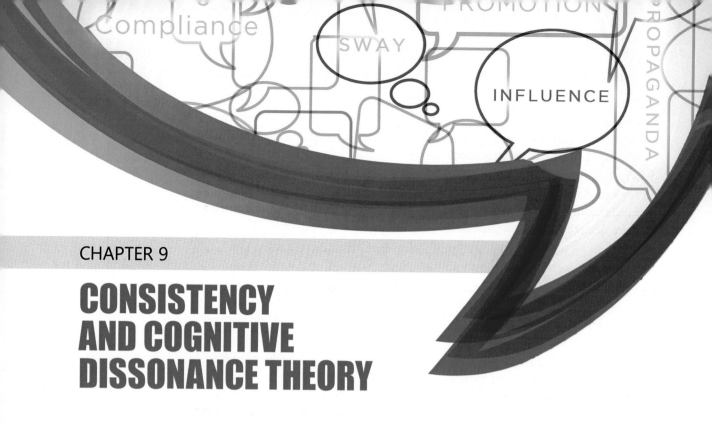

CHAPTER 9

CONSISTENCY AND COGNITIVE DISSONANCE THEORY

MARJ AND LARRY'S APPLE ADVENTURE

Our dog chewed the power cord for our iMac®, which is our home computer that we all share. Our iMac is just two years old and is in our home office on the second floor. In need of a new power cord, one Saturday morning we made the trek to the Apple Store to get what we needed. The store was packed and it took a while to get a salesperson to help us locate the correct power cord. While we waited we looked at the new MacBook Pro® and the new iPad®. The MacBook Pro seemed so sleek and compact compared to our iMac. It was light weight and so easy to use. The iPad was fun with incredible graphics. A salesperson was finally able to help us, and after a short discussion on what we needed, he went to the back to see if they had a power cord in stock. We had more time to explore and play with the MacBook and iPad. Upon his return with the power cord we made our purchase and went to lunch. During lunch all we could talk about were the MacBook and iPad and how great they were. After lunch, Larry tentatively suggested we go back to the Apple Store and ask about wireless networks. A few hours later we left the Apple Store with a MacBook Pro, two iPads, and an Airport Base for wireless. We woke up this morning expecting to spend less than $100; instead we spent $3000 and we are ecstatic. How can this be?

In the situation described, Larry and Marj behaved very inconsistently. Upon setting out for the Apple Store, all they wanted was a power cord. Buying a power cord would have been consistent with their frugal and practical values and previous buying behavior. Instead, they went nuts, spent a lot of money, and came home with more than they needed. To top it off, they were pleased with their decision. This doesn't seem to make sense. Their behavior was inconsistent with their beliefs and values. To help us make sense of this situation and how they were persuaded, we use a family of theories known as consistency theories.

LEARNING OBJECTIVES

- EXPLAIN HOW COGNITIVE DISSONANCE THEORY BUILDS ON THE BALANCE AND CONGRUITY THEORIES.
- EXPLAIN HOW DISSONANCE IS CREATED AND HOW IT IS REDUCED.
- DESCRIBE AND GIVE EXAMPLES OF THE CONTEXTS IN WHICH DISSONANCE OCCURS.
- EXPLAIN THE NECESSARY CONDITIONS FOR COGNITIVE DISSONANCE TO OCCUR.

CONSISTENCY

Social judgment theory was the first *cognitive theory* introduced. By cognitive theory we mean a theory that examines how receivers process persuasive messages. In this chapter we explore another cognitive theory that focuses on the human need for consistency. Cognitive dissonance theory proposes that humans are motivated to be consistent in their thoughts and behaviors. There is a great deal of support for this proposition, although an alternative view is explored at the end of this chapter with a discussion of self-perception theory. But first we will discuss the role of consistency in persuasion.

Fritz Heider (1946; 1958) was the first to examine consistency with the development of balance theory (see Chapter 7 for more on Balance Theory). Heider hypothesized that people desired consistency in their interpersonal relationships. Specifically, people want their friends to like the same things they do. For example, if I like Jeff and I like *Star Wars*, I want Jeff to also like *Star Wars*. Such a situation is balanced and comfortable. If Jeff doesn't like *Star Wars*, imbalance is created and I become motivated to either like Jeff less or like *Star Wars* less to create balance. Some support was found for this theory but it never met the criteria for a good theory (see Chapter 7). During this same period, Osgood and Tannenbaum (1955) developed congruity theory that provided a more complex explanation of the human need for consistency. Congruity theory provided evidence that consistency was important, but it was not very good at predicting when attitude would change. However, the research on balance and congruity theories indicated that consistency was an important part of how people behaved and processed information. The development of cognitive dissonance theory provided a useful explanation for why consistency was important in the persuasion process.

COGNITIVE DISSONANCE THEORY

Leon Festinger (1957) developed the most accepted consistency theory that still has adherents today: the **cognitive dissonance theory**. This theory built on the knowledge generated by balance theory and congruity theory, and it has continued to be modified as more research is conducted. Festinger started with what he referred to as **cognitions**, or bits of knowledge that individuals have. Cognitions can be bits of knowledge such as "I ate pancakes for breakfast" or can be attitudes, beliefs, or values such as those discussed in Chapter 2. Think of the human mind as a vast network of cognitions.

Individual cognitions have one of three relationships with one another. A **dissonant relationship** involves two cognitions that are inconsistent with one another. In the example of Larry and Marj's computer purchase, the cognition of buying a laptop, two iPads, and a wireless setup is inconsistent, or dissonant, with the cognition "we need a new power cord for our computer." A **consonant relationship** involves two cognitions that are consistent with one another. In this case, "buying a power cord" would be consistent, or consonant, with the belief "we need a power cord." An **irrelevant relationship** involves two cognitions that a person perceives as unrelated. For instance, the cognition "I eat cheese" is most likely perceived as irrelevant to the cognition "I bought a laptop and two iPads." It is important to understand that the decision about what is dissonant, consonant, or irrelevant is up to the receiver. Each person gets to connect his or her own cognitions according to his or her own sense of what constitutes a consistent, inconsistent, or irrelevant relationship. When two cognitions have a dissonant relationship, cognitive dissonance occurs. **Cognitive dissonance** is an aversive motivational state or, in other words, it is unpleasant and people are motivated to eliminate it. When a person experiences cognitive dissonance, there is pressure to change one's cognitions and to regain consistency. In Larry and Marj's situation, we would expect them to feel cognitive dissonance over their shopping extravaganza and to be motivated to eliminate it and regain consistency. Before delving into dissonance reduction, we first need to discuss how much dissonance Larry and Marj experienced.

MAGNITUDE OF DISSONANCE

According to cognitive dissonance theory, a dissonant relationship between cognitions (or the perception of inconsistency) leads to pressure for change. However, not *all* dissonance results in change. Festinger argued that the **magnitude of dissonance,** or the amount of dissonance, varies and that the magnitude of dissonance affects the pressure for change. Not all inconsistencies bother us enough to warrant changing our attitudes or beliefs. If Jim likes peas but finds out that his good friend Bob does not, that finding probably will not make Jim feel uncomfortable enough to need to change how he feels about Bob or peas. Of course, if Jim makes his living selling peas, that could be a different story. Festinger argued that the greater the magnitude or level of dissonance, the greater the pressure for change. So, did Marj and Larry experience enough dissonance to experience pressure to change their attitudes, beliefs, or behaviors?

The magnitude of dissonance is a result of three key factors: the **importance** of the cognitions, the **ratio** of dissonant to consonant cognitions, and the degree of **cognitive overlap**. First, the more important the cognitive elements involved, the more dissonance that will likely be elicited. For example, a cognitive inconsistency related to a life-or-death question, such as driving when drunk, would generate more pressure to resolve the inconsistency than a conflict regarding vegetables. Again, the receiver determines the relationships, and the perception of importance is in the receiver's mind. Larry and Marj believe strongly in living frugally and only spending on important things. These are pretty important beliefs to them. These beliefs are inconsistent with their extravagant purchase and with the amount of money spent—it is quite likely that Larry and Marj are experiencing a lot of cognitive dissonance.

A persuader can try to raise the magnitude of dissonance by trying to raise the *importance* of the issue for the receiver. For example, antismoking campaigns have tried to increase the importance of the health hazards of smoking by emphasizing the damage done to children and family members around the smoker or the importance of the smoker being alive and healthy for loved ones. This is an effort to raise the importance of the issue. Once the magnitude or level of dissonance is large enough, the receiver feels pressured to reducethe dissonance in some way.

In addition to the importance of cognitions, the *ratio* of dissonant to consonant elements also determines the magnitude of dissonance. Most of us have multiple cognitions, or pieces of information, about any given topic. Many times, some of the cognitions are consonant and some are dissonant. The greater the number of dissonant elements in comparison to consonant elements, the more pressure there is to change or the higher the magnitude of dissonance will be.

Let's take the example of smoking and the cognition "I smoke cigarettes" and consider consonant and dissonant cognitions. On the consonant or consistent side with smoking are cognitions such as "smoking keeps my weight down," "smoking calms me down," "smoking makes me more comfortable in social settings," "I need the nicotine," and "I like the flavor of cigarettes." On the dissonant side are cognitions such as "smoking causes lung disease," "smoking causes cancer," "smoking offends other people," and "smoking is very expensive." This example has five consonant cognitions and four dissonant cognitions, a 5:4 ratio. Ignoring the importance of individual cognitions for a moment, the more consonant cognitions that are present, the less dissonance that will be experienced. The antismoking forces have developed as many arguments against smoking as possible with the hope of adding dissonant cognitions to smokers' cognitive structures to increase the magnitude of dissonance to a level that requires action by the receiver. The Centers for Disease Control and Prevention (CDC) has launched several antismoking campaigns over the years, such as the "Tips from Former Smokers," that uses true images and stories of smokers. These public service announcements similar to the one shown in Figure 9.1 attempt to create dissonance by adding important dissonant cognitions.

Google "CDC Smoking Campaigns" to see some of the messages on anti-smoking. Are these messages likely to arouse dissonance in smokers?

The third factor that influences the magnitude of dissonance experienced is the degree of *cognitive overlap* between the choices facing the subject. *The less cognitive overlap between the alternatives, the greater the dissonance experienced.* Cognitive overlap refers to the similarity of the choices available. The greater the similarity, the greater the cognitive overlap. Suppose you received an inheritance of $20,000. In deciding what to do with your inheritance, one option would be to replace your old car, an action that would be practical and greatly needed. Another option would be to splurge the bulk of the inheritance on a vacation through Europe, an action less practical that you don't necessarily need but would be wonderful. In this case, there is little similarity between buying a car and going to Europe, so there is little cognitive overlap. If you were choosing between these two options, you would likely experience a good deal of dissonance. On the other hand, if you were choosing between two different models of cars (e.g., a Toyota and a Honda), there is a great deal of cognitive overlap and therefore you would experience less dissonance than in the first example.

Persuaders often send messages to increase the magnitude of dissonance in order to increase the level of cognitive dissonance. The greater the dissonance, the more likely the target of the message is to feel pressured to do something to resolve the dissonance. Advertisers hope you will buy their products, and social movements such as Mothers Against Drunk Driving (MADD) hope you will support their cause. At other times, however, persuaders may try to help reduce the dissonance in order to prevent the targeted recipient of the message from changing attitudes or behaviors that are favorable to the persuader. For example, the tobacco industry has tried to reduce dissonance about smoking with advertisements about smokers' rights and the danger of governmental control. Attempting to alter the magnitude of dissonance is one option available to persuaders with cognitive dissonance.

It should be noted that there is no magic level of dissonance that works for everyone. Each person has his or her own level of tolerance for inconsistency, and it is up to the receiver to decide how much dissonance is enough to warrant change. Different people have different tolerances for dissonance, much as different people have different personality characteristics.

DISSONANCE REDUCTION

Once the magnitude of dissonance is sufficient to generate action of some kind to reduce the dissonance, the next question becomes what steps might be taken to lead to **dissonance reduction**. Most persuaders would like the receiver to *change behavior*, and this is one option. Companies want consumers to buy their products, politicians want votes, charities want financial contributions, and social causes want action. Changing behavior is one way to reduce dissonance, but it is not the only option available. Dissonance can be reduced by changing attitudes, beliefs, and intentions, as well as actual behavior. Dissonance reduction is a cognitive process that explains how people justify their actions.

Our discussion of magnitude of dissonance points toward ways to resolve dissonance. Recall that the importance of cognitions impacts the magnitude of dissonance. Therefore the receiver can *change the importance* of certain cognitions to reduce dissonance. For example, deciding that the cognition about the cost of smoking is not so important after all would be one way to reduce dissonance without changing behavior. Rather a cognition is changed so that it is more consistent with behavior.

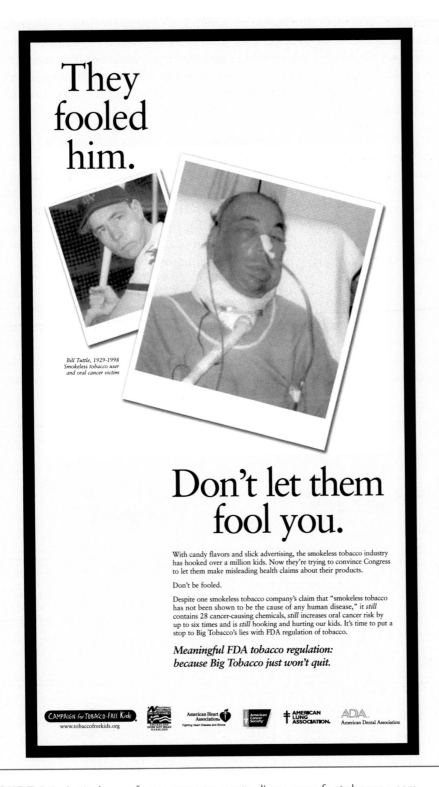

FIGURE 9.1 Antitobacco forces want to create dissonance for tobacco users.

A second way to achieve dissonance reduction is to *change the ratio* of consonant to dissonant cognitions. The receiver may identify more reasons or cognitions that are consistent with his or her behavior to reduce the dissonance. For instance, the individual could decide that smoking also enhances his or her concentration, creating a more consonant situation for the receiver. Again, cognitions are changed in order to reduce dissonance.

Robert Abelson (1959, 1963, 1968) proposed several options for dissonance reduction other than changing behavior. One option is *denial.* This involves the receiver simply choosing to disbelieve or reject information that would otherwise create dissonance. Denial is used in many other situations. Smokers may engage in denial in order to continue to smoke without experiencing dissonance. For example, Sam may point to Uncle Ray who smoked for years and died at 101 in order to deny the health hazards of smoking. When individuals use denial when faced with dissonant cognitions, neither behavior nor attitude changes. Denial maintains the status quo.

Bolstering is another option for dissonance reduction. This refers to adding consonant elements to reduce the ratio of dissonant to consonant elements. The more consonant elements there are, the less dissonance the receiver is likely to experience. A smoker who wants to continue to smoke might bolster his or her consonant cognitions by referring to others who smoke without health hazards, use weight control as a positive health benefit, emphasize the pleasure of smoking, and focus on smokers'

FIGURE 9.2 Cognitive dissonance in action.

rights issues. Adding more positives helps counter the dissonance caused by inconsistent evidence. When bolstering is used, the individual is essentially strengthening beliefs and attitudes that support the individual's behavior or decision. This may represent an attitude shift.

A third option is *transcendence*. This refers to values that are more important than the issues causing the dissonance. The superior value transcends the lesser inconsistent value. This is an example of altering the importance of cognitions. At times this is used to justify behaviors that to others appear to be very inconsistent. An example can be drawn from current controversy over abortion. Some members of the antiabortion faction have chosen to kill doctors who provide abortions as a means of protest. Because the main argument against abortion is that it involves taking a human life, the idea of taking a human life as protest would seem to be inconsistent or dissonant to many. Those who support this type of action have argued that their approach isn't dissonant. The value of protecting hundreds or thousands of unborn children in the future by killing one doctor transcends the inconsistency for these individuals. Similarly, smokers might argue that the pleasure received from smoking transcends the value of living a few more years without the pleasure of smoking for many years.

Finally, *differentiation* is an option for dissonance reduction. This refers to splitting the attitude object into acceptable or consistent parts and unacceptable or inconsistent parts. In this case, a smoker might differentiate between filtered cigarettes and unfiltered cigarettes. Smoking unfiltered cigarettes would cause dissonance because of health concerns, but smoking filtered cigarettes would be safer. Alternatively, a smoker might think that it is excessive smoking of two or more packs a day that harms health, while moderate smoking of a half pack or less each day is safe. In both cases, the offending object, smoking, was broken or differentiated into consistent and inconsistent parts.

When a person experiences cognitive dissonance, he or she is motivated to reduce the dissonance and uses one or more of the strategies we have discussed. Reduction of cognitive dissonance involves either changing one's behavior or changing one's cognitions. Changing one's cognitions is essentially changing one's attitudes and beliefs. As persuaders, we are interested in changing attitudes, beliefs, and behaviors. When we create situations in which receivers experience cognitive dissonance, we create an opportunity to influence the receivers' attitudes, beliefs, and/or behaviors.

COGNITIVE DISSONANCE CONTEXTS

In what kinds of situations is cognitive dissonance likely to occur? In general, there must be a conflict between one's cognitions for dissonance to occur. Dissonance has been studied in four contexts or situations: induced compliance, hypocrisy, decision making, and effort justification. Dissonance is probably not limited to these contexts, but the research on these contexts provides us with the key situational factors that create dissonance. Of course, when a theory explains what causes a phenomenon, we can better predict and control that phenomenon.

INDUCED COMPLIANCE

The initial study conducted by Festinger and Carlsmith (1959) is a classic example of **induced compliance** research. The researchers created a very boring task involving research participants—in this case undergraduate college students—putting spools on a tray and turning pegs for an hour. The research participants were told this was an experiment examining performance on the task. After the boring task, the researcher asked the participants for help with another part of the experiment. Participants were asked to tell a participant waiting to complete the study that the boring task they had just completed was enjoyable and interesting so future participants would have a positive expectation going into the experiment. The person posing as a waiting participant was really a confederate working for the experimenters. Half of the participants were offered $1 for performing this task; the other half were offered $20 (remember this is 1950s money). An additional group of students who completed the boring task but were not asked to talk to the waiting participant served as a control group.

Google "How much was a dollar worth in 1959" to see how much $1 and $20 was worth in 1959.

Search for "A Lesson in Cognitive Dissonance" on YouTube to see how the experiment was conducted.

The task was considered to be a **counter-attitudinal behavior** and is a key characteristic of the induced compliance context. Counter-attitudinal behavior refers to individuals behaving in a manner that goes against their attitudes. In this case, the participants were well aware of how boring the task was, yet almost all of the participants (48 out of 51) agreed to tell the next participant that it was interesting. If we assume that most people see themselves as honest, telling a lie would be counter-attitudinal. In the induced compliance context, dissonance occurs as a result of a person performing a behavior that is inconsistent with his or her attitudes (counter-attitudinal behavior).

Festinger and Carlsmith (1959) predicted that dissonance would be aroused for participants paid $1 but not for those paid $20. Those in the high-paying condition were offered enough money (and remember this was 1959 dollars) so that they could tell themselves they did it for the money. They experienced little, if any, dissonance. Those in the low-paying condition were being offered a token, but not enough to justify lying to others. The $1 participants experienced dissonance and had to reduce it.

After the participants engaged in the counter-attitudinal behavior—lying to a person they believed to be the next participant—a researcher interviewed them about participating in departmental research projects. Mixed in with the survey items were questions asking the participants to rate how interesting and enjoyable the task had been. Those participants who had been paid only a $1 found the task to be significantly more interesting and enjoyable than those who had been paid $20. A control group also engaged in the boring task for an hour and was asked to evaluate how interesting and enjoyable the task was; however, they did not engage in the counter-attitudinal behavior. This group rated the experiment similar to those paid $20. Those participants who were induced to comply with a counter-attitudinal behavior developed a relatively positive attitude toward the task when paid $1 but not when paid $20.

Why did the $1 group experience more dissonance for their counter-attitudinal advocacy? Those who were paid $1 experienced dissonance but could not use the money they were paid as a justification of their behavior. They had to convince themselves that they lied to other students because the task was not really that bad. Those who were paid $20 could tell themselves they did it for the money so they experienced little dissonance. Thus, the group with the greater dissonance had to change their attitude in order to resolve the inconsistency.

Many studies of dissonance have involved inducing participants to perform a counter-attitudinal behavior. Perhaps the most interesting of these studies was conducted by Zimbardo, Weisenberg, Firestone, and Levy (1965) and involved convincing research participants to eat grasshoppers. In this experiment, half of the participants were exposed to a cold and unfriendly researcher who encouraged them to sample the grasshoppers. The other half was exposed to a warm and friendly experimenter who similarly encouraged the subjects to sample the grasshoppers. Then, those who had eaten at least one grasshopper, about half the participants, were asked to evaluate grasshoppers as food.

Cognitive dissonance theory predicts that those who ate the grasshoppers for the unfriendly researcher would rate the grasshoppers higher than those who ate them for the friendly experimenter. Why? Those who ate them for the unfriendly researcher experienced dissonance because they did not have a good reason for sampling the grasshoppers. They might tell themselves they ate the grasshoppers because they like to try new things and they like unusual foods. Those exposed to the friendly experimenter could convince themselves that they sampled the grasshoppers to please the experimenter. As a result, there would be less dissonance to resolve. With little or no dissonance to resolve, there would be no motivation to change one's beliefs about eating grasshoppers, and the grasshoppers would be rated unfavorably. This was exactly what the study results indicated. As with Festinger and Carlsmith's study, the smaller the incentive for the behavior, the greater the dissonance and the greater the attitude change. A second context, similar to induced compliance but opposite in some ways, is the hypocrisy context.

HYPOCRISY

Sometimes your target audience already has a positive attitude toward the issue of interest but does not behave in accordance with that attitude. In other words, they are being hypocritical. They say one thing but do another. The **hypocrisy** context involves situations in which individuals are reminded of their current attitude toward an issue and then reminded that their behavior is not consistent with the attitude they hold. In this case, we are more interested in changing their behavior than their attitude. An example of the hypocrisy context is that many young people believe that using condoms is an effective way to reduce the risk of contracting HIV and other sexually transmitted infections, but they do not actually use condoms and therefore put themselves at risk. A positive attitude toward condoms already exists, so messages about the benefits of condom use are not likely to be very effective. Stone, Aronson, Crain, Winslow, and Fried (1994) induced participants to feel dissonance about the inconsistency between their attitudes toward safe sex and their behavior.

Stone and his colleagues recruited 72 students who were sexually active and at risk for contracting HIV to participate in a study. Half of the participants were asked to develop a persuasive speech about HIV and safe sex targeted at high school students. These participants developed and videotaped their speeches. The real purpose of giving the speeches was for the participants to be reminded of their existing attitude and beliefs about condom use as a means of preventing the spread of HIV. The remaining participants were asked to make speech outlines but did not actually give their speeches. Half of the participants who created and taped a speech and half of the participants who only made an outline were then given a list of circumstances that "might make it difficult to use condoms" (Stone et al., 1994, p. 119). Participants were asked to read the list and then to make a list of the circumstances surrounding their own past failures to use condoms. The purpose of making this list was to make participants mindful of their behavior that was inconsistent with their attitude toward practicing safe sex. The other participants were not made mindful of their past failures to practice safe sex. Finally, participants completed a questionnaire and had the opportunity to purchase condoms and obtain additional information on HIV (in the form of brochures).

Stone and his colleagues hypothesized that the group that made the public commitment and that was made mindful of past failures to practice safe sex would experience the greatest dissonance. In this situation, the easiest way to reduce dissonance would be to bring one's behavior in line with the existing attitude. In this case, buying condoms and intending to use them in the future allowed the participants to reduce dissonance. Stone et al.'s hypothesis was confirmed. Those participants in the hypocrisy condition (commitment and mindfulness) purchased the most condoms and also intended to practice safe sex in the future.

There are two key elements to using hypocrisy successfully. The first involves making the *attitude of interest salient*. Stone and his colleagues did this by asking participants to make a videotaped speech about safe sex. Other ways than making a speech could have been used. Dickerson, Thibodeau, Aronson, and Miller (1992) asked participants to sign a poster that would be displayed to make the attitude salient. Additionally, the attitude needs to be made salient in an active way. Stone and Fernandez (2008) conducted an extensive review of hypocrisy research and argued that there needed to be some action by the participant—passive reading wasn't sufficient to generate the hypocrisy effect. In addition, Stone and Fernandez argued that hypocrisy works best when *prosocial courses of action* are involved. People have a tendency to feel more dissonance over not performing positively valued activities than neutral or antisocial actions. The second key element is making *past failures* to behave in accordance with the attitude salient. Stone and his colleagues did this by having participants create a list of the circumstances surrounding the times they had failed to practice safe sex. The failures need to be associated with a *recent context* and should be *private rather than public*. When participants were publicly called out about their hypocrisy, they attempted to justify themselves and failed to alter their behavior. Or in other words, it backfired. Therefore, to induce hypocrisy, you have to engage your audience in some activity that makes their existing attitude salient and you have to get them to privately contemplate their past failures to behave consistently.

Stone and Fernandez (2008) reviewed research on hypocrisy and found considerable support that hypocrisy can generate behavior change in applied settings outside lab settings for the research described above. They reviewed research that examined influencing consumer energy conservation, water conservation, and safer driving behaviors and found that hypocrisy approaches generated the desired behaviors across the board. In addition, they found evidence that this effect exists in other cultures. Research supporting the hypocrisy effect was reported in the United States, Canada, Australia, and Japan. This is a tried and true approach that works in the real world in multiple contexts.

The induced compliance context involved inducing the receiver to perform a counter-attitudinal behavior. Hypocrisy involves pro-attitudinal behavior, such as giving a speech about safe sex. Both the induced compliance and the hypocrisy contexts involve attitudes and behaviors that are inconsistent and result in dissonance. The dissonance creates pressure to change so that the attitude and behavior are in line with one another.

DECISION MAKING

An additional context for dissonance is **decision making**. When an individual makes a decision or choice, he or she is likely to experience dissonance. Larry and Marj's computer buying adventure is a good example of the decision-making context. The decision-making context has four stages. The first stage is *conflict*. This is when the alternatives are being evaluated and information is being gathered. Before making the purchase, Larry and Marj compared the various types of computers and technology at the Apple Store. They also asked friends and acquaintances who were knowledgeable about technology. With the way the store displayed the various products, Larry and Marj could not avoid being exposed to the new technology and ways of using it. Being unable to avoid the alternatives, they experienced conflict about which alternative to choose—stick with what they have (a single desktop computer in their home office) or the new technology (and higher price). The second stage is the *decision*. At this point the decision is made—an alternative is chosen. Obviously, Larry and Marj made a choice, and they chose to completely upgrade their information technology setup at home. The third stage is *cognitive dissonance*. Once a decision is made, we often feel dissonance about whether we made the right choice. Earlier we noted that because of the importance of the beliefs involved and the amount of money involved, Larry and Marj experienced cognitive dissonance.

Step 1–Conflict between alternatives

Step 2–Decision is made

Step 3–Cognitive dissonance is experienced

Step 4–Dissonance reduction occurs

FIGURE 9.3 Decision-Making Steps

The fourth and final stage in the decision-making context is *dissonance reduction*. We seek supporting information to help us feel better about our decision, and we tend to perceive our choice as even better than it was perceived initially. The dissonance reduction process helps us feel satisfied with the decision we made. Recall that Larry and Marj were very happy with their decision. After making the decision, they experienced dissonance. The easiest way for them to reduce the dissonance was to change the importance and ratio of consonant and dissonant cognitions. For weeks following their purchase, they read online reviews of MacBooks and iPads (on their iPad of course). Each positive review served to bolster their consonant cognitions. The importance of "being connected" and of "high-resolution graphics" increased (remember, initially they thought their home office computer was just fine), which increased the weight of these consonant cognitions. They ignored information (denial) that was inconsistent with their purchase, such as the fact that they preferred reading traditional books and newspapers rather than the online versions. Gradually, over a period of weeks, their attitudes and beliefs about their information technology needs changed so that their purchase was no longer inconsistent with their beliefs and they no longer felt cognitive dissonance. Instead, they were satisfied with their purchases and convinced that they had spent their money wisely.

EFFORT JUSTIFICATION

Have you ever wondered why members of the military are so loyal and committed to the military when the military has put them through a difficult and humiliating basic training experience? It doesn't seem to make sense that you would be more committed to a group after being abused by that group in some way. However, we observe this behavior in many ways. Hazing of various types and levels is common in fraternities, sororities, the military, and other organizations, yet these organizations typically have loyal members who willingly devote their time, energy, and money to the organization. When we expend great effort or endure great discomfort to obtain some desirable outcome, dissonance is aroused. This situation is referred to as the **effort justification** context. It is dissonant or inconsistent to perform a behavior that is unpleasant. The more unpleasant a behavior is, the more dissonance that is aroused. So, when an individual endures eating oil-soaked raw liver in order to join a fraternity (Cialdini, 1993), dissonance results. Dissonance is unpleasant, and we are motivated to reduce it. The easiest way to reduce dissonance in this type of situation is to increase the desirability of the outcome (fraternity membership in this example). By believing that the fraternity is very desirable with many wonderful benefits that will endure for a lifetime, the unpleasant behavior becomes justified. If you consider the group you are most committed to, you have probably put forth a good deal of effort for that group and have probably told yourself that it was worthwhile to do so. If you believed it was *not* worthwhile to put forth so much effort for the group, you would experience ongoing dissonance because it does not make sense to work hard for something that is not worthy of your time. You would need to find a reason, a justification, for your behavior.

The justification of effort paradigm was first demonstrated by Aronson and Mills (1959) in a study that compared severe and mild group initiations. Aronson and Mills recruited 63 college women to join a discussion group on the psychology of sex. In the severe initiation group, the women had to read aloud in front of the experimenter sexual words and passages designed to be embarrassing for the women (remember, this was in the 1950s). In the mild initiation group, women had to read aloud in front of the experimenter passages and words that were related to sex but not sexually explicit. In a control group, women did not have to read anything to be allowed into the group. After completing the initiation, women were informed that they had "passed" and were allowed into the group. The women then listened to the group discussion that was designed to be as boring and banal as possible. After the discussion, the women rated the discussion and the participants. The women who experienced the severe initiation in order to be a member of the group evaluated the discussion and the participants significantly more positively than those women who experienced the mild initiation or those in the control group. This study provided the first evidence that greater effort to belong to a group resulted in more positive evaluations of that group. Research since this study has further supported this hypothesis and indicates that the process of reducing the dissonance generated by the initiation creates the positive evaluation of the group. Our commitment to a group is probably largely influenced by the amount of effort we have put forth to be a part of that group. However, we do not experience dissonance every time we do something that is inconsistent. Certain conditions are necessary for dissonance to occur.

NECESSARY CONDITIONS FOR COGNITIVE DISSONANCE

Much research has been conducted using cognitive dissonance theory, and part of that research has led to identification of conditions necessary for cognitive dissonance to occur. One criterion is that receivers have to perceive the situation as involving **freedom of choice** rather than force. For example, if a man is engaging in a behavior or advocating a position that causes dissonance for him but he believes he is doing it because he has no choice or is forced into it, then dissonance is not aroused. The man is likely to say to himself, "I'm only doing this because I have to." Only when the target is engaging in the behavior by his own choice will those actions cause dissonance. As another example, some smokers have indicated that they would like to quit, but they believe they are so addicted to nicotine that it is not within their power to quit. The dissonance-arousing messages against smoking will not be as likely to generate behavior change because the receivers do not believe they have a choice in the matter. However, when people choose to drive after having several drinks, they are engaging in free choice. Assuming that they have a negative attitude toward drunk driving, reminding them of their attitude and their behavior (hypocrisy situation) would likely result in dissonance arousal. This is the goal of some anti-drunk-driving messages. In the dissonance studies discussed in the prior section, participants who were paid $1 to lie about the boring task and those who had the unfriendly researcher encouraging them to sample grasshoppers had freedom of choice. There was personal responsibility for the choices made.

A second criterion for cognitive dissonance is that there must be **insufficient external justification** for the behavior. This means that the person needs to look internally to find the explanation for why he or she is engaging in the behavior that causes dissonance. If there is an external reason, then the behavior does not cause dissonance. For example, imagine Mary being very friendly to Sue even though Mary dislikes Sue. If Mary can point to an external reason for being friendly, such as being at a student organization meeting where social rules call for people to be friendly to everyone present, then Mary would experience no dissonance about behaving nicely to someone she disliked. However, if Mary and Sue were alone and Mary behaved in a friendly manner, Mary would experience some dissonance over the inconsistency between her attitude and her behavior. Persuaders who use cognitive dissonance theory try to create situations where there is no external justification for the target's behavior.

In the Festinger and Carlsmith (1959) experiment involving lying to others about the boring task, those in the $20 condition had an external justification for their behavior, whereas those who were paid just $1 for this task did not. Similarly, participants with a friendly experimenter in the grasshopper sampling experiment had an external justification of wanting to please a nice person as the rationale for eating the grasshoppers. Those with the unfriendly researcher had no external reasons to explain eating the grasshopper, so the explanation to resolve the inconsistency had to be that the grasshoppers were not so bad.

APPLYING COGNITIVE DISSONANCE THEORY

The earlier descriptions of the four contexts should have illustrated to some extent how cognitive dissonance theory is applied. The human motivation for consistency is central to cognitive dissonance theory and is a key factor in applied persuasion. As illustrated in the four dissonance contexts, when people become aware of an inconsistency in their behavior, attitudes, or beliefs, they are motivated to make a change. Applying the contexts, persuaders can create situations where receivers are made aware of inconsistencies. Persuaders can also take advantage of the dissonance reduction process by providing information that is consistent with the desired attitude or belief. For example, people will experience dissonance after making a big purchase such as a computer. Providing new and positive information about the computer will help the consumer reduce dissonance by concluding that they made a wise purchase.

Similarly, car dealers often draw on both the induced compliance and effort justification situations when selling cars. If you have ever shopped for a car, one of the first things salespeople want you to do is test drive the car. Why? If you weren't interested you wouldn't take the time to test drive it. By taking the time to test drive the car, you are performing a behavior that has to be justified. The easiest way to justify it is to tell yourself that you are interested. Upon your test driving the car, the savvy salesperson will elicit positive comments about the car from you by asking questions that almost require a positive response. Now you have not only taken the time to drive the car, but you have also made positive comments about the car—more justifications must be made. Next, the salesperson is likely to get out a contract and ask you for your address, where you work, and your social security number so that the dealer can begin to arrange financing. Before you know it, you have invested over an hour of your precious time and started the paperwork necessary for buying a car. At this point, it would be rather inconsistent to say "No, I'm not interested in this car." Of course if you are aware of the tactics being used, you can avoid feeling the pressure of cognitive dissonance and walk away. So, car dealers induce you to comply with simple behaviors such as test driving the car, voicing positive thoughts about the car, and giving them information to fill out the forms. Although no single behavior is that large, with each one you have more and more to justify. In a sense, using cognitive dissonance theory is like leaving a trail of breadcrumbs. Each crumb requires a small commitment. Although each is small, each must also be justified.

The desire for consistency should also be kept in mind when constructing persuasive messages. In Chapter 5 we discussed logical appeals and evidence. First, a message must be consistent to be logical. Second, a message that presents evidence that is inconsistent with the receiver's existing beliefs or behaviors can result in cognitive dissonance. Of course, as we learned with social judgment theory (Chapter 8), information that is too discrepant will likely be rejected. So the trick is to show the inconsistency without being rejected out of hand. Researchers have repeatedly concluded that humans are most comfortable when their attitudes, beliefs, values, and behavior are consistent with one another. Persuaders who find ways to help receivers experience consistency will be more successful.

AN ALTERNATE EXPLANATION

Cognitive dissonance theory provides a good explanation of the results Festinger and others found in their studies of persuasion and influence; and recall a primary purpose of theory is to explain the phenomena that we observe. However, not everyone agreed that cognitive dissonance theory provided a good explanation. Daryl Bem (1967, 1972) thought that Festinger and his colleagues had it all wrong. Bem didn't think the research participants in Festinger and Carlsmith's (1959) study experienced dissonance. He argued that the research participants made internal attributions about their behavior and it was these attributions that caused the results. Bem (1967, 1972) proposed the self-perception theory as a better explanation of the induced compliance research results. So let's review the propositions of self-perception theory and you can decide which theory is the better explanation.

SELF-PERCEPTION THEORY

In order to understand self-perception theory we need to have some understanding of impression formation and attribution theories. Impression formation theory explains how we form impressions of people (Heider, 1958). How we relate to other people depends in part on what we think about them and why we believe they engaged in any given behavior. To make sense of other people's behavior, we create explanations for why they do things. The process of creating causal explanations for why things happen is referred to as **attributions** and the attributions we make determine the impressions we have of others. Heider's work focused on how we make attributions about others.

One of the central tenets of Heider's theory is that humans believe that behavior is *causal,* or in other words, behavior is caused by something. That cause can be **internal** or **external factors**. An **internal attribution** is when you infer the cause of the behavior as being within the person. For example, if you observe a classmate arrive late to class just about every day, you might make an internal attribution. You might suppose that timeliness is not important to your classmate; thus, you would infer that the late arrival is a result of the classmate's personality, beliefs, or attitudes.

Alternatively, you could make an external attribution about your classmate's behavior. If that same classmate regularly arrived late but was out of breath and sweaty, you might guess that the classmate had an earlier distant class that made it difficult to arrive on time. This guess would suggest that it wasn't an internal or personality characteristic that caused the behavior (late arrival), rather the external situation was the cause of the behavior—that is, an external attribution. An **external attribution** is when you infer the cause of the behavior as being outside the person. The attribution you make affects how you view the classmate. If you consider being late a negative behavior, then an internal attribution results in a different impression than does an external attribution.

" Sorry I'm late for school - My Dad held me up
with a lecture on punctuality."

FIGURE 9.4 The student depicted in this cartoon is making an external attribution about his late behavior.

TABLE 9.1 *ATTRIBUTION SUMMARY TABLE*

	CONSENSUS	CONSISTENCY	DISTINCTIVENESS
High	External	Internal	External
Low	Internal	External	Internal

The same attribution process occurs when you observe positive behavior, but the resulting impression of the individual is different. If you observed a roommate receiving an A on an exam in a persuasion class and you make an internal attribution (the roommate is bright and hardworking), your impression would be quite positive.

Harold Kelley (1967, 1971) further developed Heider's ideas about impressions and proposed attribution theory. Kelley was interested in why people made either an internal or external attribution. He examined the situational and personal factors that we use to make attributions and identified three key factors: consensus, consistency, and distinctiveness. **Consensus** refers to what most people do in a particular situation. A behavior would have high consensus if most others behave the same way in that situation. Going back to our example, if most students in the class regularly arrived on time, consensus would be low because your classmate is the only one late. You would likely make an internal attribution. When a person's behavior reflects the consensus of behavior for others, we are more likely to make an external attribution. **Consistency** refers to whether the observed behavior occurs over time. If your classmate arrived late to class only once and was on time for all other class periods (low consistency), you would likely make an external attribution. However, if your classmate arrived late to class most days (high consistency), you would be more likely to make an internal attribution and guess that the classmate did not care about being on time. **Distinctiveness** is the third factor Kelley identified. This refers to how different the behavior is across situations. For example, if the classmate who arrived late to class was also late to student organization meetings, parties, and dates, you would probably make an internal attribution because the lateness behavior was not distinctive for just one situation. On the other hand, if the classmate arrived late to class regularly but was on time for meetings, parties, and dates, you would be more likely to make an external attribution for the pattern of late arrival at class. Thus, behavior that is distinctive to a situation is more likely to be attributed to external factors. Table 9.1 summarizes how we make attributions.

Daryl Bem (1967, 1972) drew on impression formation theory and attribution theory in the development of self-perception theory. Self-perception theory relies on situational and dispositional attributions similar to attribution theory, but Bem argues that this is not just true in how we view others. Instead, we use the same attribution process to make sense of our own behavior. Within this theory, *we are observers of ourselves as we are observers of others,* and we use a similar process to make attributions about ourselves. According to self-perception theory, persuasion involves a person acting and then figuring out why he or she behaved in that way in order to understand his or her own attitudes.

SELF-PERCEPTION THEORY POSTULATES

Bem advanced two *postulates* for self-perception theory. The first is that "individuals come to 'know' their own attitudes, emotions, and other internal states partially by inferring them from observations of their own overt behavior and/or the circumstances in which this behavior occurs" (Bem, 1972, p. 2). In the previous examples of making interpersonal attributions about others, we inferred the cause of behavior by noting the behavior and any situational factors that might account for it. In persuasion, Bem suggests, receivers of messages look at themselves and make attributions in the same way.

The second postulate is that "to the extent internal cues are weak, ambiguous, or uninterpretable, the individual is functionally in the same position as an outside observer, an observer who must necessarily rely upon those same external cues to infer the individual's internal states" (Bem, 1972, p. 2). In this case, if you are the target of a persuasive message and are unaware of any situational influences on your behavior, then you are likely to make an internal attribution about your behavior. In persuasion terms, that generally means you perceive your attitudes as being in line with your behavior.

Recall the Festinger and Carlsmith (1959) study of cognitive dissonance theory involving the boring task for which participants were paid $1 or $20 to lie to others. Self-perception theory explains the results of this study using the two postulates set out by Bem. As the participants tried to decide how boring the task of putting spools on trays and turning pegs for an hour was, they were in the position of outside observers and looked to the situational cues to help them understand their internal states. Those who were paid $1 to lie to others saw a very weak situational cue for their behavior. Because the external cue was so weak, they needed to infer an internal reason for lying. In this case, it meant that participants saw their attitudes toward the task as more positive because there was no external explanation for their behavior.

Those who were paid $20 to lie to others, however, saw a situational cue that explained their behavior. They could infer that they were willing to lie for the researcher for the money (an external factor), and thus they had no reason to infer any internal reason for doing so. Those participants made a more negative evaluation of the task. If you were an outside observer, you would probably have drawn the same conclusions about another person's behavior. Thus, self-perception theory can explain the same research finding that was used to support cognitive dissonance theory.

SUPPORTING RESEARCH

Epinephrine is also known as adrenalin and is a hormone and medication. Side effects include shakiness, anxiety, sweating, and fast heart rate.

Research was conducted to support Bem's challenge to cognitive dissonance theory. To do this, research had to be designed that could demonstrate the usefulness of self-perception theory and simultaneously show the weaknesses of cognitive dissonance theory. Schachter and Singer (1962) conducted such a study that involved injecting participants with **epinephrine**. Participants were told that the study involved investigation of the effects of a vitamin mixture called "suproxin" on vision. They were then placed into four groups. Three of the groups received the epinephrine injection; the fourth was a control group. The control group was given a placebo injection of saline solution. The first epinephrine group was *informed* about the side effects to expect from receiving the injection, including an elevated heart rate, shaking hands, and warm or flushed faces. The second epinephrine group was *misinformed* about the effects of the injection; they were told that the expected side effects included numb feet, itching, and a slight headache. The final epinephrine group was left *ignorant* of the drug's effects and was told that it would cause no side effects at all.

The participants were asked to wait in the research room for about 20 minutes to let the supposed suproxin get into their system. Each participant was dealt with individually, and during the wait a confederate posing as another research participant was brought into the room. The confederate was instructed to act either *euphoric* or *angry*. In the euphoric condition, the confederate doodled on paper, made paper basketballs and shot them at wastebaskets, made paper airplanes, shot paper balls with a rubber band, and used a hula hoop that was in the room. The confederate talked about his activities and invited the participant to join him. In the anger condition, the two students were asked to fill out a long questionnaire while they waited. The confederate complained about the injection, complained about the questions, and got angry about personal and insulting questions. Finally, the confederate ripped up the questionnaire and stomped out of the room.

Participants' responses were measured by secret observers who rated participant behavior according to the level of emotion displayed. In addition, each participant filled out a questionnaire after the waiting period. Two five-point scales were used to evaluate how irritated, angry, and/or annoyed the participants felt, as well as how good or happy they felt. Finally, each participant's pulse was measured before the injection and after the waiting period.

According to self-perception theory, participants should base evaluation of their own attitudes on observations of their own behavior and the situational cues surrounding that behavior. Remember that we tend to make internal attributions for our behavior when situational cues are weak, ambiguous, or nonexistent. In the ignorant and misinformed conditions, the situational cues were weak or ambiguous about the true cause of the physiological arousal each participant experienced, so participants used the confederate's behavior to infer how they felt. In the informed condition, the participants had been given a situational explanation for the arousal they experienced; thus, no further internal explanation was needed. Therefore, self-perception theory predicts that the participants in the informed condition are affected very little by the confederate's emotional state. Those in the ignorant and misinformed conditions attribute their physiological symptoms to external factors. In those cases, the situational cues influence their attributions about their own feelings.

This is exactly what happened. Participants in the ignorant and misinformed condition were more likely to join in the behaviors of the confederate, and they were more likely to report either anger or euphoria based on the behaviors the confederate exhibited even though the physiological arousal was the same for both conditions. Thus, these participants were using situational cues that were more obvious (the behavior of the confederate) to explain their arousal because they had no other good explanation for what they experienced. Those in the informed condition were less likely to be influenced by the confederate's behavior because they had an explanation for the arousal (behavior) they observed in themselves.

The epinephrine results are not easily explained with cognitive dissonance theory because no cognitive dissonance was generated. This is an example of forming new attitudes because there were no prior attitudes about the behavior experienced after the drug injection. Bem argued that self-perception can explain and predict most of the classic cognitive dissonance theory results (such as the $1/$20 study) and explain research results that cognitive dissonance theory cannot. The research indicates that we make attributions about our own behavior and that we may use external cues to figure out how we feel. However, cognitive dissonance theory consistently explains research results and provides useful guidance in the creation of persuasive messages and strategies.

Other research conducted in an effort to prove that cognitive dissonance does not occur in induced compliance situations was not successful, and Eagly and Chaiken (1993) concluded that Bem was wrong about cognitive dissonance. However, self-perception theory has been described as being useful for understanding attitude formation (Fazio, 1987).

STRENGTHS AND LIMITATIONS

Cognitive dissonance theory has endured and been refined, and it has been a valued perspective for many years. It applies in many situations and has very broad explanatory powers as a result. It has strong support from decades of research, and it is used in persuasion applications as various as advertising, politics, and social issues. This theory has endured because of its ability to explain at a theoretical level.

This theory also has limitations. Although broad explanatory powers is a strength, it is also a weakness. Because of the many ways to resolve dissonance, cognitive dissonance theory is difficult to disprove. If dissonance is successfully aroused and change occurs, the theory is supported. If change does not occur, the theory can explain that as well by indicating that the magnitude of dissonance was not sufficient or an alternative method of dissonance reduction such as denial was used. This breadth gives lesser *predictive* ability and *control* to those using the theory in crafting persuasive messages. Cognitive dissonance theory is not useful for creating messages intended to form new attitudes or beliefs. The limitation with control is illustrated by the theory's inability to predict *what* will change. Dissonance can be reduced by changing either attitude or behavior. The theory does not explain why attitude is changed rather than behavior, or vice versa, thus limiting control.

Finally, cognitive dissonance theory was challenged by proponents of self-perception theory, which also has strengths and weaknesses. Research on self-perception theory supports the notion that there are indeed times when people operate as outside observers of their own behavior. The centrality of the attribution process and the importance of internal and external attributions are clear in some circumstances. It also emphasizes the importance of external cues in the success or failure of persuasion attempts. Although persuaders can rarely control what goes on inside someone's head, they can often affect the setting and environment in which the persuasion occurs. Self-perception theory has also been criticized for viewing persuasion as a primarily passive process in which receivers are directed to action by external forces rather than thinking about decisions and actively deciding how to act (Smith, 1982). This is an after-the-fact justification for behavior rather than a proactive rationale before engaging in behavior. Some may support this view in some situations, but others are uncomfortable with the less active process implied by this theory.

In short, cognitive dissonance is a well-regarded theory of persuasion that offers a strong basis for persuasion research and application. As other theories are developed, we will examine a broader view of persuasion.

SUMMARY

- Consistency theories are based on the human drive to be psychologically consistent with beliefs, attitudes, and behavior.
- Cognitive dissonance theory posits that cognitions have one of three relationships: dissonant, consonant, or irrelevant.
- The magnitude of dissonance refers to the amount of dissonance a person experiences. It is a result of the importance of the elements, the ratio of dissonant to consonant elements, and the degree of cognitive overlap.
- Dissonance can be reduced by changing the behavior, changing the importance and/or ratio of dissonant elements, and through denial, bolstering, transcendence, or differentiation.
- The four major contexts in which cognitive dissonance occurs are: induced compliance, hypocrisy, decision making, and effort justification.
- Necessary conditions for cognitive dissonance to occur include aversive consequences, freedom of choice, and insufficient external justification for the behavior.
- Cognitive dissonance can be applied in persuasion by trying to generate dissonance, trying to reduce dissonance, raising the magnitude of dissonance, or directing the dissonance reduction.
- Major strengths and contributions of cognitive dissonance theory include the breadth of situations included, the greater complexity to account for multiple cognitions, consistent support from research studies, and its ability to be used in multiple applied settings.
- Factors involved in making internal and external attributions include consensus, consistency, and distinctiveness.
- Daryl Bem's self-perception theory built on the basics of Heider and Kelley's work.
- Self-perception theory is based on two postulates: (a) individuals come to "know" their own attitudes, emotions, and other internal states partially by inferring them from observations of their own overt behavior and/or the circumstances in which this behavior occurs; and (b) to the extent that internal cues are weak, ambiguous, or uninterpretable, the individual is functionally in the same position as an outside observer, an observer who must necessarily rely on those same external cues to infer the individual's internal states.

- Self-perception works best for the formation of new attitudes.
- Major limitations of cognitive dissonance theory include the difficulty in disproving the theory because of its complexity and ability to explain both success and failure in the persuasive attempt, the inability to effectively predict how the dissonance will be resolved, the inability to control the process effectively because of all the variables, the limited situations in which it functions well, and a competing theory (self-perception theory) that can explain the same findings.

KEY TERMS

Attributions—the process of creating causal explanations for why things happen.

Aversive consequences—possible outcomes that a person would want to avoid; a necessary condition for dissonance to occur.

Balance theory—the oldest of the consistency theories, sometimes referred to as the P-O-X theory.

Cognitions—bits of knowledge individuals have stored in their minds.

Cognitive dissonance theory—a consistency theory that emphasizes consistency among cognitions.

Cognitive dissonance—an aversive motivational state that people are motivated to eliminate.

Cognitive overlap—the similarity of the choices available. The greater the similarity, the greater the cognitive overlap.

Congruity theory—a consistency theory that introduced the idea of attitudes existing on a continuum.

Consensus—a rule for making attributions. A behavior would have high consensus if most others behave the same way in that situation.

Consistency—a rule for making attributions. Consistency is high if the observed behavior occurs over time.

Consonant relationship—two cognitions that are consistent with one another.

Counter-attitudinal behavior—a behavior that is counter, or against, the attitude one holds.

Decision making—a context for dissonance; after making a decision, people often experience cognitive dissonance.

Dissonance reduction—the process a person engages in to reduce cognitive dissonance that involves one or more of the following: change the behavior, change the ratio, change the importance, denial, bolstering, transcendence, and differentiation.

Dissonant relationship—two cognitions that are inconsistent with one another.

Distinctiveness—a rule for making attributions. Distinctiveness is low if the observed behavior occurs in most situations the person is in.

Effort justification—dissonance that results from enduring much or working hard to obtain a less than perfect outcome.

External attribution—the cause of behavior is attributed to something in the situation; something external to the person.

Freedom of choice—a necessary condition for dissonance to occur; the receiver needs to freely choose to engage in the dissonance-arousing behaviors.

Hypocrisy—situations in which an individual is reminded of his or her current attitude toward an issue and then reminded that his or her behavior is not consistent with the attitude he or she holds.

Induced compliance—when dissonance results from being induced to perform a counter-attitudinal behavior.

Insufficient external justification—a necessary condition for dissonance to occur; there must be little external (as opposed to internal) reason for engaging in the dissonance-arousing behavior.

Internal attribution—the cause of behavior is attributed to something internal to a person such as personality, attitude, or beliefs.

Internal factors—factors inside a person, such as personality, that cause a person to behave a certain way.

Irrelevant relationship—two cognitions that a person perceives as unrelated to one another.

Magnitude of dissonance—the amount of dissonance experienced.

REVIEW QUESTIONS

1. What two consistency theories preceded cognitive dissonance theory?
2. What are cognitions? What kinds of relationships exist between cognitions?
3. What is the magnitude of dissonance? How is it increased? What role does it play for cognitive dissonance theory?

4. What are dissonance reduction options? How does each option operate?

5. What are contexts in which dissonance occurs?

6. What are the necessary conditions for cognitive dissonance to occur?

7. What theory challenged cognitive dissonance theory?

8. What factors are involved in deciding whether a behavior is attributed to internal or external factors?

9. What are the postulates of self-perception theory?

10. How does self-perception theory explain the induced compliance context?

11. What are the strengths and weaknesses of cognitive dissonance theory?

DISCUSSION QUESTIONS

1. Balance theory, congruity theory, and cognitive dissonance theory emphasize that we like to be consistent in how we feel toward things. How important is consistency to you? Are there times when you don't care if you're consistent or not? Why?

2. Is it ethical for the tobacco industry to distract consumers with other issues in an effort to reduce dissonance in smokers? What about Mothers Against Drunk Driving trying to increase the dissonance by emphasizing the negative side of drinking and driving? What criteria would you suggest to guide ethics in this area?

3. Think about the last major decision you made. Did you experience dissonance? How did you justify your decision so that you felt good about it (had consonant cognitions)?

4. Compare the effort justification context to the group dynamics theory. How are these two approaches to persuasion similar and different?

5. Do you have any ethical concerns about using cognitive dissonance theory in persuasion (or having it used on you)? When is it acceptable to arouse dissonance and direct how it is resolved? What are some ethical issues with this process? Consider different topics and situations as you ponder these questions.

6. Think of a behavior you observed someone doing earlier today. Did you make an internal or external attribution about the behavior? Now consider why you made the attribution you did. Did you make the attribution because of observed consensus, consistency, or distinctiveness?

7. Compare self-perception theory with cognitive dissonance theory. What are the strengths of each theory? Which theory does a better job of explaining the research results?

REFERENCES

Abelson, R. P. (1959). Modes of resolution of belief dilemmas. *Journal of Conflict Resolution, 3,* 343–352.

Abelson, R. P. (1963). Computer simulation of "hot" cognition. In S. S. Tomkins & S. Messick (Eds.), *Computer simulation of personality* (pp. 227–289). New York: Wiley.

Abelson, R. P. (1968). Psychological implication. In R. P. Abelson, E. Aronson, W. J. McGuire, T. M. Newcomb, M. J. Rosenberg, & P. H. Tannenbaum (Eds.), *Theories of cognitive consistency: A sourcebook* (pp. 112–139). Chicago: Rand McNally.

Aronson, E., & Mills, J. (1959). The effect of severity of initiation on liking for a group. *Journal of Abnormal and Social Psychology, 59,* 177–181.

Bem, D. J. (1967). Self-perception: An alternative interpretation of cognitive dissonance phenomena. *Psychological Review, 74,* 183–200.

Bem, D. J. (1972). Self-perception theory. In L. Berkowitz (Ed.), *Advances in experimental social psychology* (Vol. 6, pp. 1–62). New York: Academic Press.

Burger, J. M. (1999). The foot-in-the-door compliance procedure: A multiple-process analysis and review. *Personality and Social Psychology Review, 3,* 303–325.

Cialdini, R. B. (1993). *Influence: Science and practice* (3rd ed.). New York: HarperCollins.

Cooper, J., & Fazio, R. H. (1984). A new look at dissonance theory. In L. Berkowitz (Ed.), *Advances in experimental social psychology* (Vol. 17, pp. 229–266). San Diego: Academic Press.

Cooper, J., & Worchel, S. (1970). Role of undesired consequences in arousing cognitive dissonance. *Journal of Personality and Social Psychology, 16,* 199–206.

Cooper, J., Zanna, M. P., & Goethals, G. R. (1974). Mistreatment of an esteemed other as a consequence affecting dissonance reduction. *Journal of Experimental Social Psychology, 10,* 224–233.

Dickerson, C. A., Thibodeau, R., Aronson, E., & Miller, D. (1992). Using cognitive dissonance to encourage water conservation. *Journal of Applied Social Psychology, 22,* 841–854.

Eagly, A. H., & Chaiken, S. (1994). *The psychology of attitudes.* Fort Worth, TX: Harcourt Brace Jovanovich.

Fazio, R. H. (1987). Self-perception theory: A current perspective. In M. P. Zanna, J. M. Olsen, & C. P. Herman (Eds.), *Social influence: The Ontario Symposium* (Vol. 5, pp. 129-150). Hillsdale, NJ: Erlbaum.

Fazio, R. H., Zanna, M. P., & Cooper, J. (1977). Dissonance and self-perception: An interactive view of each theory's proper domain of application. *Journal of Experimental Social Psychology, 13,* 464–479.

Festinger, L. (1957). *A theory of cognitive dissonance.* Evanston, IL: Row, Peterson.

Festinger, L., & Carlsmith, J. M. (1959). Cognitive consequences of forced compliance. *Journal of Abnormal and Social Psychology, 58,* 203–210.

Freedman, J. L., & Fraser, S. C. (1966). Compliance without pressure: The foot-in-the-door technique. *Journal of Personality and Social Psychology, 4,* 195–202.

Girandola, F. (2002). Sequential requests and organ donation. *Journal of Social Psychology, 142,* 171–178.

Gueguen, N. (2002). Foot-in-the-door technique and computer mediated communication. *Computers in Human Behavior, 18,* 11–15.

Gueguen, N., & Jacob C. (2001). Fundraising on the Web: The effect of an electronic foot-in-the-door on donation. *CyberPsychology & Behavior, 4,* 705–709.

Gueguen, N., Marchand, M., Pascual, A., & Lourel, M. (2008). The effect of the foot-in-the-door technique on a courtship request: A field experiment. *Psychological Reports, 103,* 529–534.

Heider, F. (1946). Attitudes and cognitive organization. *Journal of Psychology, 21,* 107–112.

Heider, F. (1958). *The psychology of interpersonal relations.* New York: Wiley.

Kelley, H. H. (1967). Attribution theory in social psychology. In D. Levine (Ed.), *Nebraska Symposium on Motivation* (Vol. A5, pp. 192–238). Lincoln: University of Nebraska Press.

Kelley, H. H. (1971). *Attribution in social interaction.* Morristown, NJ: General Learning Press.

Kerrick, J. (1958). The effect of relevant and nonrelevant sources on attitude change. *Journal of Social Psychology, 19,* 15–20.

Kiesler, C. A., Nisbett, R. E., & Zanna, M. P. (1969). On inferring one's beliefs from one's behavior. *Journal of Personality and Social Psychology, 11,* 321–327.

Markey, P. M. Wells, S. M., & Markey, C. N. (2001). Personality and social psychology in the culture of cyberspace. In S. P. Shohov (Ed.), *Advances in psychology research* (Vol. 9, pp. 103–124). Huntington, NY: Nova Science.

Nel, E., Helmreich, R., & Aronson, E. (1969). Opinion change in the advocate as a function of the persuasibility of his audience: A clarification of the meaning of dissonance. *Journal of Personality and Social Psychology, 12,* 117–124.

Osgood, C. E., & Tannenbaum, P. H. (1955). The principle of congruity in the prediction of attitude change. *Psychological Review, 62,* 42–55.

Rokeach, M., & Rothman, G. (1965). The principle of belief congruence and the congruity principle as models of cognitive interaction. *Psychological Review, 72,* 128–142.

Schachter, S., & Singer, J. E. (1962). Cognitive, social and physiological determinates of emotional state. *Psychological Review, 69,* 379–399.

Smith, M. J. (1982). *Persuasion and human action: A review and critique of social influence theories.* Belmont, CA: Wadsworth.

Stone, J., & Fernandez, N. C. (2008). To practice what we preach: The use of hypocrisy and cognitive dissonance to motivate behavior change. *Social and Personality Psychology Compass, 2*(2), 1024–1051.

Stone, J., Aronson, E., Crain, A. L., Winslow, M. P., & Fried, C. B. (1994). Inducing hypocrisy as a means of encouraging young adults to use condoms. *Personality and Social Psychology Bulletin, 20,* 116–128.

Tannenbaum, P. H. (1967). The congruity principle revisited: Studies in the reduction, induction, and generalization of persuasion. In L. Berkowitz (Ed.), *Advances in experimental social psychology* (Vol. 3, pp. 271–320). San Diego: Academic Press.

Tannenbaum, P. H. (1968). The congruity principle: Retrospective reflections and recent research. In R. P. Abelson, E. Aronson, W. J. McGuire, T. M. Newcomb, M. J. Rosenberg, & P. H. Tannenbaum (Eds.), *Theories of cognitive consistency: A sourcebook* (pp. 52–72). Chicago: Rand McNally.

Weiner, B. (Ed.). (1974). *Achievement motivation and attribution theory.* Morristown, NJ: General Learning Press.

Zimbardo, P. G., Weisenberg, M., Firestone, I., & Levy, B. (1965). Communicator effectiveness in producing public conformity and private attitude change. *Journal of Personality, 33,* 233–255.

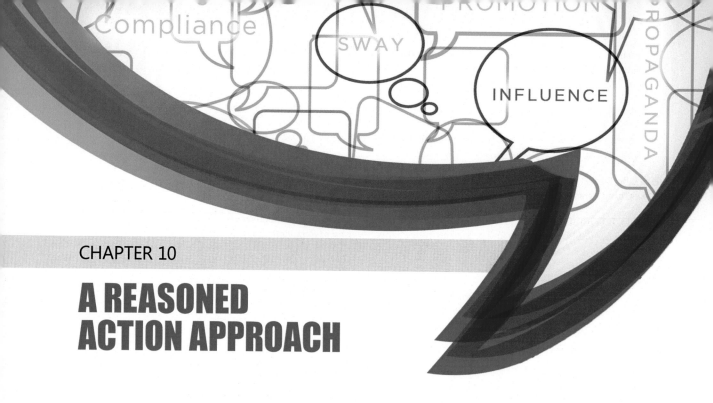

CHAPTER 10

A REASONED ACTION APPROACH

The theories we have discussed up to this point have focused on changing attitudes as a key component of persuasion. There are times, however, when we just want to change behaviors and we want to do that as quickly and efficiently as possible. AT&T launched a campaign to change people's behavior with regard to texting while driving. Several states such as Michigan and Ohio have banned texting while driving and are creating campaigns to change people's behavior.

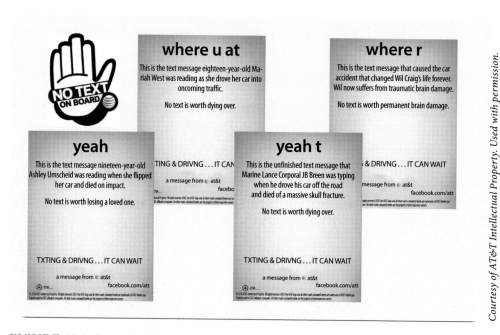

FIGURE 10.1 Txtng & Driving . . . It Can Wait

LEARNING OBJECTIVES

- GIVE EXAMPLES OF BEHAVIORS THAT ARE UNDER VOLITIONAL CONTROL.
- EXPLAIN WHEN BEHAVIORAL INTENTIONS ARE A GOOD PREDICTOR OF BEHAVIOR.
- DESCRIBE THE COMPONENTS OF THE THEORY OF REASONED ACTION AND HOW THEY RELATE TO ONE ANOTHER.
- EXPLAIN HOW BELIEF STRENGTH AND BELIEF EVALUATION CONTRIBUTE TO ATTITUDE TOWARD BEHAVIOR.
- EXPLAIN HOW NORMATIVE BELIEFS AND MOTIVATION TO COMPLY CONTRIBUTE TO SUBJECTIVE NORM.
- EXPLAIN HOW CONTROL BELIEFS AND PERCEIVED POWER OF CONTROL BELIEFS CONTRIBUTE TO PERCEIVED BEHAVIORAL CONTROL.
- DESCRIBE AND GIVE EXAMPLES OF THE STRATEGIES USED TO INFLUENCE ATTITUDE, SUBJECTIVE NORM, AND PERCEIVED BEHAVIORAL CONTROL.
- USE THE CRITERIA FOR GOOD THEORY (EXPLAIN, PREDICT, AND CONTROL) TO EXPLAIN STRENGTHS AND WEAKNESSES OF THE THEORY OF REASONED ACTION.

State governments, AT&T, and other organizations want drivers to refrain from texting while driving. The campaigns particularly target young drivers; however, teens are not the only ones who text while driving. AT&T has created an app that will automatically text a person back saying you are driving and will respond when it is safe. Parents of teens who died in car crashes caused by texting have appeared on *The Today Show* and other news venues, telling their stories and pleading for a change in behavior. These messages represent an approach to persuasion that focuses more directly on altering behavior—a challenge taken on by Ajzen and Fishbein (1980) in the development of the **theory of reasoned action** (TRA).

Search "Texting and Driving" on YouTube to find the messages intended to change our texting and driving behaviour.

The reasoned action approach to influence takes a different approach to persuasion than the theories discussed in previous chapters. If you think of a theory as a map that directs you where to go and what to look for, the theory of reasoned action is a different kind of map than social judgment theory or cognitive dissonance theory. First, the theory of reasoned action focuses on behavior as the ultimate outcome rather than attitude change, as in the case of the texting while driving public service announcements displayed in Figure 10.1. Attitude change is still important and plays a substantial role in the theory; however, it is not the primary goal. Second, an underlying assumption of this theory is that human beings follow a fairly consistent and reasoned approach in their behavior. Icek Ajzen and Martin Fishbein, the developers of this theory, assume that people make reasoned decisions about how to behave, and that much behavior is under **volitional control**. If a behavior is under volitional control, an individual has control over the behavior. Whether or not you get to class on time is, for the most part, something you control. To the extent that you depend on others (e.g., bus drivers), the less volitional control you have. You may be late to class because the bus broke down and you had to walk the rest of the way. In this situation, your behavior was less affected by the choices you made and more affected by circumstances beyond your control. Therefore, the theory of reasoned action is a map of how people make rational choices about what behaviors to engage in. This is not the map we want to use when trying to understand mindless or automatic behavior.

ATTITUDES ARE NOT ALONE

Up to this point, we have focused primarily on attitudes in our discussion of persuasion. In Chapter 3, we discussed at length how attitudes influence behavior and the possibility of behavior influencing attitudes, but overall we have focused on changing attitude as a goal of persuasion. Fishbein and Ajzen's (2010) theory of reasoned action (TRA) focuses on behavior change with attitude being only one of the factors that influence behavior. Three other factors play an important role in behavior: social pressure (subjective norm), behavioral control, and intention to perform the behavior. As we discuss in more detail later, behavioral intention is proposed as being the best single predictor of behavior, and attitude, subjective norm, and behavioral control influence intention to perform a behavior. So attitude is not the only kid on the persuasion block.

Before we discuss intentions, subjective norm, and behavioral control, let's briefly discuss Ajzen and Fishbein's (1980) approach to attitude. In Chapter 2, we defined attitude as a learned predisposition to respond in a consistently favorable or unfavorable manner to a given object. Within the theory of reasoned action, the object is always behavior—specifically, the behavior you are trying to influence—and is referred to as **attitude toward behavior**. So, if your persuasive goal is to get your fellow students to give blood at the blood drive this Friday, the only attitude of concern is your audience's attitude toward giving blood this Friday at the blood drive. This is a fairly specific attitude, as opposed to the more general attitude toward giving blood. A person might have a positive attitude toward giving blood but have a negative attitude toward giving blood this Friday because he or she has an important job interview at the same time the blood drive is going on. Attitude toward specific behavior is the focus in the TRA.

THE ROLE OF INTENTIONS

A person's intention to do something is the best predictor of whether he or she will actually perform the behavior. For example, if you raise your hand in class to answer a question (behavior), you probably intended to do so. **Behavioral intention** is a psychological concept best described as an expectation or a plan. An intention is a plan for how you are going to behave. As stated previously, intention is the best predictor of behavior in general; however, this is not always the case. Three factors influence the intention–behavior relationship. By **intention-behavior relationship** we mean the extent behavioral intentions influence behavior. The first factor has to do with **volition**. As mentioned previously, an assumption of Ajzen and Fishbein's is that behavior is under volitional control. If a behavior is not under volition, intention will not be a good predictor of behavior. For example, suppose that Mikhail intends to marry Natasha. But he does not have complete control over marrying her. Natasha has to say yes to Mikhail's proposal. So Mikhail's behavioral intention may not be a very good predictor of his behavior; Natasha may say no. Volition should be thought of as a continuum. At one extreme are those behaviors over which you have complete control (e.g., wearing underwear); at the other extreme are those behaviors over which you have no control (e.g., being late because the bus broke down); and in between are a whole range of behaviors influenced by both you and circumstances beyond your control. Intentions are a good predictor of behavior to the extent that it is under volitional control.

The other two factors affecting the intention-behavior relationship are related to how intentions are measured. You may be asking why we would want to measure intentions rather than direct behavior. There are two reasons we are concerned about measuring intentions and behavior. The first reason is that, to study persuasion, we have to be able to measure the variables of interest. If we think that intentions influence behavior and want to test the relationship, we have to measure it. The second reason concerns applied persuasion. In applied situations we frequently have to demonstrate the effectiveness of our messages and campaigns. We may ultimately want to influence people's behavior, but it is often much easier and less expensive to measure individuals' behavioral intentions. If we can measure behavioral intentions, and intentions are predictive of behavior, then we are relieved of the burden of measuring actual behavior. Also, in long-term campaigns, such as political races, measuring behavioral intentions may be a way of assessing the effectiveness of the campaign along the way. So, regardless of whether your interest is in research or in applied persuasion, measuring intentions and behavior is relevant.

Intentions are a good predictor of behavior as long as the measures correspond to one another. The second factor that influences the intention–behavior relationship is **correspondence**. The measures of intention and behavior must correspond with one another, or, in other words, have the same dimensions. For intentions and behavior to correspond, they need to match in terms of *action, target, context*, and *time*. We discussed these factors in Chapter 3 regarding measuring attitudes and behavior. These factors are useful guidelines for the measurement of attitudes as well as behavioral intentions and behavior. Let's say you want to influence people to recycle where you work. You plan first to measure your colleagues' intentions to recycle and then their actual recycling behavior. Your measures of intention and behavior must measure the same action. In this case, *action* is recycling—or more specifically, putting recyclables into a recycling bin. The *target* refers to what you want people to recycle. Do you want them to recycle newspapers, bottles, aluminum cans, plastic (what type of plastic?), old tires, or motor oil? The list could go on. For your workplace campaign, you may focus on paper. This is the target, and both the measure of intention and the measure of behavior must focus on this target. *Context* refers to where you want people to recycle. Do you want people to recycle at home, at work, or in public places? In this case you're focusing on your specific workplace. Again, the measures of intention and behavior must focus on the same context. *Time* is the last element in correspondence. When do you want the behavior to occur? In our recycling example, you probably are interested in people doing this indefinitely; however, you may focus on a narrower time frame such as within the next month during the recycling mania campaign. If your measure of intention and your measure of behavior do not correspond on one or more of these elements, your measure of intentions will not predict behavior well.

For example, if we asked people if they intended to recycle within the next month, they may say yes because they intend to recycle bottles and cans at home. When we measure their behavior (recycling paper at work), they indicate that they did not do this. The measure of intention does not predict the measured behavior. Therefore, the four elements—action, target, context, and time—act as a guide for how to define the behavior we want to influence and how to measure both the behavior and the intention. These elements are useful in developing good measures but are also useful in helping clarify what specific behavior we want to influence. Intentions are a good predictor of behavior as long as the measures of each correspond with one another.

The third factor in the intention–behavior relationship is the amount of **time** between the measurement of intentions and the performance of the behavior. Intentions are a better predictor of behaviors when the measurement occurs right before the performance of the behavior. The more time that passes after intentions are measured, the greater the likelihood that something will happen to change intentions and therefore change behavior. During a presidential election year, for example, numerous pollsters ask people for whom they intend to vote. A poll taken in April is often not very accurate in predicting who will win the election, but a poll taken the day before the election is usually very accurate in predicting who will win. Therefore, we have to recognize that intentions can and will change over time. This is particularly true if there are a number of steps in performing a behavior. For example, if you intend to move from Chicago to San Francisco, there are several things that have to happen. You have to find a job, find a place to live, sell your place in Chicago, and move all of your belongings. Your intentions might change as a result of one of these steps, making your earlier intentions inconsistent with your final behavior.

SUBJECTIVE NORM

Earlier we stated that social pressure was one of three things that influence behavioral intention. Social pressure from an important other is called a **subjective norm**. Important others are the people whose opinions you care about. Your subjective norm for a specific behavior such as refraining from texting while driving involves what you believe important others (people who are important to you regarding texting while driving) want you to do and how willing you are to comply with their wishes. So you may feel intense social pressure (high subjective norm) if your best friend (important other) really wants you to check a text while you're driving and you very much want to please your best friend.

PERCEIVED BEHAVIORAL CONTROL

In addition to your attitude toward the behavior and the social pressure you experience to perform (or not perform) a behavior, your beliefs about the level of control you have over the behavior determine your behavioral intention. **Perceived behavioral control** is the extent a person believes he or she is capable of performing a behavior and has control over whether it is performed or not (Fishbein & Ajzen, 2010). For example, do you have perceived behavioral control over texting? We're guessing that you feel capable of texting, but do you perceive control over whether or not you engage in texting? What would happen if you quit texting? Is that a choice you can make?

Your perceived behavioral control along with your subjective norm for a behavior and your attitude toward the behavior influences your intention to perform the behavior. Sometimes your attitude toward the behavior has a stronger influence on your intention, and sometimes your subjective norm or perceived behavioral control has a stronger influence on your intention, but these are the three factors that always influence your intention to perform a behavior.

THE MODEL

A visual representation of the theory of reasoned action is shown in Figure 10.2. Notice the arrow going directly from "Intention to perform behavior" to "Behavior." This arrow indicates that intention has a direct impact on behavior, just as we have been discussing. Arrows are also leading from "Attitude toward behavior," "Subjective norm," and "Perceived behavioral control" to "Intention to perform behavior." These arrows indicate that attitude and subjective norm have a direct impact on intentions. In other words, the three influences on intentions are attitude, subjective norm, and perceived behavioral control. However, these three components do not necessarily have an equal impact on intention. Recall that we said that sometimes attitude has a bigger influence on intention and sometimes subjective norm has a bigger influence, and sometimes perceived behavioral control dominates intention. Notice the factors contributing to attitude toward behavior, subjective norm, and perceived behavioral control. We discuss these concepts in more detail in the following text. The model in Figure 10.2 is a visual way of describing the relationships hypothesized by TRA.

MEASURING AND PREDICTING ATTITUDE TOWARD BEHAVIOR

Earlier we discussed how Ajzen and Fishbein defined attitude and noted the similarities between their definition and the definition we presented in Chapter 2. In the TRA, Ajzen and Fishbein also specify the relationship between attitudes and beliefs and provide us with a formula for predicting attitudes. Ajzen and Fishbein state that attitude toward behavior is a function of beliefs about the behavior. More specifically, a person's attitude is a result of the strength with which he or she holds those beliefs

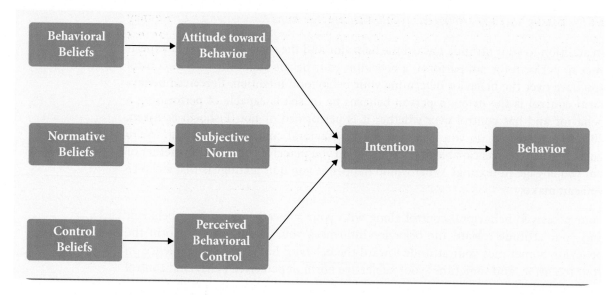

FIGURE 10.2 Theory of reasoned action.

and how he or she evaluates those beliefs. The beliefs we have about the behavior are referred to as **behavioral beliefs**. Behavioral beliefs are beliefs about a behavior that we view as most important. Behavioral beliefs frequently involve the consequences of performing a behavior. We may have dozens of beliefs about a particular behavior, but only some of them will be salient (important) at the time we are formulating an intention to perform or not perform a behavior. Ajzen and Fishbein estimate that we typically have six to nine behavioral beliefs about any particular behavior.

How do we find out what a person's behavioral beliefs are? The best way is to ask that person. When Strader and Katz (1990) wanted undecided students at a junior college to enroll in the nursing program, they first asked 120 students to list what they believe are the advantages and disadvantages of signing up for a career in nursing. Students expressed 407 beliefs. The most frequently listed beliefs would be considered the most salient for the students at the junior college. Ajzen and Fishbein (1980) recommend selecting about 10 behavioral beliefs. Strader and Katz identified the 11 most frequently mentioned beliefs:

1. Sense of accomplishment helping others
2. Good salary
3. Exposure to unpleasant sights and smells
4. Length of study program
5. Bad hours
6. Working with illness and death
7. Opportunities for the future
8. Relief that career decision is made
9. Meeting interesting people
10. Difficulty of study courses
11. Female profession

How strongly we hold a behavioral belief is referred to as **belief strength**. We may hold some beliefs very strongly, or, in other words, we believe beyond a doubt that the belief is true and likely to occur. For other beliefs, we may not feel as certain that the belief is really true. For example, you may believe that communication is a great major that will help you be successful in life; however, you may also have some doubts, making this belief weaker than your belief that the sky is blue. Belief strength is measured with a semantic differential scale that assesses how strongly an individual holds each behavioral belief. Below is an example of how Strader and Katz (1990) measured belief strength of the first behavioral belief listed above.

My signing up for a career as a registered nurse within the next month would mean I made a choice that gives me a sense of accomplishment helping others.

Likely   +3   +2   +1   0   –1   –2   –3   Unlikely

If you are particularly astute, you may have noticed that, by definition, behavioral beliefs are strongly held beliefs, making the measurement of belief strength redundant. If you were to identify one person's behavioral beliefs, there is no question that all of his or her behavioral beliefs would have a high (+2 or +3) belief strength. However, if you have targeted a large group of people, such as all undecided students at a junior college, and have elicited behavioral beliefs from a sample as we discussed above, and have taken the 10 or so most frequently listed beliefs, you need to measure belief strength. The reason is that, when you use the most frequently listed beliefs (what Ajzen and Fishbein call modal behavioral beliefs), not everyone in your audience will hold these beliefs. These were simply the most commonly held beliefs. Some members of the audience may not hold these beliefs at all. So the measurement of belief strength becomes important for predicting attitude for a large group of people.

Belief evaluation refers to how we feel about each of our behavioral beliefs. Do we view the belief as being positive about the behavior or negative? For instance, a behavioral belief I have about visiting New York City is that a lot of people are there. I may see this as a positive thing. I may find all the people to be exciting, interesting, and invigorating. On the other hand, I may view the large number of people in New York City as a negative. I might think it is too crowded and feel overwhelmed or in danger because of all the people. Obviously, evaluating a belief negatively has very different consequences for attitude than evaluating a belief positively. Belief evaluation is also measured with a semantic differential scale. Again drawing on Strader and Katz's study, the item used to measure belief evaluation for the first behavioral belief is shown below.

How bad or good for you would it be to have a sense of accomplishment helping others?

Good   +3   +2   +1   0   –1   –2   –3   Bad

At this point, we have defined belief strength and belief evaluation and discussed how to measure each. You may be wondering "So what?" The usefulness of this information is that it allows us to understand how an attitude develops as well as to predict attitude. Recall from Chapter 7 our discussion of theory. We discussed that theory helps us explain, predict, and control. Having information about the beliefs held by the audience not only helps us understand why they behave as they do but also helps us predict what they are likely to do. It also gives us the information we need to influence their behavior. You know what beliefs need to be changed and how they need to be changed in order to successfully change attitude.

Attitude toward behavior is a function of the belief strength and belief evaluation of one's behavioral beliefs. Ajzen and Fishbein specify this relationship in a mathematical formula shown here.

$$A_B = \Sigma b_i e_i$$

The A_B refers to attitude toward the behavior. The sigma sign, Σ, is the statistical symbol for sum. The b_i refers to the belief strength for each behavioral belief, and e_i refers to the belief evaluation for each behavioral belief. This formula is telling us that attitude (A_B) is a result of how strongly a person holds behavioral beliefs about a behavior multiplied by whether those beliefs are evaluated positively or negatively. The fact that the equation tells us to multiply belief strength and belief evaluation, rather than add them, is important. If you add them, each component is independent and carries its own weight individually. By multiplying, the components are interdependent, and it is the *interaction* of the components that influences attitude toward behavior.

This formula has theoretical and practical importance. On a theoretical level it tells us how these variables are related to one another. On a practical level it tells us exactly what information we need from our audience in order to understand their attitude. To calculate a person's attitude toward the behavior (A_B), you first multiply the belief strength (as marked on a scale like the one shown above) by the belief evaluation (as marked on a scale) for each behavioral belief. Once you have done this for each behavioral belief, you then sum (Σ) the products as is shown in Table 10.1. The result is a score that indicates the direction and intensity of the person's attitude toward the behavior.

TABLE 10.1 *PREDICTING ATTITUDE*

BEHAVIORAL BELIEFS	b_i	e_i	$b_i \times e_i$
1. Sense of accomplishment helping others	+2	+3	+6
2. Good salary	−2	+3	−6
3. Exposure to unpleasant sights and smells	+3	−3	−9
4 Length of study program	+2	−2	−4
5. Bad hours	+2	−3	−6
			−19

MEASURING AND PREDICTING SUBJECTIVE NORMS

Recall that the two factors that predict intention to perform a behavior are attitude toward the behavior and subjective norm. We have discussed the attitude toward behavior component; now let's discuss the subjective norm component. Above we defined subjective norm as the social pressure a person feels from important (salient) others to perform or not perform a behavior. Subjective norm is the result of two things: normative beliefs and motivation to comply. **Normative beliefs** are a person's beliefs about what salient others want him or her to do regarding the behavior in question. When Strader and Katz (1990) asked students to list advantages and disadvantages of signing up for the nursing program, they also asked the students to list the persons or groups of persons who would influence their decision. This task provided Strader and Katz with a list of salient others that included mother, father, brother, sister, girlfriend, boyfriend, spouse, and friends. The normative beliefs were what the students thought those salient others wanted them to do regarding signing up for the nursing program. It's important to remember that normative beliefs are your audience's beliefs—not their salient others' beliefs. Normative beliefs are also measured with a semantic differential scale such as the one shown below.

My mother thinks
    I should   +3   +2   +1   0   −1   −2   −3   I should not
            sign up for a career in nursing within the next month.

To predict subjective norm, you need your audience's normative beliefs and their motivation to comply with their salient others. **Motivation to comply** simply refers to how willing your audience is to go along with what they think their salient others want them to do. For example, Alice may have the normative belief that her mother wants her to sign up for the nursing program, but she may not be at all motivated to comply with her mother's wishes. As shown below, motivation to comply is measured with a scale somewhat similar to those used to measure belief strength, belief evaluation, and normative beliefs.

How much do you want to do what your mother wants you to do regarding signing up for a career as a registered nurse within the next month?

_____ Not at all (0)

_____ Slightly (+1)

_____ Moderately (+2)

_____ Strongly (+3)

The motivation to comply scale does not contain negative numbers as did the scales for normative belief, belief strength, and belief evaluation. Ajzen and Fishbein (1980) state that it is unlikely people will be motivated to do the opposite of what their salient others think they should do, so therefore it is not necessary to measure how motivated they are to do what the salient others think they *should not* do.

Similar to the prediction of attitude toward behavior, Ajzen and Fishbein (1980) provide a mathematical formula for predicting subjective norm. As with the formula for attitude, this formula tells us the relationship among the variables and has both theoretical and practical importance.

$$SN = \Sigma NB_i MC_i$$

Similar to the formula for attitude, SN refers to subjective norm, Σ is the statistical symbol for sum, NB_i refers to the normative beliefs the audience has regarding each salient other, and MC_i refers to motivation to comply with each salient other. Similar to the formula for attitude, subjective norm results from normative beliefs and motivation to comply, and again these two variables are multiplied, not added. Again, by multiplying, the components are interdependent. To calculate the subjective norm, you multiply the normative belief for each salient other (as measured by a scale like the one shown previously) by the motivation to comply (as measured by a scale like the one previously), and then all of the products are summed. The result is a score indicating the degree of social pressure a person is experiencing to either perform or not perform the behavior.

MEASURING PERCEIVED BEHAVIORAL CONTROL

As in the case of attitudes toward behavior and subjective norms, perceived behavioral control is the result of two factors being combined according to the following formula:

$$PBC = \Sigma c_i p_i$$

Here, PBC refers to the level of perceived behavioral control over the targeted behavior. The two factors that are multiplied to find the perceived behavioral control are represented by the c_i and the p_i. The c refers to the control belief. **Control beliefs** are beliefs about specific factors that may facilitate or interfere with the performance of the behavior. For example, believing in one's ability to obtain a loan to pay tuition is a control belief. Getting a loan would facilitate enrolling in a nursing program. The p refers to the **perceived power**, which is the perceived ability of the control belief to facilitate or inhibit the performance of the behavior. For example, if we consider the control belief about getting a loan, perceived power is my perception that the loan will cover tuition. A summary of the formulas from TRA is shown in Figure 10.3.

Control beliefs, like behavioral and normative beliefs, are identified by asking a sample of your target population a series of questions about the behavior in question. Once we have identified common control beliefs, we can assess the strength and power of each control belief. Strader and Katz did not measure perceived behavioral control; however, if they had, they would have had to first survey a sample to discover what factors students believed would either interfere with or facilitate them enrolling in a nursing program. Students may have had control beliefs about ability to pay tuition, transportation to clinic sites, and the ability to work with blood and other bodily fluids. To measure this last control belief, the following question would be used:

How likely is it that you will be able to handle blood and other bodily fluids while training to be a nurse?

| Extremely Likely | +3 | +2 | +1 | 0 | −1 | −2 | −3 | Extremely Unlikely |

To measure perceived power for this control belief, the following question would be used:

My being able to handle blood and other bodily fluids while training to be a nurse would make it

| Easier | +3 | +2 | +1 | 0 | −1 | −2 | −3 | More difficult for me to enroll in a nursing program |

$$A_B = \Sigma\, b_i e_i$$

$$SN = \Sigma\, NB_i MC_i$$

$$BhI = A_{B(w1)} + SN_{(w2)} + PBC_{(w3)}$$

BhI	=	behavioral intention
A_B	=	attitude toward behavior
b_i	=	belief strength for each salient belief
e_i	=	belief evaluation of each salient belief
SN	=	subjective norm
NB_i	=	normative belief for each salient other
MC_i	=	motivation to comply with each salient other
PBC	=	perceived behavioral control
Σ	=	statistical symbol for sum
i	=	is used to represent each individual belief
w_1	=	the relative weight of the attitude toward behavior (A_B)
w_2	=	the relative weight of the subjective norm (SN)
w_3	=	the relative weight of the perceived behavioral control (PBC)

FIGURE 10.3 TRA formulas

We could repeat these measures for as many control beliefs as existed and use the data to predict perceived behavioral control just as we used the data on individuals' strength and evaluation of behavioral beliefs to predict attitude toward behavior. In some research, scholars measure perceived behavioral control directly, rather than by measuring control beliefs and perceived power.

To summarize the relationships among the variables outlined in TRA, Fishbein and Ajzen provide the following formula:

$$BhI = A_{(w_1)} + SN_{(w_2)} + PBC_{(w_3)}$$

In this formula, BhI refers to behavioral intention, and the formula states that behavioral intention is a result of attitude toward behavior plus subjective norm, plus perceived behavioral control. The w_1, w_2, and w_3 refer to the relative weight placed on each of the three components, respectively. Recall from our previous discussion that sometimes attitude is more important and sometimes subjective norm or perceived behavioral control is more important in determining behavioral intentions. The relative weights are derived from a multiple regression analysis of the variables. Note here that attitude toward behavior, subjective norm, and perceived behavioral control are added together and not multiplied. The three components act *independently* on intention rather than interdependently.

SO NOW WHAT DO YOU DO WITH IT?

At this point, we have reviewed how TRA explains human behavior. We have discussed the relationship between attitudes and beliefs and how the normative, attitudinal, and control components influence intention. As mentioned above, this information is useful not only for explaining but also for predicting how people will behave, and for developing persuasive messages for influencing their attitudes and behavior. In this section, we discuss how TRA directs us to approach a persuasive situation. One nice thing about TRA is that it provides some very specific strategies for constructing persuasive messages.

USING TRA TO CHANGE ATTITUDES

Attitude toward behavior is a function of behavioral beliefs about the behavior. Change the beliefs and the attitude is likely to change. Notice that we said "beliefs," meaning more than one. If you were to change one or two behavioral beliefs, attitude may not change in any significant way. There is no magic number of how many beliefs have to be changed, but a general rule is that the more beliefs you change the more likely that attitude will change in a significant and meaningful way. Specifically, there are three strategies for changing a person's attitude. First, you can *add a new behavioral belief*. This is equivalent to giving a person new information. For example, in their study, Strader and Katz (1990) could have added a behavioral belief about the shortage of nurses (assuming there was a shortage at the time) by telling students about this shortage and the need for nurses in a variety of specialties. Alternatively, Strader and Katz could have provided information about opportunities in nursing that students were unaware of. Whenever we learn new information, we develop new beliefs, so this strategy of adding a new behavioral belief is essentially providing your audience with new information. Second, you can *change the belief evaluation*. Strader and Katz used the following message to change the belief evaluation of the behavioral belief "bad hours."

> *Many students do not understand the flexibility nurses have with their hours. Most of your friends get up early in the morning, leave late in the evening, and have to fight rush hour traffic all of their life. Nurses are flexible and can choose whenever they want to work. Most nurses can choose the type of schedules that accommodate their life style. If you are a night person who likes basking in the sun during the day and wants to make extra money, nights may be for you. If you are a morning person, you can find a job in or outside the hospital on a day shift.*

This message is attempting to change how students evaluate their belief about the hours that nurses have to work. By changing the belief evaluation from negative to positive, the attitude toward becoming a nurse becomes a little more positive.

Third, you can *change the belief strength*. For example, a behavioral belief listed by the students in Strader and Katz's study was that there would be opportunities for the future. Assuming that the audience did not believe this very strongly, a message could be created to convince students that really good opportunities are available in the nursing field. Enhancing the belief strength of positive beliefs or, conversely, reducing the belief strength of negative beliefs leads to a more positive attitude.

USING TRA TO CHANGE SUBJECTIVE NORM

Subjective norm is the social pressure a person feels to perform or not perform a behavior and, along with attitude and perceived behavioral control, it influences intention. Subjective norm is based on normative beliefs about salient others and, therefore, to change subjective norm, normative beliefs must be changed. Similar to attitude, there are three strategies for influencing subjective norm. First, you can *add new normative beliefs* about new salient others. This means suggesting to your audience that they should be concerned about the opinions of a particular person who is not currently a salient other. For instance, in the Strader and Katz study, teachers were not listed as salient others. Strader and Katz could have constructed a message telling students that their teachers think nursing is a good career choice and that the students should be concerned with what their teachers say.

Second, you can *change existing normative beliefs*. This strategy involves messages that attempt to convince the audience that their salient others want them to do something other than what they currently think their salient others want them to do. For example, in their study, Strader and Katz (1990) found that students believed their parents did not want them to sign up for the nursing program. A message based on changing normative beliefs would involve telling students that their parents really would be supportive of them signing up for the nursing program. This could be a tough sell depending on who the salient others are and the closeness of the relationship. Third, you can *alter motivation to comply* with salient others. This strategy involves creating messages that either encourage the audience to comply with salient others (who are supportive of the behavior) or discourage the audience from complying with salient others (who are not supportive of the behavior). Strader and Katz did not attempt to influence students' subjective norms. They thought that, with the limited information they had on parental beliefs, it would be unethical to attack either the normative beliefs or the motivation to comply with a parent. It is also questionable how successful such messages would have been. How many of us are going to believe a stranger telling us that what we think our parents or friends want us to do is not what they really want us to do? However, such a strategy may work in a more interpersonal persuasion situation such as when someone is persuading his or her significant other.

Influencing the subjective norm has ethical considerations. Is it ethical to attack or question salient others who are people the audience may love and depend on? It is generally considered ethical to influence a person's beliefs about objects or behaviors such as when we attempt to influence behavioral beliefs. Trying to influence how people feel and think about salient others may be quite ethical in some situations, but is likely to be unethical in other situations such as that encountered by Strader and Katz.

USING TRA TO CHANGE PERCEIVED BEHAVIORAL CONTROL

We can use perceived behavioral control to influence persuasive success in a manner similar to how we altered attitudes toward behavior and subjective norms. By altering the audience's perceptions of perceived behavioral control, we can alter their behavioral intentions. Recall that perceived behavioral control is based on control beliefs and perceived power. Therefore, messages targeted at control beliefs and perceived power could be used to alter perceived behavioral control. For example, if potential nursing students believed they could not handle blood and had low perceived power over this factor, their low perceived behavioral control would likely lead them to not choose nursing as their major. We could create a message that targeted this control belief and perceived power. However, sometimes extensive interventions are needed to change people's perceived behavioral control. For example, sometimes perceived power is based on real skills and abilities. No amount of messaging will change that. Rather, some type of training is needed to help people develop a skill set so that they have both real and perceived power over the factors preventing them from engaging in the behavior. Perceived behavioral control is of particular importance in certain situations. For example, a common barrier in getting people to stop smoking is that many smokers don't believe they actually *can* quit. Many smokers are well aware of the health hazards of smoking and are well aware of broad-based social disapproval for smoking. No change in behavior is likely to occur, however, unless the smokers are convinced that stopping smoking is actually within their control. Altering their perceived behavioral control by providing information about the effectiveness of nicotine patches, hypnosis, or other smoking cessation programs can alter the smokers' sense of perceived behavior control so that they can have stronger behavioral intentions toward quitting smoking. This is illustrated in the advertisement shown in Figure 10.4. Perceived behavioral control is often applied in health situations such as sexual decision making among women (McCabe & Killackey, 2004) and condom use (Basen-Engquist & Parcel, 1992), as well as in other contexts such as hunting behaviors (Hrube, Ajzen, & Daigle, 2001).

An additional strategy revolves around the relative weight of the attitudinal, normative, and control components. Recall that sometimes attitude toward behavior is more heavily weighted (has more influence on behavioral intentions), but at other times subjective norm is more heavily weighted. For instance if a person's attitude and subjective norm are in opposition, a strategy for influencing intention is to target the relative weights. For example, suppose Jane has a very positive attitude toward entering the nursing program, but she is also experiencing intense social pressure from her salient others to *not* enter the nursing program. If she places more weight on her attitude, she will most likely enroll in the nursing program. On the other hand, if she places more weight on her subjective norm, she is unlikely to enroll in the program. If Jane is placing more weight on the subjective norm and we want to influence her to enter the nursing program, a possible strategy is to convince her to place more weight on her attitude than on her subjective norm. A message such as "It's your life and your career; you should do what you want" is geared at increasing the weight placed on the attitudinal component. The same applies to perceived behavioral control. Sometimes this component is heavily weighted and is the primary reason a person does not engage in a behavior that they view positively and feel social pressure to perform.

When creating a persuasive message, TRA provides us with nine strategies: (a) add a new behavioral belief, (b) alter belief evaluations, (c) alter belief strength, (d) add a new salient other, (e) alter normative beliefs, (f) alter motivation to comply, (g) alter control beliefs, (h) alter perceived power, and (j) alter the relative weights. TRA specifies what kinds of things we need to learn about our audiences and what the message

The Commit® stop smoking lozenge is clinically proven to help you quit smoking, even if you've tried before. The 4 mg lozenge actually doubles your chances of quitting† It works fast to help keep your cravings under control. And, it keeps working to help protect you from cravings even after the lozenge is gone.

www.commitlozenge.com

REAL HELP. REAL HOPE.

*Vs. placebo. Use as directed, take one lozenge, every 1-2 hours. Individual results may vary. Support program improves chances of success. © 2004 GlaxoSmithKline Consumer Healthcare, L.P.

Courtesy GlaxoSmithKline, with permission.

FIGURE 10.4 How does this address perceived behavioral control?

should target. Combining what we learned about source, message, and channel factors in Chapters 4, 5, and 6 with the TRA theoretical framework allows us to create powerful and effective persuasive messages and interventions.

USING TRA TO CHANGE BEHAVIOR

Whether to use the TRA or TPB depends on the nature of the behavior and your audience's beliefs about that behavior. Recall that the TRA was developed to explain volitional behavior. Whether behavior is volitional or not is somewhat of a perception. When the target behavior is under volitional control but the audience lacks confidence or believes "they can't perform the behavior," your persuasive message needs to address control beliefs. Many health-related behaviors fall into this category. Whether a person smokes or not is within his or her control, but he or she may not "feel" in control; in other words, he or she may have negative control beliefs. Therefore, to successfully influence this person to stop smoking; you would need to address his or her control beliefs as well as his or her behavioral and normative beliefs. Regardless of whether you employ the TRA or TPB, both theories direct you first to learn about your audience. An underlying premise of these theories is that you have to understand a person's existing beliefs in order to influence his or her behavior. The TRA is similar to social judgment theory in this respect. That theory also directed the persuader to understand the audience. Once you have information about your audience's behavioral, normative, and control beliefs underlying their intentions to perform a behavior, you can begin to construct persuasive messages to alter those beliefs. If you're thinking that this sounds like a lot of work, you're right, it is; however, it is also quite effective.

Quine, Rutter, and Arnold (2001) used a reasoned action approach to influence British adolescents between 11 and 15 years old to wear bicycle helmets. In an earlier study, they had identified British adolescents' beliefs about wearing bicycle helmets (Quine, Rutter, & Arnold, 1998) and discovered that adolescents held two beliefs that reduced their perceptions of control: "Even if I wanted to, I might not be able to wear a helmet while cycling to and from school because doing up and adjusting the straps is too much effort" and "Even if I wanted to, I might not be able to wear a helmet while cycling to and from school because there is nowhere to keep it during lessons." Quine and her colleagues developed a persuasive message designed to influence students' behavioral, normative, and control beliefs. They identified 97 adolescents who regularly rode their bikes to school but did not use helmets. Half of these adolescents were given the booklet shown in Figure 10.5. The other half were given a booklet on taking a cycling proficiency and maintenance course (control group). Quine and her colleagues then measured the adolescents' behavioral, normative, and control beliefs; their intention to wear a helmet; and whether they wore a helmet when biking to and from school immediately after reading the booklet and 5 months later. At the 5-month mark, 25 percent of adolescents who were given the persuasive message reported wearing a helmet when biking to school, but none of the adolescents in the control group reported wearing a helmet. This study demonstrates the effectiveness of using TRA to guide the creation of a persuasive message.

Bright, Manfredo, Fishbein, and Bath (1993) drew on TRA to influence people who visited Yellowstone National Park about the National Park Service's controlled burn policy. People would have a high level of volitional control over supporting the National Park Service's policy, both in real terms as well as perceived control. Therefore, TRA was very appropriate in this situation. Earlier research done by Manfredo, Fishbein, Hass, and Watson (1990) identified common beliefs held by the public about the controlled burn policy. Bright et al. (1993) then surveyed 407 people entering Yellowstone Park about their behavioral beliefs, attitude, normative beliefs, motivation to comply, and intentions to support the controlled burn policy. Of these people, 66.3 percent had a positive attitude and 33.7 percent had a negative attitude toward the controlled burn policy. From the audience's behavioral beliefs, Bright and

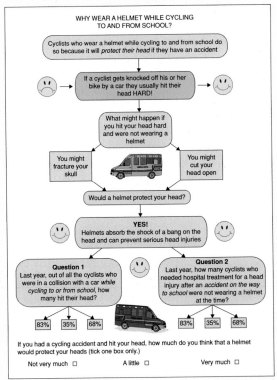

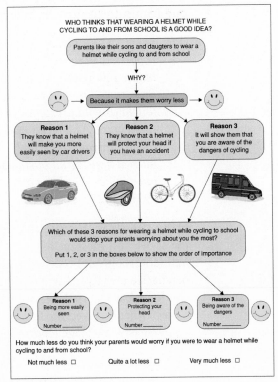

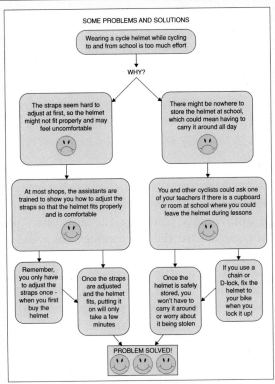

FIGURE 10.5 Why wear a helmet while cycling to and from school?

Message from Quine et al. p. 333. Reproduced with permission from The British Journal of Clinical and Social Psychology, © The British Psychological Society.

his colleagues wrote two persuasive messages: one supporting the burn policy and one against the controlled burn policy. The anti messages:

> Some experts object to the controlled burn policy because they do not believe it is possible to control fires once they have been allowed to develop into a larger blaze. Yellowstone National Park was an example of this. The summer of 1988 fires started in mid-June but, because of the controlled burn policy, were not fought as wild fires until July. By that time, the fire was beyond the control of firefighters. As a result, more than 40% of the park was burned. Furthermore, the fire spread to privately owned land where it destroyed valuable timber and burned homes and businesses. Many people now believe that the controlled burn policy should be abandoned and all forest fires suppressed. (Bright et al., 1993, pp. 270–271)

Half of those with a positive attitude toward the controlled burn policy received the above anti message as a part of a follow-up questionnaire in the mail. The other half (control group) received the same questionnaire but did not receive any type of persuasive message. The questionnaire consisted of the same questions as the survey conducted at the park. Those with a negative attitude toward the controlled burn policy either received the following pro message with the follow-up questionnaire or no persuasive message (control group). The pro message:

> Some experts support the controlled burn policy because it allows areas to remain as natural as possible. By allowing fire, forests are actually healthier. Within months after the burn, vegetation begins to grow. Compared to matured stands of trees, vegetation which grows after fires provides much better sources of food for animals such as bear, bison, elk and deer. In fact, forest fires are directly responsible for the death of a very small proportion of animals. Rather, as a result of fires, populations of wildlife will frequently increase. In addition to allowing for natural environments, many have noted that the controlled burn policy, as it did in Yellowstone, can actually improve the scenery and make it a more interesting place to visit. (Bright et al., 1993, p. 271)

These messages based on the audience's behavioral beliefs were generally quite effective, particularly for those with an initial positive attitude toward the burn policy. The individuals receiving the anti-burn policy message had a more negative attitude toward the burn policy than did the control group that did not receive a persuasive message. Those people receiving the positive message (initially had a negative attitude toward the burn policy) did not experience an attitude change. Bright et al. believed that the lack of success for the positive message was due to the message source. A pro-burn message would have been expected from the Park Service and its representatives, whereas an anti-burn message would have been unexpected. The unexpected nature of the anti-burn message may have resulted in greater source credibility. This expectancy disconfirmation in relation to source credibility was discussed in Chapter 4 and illustrates the importance of attending to all aspects of the process when designing a persuasive message.

STRENGTHS AND LIMITATIONS

A major strength of the TRA from a communication point of view is that the model is receiver oriented. The model focuses on the receiver's attitudes toward behavior, subjective norms, and perceptions of behavioral control and how these influence intention and behavior. Therefore, the model directs persuaders to understand their audience. Audience analysis becomes a requirement in the persuasion process. It's not just "what you say" to the receiver. Your message must be specifically directed at the receiver's beliefs and perceptions, both behavioral and normative. Another strength of the TRA approach is that it explains the relationship between attitudes, beliefs, and behaviors, as well as the relationship of attitudes and social pressure to perform a behavior that people experience. One important strength of the TRA is that it is well supported by research. TRA has successfully predicted individuals' behaviors. The TRA has been applied to a variety of behaviors, including voting, family planning, consumer purchases (Ajzen & Fishbein, 1980), seat belt use (Budd, North, & Spencer, 1984), eating in fast-food restaurants (Brinberg & Durand, 1983), seeking dental care (Hoogstraten, de Haan, & ter Horst, 1985), antipollution behavior (Hamid & Cheng, 1995), pediatrician recommendations for patients to get the human papillomavirus vaccination (Roberto, Krieger, Katz, Goei, & Jain, 2011), and AIDS prevention behavior (Cochran, Mays, Ciarletta, Caruso, & Mallon, 1992). The TRA approach is often applied in the health communication context. A consequence of the ability of the TRA to predict behavior is that it allows us to have some measure of control over our audience's behaviors. The TRA provides specific strategies for influencing a person's beliefs and subsequent attitude and subjective norm. Because the theory is described so specifically, it provides us with very clear and relatively simple strategies for developing a persuasive message.

Although the TRA has proved to be useful in a variety of situations, it has some limitations. One main criticism of the TRA approach is the emphasis on a specific behavior. Often, a behavior of interest is the culmination of several behaviors such as weight loss or obtaining a degree. Obtaining a college degree is a behavior, but it results from many other behaviors such as attending class, writing papers, reading books, and taking tests. To most effectively predict obtaining a college degree, we would need to understand the intention to perform each of the many underlying behaviors. This would be a mammoth task that few of us would be willing to undertake. However, because TRA does focus on specific behaviors, it can help us better understand the behaviors we are trying to influence.

An additional limitation of the theory involves the relative weights component. To obtain the relative weights, one must have not only the person's attitudinal, normative, and perceived behavioral control data but also the person's behavioral intention to conduct the multiple regression analysis that provides the relative weights. In other words, there is no way for a practitioner to obtain the relative weights without also knowing a person's behavioral intention. This is a limitation in applied settings.

One last criticism of the TRA approach is that it does not include previous behavior in the model. A person's previous experience with a behavior has been found to influence both the intention to perform a behavior and the actual performance of the behavior (see Eagly & Chaiken, 1993, for a review). Recall from Chapter 3 that attitudes formed through direct experience are more predictive of behavior. Current behavior may be somewhat based on whether or not we have performed the behavior before. Fishbein and Azjen (2010) acknowledge the role of previous behavior and experience, but the theory does not specify (explain) exactly how it impacts the attitudinal, normative, and control components. In order to predict and control, a theory must provide a specific explanation of how components are related to one another. Previous behavior is a predictor of future behavior and shouldn't be ignored. When we look at efforts to change behaviors on which we would expect past behavior to have influence, such as losing weight and exercising, we find these efforts are often unsuccessful. The theory of reasoned action is a very useful theory of influence for such behaviors and increases our ability to influence such behaviors; however, it is not a magic bullet that will give you the ability to influence anyone at any time. Of course, no theory is a magic bullet.

SUMMARY

- The TRA explains how people make behavioral choices.
- Behavior change is the primary focus of the TRA.
- The best predictor of behavior is intention to perform the behavior.
- Attitude toward behavior, subjective norm, and perceived behavioral control influence intention.
- The three situations for which intention to behave does not predict behavior are when behavior is not under volitional control, when the measure of intentions and the measure of behavior do not correspond with one another, and when too much time elapses between the measurement of intentions and the measurement of behavior.
- The social pressure a person experiences to either perform or not perform a behavior is referred to as subjective norm.
- The strength with which a person holds behavioral beliefs, along with how he or she evaluates those beliefs, determines attitude toward behavior.
- A subjective norm is determined by the normative beliefs a person holds about his or her salient others and how motivated he or she is to comply with those salient others.
- Perceived behavioral control is determined by an individual's control beliefs and perceived power.
- The three strategies for influencing attitude are to add a new behavioral belief, to change belief evaluation, and to change belief strength.

- The three strategies for influencing a subjective norm are to add new normative beliefs, to change existing normative beliefs, and to change the motivation to comply.
- An additional strategy for influencing behavioral intentions is to alter the relative weights of the attitudinal and normative components.
- The TRA directs persuaders first to assess their audience's beliefs and then to develop persuasive messages based on those beliefs.
- Altering perceptions of behavioral control can alter behavioral intentions and ultimate behavior.
- Strengths of the TRA are that it is receiver oriented, it is able to explain the causes of behavior, it is able to predict behavior, and it provides persuaders with a measure of control over their audience.
- Limitations of TRA are a focus only on specific behaviors and not complex behaviors and the exclusion of previous behavior in the models.

KEY TERMS

Attitude toward behavior—an attitude toward a specific behavior.

Behavioral beliefs—beliefs about a behavior that we view as most important and that frequently involve the consequences of performing a behavior.

Behavioral intention—a psychological concept best described as an expectation or a plan. An intention is a plan for how you are going to behave.

Belief evaluation—how positive or negative we feel about each of our behavioral beliefs.

Belief strength—how strongly we hold a behavioral belief.

Control beliefs—beliefs about the likelihood of having the opportunities and resources necessary to perform the behavior and the frequency that a control factor will occur.

Correspondence—the measures of intention and behavior, which must be measured on the same dimensions (action, target, context, and time).

Intention-behavior relationship—the extent that behavioral intentions will influence actual performance of the behavior.

Motivation to comply—how willing individuals are to go along with what they think their salient others want them to do.

Normative beliefs—a person's beliefs about what salient others want him or her to do regarding a specific behavior.

Perceived behavioral control—an individual's perception of the level of control he or she has over a behavior.

Perceived power—the perceived ability of the control belief to facilitate or inhibit the performance of the behavior.

Subjective norm—the social pressure a person feels from salient (important) others to perform or not perform a behavior.

Volitional control—if a behavior is under volitional control, an individual has control over the behavior.

REVIEW QUESTIONS

1. What types of behavior do you have volitional control over?
2. How do Ajzen and Fishbein define attitude?
3. What three factors influence the intention–behavior relationship?
4. How do action, target, context, and time affect the correspondence between intentions and behaviors?
5. What are behavioral beliefs, belief strength, and belief evaluation? How do these relate to attitudes?
6. What are salient others, normative beliefs, and motivation to comply? How do these relate to subjective norm?
7. What are control beliefs and power of control factors? How do they relate to perceived behavioral control?
8. What are the strategies for changing a person's attitude and for changing a person's subjective norm?
9. When would it be appropriate to alter the relative weights of the attitudinal and normative components in an effort to influence behavioral intentions?
10. What does the TRA direct persuaders to do when attempting to change an audience's behavior?
11. What are the strengths and limitations of the TRA?

1. Identify three behaviors you have performed today. To what extent did you have volitional control over each of these behaviors?

2. Think about a behavior you have recently performed, such as accepting a job or internship, buying a car, or giving blood. To what extent was your behavior a result of your attitude toward that behavior as compared to the social pressure (subjective norm) you felt from others to perform that behavior?

3. Think of a behavior over which you have a high level of perceived behavioral control. Why do you feel you have control over that behavior? Now think of a behavior that you would like to do, but don't because you have low perceived behavioral control. What makes this behavior different from the one you have control of?

4. In the formula for predicting attitude, belief strength and belief evaluation are multiplied. How would the predictions of the theory be different if belief strength and belief evaluation were added rather than multiplied?

5. Think of a time when your behavior was more influenced by your attitude than by your subjective norm, and think of a time when your behavior was more influenced by your subjective norm than by your attitude. How were these two situations different and similar?

6. Under what circumstances would it be ethical to influence any aspect of subjective norm? What about persuasive situations in advertising, politics, and social issues—what criteria would you suggest for ethical influence of subjective norms?

7. What ethical criteria would you suggest for attempts to alter the weight of attitudes toward behavior versus subjective norms? When is it all right to tell receivers that they should not care about normative groups or that they should care more about normative groups?

REFERENCES

Ajzen, I. (1985). From intentions to actions: A theory of planned behavior. In J. Huhl & J. Beckmann (Eds.), *Action control: From cognition to behavior* (pp. 11–39). New York: Springer-Verlag.

Ajzen, I. (1991). The theory of planned behavior. *Organizational Behavior and Human Decision Processes, 50,* 179–211.

Ajzen, I., & Fishbein, M. (1980). *Understanding attitudes and predicting social behavior.* Englewood Cliffs, NJ: Prentice-Hall.

Basen-Engquist, K., & Parcel, G. S. (1992). Attitudes, norms, and self-efficacy: A model of adolescents' HIV-related sexual risk behavior. *Health Education Quarterly, 19,* 263–277.

Bright, A. D., Manfredo, M. J., Fishbein, M., & Bath, A. (1993). Application of the theory of reasoned action to the National Park Service's controlled burn policy. *Journal of Leisure Research, 25,* 263–280.

Brinberg, D., & Durand, J. (1983). Eating at fast-food restaurants: An analysis using two behavioral intention models. *Journal of Applied Psychology, 13,* 459–472.

Budd, R. J., North, D., & Spencer, C. (1984). Understanding seat belt use: A test of Bentler and Speckart's extension of the "theory of reasoned action." *European Journal of Social Psychology, 14,* 69–78.

Cochran, S. D., Mays, V. M., Ciarletta, J., Caruso, C., & Mallon, D. (1992). Efficacy of the theory of reasoned action in predicting AIDS-related sexual risk reduction among gay men. *Journal of Applied Social Psychology, 22,* 1481–1501.

Eagly, A. H., & Chaiken, S. (1993). *The psychology of attitudes.* Fort Worth, TX: Harcourt Brace Jovanovich.

Fishbein, M. & Ajzen, I. (2010). *Predicting and changing behavior: The reasoned action approach.* New York: Psychology Press.

Hamid, P. N., & Cheng, S. (1995). Predicting antipollution behavior: The role of molar behavioral intentions, past behavior, and locus of control. *Environment and Behavior, 27,* 679–698.

Hoogstraten, J., de Haan, W., & ter Horst, G. (1985). Stimulating the demand for dental care: An application of Ajzen and Fishbein's theory of reasoned action. *European Journal of Social Psychology, 15,* 401–414.

Hrube, D, Ajzen, I., & Daigle, J. (2001). Predicting hunting intentions and behavior: An application of the theory of planned behavior. *Leisure Sciences, 23*(3), 165–179.

Liska, A. E. (1984). A critical examination of the causal structure of the Fishbein/Ajzen attitude behavior model. *Social Psychology Quarterly, 47,* 61–74.

Manfredo, M. J., Fishbein, M., Hass, & Watson, A. E. (1990). Attitudes toward prescribed fire policies: the public is widely divided in its support. *Journal of Forestry, 8,* 19–23.

McCabe, M. P., & Killackey, E. J. (2004). Sexual decision making in young women. *Sexual and Relationship Therapy, 19*(1), 15–28.

Quine, L., Rutter, D. R., & Arnold, L. (1998). Predicting and understanding safety helmet use among schoolboy cyclists: A comparison of the theory of planned behavior and the health belief model. *Psychology and Health, 13,* 251–269.

Quine, L., Rutter, D. R., & Arnold, L. (2001). Persuading school-age cyclists to use safety helmets: Effectiveness of an intervention based on the theory of planned behavior. *British Journal of Health Psychology, 6,* 327–345.

Roberto, A. J., Krieger, J. L., Katz, M. L., Goei, R., & Jain, P. (2011). Predicting pediatricians' communication with parents about the human papillomavirus (HPV) vaccine: An application of the theory of reasoned action. *Health Communication, 26,* 303–312.

Strader, M. K., & Katz, B. M. (1990). Effects of a persuasive communication on beliefs, attitudes, and career choice. *Journal of Social Psychology, 130,* 141–150.

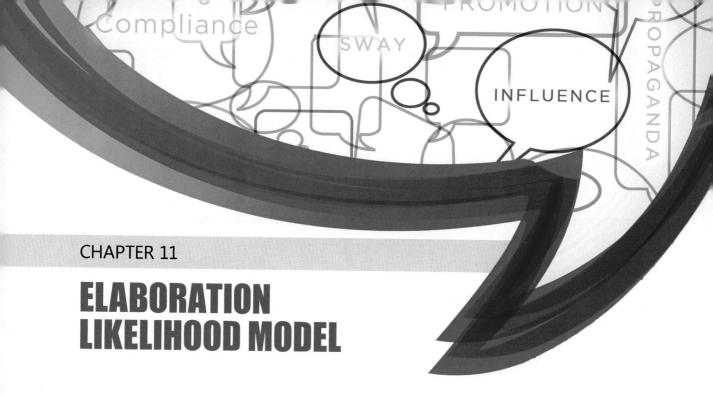

CHAPTER 11

ELABORATION LIKELIHOOD MODEL

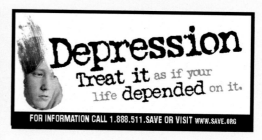

Used with permission of SAVE.

FIGURE 11.1 Two versions of the same message—which is most persuasive?

LEARNING OBJECTIVES

- DESCRIBE ELABORATION.
- EXPLAIN THE TWO ROUTES TO PERSUASION AND HOW THEY ARE DIFFERENT FROM EACH OTHER.
- EXPLAIN HOW MOTIVATION AND ABILITY DETERMINE WHICH ROUTE TO PERSUASION IS TAKEN.
- DESCRIBE FACTORS THAT INFLUENCE MOTIVATION TO PROCESS AND ABILITY TO PROCESS.
- EXPLAIN HOW ATTITUDE IS INFLUENCED IN THE TWO ROUTES TO PERSUASION.
- EXPLAIN OBJECTIVE AND BIASED PROCESSING OF MESSAGES.

Which of the two messages in Figure 11.1 do you think is more persuasive? Both are sending a message about the need to treat depression, but Message A provides rational information about why depression needs to be treated. Message B contains only 10 words and provides little rational information. In general, do you think that messages containing rational arguments are more effective or that messages relying on attention-getting visuals and snappy catchphrases are more effective? When a message contains rational arguments as Message A does, do you take the time to read or listen to them and consider them?

The theories we have discussed so far in this book have assumed that people are rational and carefully consider the persuasive messages they receive. How true do you think this assumption is? Social judgment theory, cognitive dissonance theory, and the theory of reasoned action all assume that people think rationally when receiving a persuasive message. These theories do a good job of explaining, predicting, and controlling persuasion in some situations, but other situations are beyond the scope of each theory. A good deal of research supports this rational approach, but a good deal of research also does not support it. For example, sometimes source credibility is an important factor and sometimes it is not. Sometimes including evidence in a message is effective and sometimes it is not. Petty and Cacioppo (1981, 1986) noticed these inconsistencies in research findings and the limited scope of each prior theory and developed the elaboration likelihood model to address these concerns.

ELABORATION

The **elaboration likelihood model (ELM)** focuses on different ways people respond to persuasive messages. **Elaboration** refers to the amount of thinking the receiver engages in about the content of a message. Elaboration can be thought of as a continuum, ranging from no thinking at all about the content of the message to extensive thinking about the message. The theory is called the elaboration likelihood model because it makes different predictions depending on how likely it is that the receiver will elaborate on the message.

TWO ROUTES TO ATTITUDE CHANGE

Petty and Cacioppo (1981, 1986) argued that people process information differently depending on the circumstances. Sometimes a **central route** is used to process persuasive messages. The central route involves *high elaboration,* or the receiver focusing on and thinking about the content of the message. This is active involvement that involves expending *cognitive energy* to think about and process the message. Theories that assume that receivers use rational thought and consider arguments in the message are most useful in understanding the central route to persuasion.

However, we do not always think carefully about each message directed at us. Indeed, it would be difficult to pay close attention to every message bombarding us from signs on buses and flyers posted around campus to Internet and television messages and speakers we are exposed to every day. Instead, we often use the **peripheral route** to process messages. The peripheral route involves low elaboration of the message, and rational thought does not play a key role here. When receivers are engaged in the peripheral route, there is little thinking about the content of the message or the arguments it contains and little cognitive energy is exerted. In fact, Petty and Cacioppo suggest that most of us are *cognitive misers* and choose to use as little cognitive energy as possible on most messages. When we employ the peripheral route and use a minimum amount of brainpower, we tend to rely on peripheral cues to help us decide how to respond to a message. **Peripheral cues** are factors that help us quickly decide how to process the message without having to engage in much elaboration. You can think of peripheral cues as shortcuts. Peripheral cues include things such as source credibility or the presence of evidence and are explained in more detail later in this chapter.

WHICH ROUTE TO USE?

ELM is different from the other theories we have discussed. Rather than assuming that persuasion works the same in all circumstances, ELM predicts two ways that persuasion works. One is the central route, and the other is the peripheral route. Why do we use one route over another when exposed to a message? We need to be able to predict which route receivers will use in order for ELM to be a good theory. Knowing why people use a particular route to process the information also helps us explain and control the persuasive process.

Whether a person uses the central route or the peripheral route when processing a message depends on two characteristics: the levels of receiver *motivation* and *ability* to process the information in the message. If the receiver is missing either of these characteristics, the receiver will use the peripheral route to process the message. A receiver must be both motivated *and* able to engage in elaboration to take the central route. **Motivation** refers to how much the receiver wants to elaborate on the message; **ability** refers to how capable the receiver is of elaborating on the persuasive message. If either motivation or ability is missing or low, the receiver will engage in low elaboration or "peripheral processing." Thus, for central processing to occur, the receiver must have a reason to think about the content of the message (motivation) and must be capable of doing so (ability). Otherwise, peripheral processing is the result.

MOTIVATION TO PROCESS

Of course, this means we have to understand what affects the motivation and ability of receivers regarding persuasive messages. A number of factors that affect these processes have been identified. Let's start with motivation. We discuss five factors that affect motivation. This is not an exhaustive list; additional factors can affect **motivation to process** a message. One of the most important factors for motivation involves the level of **personal relevance** of the topic, sometimes referred to as the level of **personal involvement** with the topic. As you might predict, the more important the topic is to you personally, the more motivated you are to think carefully about the message and centrally process it. Conversely, the less important the issue is to you personally, the less motivated you are to think carefully about the message. When personal involvement is high, motivation to process is greater, and you are more likely to take the central route. In Chapter 8, we discussed the concept of ego-involvement as a factor in social judgment theory. The concepts of ego-involvement and personal involvement are defined somewhat differently. As we stated in Chapter 8, ego-involvement refers to a person's commitment to an issue and is related to a person's self-concept and self-esteem (Sherif, Sherif, & Nebergall, 1965). Personal involvement refers to whether an issue or topic is relevant to the receiver's interests or goals. In Chapter 6 we discussed involvement as a receiver characteristic that influenced how a person responds to a persuasive message. Our discussion of "outcome-relevant involvement" in Chapter 6 was based on the elaboration likelihood model. We will use the terms "personal involvement" and "personal relevance" interchangeably because if we perceive something as relevant, we are more involved with the topic.

To understand your audience, you need to understand how personally relevant your topic is to them. In one study, personal involvement was manipulated for college students by using the topic of coed visiting hours in residence halls (Petty & Cacioppo, 1979). To make this topic personally relevant, researchers told half of the participants that their own university was planning to implement either stricter or more lenient visitation hours. The other half of participants were in the low-relevance group and were told that a university halfway across the country was thinking about adopting either stricter or more lenient visiting hours. When an issue is affecting us directly, we are more personally involved in the issue and have greater motivation to think about it.

A second factor that affects motivation is the degree of **personal responsibility**, or, in other words, are you accountable for the message. If we think we are the only one responsible for the message outcome or consequences, we are more likely to centrally process the content than if we think others are also responsible. This factor has been examined in research by asking participants to evaluate the content or the quality of the message, with one group being told they were the only individuals asked to provide this service and the other group being told that numerous people would be providing the same evaluation (Petty, Harkins, & Williams, 1980). You probably have seen this phenomenon in editing group papers. When one person believes he or she is the only one editing a paper, that person tends to be more careful in seeking out typos and grammatical errors. However, when we believe all members of the group are doing the same editing, we tend to relax and assume others will catch errors if we fail to do so.

A third factor that affects motivation deals with the message content. When the message includes **incongruent information,** or information not consistent with what the receiver believes to be true, then the receiver has more motivation to centrally process the message and consider the content (Maheswaran & Chaiken, 1991). This is in harmony with the cognitive dissonance theory discussed in Chapter 9. Because people tend to be uncomfortable with inconsistency, they are motivated to consider the content of the message to try to resolve that inconsistency when incongruent information is present.

Finally, the fourth factor is a personality characteristic that leads some people to more routinely centrally process information, and it has been labeled **need for cognition (NFC)** (Cacioppo & Petty, 1982; Cohen, Stotland, & Wolfe, 1955). Need for cognition refers to the desire or need to think and engage in information processing. Individuals who are high in need for cognition enjoy thinking about issues even when there is no personal relevance and their thoughts have no impact on the outcome. People high in NFC tend to centrally process most messages and think more about the content. It may be that these people find thinking about a message enjoyable in and of itself. A scale developed to measure levels of NFC among participants is included in Figure 11.2. Thus, different factors of each situation include the topic, the nature of the receiver, and the circumstances surrounding the message that need to be considered when evaluating the level of receiver motivation to process the message. Understanding these factors helps us better understand the pressures for central processing and the likelihood that it will occur. Of course, motivation is only one of two central concepts that must be considered.

ABILITY TO PROCESS

Ability is the second characteristic that has to be present for central processing to occur. The receiver has to be able to comprehend the message in order to elaborate on the arguments. Similar to motivation, multiple factors affect a receiver's ability to process the message. We discuss four factors here.

How a message is structured and the words chosen determine in part whether the audience will have the ability to process the message. The message has to be comprehensible to the audience before careful processing can occur. **Message comprehension** is the first factor and goes back to the second step in the Yale approach discussed in Chapter 7; it refers to how clear the message is to the receivers. The message's organizational pattern and language choice affect message comprehension. In Chapter 5 we discussed message factors that influence persuasion, but here we are focusing on how clearly the message is presented, whether in a written, spoken, or performed format. If the message is presented in a clear fashion with language appropriate for the audience, the audience is more likely to understand the content and is more able to think about the content. If the message is unclear and/or if the language used is at an inappropriate level for the audience, they will not be able to think about the content of the message. Consider a person with a fourth-grade reading level trying to read a *New York Times* opinion page commentary on economic policy. That person is not likely to be able to grasp the content of the message clearly enough to be able to give it careful and rational thought, even if he or she is motivated to process the message.

EIGHTEEN-ITEM NEED FOR COGNITION SCALE

Item Number   *Item Wording*

1. I would prefer complex to simple problems.
2. I like to have the responsibility of handling a situation that requires a lot of thinking.
3. Thinking is not my idea of fun.*
4. I would rather do something that requires little thought than something that is sure to challenge my thinking abilities.*
5. I try to anticipate and avoid situations where there is a likely chance I will have to think in depth about something.*
6. I find satisfaction in deliberating hard and for long hours.
7. I only think as hard as I have to.*
8. I prefer to think about small, daily projects to long-term ones.*
9. I like tasks that require little thought once I've learned them.*
10. The idea of relying on thought to make my way to the top appeals to me.
11. I really enjoy a task that involves coming up with new solutions to problems.
12. Learning new ways to think doesn't excite me very much.*
13. I prefer my life to be filled with puzzles that I must solve.
14. The notion of thinking abstractly is appealing to me.
15. I would prefer a task that is intellectual, difficult, and important to one that is somewhat important but does not require much thought.
16. I feel relief rather than satisfaction after completing a task that required a lot of mental effort.*
17. It's enough for me that something gets the job done; I don't care how or why it works.*
18. I usually end up deliberating about issues even when they do not affect me personally.

*Reverse scoring is used on this item.

Note: Subjects are asked to respond to the items on scales indicating their "agreement" or "disagreement," or to rate the extent to which the statements are "characteristic" or "uncharacteristic" of them (see Cacioppo and Petty, 1982).

Adapted from Communication and Persuasion: Central and Peripheral Routes to Attitude Change by R. E. Petty and J. T. Cacioppo, 1986, Springer-Verlag.

FIGURE 11.2 Need for cognition scale.

A second factor that influences the ability to process messages is **message repetition** (Alba & Marmorstein, 1987). The more often the information is presented, the greater the chance of comprehension. This is why many public speaking texts advise you to tell the audience what you are going to tell them with a pre-summary, tell them, and then tell them what you told them with a summary. The repetition of the key points helps increase the chances of comprehension. This is also why commercials are repeated. The more often they are presented, the more likely the target audience will comprehend them. The more complex the message, the more the need for repetition. We may be able to easily comprehend a simple message hearing it only once; however, we most likely need to hear a complex message multiple times to fully comprehend it.

A third factor that influences the ability to process is **distraction**. When receivers are distracted during the message presentation, their ability to process the message is lowered. Various types of distraction have been used in research, including having white noise play in the background while participants listen to the message, having background activities such as party sounds and laughter going on next door to where participants are reading the message, telling participants to focus on the quality of the tape recording they are listening to, or having an X appear on a screen to distract them from listening closely to the message content (Buller, 1986; Petty, Wells, & Brock, 1976). Heckling has also been used to distract audience members from thinking carefully about the content of the message they are listening to. For receivers to centrally process the message, they must be able to focus on the message content. The greater the distraction, the less able receivers are to process the message.

A fourth and final factor that influences ability to process is **prior knowledge** of the topic. When receivers have greater prior knowledge of the topic, they have greater ability to process the message. This idea also makes intuitive sense. If receivers already have some knowledge and understanding of a topic, then the information in the message fits into their existing framework of knowledge. If the topic is unfamiliar to them, then it is more difficult for them to make sense of the new information. An example is when salespeople use terms like AGP, Mbps, USB connections, and gigahertz speed and thus overwhelm a person unfamiliar with computers and newer technology. If we are familiar and comfortable with these terms, we have the ability to process a message containing them.

As with motivation, the ability to process a message depends on characteristics of the receiver, the nature of the message, and the circumstances surrounding the presentation of the message. Once these multiple factors are considered, we can better explain, predict, and control whether the receiver will centrally or peripherally process the persuasive message.

The diagram in Figure 11.3 summarizes the factors that determine whether a person processes a message centrally or peripherally. The model begins with an individual receiving a message. Let's say that individual is you. First, you assess the message and determine if you are motivated to process the message. The factors discussed previously influence whether you are motivated. If you are not motivated to process, you look for a peripheral cue and process the message via the peripheral route. If you are motivated to process, you must then assess your ability to process the message. If you

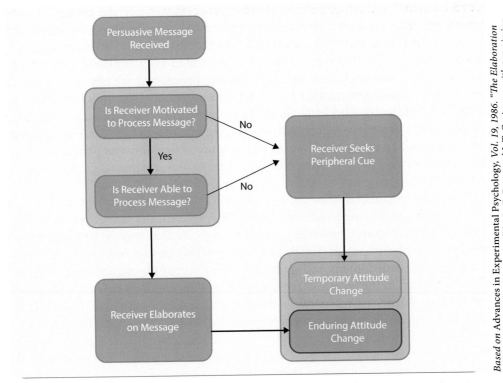

Based on Advances in Experimental Psychology, *Vol. 19, 1986. "The Elaboration Likelihood Model of Persuasion" by R. E. Petty and J. T. Cacioppo, with permission from Elsevier.*

FIGURE 11.3 The elaboration likelihood model of persuasion.

are not able to process, again you look for a peripheral cue and process the message via the peripheral route. If you are both motivated and able to process, you engage in high elaboration and centrally process the message. Notice in Figure 11.3 that both central processing and peripheral processing result in attitude change; however, one change is thought to be more stable and enduring, whereas the other change is temporary.

CENTRAL VERSUS PERIPHERAL ROUTES

Central route processing does not occur as often as peripheral route processing for most people most of the time. As we discussed earlier, we don't have the cognitive energy or even the time to think carefully about each of the thousands of messages that bombard us daily. However, many of the previously discussed persuasion theories focus on what ELM refers to as central route processing. For example, cognitive dissonance theory and the theory of reasoned action focus on rational judgments made by receivers who think about the content of persuasive messages they receive. Thus, we already have a good deal of understanding about how information may be processed in the central route. Because central route processing is rational in nature, the quality of the message is central to attitude change. When engaged in central route processing, the receiver is thinking through the message, analyzing the content, and evaluating the message. As you might expect, for the receiver to be persuaded, the message must contain high-quality information and well-constructed arguments. In Chapter 5, we discussed factors such as evidence that can be used to construct high-quality messages.

When a person engages in peripheral route processing, he or she engages in low elaboration and exerts little effort to analyze the message. To assess the quality of the information and arguments takes effort, so this information is overlooked. The receiver looks for **peripheral cues** to use as a shortcut in assessing the message. Petty and Cacioppo argue that when we use peripheral processing, we rely on peripheral cues from the environment that are sometimes described as **scripts** that allow us to function efficiently with little effort. These peripheral cues and scripts are simple decision rules we have adopted over time to make our lives easier. For example, **source credibility** and **attractiveness** of the source often serve as peripheral cues. When receivers are peripherally processing the message, peripheral cues tend to be more important than the quality of arguments. When receivers are centrally processing, these peripheral cues are less important than the quality of arguments. When we are unmotivated and/or lack the ability to centrally process messages, we seek out cues like source credibility to help us evaluate the message without careful consideration of the content. For example, if a credible person indicates that a local school levy is needed, many college students may accept the message because they are less involved in the issue and are not motivated to centrally process the message. Long-time residents are more involved in the issue, and thus are more likely to give careful consideration to the arguments about the need for the school levy and to be less influenced by the source credibility. A common script is that credible sources should be believed more than low-credibility sources. For a topic that is not personally involving, this script offers a shortcut for a decision.

Rewards or punishments associated with the message can also serve as peripheral cues. Recall our discussion of classical conditioning, operant conditioning, and social learning theory in Chapter 2. Weight loss advertisements that promise quick and easy weight loss offer a reward for purchasing the products. This reward can serve as a peripheral cue. The fine print and arguments (or lack of them) in the message content may indicate flaws, but people who are peripherally processing tend not to pay attention to those specifics. Rather, a receiver uses the promised reward as a mental shortcut to determine that purchasing the weight loss product would be wise.

The **number of arguments** in a message can also serve as a peripheral cue regardless of whether the arguments themselves are strong or weak. For those engaged in peripherally processing, simply hearing a long list of arguments may cause attitude change without knowledge about the content of the arguments. For example, Petty and Cacioppo (1984) conducted several studies and found that when audiences with low involvement were peripherally processing, six arguments and nine arguments had more of a persuasive impact than did three, regardless of argument quality. However, the number of arguments had less impact with audiences who had high involvement and were centrally processing. This effect is illustrated in Figure 11.4.

Others' reactions can also serve as a peripheral cue. When listening to a message in a group, we are typically aware of how others around us are reacting to the message. How the rest of the audience reacts to the message can serve as a cue to react either positively or negatively to the message. Axsom, Yates, and Chaiken (1987) demonstrated this principle in a study in which participants listened to an audiotaped persuasive message that included an audience's enthusiastic or unenthusiastic response.

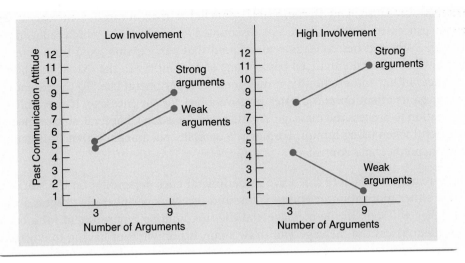

Reprinted from Advances in Experimental Psychology, Vol. 19, 1986. "The Elaboration Likelihood Model of Persuasion" by R. E. Petty and J. T. Cacioppo, with permission from Elsevier.

FIGURE 11.4 Interaction between number of arguments and involvement.

When participants had low involvement, and thus were processing peripherally, the audience responses influenced the participants' reactions to the message. When the participants had high involvement, and thus were processing centrally, the audience responses did not affect persuasion. Rather, argument quality influenced the receivers who were centrally processing the message. In this case, the response of the audience served as a peripheral cue for those engaging in little elaboration and taking the peripheral route. Di Blasio and Milani (2008) drew similar conclusions from their research. They compared participants in face-to-face decision-making groups with those in online decision making. Participants in the face-to-face groups were more likely to engage in peripheral processing than those in the online groups. These researchers argued that the physical presence of others and the social and nonverbal cues that go along with that served as distracters that led to more peripheral processing in face-to-face situations, whereas the absence of those factors allowed more central processing in the computer-mediated format.

Similarly, some studies have suggested that for those who are peripherally processing, **consensus** can serve as a peripheral cue (Hazlewood & Chaiken, 1990; Kang, 1998). In these cases, simply having poll data or study results that claim many others support the position may be sufficient to generate a positive response in those who are peripherally processing the message. This is one reason why political campaigns promote polls that show their candidate or issue is ahead in public preferences and why advertisers try to claim they have the most popular product. This is consistent with the conformity pressure discussed in Chapter 7. What others are doing can serve as a simple cue for what we should do.

After our discussion in Chapter 5 of message factors, you might think **humor** would serve as a peripheral cue, and it might in certain situations. However, people enjoy humor and are motivated to consume humorous messages. Additionally, humorous messages are often very engaging. Therefore, humorous messages sometimes enhance motivation to process rather than serving as a peripheral cue. In a study,

Nabi, Moyer-Guse, and Byrne. (2007) concluded that humorous messages were deeply processed, but they were also discounted as "just a joke," which reduced persuasion. Nabi and her colleagues also found that participants liked funny sources more, which in turn enhanced perceptions of credibility. To the extent that humor enhances liking and credibility, it may serve as a peripheral cue. To the extent that humor gains attention and creates positive affect for the message, it may enhance motivation to process the message. Again, as discussed in Chapter 5, sources need to be careful when using humor. Humor is a complex phenomenon that is difficult to explain, predict, and control.

Thus, a variety of factors can serve as peripheral cues depending on the situation. When either motivation or ability is low and receivers peripherally process a message, they will look in the message and the surrounding environment for a cue to help them assess the message and draw a conclusion without having to engage in much elaboration. However, when both motivation and ability are high, receivers engage in central processing and focus on the content of the message and ignore peripheral cues. Therefore, there are two distinct ways people process messages—peripherally or centrally—and the persuasive process differs significantly between these two routes.

ATTITUDE CHANGE IN CENTRAL AND PERIPHERAL ROUTES

Different processes are involved in attitude change with each processing route, but both can result in attitude change. Not all attitude change is equal, however. Attitudes formed through peripheral processing are more temporary, less stable, and are more susceptible to change or counter-persuasion. On the other hand, attitudes formed through central processing tend to last longer, be more stable, and be more resistant to change or counter-persuasion. In addition, attitudes formed via the central processing route tend to be better predictors of behavior than those formed through peripheral processing.

A receiver engaged in central processing is analyzing the message and carefully considering information contained in that message. Flaws in the reasoning, incorrect information, or illogical conclusions will all be noticed. Therefore, the quality of the message content is critical when an audience engages in high elaboration. In Chapter 5 we discussed factors such as evidence, logic, language, and message structure as important in creating persuasive messages. Considering these factors along with accurate and relevant information is necessary when creating messages that will be effective for an audience engaged in high elaboration.

A receiver engaged in peripheral processing is looking for a shortcut, a way to quickly process the message with the least amount of effort. Once a shortcut is found, the receiver either accepts or rejects the message and moves on. Any flaws in reasoning, incorrect information, or illogical conclusions are not likely to be noticed. Source factors and message factors that make the message look good are important in creating a message that will be effective for an audience engaged in low elaboration.

Thus, persuasion occurs differently in the two routes. Persuasion involving peripheral processing may be easier and a more common occurrence, but it is a more temporary form of attitude change. When long-term attitude change and resistance to counter-persuasion are needed, central route processing is more desirable. It may be more difficult to entice an audience to centrally process a message; however, the stronger and more stable attitude change that results often makes it worthwhile. Sometimes we seek long-term attitude change, such as in a political campaign or a social movement. On the other hand, sometimes short-term attitude change is sufficient. For example, if you are promoting a new frozen pizza by giving away free samples and receive a commission for each pizza sold, you probably are less concerned about long-term attitude change than you are with whether the consumer will buy a pizza today.

MEASUREMENT OF ELABORATION

A key issue with the development of any theory is being able to test the theory. Recall from Chapter 7 that to test a theory, a method must be designed, and the variables being studied have to be measured. Elaboration is a key issue in ELM, so to test the ELM, elaboration must be measured. If elaboration cannot be measured in a valid and reliable way, we can't test the theory. Multiple methods have been used to measure elaboration. One method is to ask research participants to **self-report** how much cognitive effort they put into evaluating a message (Petty, Harkins, Williams, & Latane, 1977). This is a simple approach, but we are not always conscious of how much thinking we put into messages. It is quite possible for self-reports to be in error; thus, this method has been used in few studies.

Argument recall has been used by some researchers as a measure of elaboration (Tyler, Hertal, McCallum, & Ellis, 1979). This has been more frequently employed as a measure of message comprehension and memory than elaboration. Recall is not an ideal measure of the elaboration engaged in by the receiver because it does not require participants to indicate personal thoughts. Just being able to re-create parts of the message does not necessarily mean that elaboration or personal thought occurred in response to the content of the message.

The most frequently used measure of elaboration is referred to as **thought listing** (Cacioppo & Petty, 1981; Cacioppo, Harkins, & Petty, 1981). With this method, research participants are asked to list what they were thinking about during the presentation of the persuasive message. By counting the different thoughts and evaluating the issue relevance of those thoughts, researchers can assess how much elaboration of the ideas occurred in the message. Receivers who generate the most issue-relevant thoughts are considered to have elaborated more and used the central route to process the message. Receivers who generate few issue-relevant thoughts are considered to have elaborated less and used the peripheral route to process the message.

TESTING ELM

ELM is one of the most widely tested and used persuasion theories today. And, as is often the case, examining ELM research provides direction on how to use ELM in everyday persuasion situations. First, we examine some of the studies Petty and

Cacioppo conducted to test the theory, and then draw on the methods used in these studies to discuss how to apply ELM to various persuasion situations.

In an early study, Petty and Cacioppo (1979) used personal relevance to test central and peripheral processing. They recruited college students and created persuasive messages that used the topic of requiring senior comprehensive exams. (A comprehensive exam is an exam given at the end of one's program that covers all main content areas of that program and must be passed in order to graduate.) This was expected to be a counter-attitudinal message for most students because it was expected that most would not embrace the idea of another hurdle to face before graduation. Petty and Cacioppo wanted some students to centrally process the message and some to peripherally process the message. To control this, they manipulated personal relevance. Recall that personal relevance influences motivation to process. One group of students was told that their own university was advocating adoption of the comprehensive exam policy, effective immediately. Presumably, these students would see the issue as personally relevant and be motivated to centrally process the message. Message language was relatively simple so that everyone would have the ability to process. Therefore, students exposed to this version of the message were expected to engage in high elaboration and centrally process the message. Another group of students heard the same message but were told that it was a policy being considered at a university across the country. Personal relevance would be low for this group, so motivation to process would be low, leading this group to engage in low elaboration and peripheral processing. Half of the students in the high-relevance condition received high-quality arguments; the other half received low-quality arguments. Half of the participants in the low-relevance condition also received high-quality arguments; the other half received low-quality arguments. You may be wondering exactly what constitutes a *high-quality argument* as opposed to a *low-quality argument*.

The messages contained arguments that had been extensively pretested to ensure they were of high or low quality but were credible to the respondents. In a pretest using different participants, high-quality arguments generated 65 percent or more positive thoughts (in a thought listing process) about the topic and 35 percent or less negative thoughts about the topic. Low-quality arguments generated 35 percent or less positive thoughts and 65 percent or more negative thoughts among participants. In both cases, the messages were tested to ensure they were credible with college students and not considered totally unbelievable. Figure 11.5 includes examples of the high-quality and low-quality arguments used in this study and several others conducted by Petty and Cacioppo.

Students were told that the messages were editorials, and they were asked to assist the Journalism Department in evaluating the quality of each editorial. After hearing the 4-minute audiotaped message containing either strong or weak arguments about the topic, participants were asked to respond to questions about their attitude on the topic, to list their thoughts, and to report how much thought they put into evaluating the message, along with other measures.

Results supported the predictions made by the elaboration likelihood model. Those in the high-relevance condition (with the message relating to their own university)

EXAMPLE STRONG ARGUMENTS

S1. The National Scholarship Achievement Board recently revealed the results of a five-year study conducted on the effectiveness of comprehensive exams at Duke University. The results of the study showed that since the comprehensive exam has been introduced at Duke, the grade point average of undergraduates has increased by 31 percent. At comparable schools without the exams, grades increased by only 8 percent over the same period. The prospect of a comprehensive exam clearly seems to be effective in challenging students to work harder and faculty to teach more effectively. It is likely that the benefits observed at Duke University could also be observed at other universities that adopt the exam policy.

S2. Graduate schools and law and medical schools are beginning to show clear and significant preferences for students who received their undergraduate degrees from institutions with comprehensive exams. As the Dean of the Harvard Business School said: "Although Harvard has not and will not discriminate on the basis of race or sex, we do show a strong preference for applicants who have demonstrated their expertise in an area of study by passing a comprehensive exam at the undergraduate level." Admissions officers of law, medical, and graduate schools have also endorsed the comprehensive exam policy and indicated that students at schools without the exams would be at a significant disadvantage in the very near future. Thus, the institution of comprehensive exams will be an aid to those who seek admission to graduate and professional schools after graduation.

S3. A member of the Board of Curators has stated publicly that alumni nationwide have refused to increase their contributions to the University because of what they feel are lax educational standards. In fact, the prestigious National Accrediting Board of Higher Education (NAB) has recently rejected the University's application for membership citing lack of a comprehensive exam as a major reason. Accreditation by the NAB enhances a university's reputation to graduate schools, employers, and demonstrates to alumni that the school is worth supporting. A recent survey of influential alumni in corporations and the state legislature has revealed that contributions would improve significantly if the exams were instituted. With increased alumni support, continued increases in tuition might be avoided.

S4. A study conducted by the Educational Testing Service of Princeton, New Jersey, revealed that most of the Ivy League schools and several of the Big 10 universities have senior comprehensive exams to maintain their academic excellence. Professors at those schools who were interviewed recently said that senior comprehensive exams assured that only high-quality and knowledgeable students would be associated with the university. This, of course, increases the prestige of current students, alumni of the school, and the university as a whole. The exams should be instituted to increase the academic reputation of the university. A national educator's publication recently predicted that within the next ten years, the top universities would have the exam policy, and the weaker ones would not.

S5. An interesting and important feature of the comprehensive exam requirement is that it has led to a significant improvement in the quality of undergraduate teaching in the schools where it has been tried. Data from the Educational Testing Service confirm that teachers and courses at the schools with comprehensive exams were rated more positively by students after the exams than before. The improvement in teaching effectiveness appears to be due to departments placing more emphasis on high-quality and stimulating teaching because departments look bad when their majors do poorly on the exam. For example, at the University of Florida, student ratings of courses increased significantly after comprehensive exams were instituted.

EXAMPLE WEAK ARGUMENTS

W1. The National Scholarship Achievement Board recently revealed the results of a study they conducted on the effectiveness of comprehensive exams at Duke University. One major finding was that student anxiety had increased by 31 percent. At comparable schools without the exam, anxiety increased by only 8 percent. The Board reasoned that anxiety over the exams, or fear of failure, would motivate students to study more in their courses while they were taking them. It is likely that this increase in anxiety observed at Duke University would also be observed and be of benefit at other universities that adopt the exam policy.

W2. Graduate students have always had to take a comprehensive exam in their major area before receiving their degrees, and it is only fair that undergraduates should have to take them also. As the Dean of the Harvard Business school said, "If a comprehensive exam is considered necessary to demonstrate competence for a masters or doctoral degree, by what logic is it excluded as a requirement for the bachelors degree? What administrators don't realize is that this is discrimination just like discrimination against Blacks or Jews. There would be a lot of trouble if universities required only whites to take comprehensive exams but not Blacks. Yet universities all over the country are getting away with the same thing by requiring graduate students but not undergraduates to take the exams." Thus, the institution of comprehensive exams could be as useful for undergraduates as they have been for graduate students.

W3. A member of the Board of Curators has stated publicly that his brother had to take a comprehensive exam while in college and now he is manager of a large restaurant. He indicated that he realized the value of the exams since their father was a migrant worker who didn't even finish high school. He also indicated that the university has received several letters from parents in support of the exam. In fact, four of the six parents who wrote in thought that the exams were an excellent idea. Also, the prestigious National Accrediting Board of Higher Education seeks input from parents as well as students, faculty, and administrators when evaluating a university. Since most parents contribute financially to their child's education and also favor the exams, the university should institute them. This would show that the university is willing to listen to and follow the parents' wishes over those of students and faculty who may simply fear the work involved in comprehensive exams.

W4. A study conducted by the Educational Testing Service of Princeton, New Jersey revealed that many universities are considering adopting comprehensive exams. Thus, any university that adopted the exams could be at the forefront of a national trend. Some professors at schools with the exams who were interviewed felt that high school students would be impressed by a university that kept pace with current trends. In fact, whether or not a school has a comprehensive exam might be a determining factor in their choice of a university. Therefore, the enrollments of universities with the exams should increase as the information about the exams spreads among high school students.

W5. An interesting and important feature of the comprehensive exam requirement is that if the exams were instituted nationwide, students across the country could use the exams to compare their achievements with those of students at other schools. Data from the Educational Testing Service confirm that students are eager to compare their grades in a particular course with those of other students. Just imagine how exciting it would be for students in the Midwest to be able to compare their scores with those of students at the University of Florida, for example. This possibility for comparison would provide an incentive for students to study and achieve as high a score as possible so they would not be embarrassed when comparing scores with their friends.

FIGURE 11.5 Examples of strong and weak arguments.

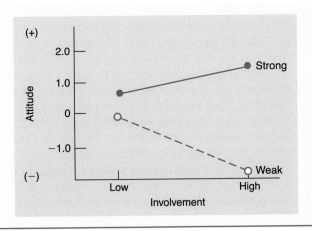

Reprinted from Advances in Experimental Psychology, Vol. 19, 1986. "The Elaboration Likelihood Model of Persuasion" by R. E. Petty and J. T. Cacioppo, with permission from Elsevier.

FIGURE 11.6 Interaction between argument strength and involvement.

listed more issue-relevant thoughts and reported thinking more about the message, indicating they engaged in high elaboration (central route). Those in the low-relevance condition (with the message relating to a distant university) listed fewer issue-relevant thoughts and reported thinking less about the message, indicating they engaged in low elaboration (peripheral route). Thus, those in the high-involvement/personal relevance condition were more likely to centrally process the message while those in the low-involvement/personal relevance condition were more likely to peripherally process the message.

Petty and Cacioppo also used both strong and weak arguments. Also recall that ELM predicts that those engaged in central processing focus more on message quality than do those engaged in peripheral processing. The graph in Figure 11.6 displays the interaction between personal relevance and argument strength. For participants in the low-relevance condition, whether they heard a message containing strong or weak arguments had little impact on their attitude toward comprehensive exams. For participants in the high-relevance condition, however, attitude change was quite different when they heard strong arguments compared to weak arguments. When strong arguments were heard, participants had a more positive attitude; when the weak arguments were heard, participants had a more negative attitude. Thus, when centrally processing, the subjects thought more about the arguments in the message and were more influenced by the strength of the arguments.

USING ELM TO INFLUENCE ATTITUDES

The elaboration likelihood model has been used in a variety of applied contexts. It has been used to design health communication campaigns (Slater, 1999), to influence beliefs of food risks (Frewer, Howard, Hedderley, & Shepherd, 1997),

In the spring of 2009, Dr. Melissa Bekelja Wanzer, Professor in the Department of Communication at Canisius College in Buffalo, NY, taught a class on persuasion using this textbook. Working in groups,

students created persuasive messages using the theories, models, and strategies they learned in class. One group of students created a set of messages that took on a life of its own. Megan Tremblay, Elyse Krezmien, Sara LaBelle, Ja'Nay Carswell, and David Jackson created a campaign titled "Check Yo Nutz" to raise awareness of testicular cancer among college age males, who have the highest incidence of this form of cancer. In September 2009, Dr. Wanzer and her students took the campaign to Roswell Park Cancer Institute in Buffalo. Administrators at Roswell Park were impressed with the students' work and agreed to collaborate with Dr. Wanzer and her students to implement a full scale campaign to increase the practice of testicular self-exams by young men and to increase awareness. In the spring of 2010, the Check Yo Nutz campaign was launched by Dr. Wanzer and her students with the help of a health communication campaign class taught by Dr. Catherine Foster at Canisius College.

The goal of the campaign was to influence college age males (*target*) to perform testicular self-exams (*behavior*) while showering (*context*) each month (*time*). Drawing on the *Yale* Model, students knew they had to get their audience's attention, so they created novel, bold, and humorous messages with a cheeky mascot named "Sammy the Squirrel" and the tag line "Check Yo Nutz." The mascot and tag line appeared on all of the message materials. The students also knew that message *repetition* was important for increasing the target audiences' *ability* to process, so a variety of materials (flyers, posters, brochures, shower cards, save the date postcards) were created and distributed using a variety of channels (social networking sites,

videos, newspapers, website, mass media, and events). Drawing on the *theory of planned behavior*, students knew they needed to change young men's beliefs about testicular cancer and testicular self-exams (TSE) in order to motivate them to intend to perform the desired behavior. Information about the symptoms, incidence and outcomes of testicular cancer (TC) were provided in the materials, as well as how to conduct a TSE. Students also understood that to influence behavior, their audience needed to engage in *central route processing* of the messages. They focused on making the messages *personally relevant* to their audience of young men to increase their motivation to process centrally. In addition, the messages were *written, repeated*, and *straightforward* in an effort to increase the target audiences' ability to process messages. The team also planned several testicular cancer awareness events: "Don't Forget Your Buddies" where Nutty Buddy ice cream cones and TC information were handed out; "Dodge These Balls, Not Yours," a dodge-ball tournament for students, faculty and staff; and "The Check Now Luau," a faculty, staff, and student dance, with Sammy the Squirrel making appearances at each event.

Not only did Dr. Wanzer and her students design and implement this campaign, they also conducted research to evaluate the effectiveness of the campaign messages and strategies. Prior to the campaign they recruited a group of 272 college males at Canisius College and had them complete a pre-test survey assessing their knowledge and awareness of TC, their intention to perform TSE and seek information, and the frequency of performing these behaviors. Two weeks after the campaign events concluded, the same college males were asked to complete a post-test survey that assessed the same variables. Concurrently a control group of 52 males at another New York state school completed the same survey and these results were compared with the experimental site.

Overall, Dr. Wanzer and her colleagues found that

> **Behavioral Intention to perform TSE measure**
> I will perform a self-examination for testicular cancer in the next month.
>
> **TSE Behavior measure**
> I perform a self-exam for testicular cancer every month.
>
> **Knowledge Questions**
> I have been exposed to information regarding testicular cancer.
> I believe that I am not at risk for testicular cancer.
> I know all of the warning signs and symptoms of testicular cancer.
> I know how to perform a self-exam for testicular cancer.
> I know where to go to find accurate information about testicular cancer.
>
> *A 5-point Likert Scale was used.*

the campaign was effective at increasing awareness of TC and increasing TSE among male students at Canisius College. There were significant increases in awareness, behavioral intention to perform TSE, and actual performance of TSE and information seeking behaviors when comparing males' responses to survey questions before and after the campaign. Also, participants at the experimental school showed statistically significant advantages over participants at the control school in all four measures of cancer awareness (i.e., exposure to TC information, knowledge of signs and symptoms, where to find TC information, and how to perform a TSE), and these effect sizes were large.

Males exposed to online campaign messages through the campaign website, Twitter, and Facebook were more likely to intend to discuss TC with a physician and perform a TSE in the next month (i.e., *behavioral intent*) than males who were not exposed to these same messages. Males who received a shower card reported greater awareness of TC and increased performance of TC behaviors (i.e., self-exams, search for TC information, etc.) than males who did not receive a shower card. One interesting outcome was that males who only read a brochure only reported greater awareness of TC, whereas males who attended one of the campaign events reported greater awareness and greater behavioral intent and actual behavior with regard to TSE.

http://www.checkyonutz.org/

FIGURE 11.7   Integrating theory, research and practice at Canisius College.

for eating disorder education (Keating, 2001), and for AIDS education (Dinoff & Kowalski, 1999). ELM has been applied to political advertising (Meirick, 2002) and social issues such as nuclear power (Katsuya, 2002) and attitudes toward rape (Heppner et al., 1995). It has frequently been applied in advertising and marketing (McCullough & Dodge, 2002; Petty & Cacioppo, 1983) and in the legal field examining jury decision-making processes (Frumkin, 2001). ELM has been used to understand how job candidates are evaluated (Forret & Turban, 1996; Larsen & Phillips, 2002) and to increase donations of blood (Hall, 1996) and organss (Skumanich & Kintsfather, 1996). It has also been used to investigate the impact of advertising on the World Wide Web (Cho, 1999; Duthler, 2001). In short, this is a versatile theory that has been broadly applied.

So, how does one go about applying this theory? If we go back to Petty and Cacioppo's (1979) study, they manipulated personal relevance in order to enhance motivation to process. If we consider the factors that influence *motivation* and *ability* to process, many of these can be manipulated by the source. The principles of ELM tell us we need to design into our message elements that will make the message relevant or in some way enhance the receiver's motivation to process the message. We also need to consider our audience's ability to process the message. Understanding our audience's existing knowledge and level of education are important to creating a message that is easy to comprehend. Additionally, channel characteristics should be considered and used to make the message easy to process. Of course you may conclude from your audience analysis that they are unlikely to engage in high elaboration.

If you successfully enhance motivation and ability to process, you must also have a really good message in terms of content that will hold up to audience scrutiny. If you expect audience elaboration to be low, you need be sure peripheral cues exist that your audience can use to quickly draw the conclusion you want. A practical approach is to design the message (or a series of messages) that contain peripheral cues for those engaged in peripheral processing AND that contain strong arguments that will be positively evaluated by those engaged in central processing. If you examine communication campaigns that contain several variations of the message, some versions are longer and contain more information (designed for central processing), and some are shorter with little content (designed for peripheral processing).

The principles of ELM can easily be combined with the principles from other theories and source and message concepts that were discussed in earlier chapters. Creators of communication campaigns rarely draw on a single theory. An example of a student-created campaign that used ELM as well as TRA, the Yale approach, and message factors such as humor is described in Figure 11.7. The students enrolled in Dr. Melissa Bekelja Wanzer's persuasion class took the concepts learned in the text to create a campaign targeted at young men to increase awareness of testicular cancer and to increase the practice of testicular self-exams. This campaign is a great example of applying theory and research to a real-life persuasive campaign (Wanzer et al., 2014).

STRENGTHS AND LIMITATIONS

Numerous strengths are associated with the elaboration likelihood model. It has been researched in a variety of settings and has been able to predict and control persuasion in real-world arenas such as advertising, marketing, politics, and health. The theory represents a step toward a covering theory that builds on prior work and includes competing theories in a larger, more systematic approach. By describing multiple routes to persuasion, preceding theories can be incorporated to explain the different paths available to process and respond to persuasive messages. ELM explains why factors such as evidence and credibility are sometimes effective and sometimes not. The theory also allows us to predict when receivers will respond to strong arguments and when they will ignore strong arguments and respond to peripheral cues. Additionally, ELM specifies factors such as personal relevance, repetition, and number of arguments that sources can use to control what route receivers use to process the persuasive message. Many persuasion theories are limited to a few situations, but ELM, with its multiple methods for processing information, is useful in a much broader range of settings.

Although the theory has advanced our knowledge about persuasion, there are some troubling aspects to the model and related research, and some questions have been left unanswered. In addition, not all research has supported the ELM predictions. A central criticism of ELM was advanced by a meta-analysis conducted by Johnson and Eagly (1989). The meta-analysis involved looking at the results of multiple ELM studies and combining them for data analysis on a broader scale. This meta-analysis found that research conducted by Petty and Cacioppo and students who studied under them were far more likely to support the ELM model than research conducted by others not associated with Petty and Cacioppo. The ability to replicate findings or support a theory with research by other scholars is an important scientific principle for all research.

The definition of argument quality—a central concept of ELM theory—was part of the difficulty other researchers had with ELM. Prior to the publication of their second book in 1986, Petty and Cacioppo had not clearly explained how they operationalized argument quality. As explained earlier, the authors defined high-quality arguments as those that generated 65 percent or more positive thoughts in a thought listing process and 35 percent or fewer negative thoughts. Conversely, low-quality arguments were those that generated 65 percent or more negative thoughts and 35 percent or less positive thoughts. So what is a high-quality argument? An argument that elicits positive thoughts. How do you elicit positive thoughts? Write a strong argument. This definition of argument quality has received much criticism, especially from the communication discipline.

Psychology scholars like Petty and Cacioppo care little about message construction and message variables. Communication scholars, however, have a long history of seeking and recommending guidelines for building good arguments. The communication standards for argument quality did not always yield the same results as Petty and Cacioppo's approach. Once other scholars understood Petty and Cacioppo's approach to argument quality, and often borrowed messages tested by them (e.g., the comprehensive exam messages discussed previously), the results became more consistent. The inability to offer guidance to prospective persuaders about how to create high- and low-argument quality messages is a weakness of the theory.

Another limitation of ELM involves individuals with a high need for cognition (NFC). These individuals do not fall into the predicted patterns of central and peripheral processing advanced by the elaboration likelihood model. Because we don't know without testing which individuals are high in NFC, we don't know when individuals will fail to follow the predicted patterns.

Other scholars (Stiff, 1994) have questioned the single-channel premise that receivers process a message either centrally or peripherally. Is it possible to do both, a parallel-processing approach? Is it always a choice of central or peripheral processing, or can we choose to do some of both with a single message? This issue is raised in response to cues that have been found to function both in central processing and peripheral processing. Source credibility is a good example. According to ELM, source credibility is a peripheral processing cue and has the most impact on receivers who are peripherally processing. Yet, in some situations, source credibility may be a legitimate part of argument quality. Political advertising is an example. Credibility is often considered an important characteristic for a politician. Although credibility has often been observed functioning as a peripheral cue, a receiver thinking carefully about the message may look at the high credibility of the politician as evidence or a reason to support the candidate. In this case, the credibility serves as part of the strength of the arguments being made. Petty and Cacioppo and other scholars debate whether ELM can explain single and parallel processing, and this issue remains an open question about the theory. If the model can explain all responses to a message, it becomes difficult to disprove the theory.

Much research has been conducted using the ELM theoretical framework, and numerous factors have been found that serve as peripheral cues and function during central processing. As more research is conducted, more knowledge is found about additional factors. Thus, we still cannot claim to know all the variables involved, and ongoing research continues to add to our knowledge and refine the model.

Finally, as Petty and Cacioppo (1986) themselves note, the theory does not answer questions about why the parts of the model operate as they do. We have already noted the lack of knowledge about what constitutes high- or low-quality arguments. In addition, we do not know why some variables are peripheral cues or why others affect how we process the information. The model answers many questions, but many are still unanswered. New theoretical models are likely to build on this knowledge base and provide more answers (and probably more questions) to our understanding of persuasion processes.

- Elaboration refers to thinking about the content and arguments of a message.
- ELM involves two routes of persuasion: a central route and a peripheral route.
- The central route involves high elaboration and expenditure of cognitive energy.
- The peripheral route involves low elaboration and use of peripheral cues.
- Both motivation (how much the receiver wants to think about the message) and ability (how capable the receiver is of processing the message) are required for central processing to occur.
- Factors that influence motivation include the level of personal relevance or involvement with the topic, personal responsibility, incongruent information, and receivers' need for cognition (NFC).
- Factors that influence ability include message comprehensibility, message repetition, distraction, and receiver prior knowledge.
- Peripheral processing cues include source credibility/source attractiveness, rewards or punishments, number of arguments, and audience reactions.
- Measures of elaboration include self-report, argument recall, and, most commonly, thought listing.
- Attitudes formed through peripheral processing tend to be more temporary, less stable over time, and more susceptible to change or counter-persuasion.
- Attitudes formed through central processing tend to last longer, be more stable, be more resistant to change or counter-persuasion, and be better predictors of behavior.
- Strengths of the ELM include broad research support, broad coverage of contexts and situations, a covering theory that includes and builds on prior theories, multiple paths for persuasion, and the ability to explain, predict, and control persuasion in real-world settings.
- Weaknesses of ELM include a lack of uniform support for the model through research, difficulty in unaffiliated researchers replicating the findings, difficulty in assessing what is needed for creating high- and low-quality arguments, inability to predict for high NFC individuals, questions about single versus parallel processing, a lack of knowledge about the totality of all variables that affect the process, and the inability of the theory to address why some of the patterns operate as they do.

KEY TERMS

Ability to process—how capable the receiver is to elaborate on the persuasive message.

Argument—a reason or series of reasons put forward to support a claim.

Argument recall—a process in which research subjects are asked to recall the arguments contained in a persuasive message.

Central route—the receiver engages in high elaboration and focuses on thinking about the content of the message.

Consensus—the perception that many or most people believe or behave a certain way.

Distraction—stimulus that distracts or diverts the receiver's attention away from the message.

Elaboration—the amount of thinking the receiver engages in about the content of a message. Elaboration can be thought of as a continuum ranging from not thinking at all about the content of the message to extensive thinking about the message.

Forewarning—when a receiver is told that he or she is about to be exposed to a persuasive message that challenges his or her beliefs.

Incongruent information—when information in a message is not consistent with what the receiver believes to be true.

Motivation to process—how much the receiver wants to elaborate on the message.

Need for cognition (NFC)—a personality predisposition that involves the need or desire to think about issues even when there is no personal relevance and their thoughts have no impact on the outcome.

Peripheral cues—simple decision rules and scripts people develop over time to allow for quick processing and decision making.

Peripheral route—the receiver engages in low elaboration of the message.

Personal relevance/involvement—the extent to which a topic is important or of value to a receiver.

Personal responsibility—the degree to which the receiver is responsible for the message outcome or consequences, such as making a decision.

Prior knowledge—the knowledge about a topic that the receiver has before being exposed to a message on the topic.

Thought listing—a process in which research participants are asked to list what they were thinking about during the presentation of a persuasive message.

REVIEW QUESTIONS

1. What is elaboration?
2. What are the routes available for processing persuasive messages? What is involved in each route?
3. What are the two factors needed for central processing to occur?
4. What factors influence motivation to process? What factors influence ability to process?

5. What are peripheral processing cues? What factors serve as peripheral processing cues?

6. How is message elaboration measured?

7. How do attitudes formed via peripheral processing differ from those formed via central processing?

8. How can ELM be used in generating persuasive messages?

9. What are the strengths and weaknesses of ELM?

DISCUSSION QUESTIONS

1. Think of a situation in which you engaged in a high elaboration. Why were you willing to put forth the effort to engage in high elaboration? In what kinds of situations are you least likely to engage in high elaboration?

2. What issues are you personally involved in? How does your personal involvement affect the way you listen to a message about that topic? Compare how you listen to messages about the topic you find personally involving with how you listen to a topic that you don't find personally involving.

3. When you are in the grocery store faced with several brands of a product and you have little experience or knowledge of the differences among the brands, what types of cues do you rely on to make a quick decision on which brand to buy?

4. Are persuaders who use peripheral cues that distract receivers from paying attention to the content of the message ethical? Should advertisers, politicians, and others cover up inadequate content by employing peripheral cues?

5. Review Chapter 5 on message factors. What makes a strong argument? What do you need to know about your audience to create a strong argument?

6. Review Chapter 4 on source factors. What source characteristics would you emphasize if you expect your audience to take the central route? What if they are taking the peripheral route?

7. Review the description of the Check Yo Nutz campaign in Figure 11.7. How did this campaign integrate ELM with other persuasion theories? Can you find other campaigns or persuasive messages that integrate principles from different theories?

8. What are the advantages and disadvantages of the four methods for measuring elaboration? Which method do you think is the best? Why?

REFERENCES

Alba, J. W., & Marmorstein, H. (1987). The effects of frequency knowledge on consumer decision making. *Journal of Consumer Research, 14*(1), 14–25.

Axsom, D., Yates, S., & Chaiken, S. (1987). Audience response as a heuristic cue in persuasion. *Journal of Personality and Social Psychology, 53*(1), 30–40.

Buller, D. B. (1986). Distraction during persuasive communication: A meta-analytic review. *Communication Monographs, 53,* 91–114.

Cacioppo, J. T., Harkins, S. G., & Petty, R. E. (1981). The nature of attitudes and cognitive responses and their relationships to behavior. In R. Petty, T. Ostrom, & T. Brock (Eds.), *Cognitive responses in persuasion.* Hillsdale, NJ: Erlbaum.

Cacioppo, J. T., & Petty, R. E. (1981). Social psychological procedures for cognitive response assessment: The thought listing technique. In T. Merluzzi, C. Glass, & M. Genest (Eds.), *Cognitive assessment.* New York, NY: Guilford Press.

Cacioppo, J. T., & Petty, R. E. (1982). The need for cognition. *Journal of Personality and Social Psychology, 42,* 116–131.

Cho, C. (1999). How advertising works on the WWW: Modified elaboration likelihood model. *Journal of Current Issues and Research in Advertising, 21*(1), 33–50.

Cohen, A., Stotland, E., & Wolfe, D. (1955). An experimental investigation of need for cognition. *Journal of Abnormal and Social Psychology, 51,* 291–294.

Di Blasio, P., & Milani, L. (2008). Computer-mediated communication and persuasion: Peripheral vs. central route to opinion shift. *Computers in Human Behavior, 24,* 798–815.

Dinoff, B. L., & Kowalski, R. M. (1999). Reducing AIDS risk behavior: The combined efficacy of protection motivation theory and the elaboration likelihood model. *Journal of Social and Clinical Psychology, 18,* 223–239.

Duthler, K. W. (2001). The influence of peripheral cues on the processing of persuasive messages on the World Wide Web. *Dissertation Abstracts International: Section A: Humanities & Social Sciences, 62*(6–A), 1983.

Forret, M. L., & Turban, D. B. (1996). Implications of the elaboration likelihood model for interviewer decision processes. *Journal of Business and Psychology, 10,* 415–428.

Frewer, L. J., Howard, C., Hedderley, D., & Shepherd, R. (1997). The use of the elaboration likelihood model in developing effective food risk communication. *Risk Analysis, 17,* 269–281.

Frumkin, L. A. (2001). The effect of eyewitnesses' accent, nationality, and authority on the perceived favorability of their testimony. *Dissertation Abstracts International: Section B: The Sciences & Engineering, 61*(8–B), 4474.

Hall, M. M. (1996). Elaboration likelihood model in a field setting: The effect of individual factors on blood donating. *Dissertation Abstracts International: Section B: The Sciences & Engineering, 57*(2–B), 1501.

Hazlewood, D., & Chaiken, S. (1990, August). *Personal relevance, majority influence, and the law of large numbers.* Poster presented at the 98th Annual Convention of the American Psychological Association, Boston.

Heppner, M. J., Good, G. E., Hillenbrand-Gunn, T. L., Hawkins, A. K., Hacquard, L. L., Nichols, R. K., et al. (1995). Examining sex differences in altering attitudes about rape: A test of the elaboration likelihood model. *Journal of Counseling and Development, 73,* 640–647.

Johnson, B.T., & Eagly, A. H. (1989). The effects of involvement on persuasion: A meta-analysis. *Psychological Bulletin, 106,* 290–314.

Kang, M. (1998). The influence of public opinion polls on public opinion: The role of motivation and ability in the elaboration likelihood model. *Dissertation Abstracts International: Section A: Humanities & Social Sciences, 59*(2–A).

Katsuya, T. (2002). Difference in the formation of attitude toward nuclear power. *Political Psychology, 23*(1), 191–203.

Keating, M. C. (2001). The effects of eating restraint and speaker characteristics on the processing of a weight-related message. *Dissertation Abstracts International: Section B: The Sciences & Engineering, 62*(6–B), 2958.

Larsen, D. A., & Phillips, J. I. (2002). Effect of recruiter on attraction to the firm: Implications of the elaboration likelihood model. *Journal of Business & Psychology, 16*(3), 347–364.

Maheswaran, D., Chaiken, S. (1991). Promoting systematic processing in low-motivation settings: Effects of incongruent information on processing and judgment. *Journal of Personality and Social Psychology, 61*(1), 13–25.

McCullough, T., & Dodge, H. R. (2002). Understanding the role consumer involvement plays in the effectiveness of hospital advertising. *Health Marketing Quarterly, 19*(3), 3–20.

Meirick, P. (2002). Cognitive responses to negative and comparative political advertising. *Journal of Advertising, 31*(1), 49–62.

Nabi, R. L., Moyer-Guse, E., & Byrne, S. (2007). All joking aside: A serious investigation into the persuasive effect of funny social issue messages. *Communication Monographs, 74*, 29–54.

Petty, R. E., & Cacioppo, J. T. (1979a). Effects of forewarning of persuasive intent and involvement on cognitive responses and persuasion. *Personality and Social Psychology Bulletin, 5*, 173–176.

Petty, R. E., & Cacioppo, J. T. (1979). Issue-involvement can increase or decrease persuasion by enhancing message-relevant cognitive responses. *Journal of Personality and Social Psychology, 37*, 1915–1926.

Petty, R. E., & Cacioppo, J. T. (1981). *Attitudes and persuasion: Classic and contemporary approaches.* Dubuque, IA: Brown.

Petty, R. E., & Cacioppo, J. T. (1983). Central and peripheral routes to persuasion: Application to advertising. In L. Percy, and A. Woodside (Eds.) *Advertising and consumer psychology* (pp. 3–23). Lexington, MA: D. C. Heath.

Petty, R. E., & Cacioppo, J. T. (1984). The effects of involvement on responses to argument quantity and quality: Central and peripheral routes to persuasion. *Journal of Personality and Social Psychology, 46*, 69–81.

Petty, R. E., & Cacioppo, J. T. (1986). *Communication and persuasion: Central and peripheral routes to attitude change.* New York: Springer-Verlag.

Petty, R. E., & Cacioppo, J. T. (1986b). The elaboration likelihood model of persuasion. *Advances in Experimental Social Psychology, 19*, 123–205.

Petty, R. E., Harkins, S. G., & Williams, K. D. (1980). The effects of group diffusion of cognitive effort on attitudes: An information processing view. *Journal of Personality and Social Psychology, 38*, 81–92.

Petty, R. E., Harkins, S. G., Williams, K. D., & Latane, B. (1977). The effects of group size on cognitive effort and evaluation. *Personality and Social Psychology Bulletin, 3*, 579–582.

Petty, R. E., & Wegener, D. T. (1991). Thought systems, argument quality, and persuasion. In R. S. Wyer & T. K. Srull (Eds.), *Advances in Social Cognition* (Vol. 4, pp. 143–161). New York: Routledge.

Petty, R. E., Wells, G. L., & Brock, T. C. (1976). Distraction can enhance or reduce yielding to propaganda: Thought disruption versus effort justification. *Journal of Personality and Social Psychology, 34*, 874–888.

Sherif, C. W., Sherif, M., & Nebergall, R. E. (1965). *Attitude and attitude change: The social judgment involvement approach*. Philadelphia: W. B. Saunders.

Skumanich, S. A., & Kintsfather, D. P. (1996). Promoting the organ donor card: A causal model of persuasion effects. *Social Science & Medicine, 43*(3), 401–408.

Slater, M. D. (1999). Integrating application of media effects, persuasion, and behavior change theories to communication campaigns: A stages-of-change framework. *Health Communication, 11*(4), 335–354.

Stiff, J. B. (1994). *Persuasive communication*. New York: Guilford Press.

Tyler, S. W., Hertal, P. T., McCallum, M., & Ellis, H. C. (1979). Cognitive effort and memory. *Journal of Experimental Psychology: Human Learning and Memory, 5,* 607–617.

Wanzer, M. B., Foster, C., Servoss, T., & LaBelle, S. (2014). Educating males about testicular cancer: Support for a comprehensive testicular cancer campaign. *The Journal of Health Communication,19,* 303–320.

Wegener, D. T., Petty, R. E. (1996). Effects of mood on persuasion processes: Enhancing, reducing, and biasing scrutiny of attitude-relevant information. In L. L. Martin & A. Tesser (Eds.), *Striving and feeling: Interactions among goals, affect, and self-regulation* (pp. 329–362). Mahwah, NJ: Lawrence Erlbaum.

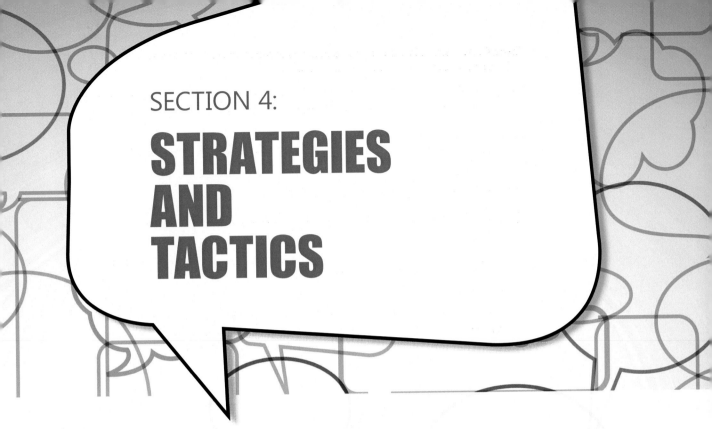

SECTION 4:

STRATEGIES AND TACTICS

U p to this point our approach to persuasion has emphasized changing attitudes and beliefs as the means to influence behavior, as well as long term rather than short term change. There is another approach to persuasion that focuses on short term behavioral change with little if any attention to changing attitudes and beliefs. This section discusses three types of tactics designed to gain short term behavioral compliance. Chapter 12 begins with a discussion of compliance and then describes three typologies of compliance-gaining tactics. Propaganda tactics and strategies are then discussed. The chapter concludes with a discussion of sequential request strategies.

CHAPTER

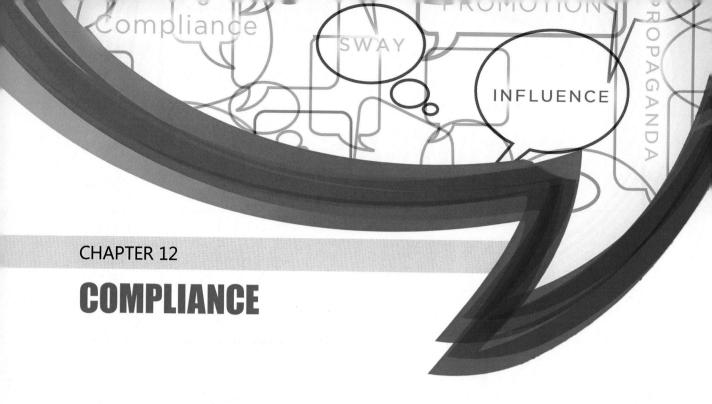

CHAPTER 12

COMPLIANCE

Julie: Nick, I have something for you.

Nick: You do! What is it?

Julie: I saw this hat yesterday and I thought it was perfect for you.

Nick: Thank you! It's great! It was really nice of you to get this for me.

Julie: Hey, Nick, I have a favor to ask of you. Would you drive me to the airport Saturday morning? I have a 6:00 a.m. flight.

Nick: *(Silence)* Yeah, I suppose I can take you.

In this dialogue is Julie using persuasion? She is clearly intending to influence Nick's behavior—specifically, to take her to the airport. However, this situation is different from most of those discussed earlier in this text. Julie is not interested in long-term attitude change, and she is not targeting a large group. Julie is using a very specific message tactic to obtain the desired behavior. In Chapter 5, we examined content choices, how a message might be structured, as well as language choices we might make when designing a message. None of these are particularly useful in analyzing Julie's strategy. In this chapter, we look at the different kinds of message **strategies** that can be used in persuasive messages. Strategies refers to the design of the message regarding the kind of argument structures or appeals that are employed as devices to persuade the audience. We examine message strategies from three perspectives. The first is compliance-gaining, which is a face-to-face interpersonal approach to influencing behavior. The second is propaganda, which is mostly used in combination with mass media to reach large audiences. The third is sequential-request strategies that involve a sequential tactic for

LEARNING OBJECTIVES

- EXPLAIN THE THREE LEVELS OF INFLUENCE.
- DESCRIBE COMPLIANCE-GAINING.
- COMPARE AND CONTRAST THE THREE COMPLIANCE-GAINING TYPOLOGIES PRESENTED.
- DESCRIBE AND PROVIDE EXAMPLES OF PROPAGANDA TACTICS.
- DESCRIBE AND PROVIDE EXAMPLES OF SEQUENTIAL REQUEST STRATEGIES.
- EXPLAIN HOW COMPLIANCE-GAINING, PROPAGANDA, AND SEQUENTIAL REQUEST STRATEGIES RELATE TO THE LEVELS OF INFLUENCE.

obtaining compliance. Julie's message strategy to get Nick to take her to the airport is classified as both a compliance-gaining strategy and as a propaganda strategy. Can you figure out which strategies she is using?

In many ways compliance is simply a different "flavor" of persuasion. Whereas persuasion is rooted in both the rhetorical and social psychological traditions, compliance has been examined in a variety of disciplines and observed in both face-to-face and one-to-many contexts. Our discussion of persuasion in previous chapters has put a good deal of emphasis on attitude and belief change as outcomes of persuasion, although behavior change has also been part of the discussion. The literature on compliance emphasizes behavior change and rarely views attitude change as an outcome of interest. Our focus in this chapter is on getting our audience to do what we want them to do; to comply with our request. Spoiler alert: these strategies are not necessarily ethical. However, the strategies and tactics discussed are commonly used and you will be better able to deal with them if you understand them. We will examine three types of strategies that are intended to gain short term behavioral compliance; compliance-gaining, propaganda, and sequential-request strategies. Before delving into these strategies and tactics, we first examine a model that is useful for organizing these strategies and for differentiating compliance-gaining from other forms of influence.

LEVELS OF INFLUENCE

Kelman (1958) developed a model that described three **levels of influence**: compliance, identification, and internalization. **Compliance** is the most basic level and involves a target being influenced to do something to gain a reward or to avoid a punishment. As long as the agent uses either a carrot or a stick as motivation, the target is willing to comply. Compliance does not involve long-term influence. There is no change in attitude, just short-term behavior change. In fact, the target will comply only to the extent that the agent keeps an eye on the target. The agent must communicate concern, control, and scrutiny to the target in order to gain and maintain compliance. The agent must demonstrate *concern* for the target complying, or in other words, let the target know he or she cares about the action. The agent must also demonstrate *control*, the ability to wield rewards or punishments. Last, the agent must be able to *scrutinize*, or watch the target to see if he or she complies (McCroskey & Richmond, 1996). If any of these three things are missing, the target is unlikely to comply. A good example is your willingness to comply with parking regulations on campus. Your university or college regularly demonstrates its *concern* by creating parking regulations and providing parking tags. You know that the university cares where you park. The university demonstrates *control* by being able to give you a ticket. If you don't pay the ticket, the punishment usually gets bigger in terms of both cost and hassle. *Scrutiny* comes in the form of parking patrol—those folks who comb the parking lots checking parking tags. Now, be honest with yourself, how likely is it that you would comply with the parking regulations if you *knew*: (a) no one cared, (b) there was no ticket or consequence, or (c) no one was patrolling the lots?

Strategies that lead to compliance are useful because you do get the behavior you're looking for; however, maintaining compliance can be a real hassle. The hassle factor often translates into high cost. Using the university parking as an example, just think of how much money the university would save if everyone just complied and it didn't have to implement all the control and scrutiny measures. Although at times short-term compliance is exactly what we want, at other times it is completely inappropriate (e.g., when we're trying to build a loyal customer base for long-term sales). The other two levels of influence are more useful in these situations.

Identification occurs when a target accepts influence from an agent because he or she wants to be associated with the agent. This is similar to conformity pressures that were discussed in Chapter 7 under *group dynamics* and the source factor of identification and similarity discussed in Chapter 4. College students often identify with peer groups such as a sorority or fraternity. They willingly comply with certain behaviors such as mode of dress and study habits in order to be identified with the group. With this level of influence, the target's willingness to comply will probably last as long as the identification lasts. Once the college students graduate and move away, the influence wanes right along with their identification with those peer groups. New groups will replace the sororities and fraternities, who students identify with and be influence by, such as employers. Identification involves attitude change, although not permanent attitude change. Identification draws heavily on the relationship between the source and the receiver. We tend to identify with people we like, respect, and want to be associated with. We are willing to go along with what they ask so that we can be associated with them. The primary advantage of identification over compliance for the source is that there is no need for surveillance as there is with the compliance level.

The last level of influence, **internalization**, involves long-term attitude change. When a receiver is influenced at the internalization level, he or she accepts the behavior as being best or most appropriate and will perform the behavior regardless of who approves or provides rewards. If you are reading this textbook because you believe it is an appropriate and useful way to learn, you have probably been influenced to read textbooks at the internalization level. If you are reading this book because you like your professor and want to please him or her, you have probably been influenced to read at the identification level. If you are reading this book because there is an exam tomorrow and you don't want to fail, you have probably been influenced to read at the compliance level.

Most of the information in this text has been devoted to helping you understand influence at the internalization and identification levels. These two levels are necessary for many of persuasive goals, particularly those that require life style changes like healthy eating and exercise. In this chapter our focus is on the compliance level of influence, which is often relevant in interpersonal situations with friends, family, neighbors, and coworkers.

COMPLIANCE-GAINING TYPOLOGIES

Compliance-gaining focuses primarily on face-to-face interactions between two persons, rather than in public forums of one to many as persuasion often does. Wheeless, Barraclough, and Stewart (1983) offer a useful definition of **compliance-gaining**: "communicative behavior in which an agent engages so as to elicit from a target some agent-selected behavior" (p. 111). Notice that different terminology is used here. Rather than referring to a persuader or source, the term **agent** is used. Similarly, the term *target* is used rather than receiver or persuadee. Compliance-gaining is the rather common act of trying to get another person to do *something*. That *something* may be getting a friend to lend you $10, your roommate to wash the dishes, or your boss to assign you a prestigious project. This definition specifically focuses compliance-gaining on influencing behavior, rather than attitude and beliefs, which was the case when we defined persuasion in Chapter 1.

The study of compliance-gaining is relatively new compared to attitude change, beginning with an article by Marwell and Schmitt in 1967. However, it was an article in 1977 by Miller, Boster, Roloff, and Siebold that began a flurry of research within the communication discipline. In trying to understand how people gained compliance, several compliance-gaining typologies were developed. Each typology consisted of numerous strategies or techniques that an agent could use to gain compliance from a target. Much effort was devoted to identifying all the various ways one can gain compliance from another. These ways are referred to as strategies or techniques (depending on the researcher). Another question that drove the research was why an agent would choose a particular strategy. This question led researchers to examine personal differences, situational differences (e.g., intimate contexts), and more recently the secondary goals of the agent. A primary **personal difference** was biological sex. One finding from this line of research was that women use more polite compliance-gaining strategies than men do (Baxter, 1984). This finding may be in part due to stereotypes about what is appropriate for each sex. Carli (2004) suggested that sex role stereotypes offer males a wider range of acceptable strategies than those available to females. More politeness may be a result of sex role expectations for women. There is also evidence that sources of persuasion employ different compliance-gaining strategies when targeting women vs. men. For example, one study found that doctors were more likely to use more strategies with women than men to get compliance with medical recommendations, and those doctors were more likely to use direct strategies (e.g., stop smoking, take medicine twice a day) with men while employing more indirect strategies (e.g., stopping smoking would be a good idea, directions for medication will be on the bottle) with women (Smith et al., 2005). **Situational characteristics** such as intimate versus nonintimate situations and dominant versus subordinate roles were also examined. Few, if any, generalizations can be made about what strategies are used in particular situations. One conclusion is that when the agent is less dominant (or less powerful) than the target, the agent will choose nonconfrontational strategies. **Secondary goals** are things the agent is trying to accomplish with the target other than gaining compliance. An example of a secondary goal involves *interaction goals* (Dillard, 1990), which is wanting to make a good impression or at least not be thought of poorly. If you are concerned about the impression you're making, this will affect which compliance-gaining strategies you choose to use. As the number of secondary goals increases, an agent's ability to formulate a socially competent message becomes more difficult (Schrader & Dillard, 1998). Trying to understand why people go about gaining compliance the way they do is complex. Despite the vast amount of research on personal and situational factors, few generalizations can be drawn from the research. One aspect of the compliance-gaining literature that is clear involves how people go about gaining compliance. Several typologies (lists) of compliance-gaining strategies have been identified. They provide us with a variety of ways to construct messages. All of the strategies are effective at gaining compliance, but some may also result in identification or internalization. When constructing a message, it is important to be mindful of your persuasive goals. Attitude change and behavior change are two different, although often related, goals. Many of the strategies listed in the typologies are very useful when attempting to influence behavior. If your primary goal is to influence attitude, some of the compliance-gaining strategies will be useful; however, the theories discussed in earlier chapters of this book will be of greater use.

MARWELL AND SCHMITT

The typology developed by Marwell and Schmitt (1967) was the first to be developed. It is widely used in compliance-gaining research, and is employed in studies looking at a variety of applied contexts ranging from business contexts such as sales (Parrish-Sprowl, Carveth, & Senk, 1994) and improving tipping in restaurants (Seiter & Weger, 2010) to health contexts such as encouraging use of multivitamins (Ferrara et al., 2011). This is the only typology presented here that was developed using a deductive approach. By **deductive approach**, we mean that Marwell and Schmitt derived the strategies from theory and previous research. Compare this method to the **inductive approach**, which derives strategies from individual observations. In a sense, Marwell and Schmitt started at an abstract level and worked their way down to specific strategies. Researchers using the inductive approach started out at a very concrete level with hundreds of observations (individual responses to a question like "How do you get your neighbor to turn down his music?") and worked their way up to the strategies. Thus, Marwell and Schmitt's compliance-gaining typology was developed by using a method different from that used in developing the other typologies we discuss.

Marwell and Schmitt identified 16 strategies, shown in Table 12.1. As you read through the strategies, you will see several that are consistent with French and Raven's

TABLE 12.1 *MARWELL AND SCHMITT'S (1967) COMPLIANCE-GAINING TECHNIQUES*

1. Promise	(If you comply, I will reward you) "You offer to increase Dick's allowance if he increases his studying."
2. Threat	(If you do not comply, I will punish you) "You threaten to forbid Dick the use of the car if he does not increase his studying."
3. Expertise (Positive)	(If you comply, you will be rewarded because of "the nature of things") "You point out to Dick that if he gets good grades he will be able to get into a good college and get a good job."
4. Expertise (Negative)	(If you do not comply, you will be punished because of "the nature of things") "You point out to Dick that if he does not get good grades he will not be able to get into a good college or get a good job."
5. Liking	(Actor is friendly and helpful to get target in "good frame of mind" so that he will comply with request) "You try to be as friendly and pleasant as possible to get Dick in the 'right frame of mind' before asking him to study."
6. Pre-Giving	(Actor rewards target before requesting compliance) "You raise Dick's allowance and tell him you now expect him to study."
7. Aversive Stimulation	(Actor continuously punishes target making cessation contingent on compliance) "You forbid Dick the use of the car and tell him he will not be allowed to drive until he studies more."
8. Debt	(You owe me compliance because of past favors) "You point out that you have sacrificed and saved to pay for Dick's education and that he owes it to you to get good enough grades to get into a good college."
9. Moral Appeal	(You are immoral if you do not comply) "You tell Dick that it is morally wrong for anyone not to get as good grades as he can and that he should study more."
10. Self-Feeling (Positive)	(You will feel better about yourself if you comply) "You tell Dick he will feel proud if he gets himself to study more."
11. Self-Feeling (Negative)	(You will feel worse about yourself if you do not comply) "You tell Dick he will feel ashamed of himself if he gets bad grades."
12. Altercasting (Positive)	(A person with "good" qualities would comply) "You tell Dick that since he is a mature and intelligent boy he naturally will want to study more and get good grades."
13. Altercasting (Negative)	(Only a person with "bad" qualities would not comply) "You tell Dick that only someone very childish does not study as he should."
14. Altruism	(I need your compliance very badly, so do it for me) "You tell Dick that you really want very badly for him to get into a good college and that you wish he would study more as a personal favor to you."
15. Esteem (Positive)	(People you value will think better of you if you comply) "You tell Dick that the whole family will be very proud of him if he gets good grades."
16. Esteem (Negative)	(People you value will think worse of you if you do not comply) "You tell Dick that the whole family will be very disappointed (in him) if he gets poor grades."

Note: Excerpts from *Dimensions of Compliance-Gaining Behavior* by G. Marwell and P. R. Schmitt, 1967.

power bases discussed in Chapter 4. For example, the expertise strategies are clearly related to the expertise power base. The liking strategy represents referent power, and aversive stimulation represents coercive power. Marwell and Schmitt's typology is important because it was the impetus behind a great deal of research on compliance-gaining; however, it is incomplete. One group of researchers found that 72 percent of the strategies participants said they would use to get a friend to repay a loan were not represented in Marwell and Schmitt's typology (Cody, McLaughlin, & Jordan, 1980).

SCHENCK-HAMLIN, WISEMAN, AND GEORGACARAKOS

The typology developed by Schenck-Hamlin, Wiseman, and Georgacarakos (1982) consists of the 14 strategies shown in Table 12.2. This typology was developed using an inductive approach with responses from more than 200 participants. Participants responded to situations such as the following, "Your roommate is playing his/her stereo loudly the night before you must take a mid-term examination

TABLE 12.2 *SCHENCK-HAMLIN, WISEMAN, AND GEORGACARAKOS' (1982) COMPLIANCE-GAINING STRATEGIES*

STRATEGIES BASED ON SANCTION

Ingratiation: Actor's proffered goods, sentiments, or services precede the request for compliance. They range from subtle verbal or nonverbal positive reinforcement to more blatant formulas of "apple polishing" or "brown-nosing." Manipulations in behavior include gift giving, supportive listening, love, and affection, or favor-doing.

Promise: Actor's proffered goods, sentiments, or services are promised the target in exchange for compliance. This may include a bribe or trade. A variant is compromise, in which gains and losses are perceived in relative terms, so that both actor and target give in order to receive. Sometimes compromise is called trading off, log-rolling, or finding a "middle-of-the-road" solution.

Debt: Actor recalls obligations owned him or her as a way of inducing the target to comply. Past debts may be as tangible as favors or loans, or as general as the catchall, "after all I've done for you . . ."

Esteem: Target's compliance will result in automatic increase of self-worth. Actor's appeal promises this increase in areas of target's power, success, status, moral/ethical standing, attention and affection of others, competence, ability to handle failure and uncertainty well, and/or attempts to aspire. "Everyone loves a winner" is the fundamental basis for appeal. "Just think how good you will feel if you do this."

Allurement: Target's reward arises from persons other than the actor or target. The target's compliance could result in a circumstance in which other people become satisfied, pleased, or happy. These positive attitudes will be beneficial to the target. "You'll always have their respect" is an example.

Aversive Stimulation: Actor continuously punishes target, making cessation contingent on compliance. Pouting, sulking, crying, acting angry, whining, "the silent treatment," and ridicule would all be examples of aversive stimulation.

Threat: Actor's proposed actions will have negative consequences for the target if he or she does not comply. Blackmailing or the suggestion of firing, violence, or breaking off a friendship would all be examples of threats.

Guilt: Target's failure to comply will result in automatic decreases of self-worth. Areas of inadequacy might include professional ineptness, social irresponsibility, or ethical/moral transgressions.

Warning: Target's punishment arises from persons other than the actor or target. The target's noncompliance could lead to a circumstance in which other people become embarrassed, offended, or hurt. Resulting negative attitudes from those people will have harmful consequences for the target. "You'll make the boss unhappy" and "What will the neighbors say?" are examples.

STRATEGIES BASED ON NEED

Altruism: Actor requests the target engage in behavior designed to benefit the actor rather than the target. Presentation of some personal need and asking for help is typical. Intensity of the appeal may be manipulated by making the target feel unselfish, generous, self-sacrificing, heroic, or helpful. "It would help me if you would do this" and "Do a favor for me" exemplify the direct approach of the altruistic strategy. Two variants are sympathy ("I am in big trouble, so help me") and empathy ("You would ask for help if you were me").

STRATEGIES BASED ON EXPLANATION

Direct Request: The actor simply asks the target to comply. The motivation or inducement for complying is not provided by the actor, but must be inferred by the target. The actor's message appears to offer as little influence as possible, so that the target is given the maximum latitude of choice. "If I were you, I would . . ." and "Why don't you think about . . ." are instances of direct request.

Explanation: One of several reasons are advanced for believing or doing something. A reason may include the following: (1) credibility, "I know from experience." The reason for complying is my trustworthiness, integrity, exemplary action, or expertise; (2) inference from empirical evidence, "Everything points to the logic of this step." The reason for complying is based on the following evidence.

Hinting: Actor represents the situational context in such a way that the target is led to conclude the desired action or response. Rather than directly requesting the desired response, the actor might say, "It sure is hot in here," rather than directly asking the target to turn down the heat.

STRATEGIES BASED ON CIRCUMVENTION

Deceit: Actor gains target's compliance by intentionally misrepresenting the characteristics or consequences of the desired response. "It's easy," when in fact is neither simple nor easy. "By doing this, you'll be handsomely rewarded," but the actor does not have the ability to give that reward.

in a class. You need to ask him/her to turn it down, even though your roommate has been known to get irritated at the prospect" (Schenck-Hamlin et al., 1982, p. 93). Schenck-Hamlin et al.'s goal was to identify the properties of compliance-gaining strategies and not just the types of strategies people used. They identified four major properties of compliance-gaining strategies. The *first property* is whether the agent's *intent is revealed* in the message. For all the strategies in Table 12.2 except for hinting and deceit, the agent's intent is revealed. The *second property* is whether the agent is *manipulating some reward or punishment*. For example, the promise strategy is based on a reward to be received in the future. The guilt strategy is based on punishment. The *third property* is whether the agent *controls the reward or punishment*. The ingratiation strategy is an example of the agent being in control of the reward, and for the allurement strategy a third party is in control of the reward (e.g., "Your classmates will really respect you if you do this"). The *fourth property* is whether a *rationale* for the agent's desired compliance is given. The strategies of direct request, explanation, and hinting all provide a rationale; however, the rationale is tacit (not revealed) in direct request and hinting. Schenck-Hamlin et al. used these major properties as well as additional properties to classify the 14 compliance-gaining strategies into four categories as shown in Table 12.2. The categories consist of strategies based on sanction, strategies based on need, strategies based on explanation, and strategies based on circumvention. Focusing on the properties gives us a better understanding of what exactly we are doing when we are gaining compliance and provides us with a way to more completely describe compliance-gaining behavior.

If you compare these strategies to those of Marwell and Schmitt, you will see some overlap. Both typologies have promise, debt, esteem, aversive stimulation, threat, and altruism. So even though the two typologies were developed by using different methods (inductive vs. deductive), similar strategies were identified. Schneck-Hamlin et al.'s approach provides us with an understanding of how compliance-gaining strategies are similar and different from one another and gives us a more in-depth understanding of the strategies.

KEARNEY, PLAX, RICHMOND, AND MCCROSKEY

The behavior alteration techniques (BATs) were developed through a series of studies conducted by Kearney, Plax, Richmond, and McCroskey (1984) (see Richmond & McCroskey, 1992, for a review). They used an inductive approach to develop a typology of the 22 strategies shown in Table 12.3. This typology differs from the others in that it was developed and studied within a single context: the classroom. Teachers were asked to describe how they got students to comply with their requests. These descriptions were the basis for the 22 strategies. In a series of seven studies, Kearney et al. determined that both teachers and students agreed these were strategies used by teachers. One finding of interest was that the strategies used by teachers influenced students' learning and motivation to study. In other words, how teachers went about getting students to follow directions, complete assignments, and so on influenced how positively students felt toward what they were being taught, how much they thought they were learning, and how willing they were to study.

TABLE 12.3 *BEHAVIOR-ALTERATION TECHNIQUES AND MESSAGES USED BY INSTRUCTORS*

TECHNIQUE (BATS)	SAMPLE MESSAGES (BAMS)
1. Immediate Reward from Behavior	You will enjoy it. It will make you happy. Because it is fun. You will find it rewarding/interesting. It is a good experience.
2. Deferred Reward from Behavior	It will help you later on in life. It will prepare you for getting a job (or going to graduate school). It will prepare you for achievement tests (or the final exam). It will help you with upcoming assignments.
3. Reward from Teacher	I will give you a reward if you do. I will make it beneficial to you. I will give you a good grade (or extra credit) if you do. I will make you my special assistant.
4. Reward from Others	Others will respect you if you do. Others will be proud of you. Your friends will like you. Your parents will be pleased.
5. Self-Esteem	You will feel good about yourself if you do. You are the best person to do it. You are good at it. You always do such a good job. Because you're capable!
6. Punishment from Behavior	You will lose if you don't. You will be unhappy. You will be hurt if you don't. It's your loss. You'll feel bad.
7. Punishment from Teacher	I will punish you if you don't. I will make it miserable for you. I'll give you an "F." If you don't do it now, it will be homework tonight.
8. Punishment from Others	No one will like you. Your friends will make fun of you. Your parents will punish you if you don't. Your classmates will reject you.

9. Guilt		If you don't, others will be hurt. You'll make others unhappy. Your parents will feel bad. Others will be punished if you don't.
10. Teacher-Student Relationship: Positive		I will like you better if you do. I will respect you. I will think more highly of you. I will appreciate you more if you do. I will be proud of you.
11. Teacher-Student Relationship: Negative		I will dislike you if you don't. I will lose respect for you. I will think less of you if you don't. I won't be proud of you. I'll be disappointed in you.
12. Legitimate Higher Authority		Do it, I'm just telling you what I was told. It is a rule; I have to do it and so do you. It's a school rule/policy.
13. Legitimate Teacher Authority		Because I told you to. You don't have a choice. You're here to work! I'm the teacher; you're the student. I'm in charge, not you. Don't ask, just do it.
14. Personal (Student) Responsibility		It's your obligation. It's your turn. Everyone has to do his/her share. It's your job. Everyone has to pull his/her own weight.
15. Responsibility to Peers		Your group needs it done. The class depends on you. All your friends are counting on you. Don't let your group down. You'll ruin it for the rest of the class.
16. Normative Rules		The majority rules. All of your friends are doing it. Everyone else has to do it. The rest of the class is doing it. It's part of growing up.
17. Debt		You owe me one. Pay your debt. You promised to do it. I did it the last time. You said you'd try this time.
18. Altruism		If you do this, it will help others. Others will benefit if you do. It will make others happy. I'm not asking you to do it for yourself; do it for the good of the class.
19. Peer Modeling		Your friends do it. Classmates you respect do it. The friends you admire do it. Other students you like do it. All your friends are doing it.
20. Teacher Modeling		This is the way I always do it. When I was your age, I did it. I had to do this when I was in school. Teachers you respect do it.
21. Expert Teacher		From my experience, it is a good idea. From what I have learned, it is what you should do. This has always worked for me. Trust me, I know what I'm doing. I had to do this before I became a teacher.
22. Teacher Feedback		Because I need to know how well you understand this. To see how well I've taught you. To see how well you can do it. It will help me know your problem areas.

Note: From Power in the classroom by Virginia Richmond and James McCroskey. Copyright © 1992 by Lawrence Erlbaum Associates, Inc. Reprinted by Permission.

Strategies based on reward, referent, and expert power were found to be most positively associated with student learning. These are referred to as **prosocial strategies**. Strategies based on coercive and legitimate power are referred to as **antisocial strategies**, and as you might expect, were most negatively associated with student learning. Very similar results were found in organizational settings. Supervisor use of prosocial strategies was associated with greater satisfaction by subordinates (Richmond, McCroskey, & Davis, 1986). You might also be curious about how students go about getting compliance from their instructors. Golish (1999) asked students how they went about getting teachers to comply and identified 19 compliance-gaining strategies; some of them are unique, while others overlap with strategies already discussed.

The 22 **behavior alteration techniques** (BATs) and corresponding **behavior alteration messages** (BAMs) are shown in Table 12.3. BATs refer to a strategy type and BAMs provide examples of what a person might say when using that strategy. When examining the BATs, you'll see a strong relationship to French and Raven's (1959) power bases (discussed in Chapter 4). BATs 1 through 5 are clearly based in reward power and are prosocial in nature. Using these strategies is effective in gaining compliance and has little impact on the relationship between the agent and the target. In other words, if you use reward-based compliance-gaining strategies to get your roommate to wash the dishes, your roommate is likely to comply, and there won't be any hard feelings as a result of your request. The next four BATs (6 through 9) are based in coercive power and are more antisocial. These BATs are also likely to be effective in gaining compliance; however, the relationship is more likely to be hurt in some way. If you use a BAT based in coercive power to get your roommate to wash dishes, there may be hard feelings afterward. Two BATs (12 and 13) are based in legitimate power. Similar to coercive power-based BATs, these two BATs are effective at gaining compliance but can hurt the relationship. Referent power is reflected in peer and teacher modeling (BATs 19 and 20). These are prosocial and most effective if used in an indirect manner. The last two BATs (21 and 22) are based in expert power and, like the referent power-based BATs, are prosocial and most effective if used indirectly.

When deciding how to gain compliance from someone, you have many options. Although all the strategies (in all three typologies) are effective in gaining compliance in some circumstances, they are not equal. As was discussed with the BATs, different techniques affect relationships differently. If a person is really important to you, selecting prosocial strategies is probably the best way to go so as not to harm the relationship. Another issue that is rarely addressed by the research on compliance-gaining is the ethical implications of different strategies. Deceit, as listed in Schneck-Hamlin et al.'s typology, is certainly a technique for gaining compliance, but how ethical is it to use it? Similar questions arise for the threat and guilt techniques. Is it ethical to use these techniques? We strongly encourage you to think about the ethical implications of using particular compliance-gaining strategies. The ethical implications of persuasion are discussed in greater depth in Chapter 13.

Understanding the various strategies used to gain compliance makes you better able to respond when others use these strategies on you. When you recognize that a person is using guilt to get you to comply with her or his request, you probably won't feel guilty in response to the message. You are then in a better position to make a rational decision on whether to comply or not. Another benefit of understanding these compliance-gaining strategies is that it increases your options. You now have a broader repertoire of strategies to draw on when seeking compliance from someone.

The compliance-gaining typologies reviewed here provide you with a variety of ways to construct a message in order to influence someone. Compliance-gaining is grounded in interpersonal communication and focuses on influencing behavior in primarily one-on-one interactions. The opposite of interpersonal influence is mass influence. In addition to studying the message techniques used in interpersonal settings, scholars have examined message techniques used with mass audiences. Propaganda consists of a variety of message strategies that have been frequently used to influence large audiences such as the general public.

PROPAGANDA

Propaganda is one of those terms whose definition we often think we know, but we often have a difficult time defining it. It is one of those things that people often believe they will "know when they see it." Propaganda is a type of persuasion and one of the many terms that fall under the broader umbrella of influence. Propaganda carries a negative connotation for many people. We often say that what *we* are engaged in is persuasion, but what *other people* whom we disagree with are engaged in is propaganda. Indeed, in just about every political campaign, politicians hurl accusations of propaganda attempts at each other. Some have argued that propaganda is simply a term for persuasion we disagree with.

Cole (1998), in *The Encyclopedia of Propaganda,* defined propaganda more neutrally as:

> any systematic attempt to influence opinion on a wide scale. It is a form of communication that seeks to promote or discourage attitudes as a means of advancing or injuring an organization, an individual, or a cause. Propaganda proceeds by deliberate plan for calculated effects. It usually addresses a mass audience through mass media or is targeted at special audiences and media that provide access to mass opinion (p. 606).

The use of the term *mass* means to reach large audiences as opposed to one-on-one interpersonal interaction and is consistently used to distinguish propaganda from other forms of influence.

Jowett and O'Donnell (1999) argued that persuasion involves interactions and attempts to satisfy the needs of both the sender and the receiver, whereas propaganda is designed only to meet the needs of the sender. Sproule (1994) added that propaganda attempts "to conceal both their persuasive purpose and lack of sound supporting reasons" (p. 8). Thus, drawing on these various approaches, we define **propaganda** as a type of persuasion that involves mass audiences with a purpose of achieving the goals of the persuader and that often involves emotional appeals, concealment of purpose, and lack of sound support. The focus on achieving the goals of the persuader raises a number of ethical concerns.

Search "propaganda strategies" on both Google and You Tube. You will find a variety of definitions and several examples, not all of them useful. What definitions and examples are consistent with what you have learned about persuasion and propaganda?

ETHICAL ISSUES IN PROPAGANDA

We often think of *propaganda* as being used for a bad purpose, such as Hitler's influencing people to hate certain groups and engage in the Holocaust. We all agree that the Holocaust and the rhetoric that led up to it was unethical, but what about outcomes we agree with? Based on the characteristics identified, propaganda can also be used for positive outcomes. For example, some public service campaigns targeted at eliminating distracted driving could be considered propaganda. Are these campaigns unethical? We are more likely to label campaigns we disagree with as propaganda than those we perceive as prosocial. This raises the question whether the *ends* justify the *means.* If propaganda is used for good outcomes, does that make it ethical? The Institute for Propaganda Analysis and other propaganda scholars have focused more on the ethics of the *means* than on the *ends.* Consider the methods identified in the definition of propaganda provided previously. Is the use of emotional appeals unethical? What about concealing one's purpose in persuasion and/or using unsound reasoning processes? These issues are discussed in more depth in Chapter 13, but you should be thinking about the ethics of the practices as they are presented.

PROPAGANDA TACTICS

Several tactics have been associated with propaganda. These tactics all have a common purpose of misleading people or directing receivers' attention to factors that are not central to the issue, with the overall goal of gaining compliance. The Institute for Propaganda Analysis (Lee and Lee, 1972) identified commonly used **propaganda tactics**. Although propaganda is generally described as a mass mediated event, these tactics can be used in interpersonal influence as well. We describe ten commonly used propaganda tactics, however there are others that have also been identified.

The first tactic is **name-calling**. This refers to giving someone or some concept a negative label with no proof or justification for it being an accurate label. The negative name is designed to cause receivers to reject the person or concepts without further consideration. Name-calling is frequently used in politics and was particularly prevalent in the 2016 presidential race. Donald Trump frequently labeled his opponents as "stupid" or as "losers." Even labeling a persuasive message as being "propaganda" can be an example of name-calling. Language labels can carry powerful weight when the receivers do not question the appropriateness of the labels.

The reverse of this tactic is called **glittering generality**. This refers to using virtuous words or labels with no proof or justification for it being an accurate label. Terms such as democracy, free speech, motherhood, and all natural all convey positive meanings to Americans. Glittering generality is when a persuader uses such words to get the audience to accept the message as positive without any proof. The positive name is designed to cause receivers to embrace the person, idea, or object without further consideration.

Go to NBC's "The More You Know" website and view the latest campaigns. How many use testimonial?

Testimonial is a tactic that refers to having a valued person express support, or offer testimony, about the value (or lack thereof) of the targeted person or concept. Testimony is used in a variety of persuasive formats, and we often think of it as being critical in courtroom settings. The kind of testimony that is treated as a propaganda tactic is when that testimony is from an individual without particular expertise in that field. For example, popular movie stars or musicians have been called on to endorse political candidates. Although those figures are entitled to their opinions, they are not asked for their support because of their perceived political expertise, rather they are called on because loyal followers will support causes promoted by their favorite stars. Athletic stars are called on to appear in antidrug commercials, and television stars regularly dispense family advice in NBC's "The More You Know" series of public service announcements. Again, these figures are not represented as having special knowledge in these areas, but they are used to attract attention and garner support simply because they are well known and well-liked by the audience. One of the authors received a solicitation from Feed the Children, a nonprofit organization that helps children. Feed the Children was asking for a donation and used testimony from three well-known stars (among a certain age group)—Garth Brooks,

Melanie Griffith, and B. B. King—as a means to increase donations. For example, next to Garth Brooks' picture was the quote: "*If there is a need,* Feed the Children *will be there.* Feed the Children *isn't just an organization, it's people helping people,*" which is a good example of the testimony tactic.

Card stacking or **case making** is another propaganda tactic used frequently. This involves arranging facts and pieces of information (which may be true or false by themselves) to attempt to prove the speaker's position, even if it is false. Anytime we construct an argument we arrange our evidence to best make our point, but card stacking refers to arranging the facts with only the source's best interest in mind. The term "card stacking" comes from the gambling world where someone "stacks the deck" so that they will win. Card stacking is not about helping an audience understand an issue; it is about furthering the persuader's goals regardless of the impact on the audience.

Another tactic identified by the Institute for Propaganda Analysis is called **bandwagon**. This tactic is based on the concept of "everyone else is doing it, why aren't you?" People don't like to be left out, and this tactic relies on social norms and conformity. This is why politicians all want to present polls showing that they are in the lead in public opinion. They hope that others will jump on the bandwagon of support if it appears that the majority of the public is in favor of the politician or the cause. In simple terms, this tactic attempts to portray the person or concept as being the one preferred by the most people so others will support the winner as well. Recall from our discussion of the elaboration likelihood model that consensus can serve as a peripheral cue. The bandwagon tactic is an example of consensus. When people are peripherally processing a message, the bandwagon tactic can serve as a peripheral cue to agree with the message.

A tactic in direct contrast to bandwagon is **appeal to exclusivity**. This approach suggests that rather than being the choice of the most people, the recommended product or idea is only for the most selective or choosy audiences. Browse through a magazine such as *Garden & Gun*, *Town & Country*, or *Architectural Digest* that targets a high income demographic and examine the ads. Exclusivity is frequently used to make products more appealing. The advertisement shown in Figure 12.1 is appealing to exclusivity by describing the jewelry collection as "The Rare and the Extraordinary" along with indicating that an appointment is suggested to buy the jewelry.

A bold propaganda tactic is called the **big lie**. This is telling an untruth in the hopes that when people hear it enough, they will believe it to be true without any proof needed. During the

Courtesy of Rare 1 Corporation, Gem Cutters & Private Jewelers.

FIGURE 12.1 Appeal to exclusivity.

Google "Debunking Myths" and you will find several examples of "big lies" that many people believe.

McCarthy era in the 1950s, all Senator McCarthy had to do to ruin a person's life was to stand on the Senate floor and label him or her a communist. This is an example of both name-calling and the big lie. No supporting evidence was needed, and the label was enough to carry weight. Similarly, today, *urban legends* abound. These are lies about an organization or its products that spread quickly without any proof they are true. The Internet has made transmission of these big lies quite easy and speedy. For example, KFC was accused of using genetically engineered meat instead of chicken in its products. Procter and Gamble has wrestled for years with rumors of profits being contributed to satanic worship. The more often a lie is stated and repeated, the more strongly it is believed and the harder it is to change that belief.

An additional tactic is called **bait and switch**, and it is used frequently in sales settings. This involves using a great claim in an advertisement to lure customers to the store, and once they are there, the seller tries to convince them to move up to a higher cost (and higher profit) item. For example, a store might advertise a mattress set for only $100. When customers come in, they are encouraged to lie on the lumpy, uncomfortable mattress set with the low price and then compare it to a top-of-the-line, comfortable (and much more expensive) set right next to it. Many customers leave with the higher priced item, but they would probably not have gone to that store in the first place without the advertised sale-priced item.

Scarcity is a commonly used tactic to make something be perceived as more valuable and desirable. When *supplies are limited* or a sale price is *only available to first 50 customers*, scarcity is being used to enhance the value of the opportunity. When a product or opportunity is scarce, there is a greater chance we will be denied access to it; our freedom to choose is limited. We react to the scarcity by perceiving it as far more desirable than if supplies were abundant. Collectables are created for every large event such as the World Series or Olympics and are scooped up by fans who perceive a high value because there will only be one 50th Super Bowl.

A final propaganda tactic is called **reciprocity**. This is when the persuader gives something to the targeted receiver and expects the receiver to feel compelled to accommodate the persuader. The "pre-giving" compliance-gaining strategy in Marwell and Schmitt's typology in Table 12.1 is an interpersonal version of reciprocity. Hari Krishna followers in airports used this tactic. They gave out flowers or books as "gifts" to airport visitors and then requested donations for their cause. Many people felt compelled to give at least something even though they didn't want the flower or book in the first place. Nonprofit organizations frequently use the reciprocity tactic. In a solicitation letter from Habitat for Humanity International, the first two paragraphs read as follows:

> *"Here they are! A selection of all occasion greeting cards—sent just for you! I'm sending them to you in the spirit of friendship and in the hope you'll read this story about some children I'm concerned about ..."*

Accompanying this letter were five greeting cards with envelopes. Clearly, Habitat for Humanity International was hoping that the recipient would feel obligated to reciprocate the gift of greeting cards. One of the authors has a collection of such gifts that includes calendars, cards, address labels, a charm, flower seeds, and a lapel pin, which illustrates the frequency the reciprocity tactic is used in fundraising. Reciprocity creates a sense of obligation in respondents regardless of what they think of the cause or product.

Both cognitive dissonance theory and self-perception theory explain the reciprocity effect. Cognitive dissonance theory emphasizes the need to be consistent. If we consider ourselves polite, it would be inconsistent to accept a gift without saying thank you in some way. Making a donation is clearly the "thank you" the organization is looking for. A self-perception theory explanation of the reciprocity effect is that we need to find an explanation for our behavior. If we accept the gift or service offered and there are no obvious external justifications, we assume that we accepted the gift or service because we value that organization.

All of these propaganda tactics are used in multiple contexts, and you are likely to see them if you look for them in advertisements, public service campaigns, political campaigns, sales contexts, and many other persuasive settings. They have been labeled propaganda by those who study this aspect of social influence, and they raise ethical questions. Again, these can be used for purposes perceived to be good as well as those we disagree with, but being aware of their existence is the first step in deciding how you choose to respond to these tactics.

Propaganda tactics and compliance-gaining strategies describe how messages can be constructed to achieve compliance. A third approach to compliance involves sequential request strategies. These are similar to compliance-gaining strategies, but are more formulaic and specify the order that certain types of requests should be made. Sequential request strategies are designed to gain compliance, not change attitudes or beliefs.

SEQUENTIAL REQUEST STRATEGIES

If you have ever worked in sales or solicited donations for a cause, you may have been trained in sequential request strategies. A **sequential request strategy** is a script specifying what you ask for and how you respond. Two commonly used sequential request strategies are door-in-the-face and foot-in-the-door.

DOOR-IN-THE-FACE

Suppose a high school student wants permission to drive his dad's Audi on prom night. A **door-in-the-face (DITF)** approach would be to request use of the Audi and $2000 for prom expenses. When this request is refused, the teen would request the use of the Audi to go to the prom—what he really wanted to begin with. The structure of the DITF strategy is that a large request is made that will be refused. Immediately following the refusal, the desired request, which is much more reasonable, is made. Cialdini and his colleagues (1975) developed the DITF and conducted an experiment to test it. In this study experimenters approached people walking on the street, and introduced themselves as being from the County Youth Counseling Program. Experimenters made one of three requests. The DITF condition involved the experimenters making an extreme request. The request was to volunteer to work as an unpaid counselor at the juvenile detention center for two hours per week for two years. After the person on the street rejected the request (which all of them did), the experimenter made a smaller request of volunteering to chaperone a group of kids to the zoo that would require a two-hour commitment. The small request condition involved experimenters only making the small request. A third condition involved both the extreme and small requests being made and giving the participant the option to choose one of them. The results were quite clear: 50% of the participants in the DITF condition complied with the small request, 25% complied when only asked to perform the small request, and only 16.7% complied with the small request when given a choice between the two options. The DITF strategy was clearly more effective.

In a similar study, Gueguen (2014) used the DITF technique to increase blood donation at a university in France, and examined both verbal and behavioral compliance. Additionally, Gueguen wanted to see if the DITF would be equally effective if there was a delay between the request and the behavior. Like Cialdini, Gueguen found the DITF technique resulted in greater compliance, but also found that behavioral compliance was greater when there was no delay between being asked to donate blood and having the opportunity to give than when there was a delay. Cialdini et al. (1975) argues that the DITF works because of the reciprocity norm. When we make a concession, our partner is pressured to reciprocate by also making a concession. In the case of the DITF, when the experimenter makes the smaller request, he/she has made a concession, so the research participant feels obligated to reciprocate. The pressure to reciprocate declines as time passes.

The door-in-the-face (DITF) strategy is often fairly effective and is frequently used by nonprofit organizations. In fact, research has found that the DITF strategy is more effective for nonprofits than for commercial organizations (O'Keefe & Figgé, 1997). One explanation for why the DITF strategy works is guilt; in other words, we need to meet our social responsibility to help someone (Turner, Tamborini, Limon, & Zuckerman-Hyman, 2007). O'Keefe and Figgé (1997) explain that DITF is a guilt appeal message. When a receiver rejects the first request, he or she experiences guilt. By accepting the second request, the guilt is alleviated. For DITF to be effective, rejection of the first request must result in guilt feelings by the receiver, and acceptance of the second request must reduce the guilt. Turner et al. (2007) found some support for this explanation when the message receivers were friends, but not when the message receivers were strangers. Turner et al. also found support for an alternate explanation based in reciprocity when the message receivers were strangers. The reciprocity explanation assumes that the request is perceived as a negotiation and that the receiver is obligated to engage in the negotiation. When the source makes the smaller request (a concession from the first large request), the receiver feels obligated to reciprocate the concession and agree to the request. Turner et al. concluded that friends and strangers process a DITF situation differently. Regardless of why the DITF strategy is effective, it gains short-term compliance and does not result in long-term attitude change. Persuaders also must be careful not to anger receivers by making too large of an initial request, which might result in anger and a refusal to negotiate. Persuaders should also consider the ethical implications of using guilt to influence.

FOOT-IN-THE-DOOR

A second strategy our high school student could use to acquire use of his dad's Audi for prom is **foot-in-the-door (FITD)**. In this case, he might first request permission to drive the Audi to run a quick errand—a small request that would probably be granted. Following this small request, the student asks to drive the Audi to prom. The structure of the FITD is to make a very small request that will be accepted. Following the performance of the first request, a second, larger request is made. Freedman and Fraser (1966) introduced the FITD technique with a classic experiment. Two fake organizations were created for the purpose of the study. One was called the Committee for Traffic Safety, and the other the Keep California Beautiful Committee. The resident participants were sorted into five groups. One group was a control group, and no initial request was made of these people. The second and third groups were asked to put a sticker in their windows for either the Committee for Traffic Safety or the Keep California Beautiful Committee. The final two groups were asked to sign a petition for one of the two committees. The four experimental groups were being asked for an initial small favor to support a good cause.

Two weeks later, a researcher representing himself or herself as a member of another fake group called Citizens for Safe Driving went to the home of each resident in the four experimental conditions and those in the control group. In this case, the residents were asked to place a large, poorly lettered sign in front of their homes. They were told it would block much of the front of their homes and needed to stay for over a week. In addition, the signs would leave a large hole in the yards when they were removed. This was a large request. Over 55 percent of the residents who had been asked to comply with the initial small favor agreed to put the signs in their yards despite the drawbacks of their appearance and the large hole left behind. However, less than 20 percent of the control group agreed to put the signs in their yards. No difference in compliance rates was found between those who had been initially approached by the Traffic Safety Committee and the Keep California Beautiful Committee. The kind of initial request (petition or window sticker) also did not make a difference in compliance rates. The type of initial request is not important, but getting people to go along with an initial request is key. Substantial research on FITD has been conducted since Freedman and Fraser's work, with results indicating that the strategy works sometimes but not always. A study conducted in France (Gueguen, Marchand, Pascual, & Lourel, 2008) found that FITD worked better than a control group for initiating a date with a stranger. In this study, young women were approached by a young man they did not know (one of three confederates working for the researcher) and either asked for a light for a cigarette or directions to a location (initial request). Following the small initial request, the young man asked the women to join him for a drink. The control condition involved the young man asking the young woman to join him for a drink without an initial request. Only about 3 percent of the control group agreed to join the male for a drink, whereas 15 to 16 percent of those in the FITD conditions involving the initial request for a light or directions agreed to have a drink with the confederate. Thus, FITD led to a significantly higher success rate in this context, but the success rate was far from a sure thing.

Recent research has also found that the FITD strategy works in an online environment such as signing an electronic petition or providing online assistance to others (Gueguen, 2002; Gueguen & Jacob, 2001; Markey, Wells, & Markey, 2001). Burger (1999) reviewed more than 50 studies using meta-analysis to refine our understanding of the FITD strategy. Burger concluded that the more involved the receivers are with the initial request the more likely they are to comply with the second request. Second, if receivers perform the initial request as opposed to simply agreeing to perform it, they are more likely to comply with the second request.

Burger (1999) identified two additional factors that affect the effectiveness of the FITD strategy. The first is the *timing of the second request*: Does it immediately follow the first request, or is it delayed? Girandola (2002) specifically tested the timing of the request in a study on organ donation. Research participants were first asked to complete a five-question survey on organ donation (initial request) and then either immediately or three days later were asked if they were willing to become organ donors. Participants were significantly more willing to become organ donors when the request came three days after the initial request.

The second factor identified by Burger (1999) was whether the *person making the second request was the same or a different person making the first request*. Girandola (2002) also examined this factor in his study. In addition to some participants receiving the second request three days after the initial request, for some participants the second request came from the same person who made the first request, and for other participants the request was made by a different person. Girandola's results were interesting: There was greater compliance when the same requester made a delayed request. If the requester was different for the two requests, the delay did not matter much. Why are these two factors important? Girandola explains that the *norm of reciprocity* dictates that requests and concessions are carried out in a reciprocal manner. In other words, if I ask a favor *of* you, I need to do a favor *for* you before I can ask a second favor. Therefore, when the same requester asks for the second favor immediately after the first, she or he is violating the norm of reciprocity. Girandola found that when the second request was delayed, it did not matter much if the requester was the same or not. This result most likely occurred because the norm of reciprocity was weakened by the delay; we don't keep that close track of whose turn it is to ask a favor.

Seeking compliance is a form of persuasion that focuses on short-term behavior. The strategies discussed here are all generally useful in gaining compliance; however, their use should be tempered by your ethical standards. These strategies can clearly be used in a manipulative fashion. Just because you can, doesn't mean you should. Several of the propaganda strategies are used to seek compliance, but some are geared toward attitude and belief change. Name-calling, glittering generality, the big lie, and card stacking are designed to change beliefs and attitudes with a secondary focus on behavior. Propaganda strategies are often thought of as manipulative and the ethics of these strategies is often questioned. Chapter 13 describes different ethical perspectives that we use to further discuss tactics such as the big lie, card stacking, and emotion.

- Kelman's model describes three levels of influence—compliance, identification, and internalization—which relate to French and Raven's five power bases (see Chapter 4).
- Compliance-gaining is a type of persuasion involving interpersonal communication with an emphasis on behavioral change.
- Personal differences, situational differences, and secondary goals of the agent affect why a particular compliance-gaining strategy is chosen.
- Compliance-gaining is rooted in the concept of power.
- Researchers wanted to understand what kinds of compliance-gaining strategies are used. As a result, typologies of compliance-gaining strategies were generated by using both inductive and deductive approaches.
- The typologies developed included Marwell and Schmitt's 16 strategies; Schenck-Hamlin, Wiseman, and Georgacarakos' 14 strategies; and Kearney, Plax, Richmond, and McCroskey's 22 behavior alteration techniques.
- Propaganda is a type of influence focusing on mass audiences that carries negative connotations and raises ethical questions.
- The Institute for Propaganda Analysis identified several propaganda tactics.
- Sequential request strategies are formulaic approaches to compliance-gaining and consist of door-in-the-face and foot-in-the-door.

KEY TERMS

Agent—the source of a compliance-gaining message.

Antisocial strategies—compliance-gaining strategies based on coercive and legitimate power.

Appeal to exclusivity—a propaganda tactic that communicates that the recommended product or idea is only for the most selective or choosy audiences, rather than being the choice of the most people or common folks.

Bait and switch—a propaganda tactic frequently used in sales settings. It involves using a great claim in an advertisement to lure customers to the store, and once they are there, the seller tries to convince them to move up to a higher cost (and higher profit) item.

Bandwagon—a propaganda tactic that communicates that everyone is doing it, so the receiver should too.

Big lie—a propaganda tactic that involves telling an untruth in the hopes that when people hear it enough, they will believe it to be true without any proof needed.

Card stacking or Case making—a propaganda tactic that involves arranging facts and pieces of information (which may be true or false by themselves) to attempt to prove something that isn't really the case.

Compliance—the most basic level of influence, it involves a target being influenced to do something to gain a reward or to avoid a punishment.

Compliance-gaining—communicative behavior in which an agent engages to elicit from a target some agent-selected behavior.

Deductive approach—conclusions are made through a process of reasoning from theory.

Door-in-the-face (DITF)—initially making a very large unreasonable request that the target is likely to turn down and then later making the critical request.

Foot-in-the-door (FITD)—initially making a very small request that the target is likely to agree to and then later making the larger critical request.

Glittering generality—a propaganda tactic where someone or some concept is given a positive label with no proof or justification for it being an accurate label.

Identification—occurs when a target accepts influence from an agent because he or she wants to be associated with the agent.

Inductive approach—a method of reasoning that begins with observation and then moves from observation of particular events to general principles or hypotheses.

Internalization—long-term attitude change. A target accepts the behavior as being best or most appropriate and will perform the behavior regardless of who approves or provides rewards.

Levels of influence—Kelman's model of three types of influence that build on one another. Compliance is the basic level, then identification, then internalization.

Name-calling—a propaganda tactic where someone or some concept is given a negative label with no proof or justification for it being an accurate label.

Propaganda—a type of persuasion that involves mass audiences with a purpose of achieving the goals of the persuader, and it often involves emotional appeals, concealment of purpose, and a lack of sound support.

Prosocial strategies—compliance-gaining strategies based on reward, referent, and expert power.

Reciprocity—a propaganda tactic that involves the persuader giving something to the targeted receiver and expecting the receiver to feel compelled to accommodate the persuader.

Scarcity—a propaganda tactic that involves creating the perception that something is rare or scarce in order to increase its perceived value.

Secondary goals—things the agent is trying to accomplish with the target other than gaining compliance.

Select the issue—a propaganda tactic that involves arguing that something is what really matters, regardless of any proof or compelling rationale that makes it the most important concept.

Sequential request strategy—a script specifying what you ask for and how you respond.

Target—the receiver of a compliance-gaining message (the person the compliance is targeted at).

Testimonial—a propaganda tactic where a valued person expresses support, or offers testimony, about the value (or lack thereof) of the targeted person or concept.

REVIEW QUESTIONS

1. What are the three levels of influence?
2. How does using a deductive approach to develop a compliance-gaining typology differ from using an inductive approach?
3. What is compliance-gaining?
4. Which strategies in Marwell and Schmitt's typology are based in reward power? Coercive power? Legitimate power? Referent power? Expert power?
5. What are the four major properties of compliance-gaining identified by Schenck-Hamlin, Wiseman, and Georgacarakos?
6. Which behavior alteration techniques are based in reward power? Coercive power? Legitimate power? Referent power? Expert power?
7. How do prosocial and antisocial strategies differ from each other? Why should you use prosocial strategies?
8. How is propaganda defined? How does this differ from the definition for persuasion?
9. How does compliance-gaining differ from propaganda and persuasion?
10. What are the two sequential request strategies and how do they work?

DISCUSSION QUESTIONS

1. Think of the people and groups you identify with most. What are some behaviors you perform (e.g., dress, study habits, hobbies, etc.) mostly because you identify with those people or groups?
2. Are there any ethical differences between targeting compliance versus identification versus internalization? Are there any situations in which you would find seeking one level of influence less ethical than other levels?

3. Think of a time when you tried to gain compliance from someone and it was somewhat difficult. Which compliance-gaining strategies did you use (examine the typologies in Tables 12.1, 12.2, and 12.3)? Did the target of your compliance-gaining use any of the strategies in trying to resist your efforts?

4. Look up Golish's (1999) list of compliance-gaining strategies students use on teachers and compare it to the other typologies. How much overlap is there? Have you ever engaged in any of the strategies identified by Golish?

5. Are any ethical issues involved in selection of compliance-gaining strategies? Are we simply concerned with what is most effective in any given situation, or are there ethical issues we should take into account as well? Do you find any of the compliance-gaining strategies to be inherently ethical? Inherently unethical?

6. Which propaganda tactics do you think are most commonly used? Which do you feel are the most unethical? Do these two lists overlap at all?

7. Do you find any of the propaganda tactics to be always unethical no matter how or why they are used? What criteria would you suggest be employed to evaluate the ethics of propaganda tactics across situations?

8. Have you ever used the DITF or the FITD sequential request strategies? Were they effective?

9. Has someone ever used the DITF or the FITD sequential request strategies on you? Did you comply with the request?

REFERENCES

Baxter, L. A. (1984). An investigation of compliance-gaining as politeness. *Human Communication Research, 10,* 427–456.

Brown, J. A. C. (1963). *Techniques of persuasion, from propaganda to brainwashing.* Baltimore: Penguin Books.

Burger, J. M. (1999). The foot-in-the-door compliance procedure: A multiple-process analysis and review. *Personality and Social Psychology Review, 3,* 303–325.

Carli, L. L. (2004). Gender effects on social influence. In J. S. Seiter & R. H. Gass (Eds.), *Perspectives on persuasion, social influence, and compliance gaining* (pp. 138–148). Boston: Allyn & Bacon.

Cialdini, R. B., Vincent, J. E., Lewis, S. K., Catalan, J., Wheeler, D., & Darby, B. L. (1975). Reciprocal concessions procedures for inducing compliance: The door-in-the-face technique. *Journal of Personality and -Social Psychology, 31,* 206–215.

Cody, M. J., McLaughlin, M. L., & Jordan, W. J. (1980). A multidimensional scaling of three sets of compliance-gaining strategies. *Communication Quarterly, 28,* 34–46.

Cole, R. (Ed.). (1998). *The encyclopedia of propaganda: Volume 2.* Armonk, NY: M. E. Sharpe.

Dillard, J. P. (1990). A goal-driven model of interpersonal influence. In J. P. Dillard (Ed.), *Seeking compliance: The production of interpersonal influence messages* (pp. 41–56). Scottsdale, AZ: Gorsuch Scarisbrick.

Ferrara, M., Kopfman, J., Hall, E. D., Navon, E., & Septor, K. (2011). Talk to take: Multiviamin usage in college-aged women. *Journal of Communication in Healthcare, 4*(4), 271–280.

Freedman, J. L., & Fraser, S. C. (1966). Compliance without pressure: The foot-in-the-door technique. *Journal of Personality and Social Psychology, 4,* 195–202.

French, J. R. P., & Raven, B. (1959). The bases of social power. In D. Cartwright (Ed.), *Studies in social power* (pp. 150–167). Ann Arbor, MI: Institute for Social Research.

Girandola, F. (2002). Sequential requests and organ donation. *Journal of Social Psychology, 142,* 171–178.

Gueguen, N. (2002). Foot-in-the-door technique and computer mediated communication. *Computers in Human Behavior, 18,* 11–15.

Gueguen, N., & Jacob C. (2001). Fund-raising on the Web: The effect on electronic foot-in-the-door on donation. *CyberPsychology & Behavior, 4,* 705–709.

Gueguen, N., Marchand, M., Pascual, A., & Lourel, M. (2008). The effect of the foot-in-the-door technique on a courtship request: A field experiment. *Psychological Reports, 103,* 529–534.

Golish, T. D. (1999). Students' use of compliance gaining strategies with graduate teaching assistants: Examining the other end of the power spectrum. *Communication Quarterly, 47*(1), 12–32.

Gueguen, N. (2014). Door-in-the-face technique and delay to fulfill the final request: An evaluation with a request to give blood. *The Journal of Psychology, 148,* 569–576.

Jowett, G. S., & O'Donnell, V. (1999). *Propaganda and persuasion* (3rd ed.). Thousand Oaks, CA: Sage Publications.

Kearney, P., Plax, T. G., Richmond, V. P., & McCroskey, J. C. (1984). Power in the classroom IV: Alternatives to discipline. In R. Bostrom (Ed.), *Communication yearbook 8* (pp. 724–746). Beverly Hills, CA: Sage.

Kelman, H. C. (1958). Compliance, identification, and internalization: Three processes of attitude change. *Journal of Conflict Resolution, 2,* 51–60.

Lee, A. M., & Lee E. B. (1972). *The fine art of propaganda.* New York: Octagon Books. (Original work published in 1939.)

Marwell, G., & Schmitt, D. R. (1967). Dimensions of compliance-gaining behavior: An empirical analysis. *Sociometry, 30,* 350–364.

McCroskey, J. C., & Richmond, V. P. (1996). *Fundamentals of human communication: An interpersonal perspective.* Prospect Heights, IL: Waveland.

Miller, G., Boster, F., Roloff, M., & Siebold, D. (1977). Compliance-gaining message strategies: A typology and some findings concerning effects of situational differences. *Communication Monographs, 44,* 37–51.

O'Keefe, D. J., & Figgé, M. (1997). A guilt-based explanation of the door-in-the-face influence strategy. *Human Communication Research, 24,* 64–81.

Parrish-Sprowl, J., Carveth, R., Senk, M. (1994). The effect of compliance-gaining strategy choice and communicator style on sales success. *The Journal of Business Communication, 31*(4), 291–310.

Richmond, V. P., & McCroskey, J. C. (Eds.). (1992). *Power in the classroom: Communication, control, and concern.* Hillsdale, NJ: Lawrence Erlbaum.

Richmond, V. P., McCroskey, J. C., & Davis, L. M. (1986). The relationship of supervisor use of power and affinity-seeking strategies with subordinate satisfaction. *Communication Quarterly, 34,* 178–193.

Schenck-Hamlin, W. J., Wiseman, R. L., & Georgacarakos, G. N. (1982). A model of properties of compliance-gaining strategies. *Communication Quarterly, 30,* 92–100.

Schrader, D. C., & Dillard, J. P. (1998). Goal structures and interpersonal influence. *Communication Studies, 49,* 276–293.

Seiter, J. S., & Weger, H. (2010). The effect of generalized compliments, sex of server, and size of dining party on tipping behavior in restaurants. *Journal of Applied Social Psychology, 40*(1), 1–12.

Smith, V. A., DeVellis, B. M., Kalet, A., Roberts, J. C., & DeVillis, R. F. (2005). Encouraging patient adherence: Primary care physicians' use of verbal compliance-gaining strategies in medical interviews. *Patient Education and Counseling, 57,* 62–76.

Sproule, J. M (1994). *Channels of propaganda.* Bloomington, IN: ERIC/EDINFO Press.

Turner, M. M., Tamborini, R., Limon, M. S., & Zuckerman-Hyman, C. (2007). The moderators and mediators of door-in-the-face requests: Is it a negotiation or a helping experience? *Communication Monographs, 74,* 333–356.

Wheeless, L. R., Barraclough, R., & Stewart, R. (1983). Compliance-gaining and power in persuasion. In R. N. Bostrom (Ed.), *Communication yearbook 7* (pp. 105–145). Beverly Hills, CA: Sage.

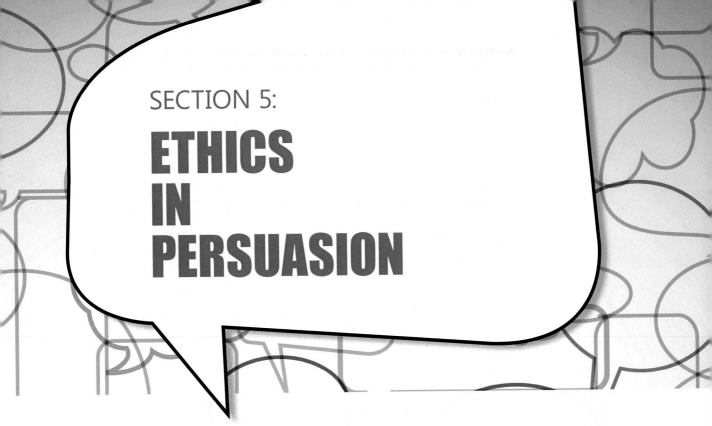

SECTION 5:

ETHICS IN PERSUASION

The previous 12 chapters have helped you understand how to be persuasive. The focus of this section is on the ethics of using those persuasive strategies. Chapter 13 discusses seven perspectives or approaches to ethics and draws heavily on Richard Johannesen's work. This chapter is written so that it can be read and discussed at any point in a course. It does not need to be read last. This chapter could be used as a framework with which to evaluate and discuss the various theories and concepts of persuasion, or it could be used as a way to summarize and conclude the topic of persuasion at the end of a course.

CHAPTERS

CHAPTER 13

ETHICS

Liam, a college student eager to make money for college expenses, decided to sell a line of powdered diet shakes from the Acme Corporation called Fat Melt. Liam found the information about the company and its product online and ordered the starter kit that included a case of the product along with a packet of materials. The materials described the product, suggested selling points, and included a set of glossy, full-color brochures to use in selling the product to others. Liam knew that lots of his female friends were constantly on one kind of diet or another, so he guessed that his campus would be a good market for this product. Liam was very effective in his efforts to persuade students on his campus to try the product. He sold over a dozen cases of the product in the first two months alone.

During the third month of his sales campaign, two of his customers were hospitalized, and the doctors concluded that Fat Melt was responsible for serious kidney damage in both of them. One of the ill customers recovered but faced permanent kidney damage. The other hospitalized customer died despite all the doctor's efforts. The following week, three other customers were hospitalized with lesser illnesses, but the doctors again concluded that Fat Melt was at fault.

Liam faced an ethical dilemma. Was he ethically responsible for the health issues of his customers tied to the product he sold them? Was he responsible for the one customer who died? Liam's friends were split. Some decided he was to blame; others decided it was not his fault. What is your conclusion? Is Liam ethically responsible for the negative effects of the product he sold?

Let's add more information and see if your evaluation changes. Suppose the guidelines on the bottles of Fat Melt and in the brochure indicated that the shakes were to be used as a supplement for breakfast and lunch but that a normal meal was to be eaten for dinner. In addition, the guidelines also advised customers not to use the product for more than 30 consecutive days. In this case, all the ill customers failed to follow the guidelines. The most seriously ill patients used the shakes for all three daily meals and carried

LEARNING OBJECTIVES

- EXPLAIN WHY PERSUASION HAS ETHICAL IMPLICATIONS.
- EXPLAIN HOW CULTURE INFLUENCES ETHICAL STANDARDS.
- USE THE SEVEN ETHICAL PERSPECTIVES TO EVALUATE THE ETHICS OF VARIOUS PERSUASIVE MESSAGES.
- DISCUSS MAJOR ETHICAL ISSUES, INCLUDING WHETHER THE END JUSTIFIES THE MEANS, WHETHER IT IS ETHICAL TO USE EMOTIONAL APPEALS, AND WHETHER RESPONSIBILITY IN PERSUASION LIES WITH THE SOURCE OR THE RECEIVER.

on this pattern for more than two months. With this information, would you hold Liam ethically responsible for the consequences of his persuasive sales pitch?

What other information would you want to know about this situation? Would knowing the methods that Liam used in his persuasive sales pitches affect your response? What would you have wanted Liam to do in order to be ethical in his persuasive efforts?

ETHICAL NATURE OF PERSUASION

The scenario described here represents an ethical challenge associated with using the persuasion principles discussed in this book. As you have considered various applications of persuasion in this book, you probably noticed that, at times, persuasion was employed as a tool to enhance society, but that, at other times, persuasion was used as a weapon with undesirable outcomes. Gun enthusiasts have argued that "guns don't kill people, people kill people" in an attempt to portray guns as a neutral weapon that can be used by people for good or evil purposes. Persuasion is often looked at in a similar way. Persuasion is a powerful tool. Throughout the book, we have discussed what works and what does not work, and we have offered guidelines designed to help you be more successful in your persuasive attempts. The central question in this chapter, however, is not what *can* be done or what *works*, but rather what *should* be done in persuasive messages.

As defined in Chapter 1, persuasion involves symbolic communication between two or more persons with intent to change, reinforce, or shape attitudes, beliefs, and/or behaviors of the receiver. Because persuasion involves intentionally trying to change some aspect of another person, by most standards, persuasion involves ethics. When we behave intentionally, we have a great deal of responsibility for the outcome. Because Liam intended to sell a product in the scenario presented, many of you probably held him responsible for the consequences of his persuasive efforts. However, Liam did not intend to cause harm to his customers, so some of you probably decided that he was not responsible for the problems associated with his product. How do we decide where to draw the line?

As a society we clearly distinguish between outcomes that are a result of intentional behavior and those that occur by accident. This can be seen in how we treat the killing of another person. If you intentionally kill someone, you will most likely spend most of your life in prison or even receive the death penalty. If, however, you kill someone accidentally with absolutely no intent to harm (e.g., in a car accident as a result of a mechanical failure), it is unlikely that you would receive any jail time, as it would not represent willful misconduct or gross negligence in legal terms. Nilsen (1974) argues that society should hold people responsible for outcomes of persuasion that are intended, but he also extends this responsibility to foreseeable consequences of the persuasive behavior. If Liam knew that the product was likely to be abused by customers and that negative consequences such as the serious kidney damage or death were foreseeable, then, according to Nilsen's view, Liam is ethically responsible for the illness and death even though he did not intend those to occur. If we decided that Liam could not have predicted these outcomes and couldn't do anything to prevent them, then Liam would not be ethically responsible for the results. Nilsen and others have argued that we have an ethical obligation to consider the potential consequences before engaging in any persuasive attempts. The outcomes of a source's use of persuasion will be evaluated by the receiver and often by other bystanders (e.g., the public) and judged not only as effective or ineffective but also as ethical or unethical.

The term **ethics** refers to principles or guidelines for what is right and wrong and is often used interchangeably with *morals*. An individual or group's ethical standards are closely linked to their culture. Within a culture, individuals share expectations for what and how things will happen. For instance, when you go into a bank, you know and expect to wait in line, giving the person in front of you adequate space to conduct business with a certain level of privacy. You don't crowd in and look over his or her shoulder. This expectation is based in the U.S. culture. In another culture, the expectations for behavior in a bank may be different. Ethics are also linked to cultural values. A predominant value in the United States is individualism. We assume that individuals should run their own lives, make their own decisions, and be free to succeed or fail. We strongly value free choice and freedom of speech. Our values and expectations influence what we believe to be right and wrong. In the United States we usually view anything that infringes on free speech as wrong. Our cultural values for individualism and free speech have a strong influence on what we believe to be right and ethical. Culture and ethical standards are intertwined—one influences the other. When you move from one culture to another, ethical standards change hand in hand with the culture.

RULES-BASED APPROACHES TO ETHICS

On the surface, ethics may seem like a fairly simple and straightforward concept. Many believe that ethical guidelines should be followed in order for persuasion to be ethical, and these guidelines may involve rules about what to do in ethical persuasion and rules for what should not be done in order to be ethical. Jaska and Pritchard (1994) reviewed a large body of research and created the five guidelines for ethical persuasion presented in Figure 13.1. Their guidelines are based on multiple philosophical perspectives. There is a certain amount of ambiguity in the guidelines, but they do provide fairly straightforward guidelines on what is and is not ethical. Review Jaska and Pritchard's guidelines in Figure 13.1 and then review Liam's situation. How do you evaluate Liam's actions on the basis of these guidelines?

Others have offered more specific advice. Minnick (1957) broke persuasion into three categories: practices that are always unethical, practices that are always ethical, and practices that could be ethical or unethical, depending on the circumstances surrounding their use. The unethical group includes lying, distorting

1. The use of persuasion should reinforce, or at least be consistent with, democratic processes in a free society. Dissent, discussion, argument, debate, and persuasion in general are fundamental democratic values. However, when communication fails to permit listeners to make rational choices, freedom itself is endangered. Freedom of speech is an important right, but it also carries with it important abilities.

2. We value persuaders who demonstrate good character and goodwill. We respond favorably to persuaders who integrate personal integrity with the integrity of ideas. We appreciate persuaders who first conduct careful and conscientious research before attempting "to make truth effective." We want persuaders to be honest, disclosing important and relevant information for the case at hand. The great Roman teacher Quintilian summarized these qualities in saying, "The perfect orator is a good man speaking well."

3. Those who attempt to persuade others should consider the varying perspectives of listeners and others who may be affected by the communication. We respect persuaders who demonstrate that they can view a situation through the eyes of listeners as well as their own. Deceivers tend to see things from their own, often quite restricted, perspectives.

4. Both the means and ends of persuasive communication should be ethically acceptable. The means of communication include the methodological choices of the persuader—the selection of material, the testing and arrangement of ideas, the intentions of the communicator, and the use of language and delivery. The ends include the effects of the persuader's presentation. Are they beneficial or harmful? Does the persuasion bring about long-range, positive effects, or does a "quick fix" result in harm over the long term?

5. Responsibility for communication does not rest solely on the speakers. Listeners and even those not directly involved in particular communication situations also have responsibilities. Kenneth Andersen emphasizes the voluntariness of listener responses in persuasive communication, suggesting that listeners should not view themselves as passive and uncritical receivers. Nonparticipants, who have opportunities to evaluate persuasive communication even though it is not addressed directly to them, also have responsibilities. Voting, writing letters of opposition, or joining with others in organized protest are only some of the ways nonparticipants can exercise responsibility in opposing questionable modes of persuasion.

From Communication Ethics by J. A. Jaska and M. S. Pritchard.

FIGURE 13.1 Jaska and Pritchard's (1994) ethical guidelines.

evidence, using specious reasoning, and deceiving the audience about the persuader's intent. Although Minnick agrees that we can sometimes try to justify using one of these methods (e.g., telling a "white lie" to avoid hurting someone's feelings), they aren't ethical as general practice and thus should be considered unethical. The ethical group includes use of sound evidence and rigorous thinking. If the persuader has carefully researched the topic and applied strong critical thinking skills in evaluating the arguments, then the persuasive message would be ethical. Finally, the largest category includes persuasive approaches that can be considered ethical or unethical, depending on how they are used. This category includes methods such as the use of fear appeals, emotional appeals, majority opinion appeals, name-calling, and personal prestige. If these methods were employed as part of systematic thinking and evaluation of arguments to present valid evidence and sound thinking, they would be acceptable. If they were used in other manners, they would be unacceptable. These categories are more specific than those used by Jaska and Pritchard (1994), but they also require interpretation to apply to a specific situation. What do you think Minnick would say about the ethics of Liam's persuasion in selling Fat Melt?

Google "code of ethics" and "ethical guidelines" to find examples of rules based approaches to ethics.

One application of this rules-based approach to ethics that many professional organizations employ is to create a "code of ethics." Many organizations, particularly those in the communication business, have developed codes of ethics to guide their professional practices. A code of ethics is often helpful to professionals in deciding how to carry out their professional responsibilities. For instance, Figure 13.2 displays the code of ethics for professional communicators developed by the International Association of Business Communicators. This code of ethics provides some very specific guidelines for professional communicators, such as public relations professionals. For example, the second item seems quite specific, "Professional communicators disseminate accurate information and promptly correct any erroneous communication for which they may be responsible." Neither this guideline nor any of the others, however, provide guidance on how much information to provide and what to include or leave out. In most situations, it is not possible, nor desirable, to include everything. One of the responsibilities of the professional communicator is to decide what to include and what not to include. The pieces of information that are excluded can alter dramatically how the receiver interprets the message—recall the card stacking propaganda tactic discussed in Chapter 12. For example, consider an advertisement for Zocor®, a drug that reduces cholesterol. The advertisement featured former NFL coach Dan Reeves (who had heart bypass surgery) promoting a healthful diet, exercise, and Zocor to control blood cholesterol. A key piece of information in this persuasive message was that the drug Zocor could significantly lower total cholesterol. Also included in the advertisement was information about side effects and who should not take the drug. If the latter information were not included, the message would still be accurate (and therefore meet the second guideline in Figure 13.2); however, how receivers would interpret the message would be dramatically different. Would you consider such an advertisement to be ethical if the information on side effects were excluded? Drug advertisements are prevalent in magazines and on television. Find a drug advertisement in a magazine and evaluate the ad. Did the message source provide sufficient information? Is the ad ethical?

- Professional communicators uphold the credibility and dignity of their profession by practicing honest, candid, and timely communication and by fostering the free flow of essential information in accord with the public interest.

- Professional communicators disseminate accurate information and promptly correct any erroneous communication for which they may be responsible.

- Professional communicators understand and support the principles of free speech, freedom of assembly, and access to an open marketplace of ideas and act accordingly.

- Professional communicators are sensitive to cultural values and beliefs and engage in fair and balanced communication activities that foster and encourage mutual understanding.

- Professional communicators refrain from taking part in any undertaking that the communicator considers to be unethical.

- Professional communicators obey laws and public policies governing their professional activities and are sensitive to the spirit of all laws and regulations and, should any law or public policy be violated, for whatever reason, act promptly to correct the situation.

- Professional communicators give credit for unique expressions borrowed from others and identify the sources and purposes of all information disseminated to the public.

- Professional communicators protect confidential information and, at the same time, comply with all legal requirements for the disclosure of information affecting the welfare of others.

- Professional communicators do not use confidential information gained as a result of professional activities for personal benefit and do not represent conflicting or competing interests without written consent of those involved.

- Professional communicators do not accept undisclosed gifts or payments for professional services from anyone other than a client or employer.

- Professional communicators do not guarantee results that are beyond the power of the practitioner to deliver.

- Professional communicators are honest not only with others, but also, and most importantly, with themselves as individuals; for a professional communicator seeks the truth and speaks that truth first to the self.

FIGURE 13.2 Code of ethics for professional communicators, International Association of Business Communicators.

Codes of ethics are often useful; however, they are generally limited to a particular profession and are often of little help in unusual and complex situations. The same can be said for any set of "ethical rules." Another approach to ethics is to examine different ethical perspectives. A perspective is a way of looking at something. When we examine an object or issue from a different perspective, we often draw different conclusions. Although this process rarely results in clear-cut conclusions, it does give us a greater understanding of the issue at hand and helps us identify why we find some things ethical and others not ethical. Rather than give you a single set of ethical principles to guide persuasion, we offer several perspectives. Our goal is to help you examine ethical questions and make you aware of the ethical implications of the persuasive messages you send. We present several perspectives and pose several questions to consider. We hope you wrestle with each of these perspectives and use them to develop your own set of ethical principles that will guide you through both simple and complex situations.

JOHANNESEN'S ETHICAL PERSPECTIVES

Richard Johannesen is well known for his work in communication ethics. He has summarized a vast array of literature on ethics and identified seven perspectives or approaches one can take in examining ethical questions (Johannesen, 1996). We are not proposing that one of these perspectives is necessarily the best, but you may find one or more perspectives to be more acceptable to you personally. Also, we are not limited to a single perspective. A close examination of Jaska and Pritchard's ethical guidelines in Figure 13.1 reveals that the researchers used more than one perspective in developing their guidelines. We encourage you not to disregard any of the perspectives, but to try each one on and take it for a test drive as you examine persuasive messages. As you study these perspectives, keep two things in mind. First is diversity. Different people with different backgrounds are likely to draw on different perspectives. Being tolerant of different perspectives is necessary for communication competence. Developing a set of ethical principles is very desirable and is an important part of being an ethical communicator. It is important to constantly remind yourself, however, that your personal ethical principles are not necessarily better than someone else's, particularly when that someone else is different from you in some way, such as culture, ethnic background, religion, or socioeconomic status. The second thing to keep in mind is that these seven ethical perspectives are not representative of ethical perspectives from all cultures. Johannesen's work, as well as this book, uses a Western perspective. Although there may be broad ethical principles that virtually all people would find acceptable, there are often differences in applications of those ethical principles, resulting in cross-cultural disagreements about what is and is not ethical.

RELIGIOUS PERSPECTIVE

Religion often serves as a basis for what a person views as moral and ethical. Religious writings such as the Bible, Koran, or Talmud often provide criteria for ethical behavior and provide specific guidelines for how humans should behave. Many of the laws and ethical principles advocated in Western countries such as the United States are based on what has been referred to as the Judeo-Christian ethic (Day, 1991). Based on the tenets of the Old Testament, this perspective involves respect for individuals as human beings. One aspect of this is based on the Bible's Ten Commandments, which provide very specific and rigid guidelines for ethical behavior. Religions also provide more general guidelines, however, such as that people should be honest and forthcoming with one another and that people should be respectful and loving toward others. Persuasive messages that were in some way harmful to individuals would violate the guideline of being loving toward others. Different religions are likely to emphasize different values and beliefs, leading to different ethical guidelines.

If we take the example concerning the Zocor advertisement discussed previously from a Judeo-Christian **religious perspective**, leaving out the information on the

FIGURE 13.3 For Better or For Worse.

side effects could be considered unethical, because doing so would not be forthcoming and respectful of individuals' needs for information. A Judeo-Christian ethic would guide the message source to include the information necessary to make an informed choice. The advertisement directs readers to speak with their doctors to help them make an informed decision. This direction from the source encourages receivers to obtain more information and is consistent with a Judeo-Christian ethic of being loving and forthcoming with information.

HUMAN NATURE PERSPECTIVE

The basic principle underlying the **human nature perspective** is that any communication that enhances or supports unique human attributes is ethical (Johannesen, 1996). Any communication that undermines unique human characteristics is unethical. A central attribute discussed by Johannesen (1996) is the human capacity to reason. The ability to use information to reason and to draw logical conclusions is considered to be a uniquely human characteristic that all humans, regardless of culture or location, possess. Therefore, any persuasive communication that undermined or reduced a person's ability to make a reasoned judgment would be considered unethical. Providing inaccurate information or misleading information would clearly be considered unethical. But, what if a minimum amount of concrete information was given in a message and, instead, it relied heavily on emotional images? Consider a request for donations to an organization devoted to aiding impoverished children. Let's say the message did not contain information on how the money would be spent or what percentage would go to administrative costs versus actually helping the children. But, the message did contain a picture of a malnourished child looking directly into the camera with sad beautiful eyes, wearing dirty, ragged clothes, with a trash-filled street and open sewer in the background. Would this message be supportive of the human capacity to reason? Another type of emotional appeal that we discussed in Chapter 5 was fear appeals. Would inducing fear detract from the receivers' ability to rely on reasoning?

Another uniquely human attribute discussed by Johannesen (1996) is the capacity of humans to use symbols. Language itself is an elaborate system of symbols that we use

Are we really crazy enough to keep doing the same things that got us into this mess?

It's America's straight jacket: A devastated economy that's addicted to imported oil. For decades we've ignored it. But now there's a plan to change all that, and create new clean energy jobs in the process. It's called a carbon cap and it will let America lead in the biggest new industry of the 21st century.

But some of the same people who brought us the worst mess since the 1930's are trying to scare us out of overhauling our economy. We're already hearing their tired scare tactics — one made up statistic after another about how bad things will be if we try anything different.

Here are the facts: A carbon cap will create new jobs in clean energy industries. There will be demand for steel for wind turbines, energy efficient windows, and thousands of other products made in America. In fact, you can see a long list of companies waiting to get started at *LessCarbonMoreJobs.org*.

And a cap is a bargain for America. For example, using estimates by the U.S. Department of Energy, the impact on household utility bills will be just pennies a day — while an MIT study forecasts savings of $20 billion a year in imported oil.

Congressman Steve Driehaus: Stand with us for New Jobs and Less Imported Oil.

CHANGE THE FUTURE FOR THE BETTER. CAP CARBON POLLUTION.

Paid for by Environmental Defense Action Fund • edf.org

FIGURE 13.4 Environmental Defense Action Fund (EDAF).

to communicate. We also use many other symbols to communicate, such as nonverbal behaviors, visual images, music, and other auditory stimuli (e.g., birds singing, waves crashing on a beach). Related to this attribute is the need of human beings for other human beings (Johannesen, 1996) and is described as the need to be appreciated and understood. Johannesen describes the implications of this standard as being that "communication is ethical to the degree that it enhances human symbol-using capacity, fulfills the need for mutual appreciative understanding, and promotes mutuality of control and influence" (p. 48). A persuasive message that in some way reduced or minimized a receiver's ability to respond would be considered unethical from this perspective. For example, communication that inhibits another person from participating in a discussion would reduce human capacity to engage in mutual control and influence and be unethical. A persuasive message that invited the other to participate in a debate would enhance the human ability to engage in mutual influence and therefore be ethical. To evaluate the case of Liam selling Fat Melt with this perspective, we need to know more about the content of the persuasive messages used to sell the product. Consider the message from the Environmental Defense Action Fund (EDAF) in Figure 13.4 and evaluate it according to the human nature perspective. Does it support the human capacity to reason and engage in mutual influence? Do aspects of the message undermine the uniquely human qualities we discussed?

POLITICAL PERSPECTIVE

Ethics from a **political perspective** vary, depending on the political government you are drawing on. Essentially, persuasion is ethical to the extent that it supports the basic values or tenets of the political system. In large part, this is based on the assumption that the values that allow the society to operate should be the values that guide evaluation of the ethics of communication within that society. Therefore, standards for determining what is considered ethical persuasion in a dictatorship would be quite different from standards used in a democracy. One must first identify the primary tenets or underlying values of a political system and then determine whether a particular persuasive message is supportive or unsupportive of those values.

Wallace (1955) identified four values he believed were basic to the democratic political system: (a) a belief in the dignity and worth of individuals, (b) a belief in equality of opportunity, (c) freedom coupled with responsible exercise of freedom, and (d) a belief in each person's ability to understand the nature of democracy. If a labor union were to tell its members how to vote and discouraged them from assessing the candidates on their own, this would violate the assumption that each person has the ability to understand the nature of democracy and therefore vote for the candidates and issues he or she believes are worthy. Another example of unethical communication from this perspective is if a person justifies her or his abuse of others by saying "this is a free country." As members of a democracy, we are free; however, as stated by Wallace, we must exercise our freedom responsibly. Using our freedom to harm others is not exercising our freedom responsibly.

Another key component of democracy identified by Johannesen (1996) is the ability to reason logically. In other words, for democracy to function as intended, all persons must be encouraged to think rationally and make logical decisions, as was discussed in the human nature perspective.

Using a political perspective based in democracy to evaluate persuasive messages requires us to determine whether the message supports the above-mentioned values (as well as other values of democracy not discussed here). Becoming more and more common over the years in political campaigns is the use of sound bites, which are short phrases that identify a particular stand on a topic but do not provide any detailed information on the topic. For example in the 2016 presidential election, Donald Trump used the sound bite, "make America great again." Does the use of sound bites support the value of logical reasoning? It is also quite common for different political groups or candidates to label their opposition. Recall from Chapter 12 the name-calling propaganda tactic. Some groups that oppose abortion label their opponents "baby killers." Do such labels support logical reasoning and other values of democracy? Political groups often rely on emotional verbal and visual messages in their persuasive messages. For instance, in a pamphlet advocating a vegetarian lifestyle, a picture of an abused calf was included. The picture of the poor calf was heart wrenching and emotional. The use of emotion has often been criticized as a means of deterring the reasoning process (Johannesen, 1996) and therefore is often considered unethical. What place does the use of emotion have in a democratic society that values logical reasoning as a basis for making choices? Take another look at the EDAF message in Figure 13.4. This is a communication about politics. Would the political perspective find this message ethical in a democracy? Why or why not?

DIALOGICAL PERSPECTIVE

The **dialogical perspective** is in many ways an interpersonal approach to ethics. Essentially, communication that supports a dialogue between communicators is ethical, whereas communication that supports a monologue is unethical. Monologue and dialogue are considered opposites, but a pure dialogue may be unattainable or, at best, rare. Therefore, an interaction need not be pure dialogue to be considered ethical, but it must be more dialogue than monologue. Much of the dialogical perspective is based on the work of Martin Buber. You may have been exposed to many of these ideas in an interpersonal communication course.

Dialogical communication promotes the development of the self and of self-knowledge. Whether communication is considered dialogue or monologue largely lies in the attitude participants have toward one another. Johannesen (1996) identifies the following six characteristics of dialogical communication. Participants are *authentic* with one another; they are honest and straightforward in communicating all relevant information. Participants are *inclusive*. They strive to understand each other's perspective. This does not mean that participants have to agree with one another; it means they seek to understand each other's reality. Participants are *confirming*. They confirm each other's inherent worth as human beings. We can confirm the worth of other people and their right to believe as they do without necessarily agreeing with them. *Presentness* is another characteristic of dialogical communication. Participants must demonstrate a willingness to become involved, to listen, and to concentrate on what is being said. This means ignoring our phone and other distractions. A *spirit of mutual equality* is another characteristic. Participants treat each other as equals and as persons despite differences in status or societal roles. The last characteristic is a *supportive climate*. Johannesen (1996) describes this as: "One allows free expression, seeks understanding, and avoids value judgments that stifle. One shows desire and capacity to listen without anticipating, interfering, competing, refuting, or warping meanings into preconceived interpretations. Assumptions and prejudgments are minimized" (p. 68). To the extent that participants' attitudes toward one another reflect these six characteristics, their interaction is described as dialogue.

Monologue in many respects is the opposite of dialogue. More specifically, monologue treats a person as an "it" that can be observed and classified. Whereas dialogue is very "other-centered," monologue is very "self-centered." Characteristics of monologue include *deception, pretense, appearance, coercion, unapproachableness, seduction, domination, exploitation,* and *manipulation* (Johannesen, 1996). When sources are involved in monologue, they are only concerned with their own needs and their own goals. The needs and goals of the receiver are irrelevant to the source. An example of a monologue is the salesperson who disregards all of your objections and concerns in order to "make the sale." This technique is often referred to as a "hard sell." The salesperson is only concerned if he or she makes a sale, not whether you need the product or service or can afford it. A salesperson engaging in a dialogue would carefully listen to your needs and goals, address your concerns, and seek to understand your perspective. The salesperson taking the dialogic perspective may be just as likely as you to conclude that you do not need the service or product being sold.

From a dialogical perspective, to the extent that a source exhibits a dialogical attitude, his or her communication is considered ethical. Even though the concept of dialogue is framed in interpersonal, face-to-face interaction, communication does not have to be face-to-face to be considered ethical or for this perspective to apply. Certainly, most mediated communication sent via the Internet or television is not face-to-face and a literal dialogue is not possible. That doesn't mean it is unethical by this standard. If a source is primarily motivated by a desire to serve his or her audience, to understand them, to answer their questions, and to give them complete and accurate information, then the source's message would be considered ethical from a dialogical perspective. If, on the other hand, self-serving interests such as profit or power primarily motivate the source, the message would not be considered ethical. Thus, media messages would have to be evaluated to determine whether they are primarily dialogical in nature (and thus ethical) or more monologue in design (and thus unethical).

SITUATIONAL PERSPECTIVE

The essence of the **situational perspective** is that each situation should be judged differently by examining the characteristics of the situation at hand. The other perspectives we have discussed allow some flexibility to accommodate situational demands, but the situational perspective avoids the use of any broad criteria. Without criteria, it is very difficult to assess what is and what is not ethical. To help us better understand this perspective, Johannesen (1996, p. 87) identifies six factors that we should use when applying the situational perspective. These factors are aspects of the situation that we should evaluate when making ethical judgments.

1. the role or function of the communicator for the audience (listeners or readers);
2. audience standards concerning the reasonableness and appropriateness of the message;
3. degree of audience awareness of the communicator's techniques;
4. degree of urgency for implementation of the communicator's proposal;
5. audience goals and values;
6. audience standards for ethical communication.

Using this perspective, a tactic such as name-calling may be viewed as ethical. If the communicator's proposal were judged to be urgent and worthwhile, then the use of name-calling could be justified and therefore ethical. Another example is the use of emotional messages in place of reasoned evidence. If the speaker served the role of motivator for the audience, then the use of emotional messages that discouraged reasoned thinking may be justified if the emotional messages motivated the audience and spurred them to action.

In many ways, the situational perspective is more complex than the other perspectives. Rather than being guided by broad principles, the situational perspective requires us to examine the context in terms of audience expectations and knowledge, the culture and society at the time of the message, the value of the persuasive goal, as well as the means being used to achieve the goal. An attractive feature of the situational perspective is that it allows flexibility in what is considered moral and ethical.

It allows for the unique situation. A major drawback of this perspective is that it requires a very high level of analysis to be conducted on every situation to determine the ethical standards that should apply. If the characteristics of the audience and their needs, the context, and the source's persuasive goals are not analyzed, the situational perspective easily becomes a way to justify almost any persuasive means imaginable. Persuaders need to guard against using a situational perspective to justify a persuasive strategy that would be deemed unethical by most other approaches. The situational approach is useful in unique situations and provides flexibility that is often needed. To use the situational approach ethically, however, the persuader needs to consider several elements of the situation and not just her or his own goals.

The situational perspective is often referred to as relativism and has been a very controversial approach to ethics. The danger of a situational perspective is that it may lead to the conclusion that ethics are always relative and that no set standards exist at all. This can lead individuals to make self-serving judgments in the middle of ethical dilemmas, and it offers few set guidelines for behavior. Some have argued that tolerance of other viewpoints and cultural differences requires taking a relativist approach to ethics. After all, who are we to judge other cultures and the values of other people? As a result, many shy away from making absolute moral judgments and argue that it always depends on the situation, the context, or other factors discussed earlier. Jaska and Pritchard (1994) argued against relativism as an approach to ethics in developing their guidelines shown in Figure 13.1. Jaska and Pritchard argue that, although we may acknowledge occasional exceptions to ethical guidelines, we can establish moral and ethical principles that we follow as a general rule. In many ways, this is similar to Aristotle's concept of the golden mean (Day, 1991). Aristotle argued against holding extreme views and encouraged persuaders to find an appropriate moderate stance that represented the best balance. This doesn't mean a literal mid-point between a strict set of ethical rules and relativism, but it does represent finding a balance between the two extremes. The factors for assessing situations provide ways to carefully assess the situation while maintaining ethical principles. Consider the case of Liam selling Fat Melt. What situational factors should be considered in deciding whether Liam was ethical or not?

LEGAL PERSPECTIVE

What is legal is considered ethical from the **legal perspective**. Essentially, laws and ethics become synonymous. This perspective provides the advantage of simplicity. It becomes quite easy to determine whether a particular persuasive message is ethical or not. If it will stand up in a court of law, it is ethical. Laws on obscenity and libel provide much of the basis for what is considered ethical communication from a legal perspective. Many of the persuasive means considered unethical by other perspectives are legal and so are considered ethical from the legal perspective. For example, within both the human nature and political perspectives, anything that reduces people's ability to reason and think for themselves, such as emotional appeals, is considered unethical. No law within the United States bans the use of emotion in persuasive messages. Although the legal perspective offers simplicity, many people find this perspective to be inadequate. Most people recognize that moral standards and legal standards are related but not the same. In fact, most people believe that the law is a poor substitute for ethics—particularly when considering persuasive communication. The simplicity of this perspective makes it appealing, however, and therefore it is used frequently. Think about how often you have heard individuals justify their behavior by saying that is was legal. One study (Tenbrunsel & Messick, 1999) found that introducing legal guidelines with economic penalties for misbehavior in a corporate setting actually increased unethical behavior over situations where there was no economic penalty for the company. The legal penalties caused participants to consider their behavior as a financial issue rather than an ethical issue, whereas the absence of penalties caused participants to view the situation as an ethical one. Thus, relying on legal guidelines alone can actually be counterproductive if ethical behavior is the desired outcome.

The legal perspective leads to another related issue. Should persuasive means considered unethical from other perspectives, such as the political perspective, be made illegal? Is it possible to effectively legislate ethics? If not, how does society apply and uphold ethical standards?

SOCIAL UTILITY PERSPECTIVE

The last perspective Johannesen (1996) discusses is **social utility**. This perspective stresses the usefulness of the persuasion to the targeted audience. Brembeck and Howell (1976) describe the social utility approach as being guided by the amount of good versus harm that results from a persuasive message. To use the social utility approach, a source first must estimate the effects of the persuasive message on the audience. The more socially useful the message, the more ethical it would be. To estimate the social utility of a message (or series of messages), the persuader must understand: "(1) the group members and their common interests, (2) ways our persuasion may help or hurt the group, and (3) favorable and adverse effects on individuals" (Brembeck & Howell, 1976, p. 245). Persuasive communication should benefit most of the people with a minimum amount of harm to individuals. For example, advocating that parents immunize their children against such diseases as polio, measles, rubella, whooping cough, and so on has social utility. Immunizations prevent millions of cases of severe illness and death among children; however, a small number of children are harmed each year by these immunizations. Using any available means to advocate that parents immunize their children may be considered ethical if we believe the benefits of having a high percentage of children immunized outweigh any possible harm. In assessing the possible harm, we would have to consider not only the minority of children harmed by the immunization but also any harm from the persuasive strategies used, such as causing panic or undue stress. From a social utility approach, whether or not something is ethical has much more to do with the outcome of the message for the audience than with the means used to accomplish the outcome. Let's consider Liam and Fat Melt one more time. Using the social utility perspective, do you find Liam's selling Fat Melt to be ethical?

ETHICS IN PROFESSIONAL PRACTICE

The ethical perspectives presented so far have been based on theoretical perspectives for evaluating the ethics of persuasive messages. An examination of ethics by those who employ persuasion in their daily lives illustrates how these theoretical approaches shape ethical principles in practice, and how they are adapted for use in applied persuasion contexts. For example, those who work in public relations, marketing, strategic communication, and/or sales are involved in the use of persuasion to accomplish their professional goals. The public relations field has drawn on these theoretical principles to develop the TARES test, which focuses on five overlapping principles for ethical persuasion: Truthfulness of the message, Authenticity of the persuader, Respect for the receiver, Equity of the persuasive appeal, and Social responsibility for the common good (Baker & Martinson, 2001). In this context, *truthfulness* requires making sure that the information is presented in a manner that not only includes the literal truth but also avoids any deception, misleading content, or lies by omission. This criterion calls for open and complete information to be shared. *Authenticity* refers to persuaders being true to their own personal standards and sincere in their motivation for persuasion. *Integrity* calls for persuaders to act in accordance with pure motives, intentions, and good will toward their audience. *Respect* for the receiver is drawn from the Johannesen's human nature perspective, and it involves treating the receivers of persuasive messages in a manner that allows them to make free, well informed, and rational choices. The self-interest of the persuader is expected to take a back seat to the interests and well-being of the targeted audience. The *equity* principle focuses on the fairness of any appeals and content, and requires persuaders to ensure that their message is not deceptive in any way. It also calls for persuaders to make sure that their message can be clearly understood by the target audience. Finally, the *social responsibility* principle calls for persuaders to ensure that their message is socially responsible for the larger context of society, and not just fair for the specifically targeted receivers of the message. Thus, a message targeting business owners who might benefit from an erosion of environmental protection laws would not be considered socially responsible if it created environmental issues for the larger society in which the businesses operated.

These principles are more specific than Johannesen's perspectives, but require the source to have a well-developed ethical perspective. Johannesen's perspectives provide a foundation for developing your own ethical standards and sense of integrity. The TARES test can be used as a rubric for evaluating any given ethical situation and a means of implementing your own ethical standards. Part of being an ethical persuader also involves understanding how the communication situation can influence ethical behavior. As explored in Chapter 6, we know that individual differences affect how we process and respond to persuasive messages. Individual differences also affect ethical judgments. For example, marketing students were asked to evaluate the ethics of a variety of sales tactics such as offering gifts, lavish entertaining of clients, using exaggerated or false promises to close the sale, withholding information from customers, and exaggerating the benefits of the product. Females evaluated these sales tactics scenarios as less ethical than did males and scored higher on a moral idealism scale than males (Donoho, Heinze, & Kondo, 2012). Thus, we need to be aware that judgments about what is ethical or not are impacted by individual differences.

In addition, we know from Chapter 6 that the channel of communication is an important part of the persuasion process, and there are channel differences for ethical communication behaviors. Xu, Cenfetelli, and Aquino (2012) conducted research using a scenario involving buying and selling shares of stock for a company, and the research participant assigned to the broker role could lie to the buyer in order to enhance his or her earnings at the expense of the purchaser. Those involved in face-to-face negotiations used less deception than those in texting situations. The lack of immediate nonverbal feedback seemed to lead to less accountability. As more and more of our communication moves online, there may be more temptation to take ethical shortcuts. Think about the persuasion you are involved in—both as a sender (now and in a future role involving persuasion in a professional context) and as a receiver—what role does ethics play?

THE BIG QUESTIONS

While discussing the ethical perspectives, we raised several questions. In the concluding section, we further address these questions, not so much by answering them, but by discussing them further. We also encourage you to discuss these questions with your professors and with your peers. Ethical questions are never easy to answer and they are almost always best addressed by seeking multiple opinions. We hope you engage in discussion using the information here to establish ethical principles to guide you in both generating and evaluating persuasive messages. It is important to have solid ethical principles before you are in the middle of a situation where objectivity could be difficult to come by. Discuss and reflect on the following issues to help you generate solid ethical principles of your own.

Google "ethical dilemmas" and analyze one or more of the dilemmas using what you've learned about ethics.

DOES THE END JUSTIFY THE MEANS?

An ongoing point of discussion in ethics is whether or not the end justifies the means. Some ethical perspectives adopt a **teleological approach** that emphasizes evaluation of the ends or outcomes of the persuasive message (Seib & Fitzpatrick, 1995). Does a worthy cause justify using means (strategies) that are less than ethical? Teleological approaches argue that the ends are the most important factor to consider in evaluating ethics. This approach leads to the question of what is a worthy cause and who decides what is worthy? Many people agree that advocating for women to receive mammograms and to do self-exams is a worthy cause that can save thousands of lives a year. But, what are the standards for determining if something is worthy? For the moment, let's assume that advocating for mammograms and self-exams is indeed a worthy cause. Would it be ethical to lie to women and tell them that their risk of breast cancer is higher than it really is to get them to schedule mammograms and to do monthly self-exams? Someone might ask, "What would be the harm?" Increased stress and worry about getting breast cancer would be one source of harm. Increased stress contributes to other health problems and can negatively impact personal relationships. From a dialogical and TARES perspective, any kind of deception would not be authentic communication and therefore would not be ethical. If you value honest, authentic communication, then using deception to accomplish your persuasive goal could not be justified. From a social utility perspective, if it could be determined that more good would come from the deception (breast cancer being detected earlier for more women) than harm to individuals, then it could be considered ethical. Are any causes so universally worthy that they justify the use of unethical means? Of course, there is no consensus on what means are unethical. Deception, threats, and violence are typically viewed as unethical; however, nations regularly spy on one another, point missiles at one another, and engage in wars. The United States has typically viewed freedom as an end that justified almost any means to preserve it. For example, waterboarding and other forms of torture have been utilized to gather intelligence information, whereas others have argued that less extreme methods actually produce better results. The use of waterboarding has been justified based on an ethical perspective that values the ends over the means. The social utility approach to ethics raises difficult questions that have no clear answers.

The opposite of the teleological approach is the **deontological approach**, which argues that the ends do not justify the means. This approach evaluates ethics on the basis of the methods (or means) employed to reach the ends. In this case, lying, deception, and name-calling would be considered unethical even if they were employed as tactics designed to achieve a good end. The approach advocated by Minnick at the beginning of the chapter represents this more rules-based perspective. Rather than get into subjective discussions of who gets to decide what a good end is, a deontological approach advocates good methods as the best way to achieve ethical outcomes. Of course, it is possible to want both good ends and ethical means. We don't necessarily have to choose between one extreme and the other.

IS IT ETHICAL TO USE EMOTIONAL APPEALS?

When discussing the human nature and political perspectives, we asked whether using emotional appeals was ethical. The human nature and political perspectives place a high value on logical reasoning. To the extent an emotional appeal subverts logical reasoning, it is viewed as unethical from these perspectives. However, many issues are inherently emotional. Issues such as abortion, starvation, torture, and murder of innocent people all involve emotion simply by their nature. Should we do our best to eliminate emotion and address these issues only with logic? Other issues also have an emotional element, but the emotional element may not be the most important one. For example, when buying life insurance, there is certainly an emotional element (your eventual death); however, you are better served if your decision to buy life insurance is made on evidence and reason rather than on emotions.

You will recall that in Chapter 4 we discussed the elements of persuasion identified by Aristotle: logos, pathos, and ethos. Even though the logos (logical) and the pathos (emotional) components of a topic can be identified separately, the two often influence one another. The emotional component in a message can serve to motivate the receiver to more carefully consider the evidence presented (centrally process the message; see Chapter 11). Seeing a picture of a starving child may motivate us to learn more about the situation and to investigate what is being done to solve the problem. Without the emotional message, we may not have taken notice of the issue. For example, in the Red Cross advertisement shown in Figure 13.5, the use of the child is certainly an emotional appeal. Is the Red Cross simply trying to motivate you to think more about the tsunami relief effort, or is it trying to subvert your reasoning processes? A message that lacked any emotional element might be boring and dry and not appeal to most receivers. Messages that contain emotional elements are not inherently unethical from any perspective. People often object to messages that rely

FIGURE 13.5 You can help ad.

only on emotion and do not include any logical component. It is often considered unethical to appeal to the emotions of the audience when the intent is to discourage them from assessing the evidence and logic of the persuasive message. If you use a picture of a starving child to get people to donate money, with the intent to arouse emotions such as guilt so the receivers won't ask how the money will be used, it would be considered unethical from several of the perspectives. However, the legal and social utility perspectives do not condemn the use of emotion. In what kinds of situations/topics would emotional appeals be appropriate and ethical?

WHO IS RESPONSIBLE—THE SOURCE? THE RECEIVER?

According to the transactional model of communication, both the source and the receiver of a message contribute to, and therefore are responsible for, the outcomes in a communication interaction, including ethics. In a transactional model of communication, both the source and the receiver contribute to the meaning created by the verbal and nonverbal messages they send. Both participants are actively involved and contribute to the outcome of the communication. The question is not, *does* the receiver have responsibility, but *how much* and in *what* situations? Johannesen (1996) suggests that receivers have two primary responsibilities. The first is to be a **reasoned skeptic**. Being a reasoned skeptic involves finding an appropriate middle ground between gullibility and close-mindedness. In other words, being a reasoned skeptic requires us to be open enough to accept new ideas and information, but not so open as to accept anything. Being a skeptic means questioning ideas and information, engaging in critical thinking. Skeptics often assume that others are not being completely honest and have something to hide. If we are too skeptical, we don't believe anything we hear, and this does not allow us to learn new things and to take advantage of opportunities. To be a reasoned skeptic means we look for reasons to not believe and we are skeptical of claims until adequate evidence is supplied. For instance, if you were shopping for a new car and a salesperson said you had to make a decision immediately or lose the great deal being offered, as a reasoned skeptic you would question that claim. You would require the salesperson to explain exactly why the same deal could not be given tomorrow or the next day. In summary, a reasoned skeptic asks questions and engages in critical thinking.

The second responsibility suggested by Johannesen is that the receiver must provide appropriate **feedback to the source**. We must be honest in our response to a source. If we do not understand a message, we must indicate such. If the source is responsible for supplying relevant information and evidence, the receiver is responsible for making some effort to understand and process that information. It would also be considered dishonest if we pretended agreement and then later condemned the message, or if we pretended to understand when we didn't. The expectation for honesty applies to both the source and the receiver of the message. If we consider it unethical for a persuader to manipulate a receiver in order to achieve his or her persuasive goal, it would also be considered unethical for the receiver to manipulate the persuader.

At this point, we have concluded that the receiver has a certain amount of responsibility in persuasion and that specifically the receiver is responsible for being a reasoned skeptic and for providing feedback to the source. Let's examine an example. Let's say you are shopping for a home theatre system. You visit several stores and encounter a wide range of home theatre systems at a wide range of prices. A salesperson at one store provides a long list of qualities for a particular, expensive model. This model is loaded with lots of features the typical consumer doesn't use, which drives the price up. You ask some questions that the salesperson answers, but you really don't know the right questions to ask and so you don't get the information you really need to make a good decision. You buy this model and later realize that you spent more money than you should have. Who is responsible? Should the salesperson have been more honest and forthcoming with objective information? Should you have been more informed? Does your response change if the shopper was a 75-year-old grandmother on a fixed income? What if the shopper had only an eighth-grade education? What if the shopper had Down syndrome?

How much responsibility lies on the receiver's shoulders depends a great deal on the availability of the information, the complexity of the information, and the ability of the receiver. When it comes to buying a consumer product such as a home theatre system, most of us would say that the receiver has some responsibility to research the product first, especially because many websites, as well as magazines such as *Consumer Reports,* can help you research a product, making such research relatively easy. Information for other topics may not be so readily available. For instance, shortly after taking office, President Obama proposed a $3.6 trillion budget. Various news reports both supported and condemned the budget; most people did not have access to the details or the economic background to be able to fully evaluate the proposal. In this situation, the source has a greater responsibility for sharing information and the receiver has less responsibility for "knowing" what everything means.

We have raised many questions in this chapter and given you a variety of approaches to generate answers. Although our society and culture provide guidelines and standards for what is ethical, these standards and guidelines often conflict with one another and are applied differently by different people. It may be uncomfortable to work through the questions and issues raised in this chapter, but we encourage you to make the effort. As a human being, you will be engaged in persuasion at multiple levels. If you choose a career that involves persuasion (and most do to some extent), you will be held accountable for the messages and strategies you choose. You cannot avoid the ethical implications of your behavior. In addition, you are certainly a consumer of persuasive messages, and that involves ethical responsibilities as well. Thinking through these issues and developing your own code of ethics now will serve you well in both your personal and professional communication.

SUMMARY

- Ethical standards are linked to cultural expectations for behavior and cultural values.
- Many organizations create codes of ethics to guide their members' behavior.
- An ethical perspective is a particular approach or lens with which to examine a situation.
- The religious perspective is based in religious writings and teaching such as the Bible or Koran.
- The human nature perspective indicates that ethical communication is that which supports uniquely human attributes.
- A message is considered ethical from the political perspective if the message supports a particular political system such as democracy.
- From the dialogical perspective, dialogue is considered ethical but monologue is not.
- The situational perspective involves applying different ethical standards to different situations. However, relativism can be dangerous.

- Communication that is legal is considered ethical from the legal perspective.
- The social utility perspective places emphasis on the usefulness of the message and its outcomes for the audience.
- The TARES perspective emphasizes truthfulness, authenticity, respect for receivers, equity, and social responsibility.
- Significant questions that must be addressed when considering ethics in persuasion are "Does the end justify the means?" "Are emotional appeals ethical?" and "Is the source or the receiver responsible?"

KEY TERMS

Deontological approach—an approach to ethics that values the means or methods more than the ends or outcomes of the persuasion.

Dialogical perspective—an interpersonal approach to ethics that asserts communication must be in the form of dialogue (rather than monologue) to be ethical.

Ethics—principles or guidelines for what is right and wrong.

Feedback to the source—a responsibility of the receiver that involves giving honest responses to a source.

Human nature perspective—an approach to ethics that asserts communication must be humanizing (rather than dehumanizing) to be considered ethical.

Legal perspective—an approach to ethics that asserts that whatever is legal is also ethical.

Political perspective—an approach to ethics that is based on the tenets and values of a particular political system such as democracy.

Reasoned skeptic—a responsibility of the receiver that involves finding an appropriate middle between gullibility and close-mindedness.

Religious perspective—ethical principles that are based on the teachings of a particular religion.

Situational perspective—an approach to ethics that asserts that the characteristics of each situation be used to determine what is and is not ethical.

Social utility perspective—an approach to ethics that uses the outcome of the persuasion to determine if the means were ethical.

TARES principles—an approach to public relations, marketing, strategic communication, sales, and professional contexts that calls for truth, authenticity, respect for receivers, equity, and social responsibility on the part of the persuader in order to be ethical.

Teleological approach—an approach to ethics that values the ends or outcomes more than the means or methods that are used to achieve the ends.

REVIEW QUESTIONS

1. What is meant by the term *ethics*?
2. How is ethics related to culture?
3. What is an advantage of a code of ethics? What is a disadvantage of a code of ethics?
4. What are the key characteristics of the seven ethical perspectives discussed?
5. What are the TARES principles and how are they used?
6. Which ethical perspectives would allow you to justify using unethical means to promote a just end?
7. Which ethical perspectives discourage the use of emotional appeals?
8. What are the two receiver responsibilities suggested by Johannesen?

DISCUSSION QUESTIONS

1. Identify one ethical principle that guides your communication behavior. Ask three peers to do the same. Compare the ethical principles of your peers to your own. How similar or different are your ethical principles? How culturally similar or different are you from those to whom you compared yourself?
2. Review the seven ethical perspectives and the TARES principles discussed in this chapter. Which ethical perspective are you most comfortable with? Why? Which ethical perspective are you least comfortable with? Why? Which do you think are used most frequently in U.S. society?
3. Does the end ever justify the means? Think about your own personal code of ethics. Do you feel comfortable using the end to justify the means? Why or why not?
4. When is it ethical to use emotion in a persuasive message, and when is it not? What does your own personal code of ethics say about the use of emotion in persuasive messages?
5. How much responsibility do you expect to have as a receiver of persuasive messages? How much responsibility do you expect of others who are receivers of messages? Do factors such as age and education affect your expectations?

REFERENCES

Baker, S., & Martinson, D. L. (2001). The TARES test: Five principles for ethical persuasion. *Journal of Mass Media Ethics, 16*(2&3), 148–175.

Brembeck, W. L., & Howell, W. S. (1976). *Persuasion: A means of social influence* (2nd ed.). Englewood Cliffs, NJ: Prentice-Hall.

Day, L. A. (1991). *Ethics in media communications: Cases and controversies.* Belmont, CA: Wadsworth.

Donoho, C., Heinze, T., & Kondo, C. (2012). Gender differences in personal selling ethics evaluations: Do they exist and what does their existence mean for teaching sales ethics? *Journal of Marketing Education, 34*(1), 55–66.

Jaska, J. A., & Pritchard, M. S. (1994). *Communication ethics: Methods of analysis* (2nd ed.). Belmont, CA: Wadsworth.

Johannesen, R. L. (1996). *Ethics in human communication* (4th ed.). Prospect Heights, IL: Waveland Press.

Minnick, W. C. (1957). *The art of persuasion.* Boston: Houghton Mifflin.

Nilsen, T. R. (1974). *Ethics of speech communication* (2nd ed.). New York: Bobbs-Merrill.

Seib, P., & Fitzpatrick, K. (1995). *Public relations ethics.* Fort Worth, TX: Harcourt Brace College Publishers.

Tenbrunsel, A. E., & Messick, D. M. (1999). Sanctioning systems, decision frames, and cooperation. *Administrative Science Quarterly, 44*(4), 684–707.

Wallace, K. R. (1955). An ethical basis of communication. *Speech Teacher, 4,* 1–9.

Xu, D. J., Cenfetelli, R. T., & Aquino, K. (2012). The influence of media cue multiplicity on deceivers and those who are deceived. *Journal of Business Ethics, 106,* 337–352.

GLOSSARY

Ability to process—how capable the receiver is to elaborate on the persuasive message.

Acceptance—the third step in the Yale approach, which means that the persuasive message was successful in achieving its goals.

Accountability—the degree to which the receiver is responsible for the knowing the content.

Age—number of years old receivers are.

Agent—the source of a compliance-gaining message.

Antisocial strategies—compliance-gaining strategies based on coercive and legitimate power.

Appeal to exclusivity—a propaganda tactic that communicates that the recommended product or idea is only for the most selective or choosy audiences, rather than being the choice of the most people or common folks.

Argument—a reason or series of reasons put forward to support a claim.

Argument recall—a process in which research subjects are asked to recall the arguments contained in a persuasive message.

Assimilation—a person perceives a message as being similar to his or her attitudinal anchor and possibly closer than it really is from an objective point of view.

Attention—the first step in the Yale approach referring to getting the audience to focus on the specific message.

Attitude—a learned predisposition to respond in a consistently favorable or unfavorable manner with respect to a given object.

Attitude accessibility—the availability of an attitude in a person's mind.

Attitude relevance—how related or connected an attitude is to a behavior.

Attitude toward behavior—an attitude toward a specific behavior.

Attitudinal anchor—the position on a particular issue that a person finds most acceptable.

Attributions—the process of creating causal explanations for why things happen.

Audience segment—a subgroup of the audience that has similar needs, wants, or characteristics that distinguish it from other segments.

Authoritarianism—a personality trait regarding to the degree to which individuals rely on authority figures and sources to guide their lives.

Aversive consequences—possible outcomes that a person would want to avoid; a necessary condition for dissonance to occur.

Bait and switch—a propaganda tactic frequently used in sales settings. It involves using a great claim in an advertisement to lure customers to the store, and once they are there, the seller tries to convince them to move up to a higher cost (and higher profit) item.

Balance theory—the oldest of the consistency theories, sometimes referred to as the P-O-X theory.

Bandwagon—a propaganda tactic that communicates that everyone is doing it, so the receiver should too.

Behavior—an individual's overt physical actions.

Behavioral beliefs—beliefs about a behavior that we view as most important and that frequently involve the consequences of performing a behavior.

Behavioral domain—a set of related behaviors.

Behavioral intention—a psychological concept best described as an expectation or a plan. An intention is a plan for how you are going to behave.

Belief—a belief links an object to some attribute.

Belief evaluation—how positive or negative we feel about each of our behavioral beliefs.

Belief strength—how strongly we hold a behavioral belief.

Beliefs-about—beliefs about characteristics of a concept.

Beliefs-in—beliefs in the existence of an object.

Big lie—a propaganda tactic that involves telling an untruth in the hopes that when people hear it enough, they will believe it to be true without any proof needed.

Boomerang effect—can happen during contrasting, when a person's anchor is moved in the opposite direction of the proposed message.

Card stacking or Case making—a propaganda tactic that involves arranging facts and pieces of information (which may be true or false by themselves) to attempt to prove something that isn't really the case.

Central route—the receiver engages in high elaboration and focuses on thinking about the content of the message.

Channel—choice of delivery system for messages.

Coercion—social influence that involves force or threat of force.

Cognitions—bits of knowledge individuals have stored in their minds.

Cognitive dissonance—an aversive motivational state that people are motivated to eliminate.

Cognitive dissonance theory—a consistency theory that emphasizes consistency among cognitions.

Cognitive overlap—the similarity of the choices available. The greater the similarity, the greater the cognitive overlap.

Cognitive theories—theories of persuasion that examine the cognitive processes involved in accepting persuasive messages.

Communication—the process by which one person stimulates meaning in the mind(s) of another person (or persons) through verbal and nonverbal messages.

Compliance—the most basic level of influence, it involves a target being influenced to do something to gain a reward or to avoid a punishment.

Compliance-gaining—communicative behavior in which an agent engages to elicit from a target some agent-selected behavior.

Comprehension—the second step in the Yale approach which refers to the audience needing to understand the message.

Conditioned response—a learned response.

Conditioned stimulus—a new stimulus that is paired with an unconditioned stimulus until it elicits the same response as the unconditioned stimulus.

Conformity—the pressure to conform to what others in a group are doing.

Congruity theory—a consistency theory that introduced the idea of attitudes existing on a continuum.

Consensus—a rule for making attributions. A behavior would have high consensus if most others behave the same way in that situation. Also in ELM can serve as a peripheral cue.

Consistency—a rule for making attributions. Consistency is high if the observed behavior occurs over time.

Consonant relationship—two cognitions that are consistent with one another.

Contrasting—when a person perceives a message as being in opposition to his or her views.

Control beliefs—beliefs about the likelihood of having the opportunities and resources necessary to perform the behavior and the frequency that a control factor will occur.

Core beliefs—beliefs that are strongly held and hard to change.

Correspondence—the measures of intention and behavior must be measured on the same dimensions (action, target, context, and time).

Counter-attitudinal advocacy—speaking in favor of positions that are against one's current attitudes.

Counter-attitudinal behavior—a behavior that is counter, or against, the attitude one holds.

Credibility—a perception of believability.

Culture—demographic receiver variable that includes things such as differences in religion, ethnic origin, economic class, and societal values of the group membership.

Danger control response—a cognitive response to a fear appeal that focuses on how to eliminate the danger or threat that is causing the fear.

Decision making—a context for dissonance; after making a decision, people often experience cognitive dissonance.

Deductive approach—conclusions are made through a process of reasoning from theory.

Deindividuated situations—situations that offer the individual more anonymity and that tend to focus less on internal states such as attitudes and feelings.

Demographic characteristics—factors such as sex, age, intelligence, and cultural aspects of receivers.

Deontological approach—an approach to ethics that values the means or methods more than the ends or outcomes of the persuasion.

Derived credibility—the nature of the credibility of a source during and after the presentation of a particular message.

Dialogical perspective—an interpersonal approach to ethics that asserts communication must be in the form of dialogue (rather than monologue) to be ethical.

Direct experience—engaging the persuasion recipients in some kind of behavior related to the topic.

Discounting model—assumes that initial attitude change is a result of both source credibility and message content; however, permanent attitude change is based on message content.

Dispositional attributions—internal attributions based on personal characteristics.

Dissonance reduction—the process a person engages in to reduce cognitive dissonance that involves one or more of the following: change the behavior, change the ratio, change the importance, denial, bolstering, transcendence, and differentiation.

Dissonant relationship—two cognitions that are inconsistent with one another.

Distinctiveness—a rule for making attributions. Distinctiveness is low if the observed behavior occurs in most situations the person is in.

Distraction—stimulus that distracts or diverts the receiver's attention away from the message.

Door-in-the-face (DITF)—initially making a very large unreasonable request that the target is likely to turn down and then later making the critical request.

Effort justification—dissonance that results from enduring much or working hard to obtain a less than perfect outcome.

Ego-defensive function—attitudes that are held to help people protect their sense of self and prevent the need to face unpleasant realities.

Ego-involvement—a person's commitment to an issue and related to a person's self-concept and self-esteem.

Elaboration—the amount of thinking the receiver engages in about the content of a message. Elaboration can be thought of as a continuum ranging from not thinking at all about the content of the message to extensive thinking about the message.

Emotional appeal—a persuasive message that relies on emotion to be persuasive.

Emotional intensity—the amount of affect expressed in the language choices of the source.

Ethics—principles or guidelines for what is right and wrong.

Ethos—the nature of the source's credibility and composed of three dimensions: good character, goodwill, and intelligence.

Evaluative consistency—consistent affective feeling toward an object.

Evaluative priming—a commonly used implicit measure of attitude.

Evidence—factual statements originating from a source other than the speaker, objects not created by the speaker, and opinions of persons other than the speaker that are offered in support of the speaker's claims.

Expertise—a primary dimension of credibility that refers to the perceived knowledge and intelligence of the source.

Extended parallel process model (EPPM)—developed by Witte and describes the two ways receivers process fear appeals and how different responses result from different ways of processing.

External factors—factors outside a person such as other people, the weather, the situation, and so on that cause a person to behave a certain way.

Fear appeal—a persuasive message that attempts to arouse the emotion of fear by depicting a personally relevant and significant threat and then follows this description of the threat by outlining recommendations presented as feasible and effective in deterring the threat.

Fear control response—an emotional response to a fear appeal that focuses on how to eliminate the fear.

Feedback to the source—a responsibility of the receiver that involves giving honest responses to a source.

Folk theory—a theory we develop through our own observations, experiences, and knowledge. It exists in our heads, and we may occasionally verbalize it to others.

Foot-in-the-door (FITD)—initially making a very small request that the target is likely to agree to and then later making the larger critical request.

Forewarning—when a receiver is told that he or she is about to be exposed to a persuasive message that challenges his or her beliefs.

Freedom of choice—a necessary condition for dissonance to occur; the receiver needs to freely choose to engage in the dissonance-arousing behaviors.

Functional matching—when the persuasive message is matched to the function the relevant attitude serves for the audience.

Glittering generality—a propaganda tactic where someone or some concept is given a positive label with no proof or justification for it being an accurate label.

Goodwill—a dimension of credibility that refers to the perceived caring on the part of the source.

Guilt appeal—a persuasive message intended to stimulate the emotion of guilt, which is often experienced when a person thinks his or her behavior does not meet his or her own standards.

Higher-order conditioning—when a conditioned stimulus acts like an unconditioned stimulus and can be paired with another stimulus.

Human nature perspective—an approach to ethics that asserts communication must be humanizing (rather than dehumanizing) to be considered ethical.

Hypocrisy—situations in which an individual is reminded of his or her current attitude toward an issue and then reminded that his or her behavior is not consistent with the attitude he or she holds.

Identification—occurs when a target accepts influence from an agent because he or she wants to be associated with the agent.

Implicit Association Test (IAT)—a commonly used implicit measure of attitude.

Impression-relevant involvement—involvement tied to the impression that the receiver's attitudes make on a public audience.

Incongruent information—when information in a message is not consistent with what the receiver believes to be true.

Indirect experience—the persuasion recipients learning about the topic from reading or other indirect means.

Individuated situations—situations that encourage individuals to focus on their internal states, including attitudes, beliefs, and values.

Induced compliance—when dissonance results from being induced to perform a counter-attitudinal behavior.

Inductive approach—a method of reasoning that begins with observation and then moves from observation of particular events to general principles or hypotheses.

Initial credibility—the credibility of a source prior to the presentation of a persuasive message.

Inoculation theory—McGuire's theory on resistance to persuasive messages.

Insufficient external justification—a necessary condition for dissonance to occur; there must be little external (as opposed to internal) reason for engaging in the dissonance-arousing behavior.

Intention-behavior relationship—the extent that behavioral intentions will influence actual performance of the behavior.

Internal factors—factors inside a person, such as personality, that cause a person to behave a certain way.

Internalization—long-term attitude change. A target accepts the behavior as being best or most appropriate and will perform the behavior regardless of who approves or provides rewards.

Involvement—occurs when receivers have a personal stake in the issue, something to gain or lose, the task is important, and/or the individual has a personal commitment to the issue.

Irrelevant relationship—two cognitions that a person perceives as unrelated to one another.

Knowledge function—attitudes that help people understand the world around them.

Language intensity—language characteristics that indicate the extent the source deviates from neutrality.

Language style—the types of words a person chooses to present a message.

Latitude of acceptance (LOA)—the range of positions along an attitude continuum a person finds acceptable.

Latitude of noncommitment (LNC)—the range of positions along an attitude continuum a person finds neither acceptable nor unacceptable.

Latitude of rejection (LOR)—the range of positions along an attitude continuum a person finds unacceptable.

Legal perspective—an approach to ethics that asserts that whatever is legal is also ethical.

Level of specificity—refers to measuring both attitude and behavior with the same amount of detail.

Levels of influence—Kelman's model of three types of influence that build on one another. Compliance is the basic level, then identification, then internalization.

Likert Scale—consists of several statements with which participants indicate their level of agreement.

Linguistic specificity—the degree to which a source makes precise reference to attitude objects in a message.

Locus of control—the degree to which an individual perceives his or her life is controlled by internal factors or external factors.

Logical appeal—a persuasive message that relies on logic and reasoning to be persuasive.

Logos—the nature of the arguments and structure of the message.

Magnitude of dissonance—the amount of dissonance experienced.

Measurement factors—how attitudes and behaviors are measured. How they are measured can influence whether attitudes and behavior are related.

Measurement specificity—the extent to which both attitude and behavior are measured in the same way with regard to the action, target, context, and time.

Medium—the mode used to transmit the message from the source to the receiver.

Message discrepancy—the difference between the position being advocated by a message and preferred position of the receiver.

Message incongruity—when a message goes against (not congruent) with the source's interests or needs.

Motivation to comply—how willing individuals are to go along with what they think their salient others want them to do.

Motivation to process—how much the receiver wants to elaborate on the message.

Name-calling—a propaganda tactic where someone or some concept is given a negative label with no proof or justification for it being an accurate label.

Narrative evidence—case stories or examples that are used to support a claim.

Need for cognition (NFC)—a personality predisposition that involves the need or desire to think about issues even when there is no personal relevance and their thoughts have no impact on the outcome.

Non-normative behavior—behavior that is not standard or typical for a situation.

Non-refutational two-sided message—a message that mentions the opposing arguments but does not refute them.

Normative beliefs—a person's beliefs about what salient others want him or her to do regarding a specific behavior.

Normative influence—a factor that can influence perceptions of credibility; refers to the influence from group norms; also referred to as identification and similarity.

Objective processing—occurs when an individual elaborates on a message in an objective or unbiased manner.

One-sided message—a message that only presents arguments in favor of a particular issue.

Outcome-relevant involvement—involvement levels based on how relevant the outcomes are to the receivers.

Parallel response model—developed by Leventhal and proposes that people have one of two responses when exposed to a fear appeal.

Pathos—the emotional appeals of the message.

Perceived behavioral control—an individual's perception of the level of control he or she has over a behavior.

Perceived power—the perceived ability of the control belief to facilitate or inhibit the performance of the behavior.

Peripheral beliefs—beliefs about issues that are less important to a person.

Peripheral cues—simple decision rules and scripts people develop over time to allow for quick processing and decision making.

Peripheral route—the receiver engages in low elaboration of the message.

Personal relevance/involvement—the extent to which a topic is important or of value to a receiver.

Personal responsibility—the degree to which the receiver is responsible for the message outcome or consequences, such as making a decision.

Persuasion—symbolic communication between two or more persons with an intent to change, reinforce, or shape the attitudes, beliefs, and/or behaviors of the receiver.

Persuasive intent forewarning—a message that forewarns the audience that they will be receiving a message that will probably attack their attitudes and beliefs; however, the topic and position of the message are not given.

Phenomena—things a person finds extraordinary and in need of explanation.

Political perspective—an approach to ethics that is based on the tenets and values of a particular political system such as democracy.

Power—the ability to get others to do what you want.

Power bases—includes five types of power: reward, coercive, legitimate, referent, and expert.

Powerful speech—the absence of powerless language features.

Powerless speech—the use of language features such as hedges or qualifiers, hesitations, tag questions, and disclaimers that create perceptions of little power.

Principle of aggregation—states that a general attitude will predict a behavioral domain but not a specific behavior.

Prior knowledge—the knowledge about a topic that the receiver has before being exposed to a message on the topic.

Pro-attitudinal advocacy—speaking in favor of positions one currently supports.

Propaganda—a type of persuasion that involves mass audiences with a purpose of achieving the goals of the persuader, and it often involves emotional appeals, concealment of purpose, and a lack of sound support.

Prosocial strategies—compliance-gaining strategies based on reward, referent, and expert power.

Psychological characteristics—aspects of the receiver that vary according to some element of the receiver's personality or psychological state.

Reasoned skeptic—a responsibility of the receiver that involves finding an appropriate middle between gullibility and close-mindedness.

Receiver characteristics—aspects of target audiences that influence how persuasive messages are processed and, ultimately, the success or failure of those messages.

Receiver—the recipient of a message.

Reciprocity—a propaganda tactic that involves the persuader giving something to the targeted receiver and expecting the receiver to feel compelled to accommodate the persuader.

Refutational message—a message in which opposing views are presented and refuted in inoculation theory.

Refutational two-sided message—a two-sided message that presents opposing arguments and then refutes them.

Refutational-different message—a message that refutes opposing arguments on an issue but not the ones contained in the preceding attack message.

Refutational-same message—a message that refutes the arguments contained in the attack message from the opposition.

Religious perspective—ethical principles that are based on the teachings of a particular religion.

Response efficacy—how effective the recommended response is in eliminating a particular threat.

Response-response consistency—expectations that responses to stimuli will be similar over time.

Retention—the fourth step in the Yale approach, which refers to the audience remembering the message.

Scientific theory—a theory that is published, tested, and offered up for review by experts.

Scripted situations—situations in which individuals know the expected behavior and therefore do not need to think in order to behave.

Secondary goals—things the agent is trying to accomplish with the target other than gaining compliance.

Selective attention and perception—our choosing to pay attention only to some of the messages bombarding us out of self-defense. We pay attention to messages that are particularly relevant to us in some way or those that attract our attention because of their use of humor, oddity, or other similar devices.

Self-efficacy—the extent the audience believes they are capable of performing the response recommended in a message.

Self-esteem—how confident, optimistic, and capable individuals perceive themselves to be.

Self-monitoring—how much an individual watches (or monitors) her or his own behavior and the response of others to it.

Semantic Differential Scale—consists of a series of paired adjectives.

Sequential Request Strategy—a script specifying what you ask for and how you respond

Severity—the grimness of the threat presented in a message.

Sex—whether a receiver is a biological male or female.

Situational attributions—external attributions based in influences around the individual.

Situational factors—characteristics of the situation in which an individual performs the behavior in question.

Situational perspective—an approach to ethics that asserts that the characteristics of each situation be used to determine what is and is not ethical.

Sleeper effect—suggests that high credibility sources have more persuasive impact immediately following the message than do low credibility sources but that, over time, the effects of credibility wear off.

Social-adjustive—attitudes held that help individuals fit the expectations of those around them.

Social-adjustive function—attitudes that are held to help us better relate to those around us.

Social comparison—our evaluation of how good our own accomplishments are by comparing ourselves to others.

Social utility perspective—an approach to ethics that uses the outcome of the persuasion to determine if the means were ethical.

Statistical evidence—an informational summary of many cases and that is expressed in numbers used to support a claim.

Stimulus-response consistency—the expectation that people will have the same response to the same stimuli over time.

Subjective norm—the social pressure a person feels from salient (important) others to perform or not perform a behavior.

Subliminal—awareness that is below consciousness.

Supportive message—a one-sided message in inoculation theory.

Supraliminal—conscious awareness.

Susceptibility—how probable it is that a particular threat will affect the audience.

TARES principles—an approach to public relations, marketing, strategic communication, sales, and professional contexts that calls for truth, authenticity, respect for receivers, equity, and social responsibility on the part of the persuader in order to be ethical.

Target—the receiver of a compliance-gaining message (the person the compliance is targeted at).

Teleological approach—an approach to ethics that values the ends or outcomes more than the means or methods that are used to achieve the ends.

Testimonial—a propaganda tactic where a valued person expresses support, or offers testimony, about the value (or lack thereof) of the targeted person or concept.

Theory—any systematically related set of ideas used to describe and/or explain phenomena.

Thought listing—a process in which research participants are asked to list what they were thinking about during the presentation of a persuasive message.

Thurstone Scale—consists of several items each representing a different level of favorableness or unfavorableness toward the attitude object.

Topic and position forewarning—a message that forewarns the audience of the topic of persuasion and the position (for or against) of the impending persuasive message.

Topic saliency—how important the topic of a persuasive message is to receivers.

Trustworthiness—a primary dimension of credibility that refers to receivers' perceptions of the source's honesty.

Two-sided message—a message that presents arguments in favor of an issue but also considers opposing arguments.

Unconditioned response—an automatic or natural response (one that is not learned).

Unconditioned stimulus—a stimulus that elicits an unconditioned response.

Utilitarian function—attitudes that benefit individuals by allowing them to avoid negative consequences and achieve positive outcomes.

Value-expressive—attitudes held that help people express their own values.

Value-expressive function—attitudes that allow people to express values that are important to them.

Value-relevant involvement—deals with central or core values for individuals.

Values—enduring beliefs that specific modes of conduct or end state of existence are personally and socially preferable to alternative modes of conduct or end states of existence.

Vested interest—having a personal stake in the outcome of a situation.

Volitional control—if a behavior is under volitional control, an individual has control over the behavior.

Yale approach—theorized that persuasion has components of attention, comprehension, acceptance, and retention.

INDEX

A

Advertisements, 5, 10, 19, 21–22, 25, 28, 75–77, 80, 88, 94, 119, 129, 143–145, 148, 155, 162–163, 165, 194, 232, 285–287, 291, 302, 322

Advertisers, 5, 22–23, 25, 71, 77, 86, 88, 129, 131, 134, 139, 143, 146, 194, 253, 267
  and modeling, 25
  outcome-relevant involvement, 131

Advertising, 10, 14, 21, 25, 71, 81, 86, 102, 121–122, 129, 134–135, 140, 146, 148, 151–152, 163, 167, 195, 210, 241, 262–263, 268–269
  balance theory, 167
  and marketing, persuasion in, 10
  and subliminal messages, 143

Age of receiver, 133–134

Antismoking messages, 99

Antitobacco forces, 195

Argument recall, 255

Arguments and involvement, interaction between, 253

Aristotle, 9

Assimilation, 175, 177–178, 180–181, 186–189, 321

Assisted-suicide, steps toward legalizing, 184–186

Attack messages, 112–114

Attention (modeling process), 24

Attitude, 220
  vs. behavior, 28
  and behavior specificity, 46–48
  and belief, 28–29
  characteristics of
    affect, 17
    consistency, 17–18
    influencing behavior, 18–19
    learned, 19
    tied to an object, 17
  definitions of, 16–18
  formation, theories of, 19–25
    classical conditioning, 20–22

    modeling, 24–25
    operant conditioning, 22–23
  functions of, 26–28
  as learned predisposition, 220
  measures, 30
    evaluative priming, 35
    galvanic skin response, 34–35
    implicit association test, 35–36
    Likert scale, 32–33
    semantic differential scale, 34
    Thurstone scale, 31–32
  predicting, 226
  and self-monitoring, 128–130
  subliminal messages influence on, 143–144

Attitude accessibility, 50–51

Attitude–behavior consistency, 51

Attitude–behavior relationship, 17
  in artificial laboratory settings, 45
  attitude towards Chinese couple, 43–44
  correlations, 44–45
  factors affecting
    attitude formation, 48–50
    cognitive processing, 50–52
    measurement issues, 45–48
    perceptions of behavioral control, 48
    situational, 52–54
  views of, 50

Attitude change, 5, 66, 80, 100–102, 115–116, 122, 126–127, 142, 150, 166, 177, 181–184, 187, 189, 199, 216, 219, 236, 246, 251, 254–255, 259, 269–270, 273–275, 295
  in central processing, 254–255
  and cognitive dissonance theory, Cognitive dissonance theory
  and discounting model, 65–66, 100
  with evidence in persuasive message, 100
  and message discrepancy, relationship between, 182–183
  in peripheral processing, 254–255
  self-perception theory and. *See* Self-perception theory
  social judgment theory and. *See* Social judgment theory
  using TRA, 230

development of, 192
dissonance reduction, 194–197
  bolstering, 196–197
  changing behavior, 194–195
  changing ratio of consonant to dissonant cognitions, 196
  denial, 196
  differentiation, 197
  tobacco users, 195
  transcendence, 197
magnitude of dissonance
  cognitive overlap and, 193–194
  factors influencing, 193
  smoking and cognition, 193
  tobacco industry, 194
  variation of, 192
reciprocity effect and, 287
strengths and limitations, 210–211
supporting research, 208–210
weaknesses of, 208
Cognitive overlap, 193–194
Cognitive processing factors, 50–52
  attitude accessibility, 50–51
  attitude–behavior consistency, 51–52
  vested interest and, 52
Cognitive theory
  cognitive dissonance theory. *See* Cognitive dissonance theory
  definition of, 191
  social judgment theory. *See* Social judgment theory
Communication, 3
  components of, 59
  definition of, 11
  influence, persuasion, coercion, and education, link between, 12
  source. *See* Source
Compliance, 271, 273
  vs. identification, 274
  strategies leading to, 274
    compliance-gaining. *See* Compliance-gaining typologies
    propaganda tactics. *See* Propaganda tactics
    sequential request. *See* Sequential request strategies
  target influence, 273–274
Compliance-gaining typologies, 272, 273, 275–282
  definition of, 275

face-to-face interactions, 275
by Kearney, Plax, Richmond, and McCroskey, 280–282
by Marwell and Schmitt, 276–278
by Schenck-Hamlin, Wiseman, and Georgacarakos, 278–280
study of, 275
  personal differences, 275–276
  secondary goals, 276
  situational characteristics, 276
Conditioned response, 20
Conditioned stimulus, 20, 160
Congruity theory, 191
Consistency theories, 190–191
Consonant relationship, 192
Contrasting, 177
Control belief, 228
Core beliefs, 29–30
Correlation, 44
CS. *See* Conditioned stimulus
Culture
  definition of, 134–135
  response to persuasive messages
    advertising slogans, 135
    Chinese and American managers, 135–136
    same-sex marriage issue, 135

D

Danger control response, 91, 94, 127
Data analysis, 161
Data collection, 160–161
Date rape attitude survey, 24–25
Deductive approach, 276
Deindividuated situations, 53
Delivery channel, credibility of
  social media channels, 69–71
  traditional media, 69
Democratic political system, values of, 307
Democratic society, participation in, 9
Deontological approach, 314
Depression treatment, persuasive message for, 244–245
Descriptive beliefs, 29
Dialogical perspective of ethics, 308–309
Discounting model, 65–66, 100
Dissonant relationship, 192
Door-in-the-face (DITF) approach, 287–288

E

F

Reward power, 71
Rock the Vote campaigns, 27–28

S

Safety belt use, public service announcement for, 8
Scientific theories, 159
Script. *See* Peripheral cues
Scripted situations, 53–54
Self-efficacy *vs.* self-esteem, 126–128
Self-esteem
    and attitude change, relationship
      between, 126–127
    definition of, 125
    and fear appeals, 126–127
    measurement, 126
    and message quality, relationship
      between, 126
    role in persuasion, 126
    vs. self-efficacy, 126–128
Self-monitoring, 128–130
    high and low, 128
    implications for persuasion, 129–130
    and response to message appeals, 128
    social-adjustive appeal, 129
    value-expressive appeal, 129
Self-perception theory
    attributions and, 207
    attribution theories, 205
      development of, 207
      external attribution, 206
      factors for attributions, 207
      internal attribution, 206, 207
    impression formation theory, 205, 207
    postulates for, 208
    reciprocity effect and, 287
    supporting research, 208–210
    usefulness of, 208–209
Semantic differential scale, 34
Sender and receiver, 4–5
Sequential request strategies, 272
    definition of, 287
    DITF approach, 287–288
    FITD approach, 289–290
Sex differences in persuadability, 132–133
Similarity and normative influence, 74–75
Similarity of source, 74–75
Situational factors
    categories of, 53
    definition of, 52

Situational perspective of ethics, 309–310
Sleeper effect, 65–66
Social-adjustive and value-expressive
    functions, 27
Social-adjustive function, 27, 128
Social judgment theory
    application in persuasive campaign,
      184–186
    assimilation and contrast effects,
      177–178
    basic premise of, 175
    boomerang effect, 178
    changing attitudes with, 181–184
    core assumption of, 177
    ego-involvement, 178–181
      contrasting and assimilation effects,
        179–181
      impact on persuasion process, 179
      LOA, LOR and LNC, 179
    influencing attitude from perspective of,
      183
    and involvement, 130
    judgments and attitude change, 177–178
    latitude of acceptance, 176–177
    latitude of noncommitment, 176–177
    latitude of rejection, 176–177
    possible positions on abortion, 175–176
    strengths and limitations, 186–187
Social media channels, credibility of, 69–71
Social utility approach, 311
Social utility perspective of ethics, 311
Source, 60
    attractiveness of, 252
    characteristics, 61
    definition of, 61
    education and experience of, 66–67
    introductions, 66–68
    and receiver, ethical perspectives of,
      316–317
Source credibility, 60, 252
    Aristotle's approach, 62–63
    concept of, 61
    construct of, 63
    definition of, 61
    derived, 62
    dimensions of, 62–64
      good character, 62
      goodwill, 62
      intelligence, 63
    effects over time, persistence of, 65–66
    with evidence in persuasive message, 100
    initial, 61–62